T0318454

Themes in Economic Analysis

This book covers diverse themes, including institutions and efficiency, choice and values, law and economics, development and policy, and social and economic measurement. Written in honour of the distinguished economist Satish K. Jain, this compilation of essays should appeal not only to students and researchers of economic theory but also to those interested in the design and evaluation of institutions and policy.

Subrata Guha is Associate Professor, Centre for Economic Studies and Planning, Jawaharlal Nehru University, and has been associated with research and teaching there since 1999.

Rajendra Prasad Kundu is Assistant Professor, Centre for Economic Studies and Planning, Jawaharlal Nehru University. He has taught at Jadavpur University and at the Delhi School of Economics, University of Delhi.

S. Subramanian is an ICSSR National Fellow affiliated with the Madras Institute of Development Studies, from where he retired as a professor. Previously, he was a consultant with the Planning Commission of India and the Bureau of Industrial Costs and Prices, Government of India.

'Satish Jain ... combined intellectual brilliance, extreme modesty and a unique gentleness in a way that I have rarely encountered since. This volume of essays by many ... leading lights of economic theory ... is an appropriate tribute to this remarkable scholar and human being.'

Abhijit Vinayak Banerjee, Massachusetts Institute of Technology, USA

'It is rare to find such a cluster of leading economic theorists coming together to pay tribute to an individual ... [but then] Satish Jain is himself a rare economist ... [with] a remarkable range of intellectual interests ... [who] is known for his personal integrity and moral courage.'

Kaushik Basu, Cornell University, USA, and the World Bank

'The contributions are of the highest quality by scholars of great eminence. I believe this volume should be of great value to all advanced level students of economic theory.'

Pulin B. Nayak, Delhi School of Economics, India

'This volume of essays ... which spans [Satish K. Jain's] wide spectrum of interests in economic theory and is characterised by ... rigour and precision ... in analysis, is a splendid tribute to his contributions to the profession.'

Deepak Nayyar, Jawaharlal Nehru University, India

Themes in Economic Analysis

Theory, policy and measurement

Essays in honour of Satish Jain

Edited by

**Subrata Guha,
Rajendra Prasad Kundu and
S. Subramanian**

Routledge
Taylor & Francis Group

LONDON AND NEW YORK

First published 2016 by Routledge

2 Park Square, Milton Park, Abingdon, Oxfordshire OX14 4RN
711 Third Avenue, New York, NY 10017

Routledge is an imprint of the Taylor & Francis Group, an informa business

First issued in paperback 2017

British Library Cataloguing-in-Publication Data
A catalogue record for this book is available from the British Library

Library of Congress Cataloging-in-Publication Data
A catalog record has been requested for this book

ISBN: 978-1-138-88797-8 (hbk)
ISBN: 978-0-8153-7594-4 (pbk)

Typeset in Sabon LT Std
by SunRise Media

Contents

Illustrations

Contributors

Sugata Bag is Assistant Professor, Department of Economics, Delhi School of Economics, University of Delhi, India.

Priyodorshi Banerjee is Assistant Professor, Economic Research Unit, Indian Statistical Institute, Kolkata, India.

Taposik Banerjee is Assistant Professor of Economics, School of Liberal Studies, Ambedkar University Delhi, India.

Amitava Bose is a former Professor of Economics, Indian Institute of Management Kolkata, India.

Archishman Chakraborty is Mel Harris Chair in Insurance and Risk Professor of Finance, Syms School of Business, Yeshiva University, U.S.A.

Satya Ranjan Chakravarty is Professor, Economic Research Unit, Indian Statistical Institute, Kolkata, India.

Nachiketa Chattopadhyay is Associate Professor, Sampling and Official Statistics Unit, Indian Statistical Institute, Kolkata, India.

Sarbajit Chaudhuri is Professor, Department of Economics, University of Calcutta, India.

Sugato Dasgupta is Professor, Centre for Economic Studies and Planning, Jawaharlal Nehru University, India.

Bhaskar Dutta is Professor, Department of Economics, University of Warwick, United Kingdom.

Krishnendu Ghosh Dastidar is Professor, Centre for Economic Studies and Planning, Jawaharlal Nehru University, India.

Subrata Guha is Associate Professor, Centre for Economic Studies and Planning, Jawaharlal Nehru University, India.

Rajendra Prasad Kundu is Assistant Professor, Centre for Economic Studies and Planning, Jawaharlal Nehru University, India.

Tapan Mitra is Goldwin Smith Professor of Economics, Department of Economics, Cornell University, U. S. A.

Anjan Mukherji is Professor Emeritus, Jawaharlal Nehru University, India, and Honorary Visiting Professor, National Institute of Public Finance and Policy, India.

Debabrata Pal is Assistant Professor, Centre for Economic Studies and Planning, Jawaharlal Nehru University, India.

Ravindra R. Ranade is Professor of Mathematical Economics, Faculty of Economics, Kagawa University, Japan.

Amal Sanyal is Associate Professor, Department of Accounting, Economics and Finance, Lincoln University, New Zealand.

Kunal Sengupta is Professor of Economics, School of Political Science and Economics, University of Sydney, Australia.

Yukie Shimono is a student at the Graduate School of Economics, Kagawa University, Japan.

Manimay Sengupta is a former Visiting Professor, Centre for Economic Studies and Planning, Jawaharlal Nehru University, India.

Ram Singh is Associate Professor, Department of Economics, Delhi School of Economics, University of Delhi, India.

S. Subramanian is Indian Council of Social Science Research National Fellow at the Madras Institute of Development Studies, India.

Foreword

At some point in the middle or late 1960s, the Department of Economics at the University of Rochester started admitting a stream of outstanding doctoral students from India. Most of them had graduated from Presidency College, Kolkata, and/or the Delhi School of Economics. The first person from this list of fine students whom I met was Dipankar Dasgupta, a second year student in the fall of 1968 when I joined the department. Dipankar was one of the handful of students in the game theory course I taught that year and has, ever since, been a friend I have stayed in touch with over the years. Later students would all have taken one of the first year compulsory theory courses from me and some took the game theory course a year later. A few contributors to this volume— Amitava Bose, Tapan Mitra and Anjan Mukjerji—are Rochester Ph.D.s whom I remember well and fondly. Anjan and I have also maintained contact over the years and, for me, it was a special treat when I served as an external dissertation reader for Anjan's student Krishnendu Ghosh Dastidar.

An impressive number of the Indian students at Rochester in those days have gone on to have distinguished careers, Satish Jain, of course, among them. When Satish was a doctoral student, I did not know him as well as the other students, probably because he was a little shy and quiet. At least he seemed so to me at that time. He came to me to ask if I would be his dissertation adviser, no doubt saying he planned something in social choice theory—a topic about which I knew a little, but in which I was far from being an expert. The Department of Political Science occupied a floor adjacent to that housing the Department of Economics and I had a close relationship with Bill Riker who was quite well versed in social choice theory. Satish might have come to me knowing of this connection. In any case, he set to work, time went by and he produced a superb dissertation with virtually no input from me.

Satish was a very rare doctoral student. Anyone who has served on a number of dissertation committees would know that while many students have good ideas, not all have the the discipline to get their work done. Others have good work habits but do not know what to work on; some students have good topics and work habits but still need a great deal of guidance as they go along. Rarely there is a student who is so talented and motivated that all he needs is to be left alone and he will produce an outstanding, finished piece of research—Satish fell into this category. When his dissertation was finished, I had no trouble recognising that he had produced something worthwhile. However, I did not have the knowledge and insight to realise what a fundamental, important result he had arrived at. My friend Bill Riker pointed this out to me. Bill, though not highly trained in mathematics, was a remarkably intelligent and insightful person and was the main force behind bringing mathematical theory to the discipline of political science. Bill was aware of the work of Allan Gibbard and Mark Satterthwaite, which, unfortunately for Satish, got published first. Whether Satish worked out his results literally at the same time as they did or was slightly ahead or behind in time, there is no doubt that his work was independently conceived and executed. It was and is a brilliant piece of research. Over my own career of roughly 40 years, I have had the pleasure of serving on doctoral committees of some very talented people, but I do not think any of them wrote a dissertation as important as Satish's and few worked so independently as him.

I join Satish's friends and colleagues in congratulating him on a fine career and wish him well in retirement.

James W. Friedman
Kenan Professor Emeritus
The University of North Carolina at Chapel Hill

Introduction*

Subrata Guha, Rajendra Prasad Kundu and S. Subramanian

THE HONOUREE

This book is a collection of essays put together by friends, colleagues and students of Satish K. Jain, as a tribute to his extraordinary scholarship, professional values, personal integrity and warm companionship towards all those that have had the good fortune to know and work with him. At the time of writing this introduction, Satish's formal career in academia is nearing its end. This book is, therefore, intended also as a retirement gift, to mark the end of an era of institutional affiliation—but, more importantly, to inaugurate a substantive new era, post-retirement, of research and mentoring.

Satish graduated with a B.Sc. from Agra College in 1968, completed his M.A. in economics from the Delhi School of Economics in 1970 and obtained his Ph.D. in economics, under the supervision of James Friedman, from the University of Rochester in 1976. Between his M.A. and Ph.D., Satish worked for a year as a lecturer at the Shri Ram College of Commerce in Delhi during 1970–71. On his return to India after completing his Ph.D., he worked at the Indian Statistical Institute, Delhi, over 1976–78, and thereafter has been on the faculty of the Centre for Economic Studies and Planning at the Jawaharlal Nehru University, Delhi, from which he is due to retire very soon, at the age of 65.

Satish is admired by those who know him for his research, his teaching and his commitment to a certain non-parochial and cosmopolitan vision for his country. In many ways, Satish is a theorist's theorist. Doing economic theory in India is at best a somewhat foolhardy venture, but to have brought it off as rigorously and imaginatively as Satish has done is a truly remarkable feat. While his interests have traversed a very wide

---

* The editors are indebted to the contributors for providing them with abstracts of their respective essays: this has been of invaluable assistance in introducing the essays in this volume.

spectrum (to which we hope the essays in this collection bear testimony), his principal scholarly contributions have been in the fields of social choice theory and law and economics.

In the theory of collective choice, Satish has to his credit a number of foundational papers on, inter alia, the method of majority decision, rights and liberty, and strategic voting. With respect to the last, namely, the manipulability of aggregation mechanisms, it is a little-known fact that two distinguished political scientists, R.G. Niemi and W.H. Riker (1976), have given Satish Jain credit for having independently arrived at a version of what is now known in the literature as the Gibbard–Satterthwaite Theorem. Niemi and Riker refer to the main result in his Ph.D. dissertation, which demonstrated that every non-trivial binary social decision rule is manipulable (Jain 1975). It is worth noting that while the Gibbard–Satterthwaite Theorem deals with voting schemes, Satish focuses on binary social decision rules, and the intersection of these two sets of rules consists only of trivial functions. Thus, leaving aside these trivial cases, the two results are independent of each other. Satish has also contributed several important papers on the relationship between rationality conditions and individual preferences in the context of voting rules. These include a significant contribution on the method of majority decision (Jain 2009a) and complete characterisations for several classes of rules, including special majority rules (Jain 1983, 1986) and non-minority rules (Jain 1984). Of considerable salience, also, is Satish's contribution to the literature on the so-called liberal paradox pioneered by Amartya Sen (1970), in terms of a comprehensive and rigorous formulation of the notion of a coherent rights-assignment (Jain 1995).

Satish's primary contribution to law and economics has been the creation of an axiomatic framework within which questions relating to efficiency of liability rules can be analysed in a systematic manner. He uses this framework to:

provide a complete characterisation of efficient liability rules (Jain 2005; Jain and Singh 2002);

demonstrate that the efficiency properties of liability rules crucially depend on how one formalises the notion of negligence (Jain 2006);

demonstrate that the conflict between the considerations involving economic efficiency and those of distributive justice, in the context of assigning liability, is not as sharp as is generally believed to be the case (Jain and Kundu 2004);

show that if liability is decoupled in the sense that the damages awarded to the victim are not equal to the liability imposed on the injurer, then no rule for liability apportionment can be efficient (Jain 2012); and completely characterise efficient incremental liability rules, a notion which he introduced into the literature by way of formalising the idea that a party held liable is made to bear only that portion of the loss which is attributable to the party's negligence (Jain 2009b).

These and several other results that he has to his credit give us interesting insights into the efficiency characteristics of rules for apportionment of losses arising from interactions involving harmful externalities. His original critique of the Coasean argument brings into sharp focus some very important implications of applying economic methodology to the analysis of law (Jain 2010).

Satish's collection of readings on law and economics (brought out as a part of the Oxford University Press's series *Readings in Economics*) is an anthology of the first importance, and his introduction is a weighty part of this significant book. Much of the economics literature in law and, indeed, in matters purporting to human welfare has been on the subject of efficiency. The introduction takes the reader through an examination of the possibility of achieving efficiency in the presence of non-negligible transaction costs without having to rely on the informationally demanding mechanism of Pigouvian taxes and subsidies. It then proceeds to deal with

the role of liability rules as an alternative to tax/subsidy schemes;

the characterisation of efficient liability rules in terms of negligence conditions;

the consequences of relaxing certain crucial assumptions underlying the 'efficiency theorems', which could result in a discovery of non-existence;

an exploration of the 'economistic' obsession with efficiency as the single guiding principle of common law;

the view that the notion of justice is exhausted by a consideration of the idea of efficiency;

an advancement of the claim that there is a precise and well-defined sense in which considerations of efficiency could threaten justice by violating basic rights;

an invitation to view the project of law and governance as being informed by social virtues other than (and possibly conflicting with) efficiency, values such as liberty, non-exploitation, basic rights, freedom and democracy; and

a treatment, touching on both abstract and practical issues, of the role of law and governance in a rapidly globalising world, which is increasingly sought to be regulated by rules and fiats issuing forth from international institutions that have neither the popular sanction nor the moral credibility of democratic legitimacy.

A first of three signature features of Satish's theoretical work resides in his skilful demonstration that the values informing much of mainstream economics are fairly impoverished—though, as he makes clear, they need not and should not be so. Second, students of economics often emerge in two forms—as moral monsters or as strident moralists, depending on what doctrinaire impulse they have been subjected to in their graduate and postgraduate courses: Satish's work points to the importance of the positive *and* the normative elements of economics, ruling out both insensitivity and shrillness as appropriate social science virtues. Third, and in a related spirit, a large corpus of his work suggests that effective criticism is not best carried out by shouting down your opponents, but by honing your analytical skills so finely that you are enabled to strike at the very heart of a defective theory—first from *within* its own perspective, and then, in a more comprehensive exercise, from *without*. Satish's approach to theoretical economics, that is, enjoins on the reader the virtues of scholarship and discipline.

Satish has taught and trained generations of students with a patience and a commitment that have endeared him greatly to them. In an academic milieu in which the inevitability of abstraction for reasoned argument has been little understood, and passionate evocations of pious sentiments have underpinned debate, he has consistently tried to instill in his students an appreciation of the value of discourse based on truly logical arguments developed with rigour and precision. Most students, especially those encountering him as an examiner for the first time, may have found his expectations to be unreasonably exacting. Yet, this impression has always been tempered by the understanding that even the least display of promise on their part would inevitably be rewarded with fulsome praise and encouragement. Those who have had the opportunity to be mentored by Satish may not have always found the going easy, but they have never been other than deeply grateful for the troubles he has taken to make serious and honest scholars out of them.

These academic virtues are part of a value system that has always characterised Satish's approach to the larger issues of life: intellectual curiosity; rigour, precision and care in evaluation; a deeply felt sense of justice; political progressiveness, marked by an embracing of cosmopolitanism and a dislike for dogmatic and doctrinaire 'judgmentalism'; sympathy with the weak and the undefended; and impatience with cant, hypocrisy and pomposity. These sentiments are reflected in his affection for Buddhist texts and detective novels alike; in his passionate appreciation of both ancient Indian systems of knowledge and modern mathematics; in the undiscriminating welcome he extends at home to all his visitors, both human and animal; and in his impartial aversion to both the inchoate individualism of the extreme right and the impregnable herd mentality of the extreme left.

No account of Satish could ever be complete without a reference to his eccentricity, which has several facets to it, and which—because Satish is Satish—endear him to his friends when these could, with equal justice, exasperate them. Anyone who has known him has a favourite 'Satish story'. Here is one from one of the editors of this volume [S. Subramanian]. On a visit to his home over 20 years ago, Subramanian, after being treated to a masterly exposition on the intricacies of liberty in a theory of social choice, was threatened with an offer of tea. Meanwhile, Satish had also got on to the subject of Buddhism. While he expounded on the subject, he placed a vessel of water and another one of milk on two adjacent gas rings. The milk was first boiled, and upon conclusion of that activity, and at a crucial juncture of the Buddhist treatise, it was discovered that the water had not been boiled. So the expounder boiled the water, only to discover that, unhappily, the milk had gone colder than was fit for decent tea. Arising from this, the milk was boiled again, to the neglect of the cooling water. An increasingly engaged speaker then boiled the water again, and then the milk again, and then ... At this stage, and in some despair over ever getting at that tea, Subramanian suggested that the contents of both vessels be heated at the same time. Satish was deeply impressed by what he called Subramanian's 'practical intelligence', and everything turned out well thereafter, with both the Buddhist discourse and the tea.

THE BOOK

We made a reference earlier to the wide spectrum of Satish's theoretical interests. This book is an attempt at reflecting on some parts of that spectrum.

The first part 'Institutions and Efficiency' features four essays. In the first essay 'Market Failures: Almost Always?', Anjan Mukherji goes beyond standard discussions of efficiency in competitive economies using $2 \times 2 \times 2$ models to establish conditions for existence and efficiency of equilibria in an economy with m individuals and n goods. He demonstrates how market failure may occur because of externalities, because of asymmetric information or because, in the absence of outside coercion, it may not be in the best interest of individual traders to execute the contracted competitive transactions at equilibrium prices. Mukherji notes that these three cases 'between them cover all types of markets'. Unfortunately, the nature of intervention required to avert market failure in each of these cases gives rise to the possibility of rent-seeking behaviour. Since 'good moral behaviour' or 'good governance' based on such behaviour may be the only way out, the author expects that 'on the balance, the markets will fail to deliver'.

The second essay 'Encompassing Interests, Regionalism and Public Investment' by Sugato Dasgupta, Bhaskar Dutta and Kunal Sengupta focuses on the roles of national and regional parties in the theory of resource allocation. The preferences of a regional party are fully aligned with the interests of its own constituency, while a national party has encompassing interests. A government composed solely of regional parties fails to internalise externalities and this results in an inefficient allocation of resources. A national party government internalises externalities because then it has encompassing interests. However, government formation is endogenous, and the authors show that a government composed solely of regional parties may be a voting equilibrium if the degree of encompassing interests of the national party exceeds a threshold level.

The third essay 'Bribe Chains in a Police Administration' by Amal Sanyal contends that a bribe chain enables offences by providing a stable arrangement for transmitting a bribe from an offender to various levels of the administration. There is a belief that the problem can be eliminated or weakened by introducing more levels of supervision and increasing the number of honest officers at various levels. The essay argues against these beliefs. It shows that it serves no purpose to increase the number of supervisory levels, nor does it help to increase the number of honest cadres in supervisory levels *per se*. Instead, ensuring that any one level is fully impervious to corruption can completely stop bribe chains and offences. The essay first develops a model of corrupt hierarchy and bribe chains and then explores its properties to establish these results.

The fourth essay 'Notes towards Rationality and Institutions' by Manimay Sengupta introduces a rationality principle which is an extension of the rationality principle in economics and game theory, and is consonant with the principle of instrumental rationality. Under standard epistemic conditions that correspond to Nash equilibria, the author shows that players' choice of strategies under this rationality principle will induce cooperation in social situations akin to the prisoner's dilemma. The result is in sharp contrast with the usual position of institutional economists that instrumental rationality is inadequate to explain observed social behaviour that often exhibits cooperation and reciprocity.

The second part 'Choice and Values' has two essays. People often make choices which according to commonly used internal consistency conditions would be considered inconsistent and, hence, irrational. Many such choices, however, one may argue, are neither inconsistent nor irrational. The internal consistency conditions suffer from a definitional constraint, owing to which they filter out many choices as inconsistent. Those popularly used in social choice theory to assess a choice function, therefore, turn out be insufficient to analyse several choice patterns. The first of these essays, 'Characterisation of a Second-Best Rationalisable Choice Function with General Domain', by Taposik Banerjee, makes an effort to address this limitation. It accepts a broader definition of rationality than is customary, and characterises choice behavior where an individual chooses a second-best element when available, and otherwise chooses a best element, without imposing any restriction on the domain of the choice function.

In 'Domain Conditions for Quasi-transitive Rationalisability', Debabrata Pal points out that a crucial problem in the choice theory literature is the so-called rationalisability of choice functions. A choice function is rationalisable if and only if it is possible to find a preference relation that generates choice sets in different environments. The essay investigates whether there is any basis to choices made by an individual in different environments. The standard literature addresses this problem by introducing a number of choice consistency conditions that, in effect, have proved to be necessary and sufficient for ordering rationalisation. Most of these choice consistency conditions are of the nature that they impose restrictions on the choice function and thereby on the choice behaviour of an individual. The essay introduces domain conditions for rationalisability that, unlike restricting the choice behaviour of an individual, place constraints on the domains of choice functions. It provides a necessary and sufficient condition for a domain over which all choice functions are rationalisable. It introduces a set of domain conditions and shows that if a domain satisfies these conditions then all choice functions defined over that domain would be quasi-transitive rationalisable.

The third part 'Law and Economics' features three essays. Ram Singh in 'Existence and Efficiency of Equilibria When Care is Multi-dimensional' argues that multidimensional care is a basic feature of reality in many accident contexts. Nonetheless, the economic models of liability rules generally take the nature of care to be uni-dimensional. In this essay, the author models the care levels to be multidimensional. Moreover, care is assumed to have verifiable as well as non-verifiable dimensions. Under this assumption, the essay examines the conditions necessary for existence of equilibrium under standard liability rules. These conditions are used to show that standard liability rules fail to induce the first-best efficient care levels with respect to not only the non-verifiable but also the verifiable aspects of care. Moreover, second-best efficiency requires some loss sharing between non-negligent parties. Therefore, the standard liability rules are not efficient even from a second-best perspective.

In the essay 'Efficiency of (1, 2)-Incremental Liability Rules: Some Results', Rajendra Kundu investigates questions on efficient apportionment of accident losses resulting from harmful interactions involving one victim and two injurers. The notion of a $(1, 2)$-incremental liability rule is introduced, and efficient rules for some classes of $(1, 2)$-incremental liability rules are completely characterised.

In 'On Breach Remedies: Contracting with Bilateral Selfish Investment and Two-sided Private Information', Sugata Bag considers a setting of bilateral selfish reliance investments and post-contractual two-sided asymmetric information. One can take it as established that comprehensive contracts can implement the first-best choice even if the parties' valuations are private information, and reliance investments are of the selfish type (with quasi-linear utilities). However, real world contracts seem to be rather simple, fixed-price incomplete contracts, which are sometimes renegotiated later. Hence, it is of interest to analyse whether breach remedies can introduce the first best in this set-up. The essay represents an effort at filling this gap in the literature, and presents a set of results by exploring the problem.

The fourth part of the book deals with the theme of 'Stratagems and Private Gains'. In the first essay on this theme 'Auctions with Ceilings', Priyodorshi Banerjee and Archishman Chakraborty argue that in symmetric common value auctions where bidders differ ex post in information quality, a seller may benefit from committing to a ceiling on allowable bids. By reducing the winner's curse facing poorly informed bidders, a ceiling encourages them to bid aggressively. This may reduce information rents earned by better-informed bidders, yielding the seller higher expected revenues compared to selling the object in a standard ascending auction or at a fixed posted price. Trade with a ceiling can be interpreted as a scenario where the object is offered for sale at a fixed price or the best offer.

Sarbajit Chaudhuri and Krishnendu Ghosh Dastidar in the essay 'Corruption in Union Leadership' develop a model of a two-stage game between a corrupt trade union leader and the management of the firm where the former negotiates for the wages of the workers in the firm. The management of the firm bribes the leader so that he keeps the wage as close as possible to the workers' reservation wage. The analysis leads to some interesting results, which could be of significance for anti-corruption policy formulation.

The fifth part of the book 'Development and Policy' has two essays. Amitava Bose's 'Alternative Models for Structural Change and Unbalanced Growth' discusses the modelling of structural changes that the Indian economy is currently experiencing. Neoclassical models are not appropriate for this. First, in contrast to the Kaldor facts that such models address, the Indian economy is clearly in the phase of *transitional* rather than balanced growth dynamics. Second, a major contemporary concern is that high growth in India has not proved to be 'inclusive'. The surplus unskilled labour of the agriculture sector is not being sucked out through increased employment in the expanding parts of the economy, viz., the services sector. Neither full-employment models of the neoclassical variety nor Lewis-type surplus labour models are appropriate in this context. An alternative to these is the tradition of the Cambridge School. The setting is that of a two-sector dual economy but the distinguishing characteristic of this tradition—in contrast to the Ricardian roots of the Lewis model—is emphasis on the role of *demand* factors and less reliance on the market-clearing role of the inter-sectoral terms of trade. However, there are some important issues of model-building that have been left open and the essay addresses some of these.

The second essay 'Public Expansion of Higher Education and a Dynamic Todaro Paradox' by Subrata Guha considers a dual economy with the addition of a public higher education sector. There is an infinitely elastic supply of physical capital available in the economy but employment in the knowledge-intensive sector of the economy, comprising the high productivity commodity-producing sector and the public education sector, is restricted to those with a threshold level of education. The essay considers how the relative size of the public education sector may influence the rate of employment growth in the knowledge-intensive sector as well as the rate of employment of qualified job seekers in that sector in the long run. A necessary and sufficient condition is derived for the existence of a dynamic Todaro Paradox—the possibility that there is a long-run trade-off between increasing the rate of employment growth and increasing the rate of employment of qualified job seekers.

The sixth part of the book 'Social and Economic Measurement' comprises four essays. In the essay 'On a Family of Indices for Envy in Situations of Income Inequality', Ravindra Ranade and Yukie Shimono examine continuous income distributions of the triangular type that are skewed to the left. Taking this as an approximation for the supposedly ideal lognormal one, the essay constructs the Lorenz curve for the distribution. The difference between the lower y per cent of the population and the proportion of that population's income $g(y)$ is taken as the basis for measuring the envy experienced by the population in question. Leaving aside, for future work, the possibility of taking positive monotonic transformations of this distance as corresponding to different notions of envy, the essay takes the distance itself as a measure of envy and, thus, arrives at an index that is nothing but the area between the diagonal and the Lorenz curve. The index involves the minimum, modal and maximum incomes as three parameters, or equivalently the range, variance and mean as the parameters of interest. The essay highlights the limits on the Gini coefficient and questions the appropriateness of using perfect equality and perfect inequality as the two goalposts that are commonly taught in classrooms.

In the essay 'On a Distance Function-Based Inequality Measure in the Spirit of the Bonferroni and Gini Indices', S. Subramanian suggests that a natural way of viewing an inequality or a poverty measure is in terms of the vector distance between an actual (empirical) distribution of incomes and some appropriately normative distribution (reflecting a perfectly equal distribution of incomes, or a distribution with the smallest mean that is compatible with a complete absence of poverty). Real analysis offers a number of distance functions to choose from. In this essay, the employment of what is known as the Canberra distance function leads to an inequality measure in the tradition of the Bonferroni and Gini indices of inequality. The essay discusses some properties of the measure, and presents a graphical representation of inequality that shares commonalities with the well-known Lorenz curve depiction of distributional inequality.

In the essay 'Measuring Vulnerability to Poverty: An Expected Poverty Index', Satya R. Chakravarty and Nachiketa Chattopadhyay note that vulnerability to poverty is defined as the magnitude of the threat of poverty. Continuing in the tradition of earlier work done by Calvo–Dercon, and Chakravarty, this essay develops an axiomatic characterisation of an expected index of vulnerability using the von Neumann–Morgernstern utility function.

Tapan Mitra's essay ' On Literacy Rankings' is concerned with one of the principal themes of the literature on literacy which posits that, taking into account the fact that literate household members generate a positive externality for illiterate members, a more equitable distribution of literates across households leads to greater effective literacy. The essay shows that the validity of this observation does not depend on the choice of a specific externality function, but applies to an entire class of externality functions, consistent with decomposable literacy indices satisfying a set of reasonable axioms. Further, the distributions of literacy rates across households that can be compared are not confined merely to extreme polar cases, but are as numerous as those that are Lorenz comparable.

In what we regard as a fitting epilogue, we conclude with an abridged version of the final chapter of Satish's Ph.D. dissertation titled 'The Stability of Binary Social Decision Rules'. We hope this will go some way in making more accessible what, in our view, is one of the most important contributions to social choice theory. And even if our effort is a belated one, nevertheless one must draw such satisfaction as one can from what the poet Gerard Manley Hopkins called 'that dismal proverb'.

REFERENCES

Jain, Satish K. 1975. 'The Stability of Binary Social Decision Rules', Unpublished Ph.D Dissertation, University of Rochester.

———. 1983. 'Necessary and Sufficient Conditions for Quasi-transitivity and Transitivity of Special Majority Rules', *Keio Economic Studies*, 20(2): 55–63.

———. 1984. 'Non-minority Rules: Characterization of Configurations with Rational Social Preferences', *Keio Economic Studies*, 21(2): 45–54.

———. 1986. 'Special Majority Rules: Necessary and Sufficient Condition for Quasi-transitivity with Quasi-transitive Individual Preferences', *Social Choice and Welfare*, 3(2): 99–106.

———. 1995. 'The Coherence of Rights', in D. Andler, P. Banerjee, M. Chaudhury and O. Guillaume (eds), *Facets of Rationality*. New Delhi: Sage Publications, pp. 104–24.

———. 2005. 'The Structure of Efficient Liability Rules', unpublished manuscript available at http://ssrn.com/abstract=1844577 and http://dx.doi.org/10.2139/ssrn.1844577 (accessed on 18 July 2014).

———. 2006. 'Efficiency of Liability Rules: A Reconsideration', *Journal of International Trade & Economic Development*, 15(3): 359–73.

———. 2009a. 'The Method of Majority Decision and Rationality Conditions', in K. Basu and R. Kanbur (eds), *Ethics, Welfare, and Measurement*, Volume 1 of *Arguments for a Better World: Essays in Honor of Amartya Sen*, pp. 167–97. New York: Oxford University Press.

———. 2009b. 'The Structure of Incremental Liability Rules', *Review of Law & Economics*, 5(1): 373–98.

———. 2010. 'The Coasean Analysis of Harmful Interactions: Some Conceptual Difficulties', available at http://ssrn.com/abstract=1627622 or http://dx.doi.org/10.2139/ssrn.1627622 (accessed on 18 July 2014).

———. 2012. 'Decoupled Liability and Efficiency: An Impossibility Theorem', *Review of Law & Economics*, 8(3): 697–718.

Jain, Satish K. and Ram Singh. 2002. 'Efficient Liability Rules: Complete Characterisation', *Journal of Economics*, 75(2): 105–24.

Niemi, R. G. and W. H. Riker. 1976. 'The Choice of Voting Systems', *Scientific American*, 234(6): 21–27.

Sen, A. K. 1970. 'The Impossibility of a Paretian Liberal', *Journal of Political Economy*, 78(1): 152–59.

PART I
INSTITUTIONS AND EFFICIENCY

1

Market Failures:
Almost Always?

Anjan Mukherji*

We shall argue that market failures are far more endemic than generally assumed. This assertion opens up the question that if the market has to be carefully nurtured, then who should look after this aspect. Hence, this essay is an attempt to clarify the nature of interventions required to restore the market. Alternatively, this discussion may be seen as an attempt at uncovering what the role of governments must include. It would appear that governments, or maybe some outside agencies, have a huge responsibility. A smaller government or a withdrawal from matters of the market will just not do. This matter, apart from being of theoretical importance, has received a great deal of attention over the years; for example, in the last election for the position of the most powerful person in the world, the US president, one of the major points of debate between the two main protagonists was the role of the government. The one who favoured a larger role, won the election but it is not as if the debate has been settled. On the contrary, the positions taken seem to have hardened. And the consequences affect not only the US economy but the entire world. In the circumstances, it seems worthwhile

* I am grateful to the National Institute of Public Finance and Policy, New Delhi, for hosting me during the tenure of the Jawaharlal Nehru National Fellowship and thereafter, when this essay was prepared. Earlier versions have been presented at various venues and comments received are gratefully acknowledged. The essay is dedicated with great affection to Professor Satish Jain on the occasion of his retirement from the position of RBI (Reserve Bank of India) Chair in Economic Theory at the Centre for Economic Studies and Planning, JNU (Jawaharlal Nehru University) New Delhi. Satish Jain has been one of the most outstanding personalities that I have come across: a very original mind, the kind seldom encountered, an outstanding teacher and a very loyal friend. In fact, my first attempt to come to terms with the matters reported here were presented in the first conference organised by Satish Jain in 2007 and I am grateful to S. Subramanian, Rajendra Kundu and Subrata Guha for providing me with an opportunity and the time frame to contribute to this volume.

to investigate matters and clarify exactly what governments should do to enable markets to prosper.

We are, thus, proceeding with the basic assumption that economies function under a system of competitive markets. This basic assumption may be considered to be a worthwhile one only if competitive markets yield interesting outcomes. We first investigate these properties, namely, the efficiency of competitive outcomes. We then proceed to demonstrate how and why these properties are dependent on some features of the underlying characteristics of the economy and, hence, go on to show how the markets, on their own, may generally be unable to satisfy these characteristics. Thus, we shall argue that markets, when left to themselves, will almost always fail.

The introduction of an agency outside the purview of the markets may be required to ensure that the missing characteristics are in place so that markets function the way they are supposed to. This outside agency may be identified with either the government or civil society. The first may be required to set up taxes and subsidies to encourage proper behaviour on the part of economic agents; the second will, in general, set up values or modes of conduct, which also elicit proper reactions from decision makers. The extent of such interventions will then be used to clarify the role of such external agencies.

However, the necessity for introducing such outside agencies and the kind of support they have to provide raises questions about incentives. And we shall discuss what needs to be done in this context. We begin by noting what the wise have said. It turns out that contrary to the lament of US President Harry S. Truman 'Give me a one-handed economist' (since all economists invariably mention 'on the one-hand ...' and then continue with 'On the other ...')', economists over the ages have spoken with a rare degree of uniformity on the role of the government or the support to foster markets. We next turn to these assertions and claims.

Received Wisdom

Chanakya, the adviser to Chandragupta Maurya, the emperor who ruled around 320 BC over Magadha, which comprised a great chunk of the sub-continent, advised as follows: 'In the interests of the prosperity of the country, a king should be diligent [and] remove all obstructions to economic activity.' Further, 'The pursuit of the people's welfare ... the economic well-being of the society is dependant on the sceptre wielded by the King. The maintenance of law and order by the use of punishment is the science of government' (Rangarajan 1992: 108, 116). During Chanakya's time, the king was the government. Notice, therefore, the stress laid on the maintenance of law and order and the fact that this was considered crucial for ensuring prosperity of the people.

Almost 2,000 years later, Adam Smith is reported to have said, 'Little else is required to carry a state to the highest degree of opulence from the lowest barbarism, but peace, easy taxes, and a tolerable administration of justice; all the rest being brought about by the natural course of things' (Stewart 1793: 38–39). Notice that here too, law and order and a 'tolerable' amount of justice are asserted to yield rich dividends.

Two hundred years later, Milton Friedman, the celebrated economist who is perhaps the leading proponent of free markets as a panacea for everything, was also very clear about what support had to be provided: '[The government's] major function must be to protect our freedom both from enemies outside our gates and from our fellow citizens: to preserve law and order, to enforce private contracts, to foster competitive markets' (Friedman 1952: 2). Notice that even Friedman realised that free markets function only if governments are sufficiently strong to maintain law and order, and are able to enforce private contracts. This may appear to be a fresh charge put on governments, but enforcing private contracts is also an essential part of maintaining peace or law and order. The agreement between all the three scholars could not have been more striking.

To add this agreement, let us consider some more contemporary scholars. Olson (1993: 56) writes, '[N]o society can work satisfactorily if it does not have a peaceful order and usually other public goods as well. Obviously anarchic violence cannot be rational for a society: the victims of violence and theft lose not only what is taken from them but also the incentive to produce any goods which could be taken by others. There is accordingly little or no production in the absence of a peaceful order. Thus, there are colossal gains from providing domestic tranquillity and other basic public goods.' In fact, Olson describes bandits to be either of the roving type or those that are stationary; and roving bandits pillage and plunder and go from place to place destroying each place as they move on. The stationary bandits maintain peace and order and make it worthwhile for people to produce for it is only then that they themselves can prosper. Once again, there is an appeal for law and order and the delivery of public goods.

Our final quotation is from Besley and Persson (2011: 5): 'state authority, tax systems, court systems and democracy co-evolve in a complex web of interdependent causality'. Therefore, the following characteristics are found to be necessary for the proper functioning of any economy:

1. Peace
2. Law and order
3. Ensuring private contracts
4. Functioning competitive markets
5. Quality public services

Clearly, we should be careful in specifying what we mean by 'proper' functioning. To make matters easy we shall take the forementioned properties to be the defining characteristics of a proper functioning economy. We shall show next why our intuitive understanding of what a proper functioning economy should be is best described thus. The received wisdom in this context lends a strong support to this view. To conduct our analysis, we need to specify the context within which we shall be confined and we proceed to do so next.

THE ECONOMY

Preliminaries
Usually the entire discussion relating to markets and their positive and normative properties is usually carried out in the context of the well-known $2 \times 2 \times 2$ models, that is, models where two scarce factors are used to produce two commodities for two individuals.[1] One aspect of these models is the fact that there are several hidden assumptions: for instance, the fact that the number of factors and the number of goods are the same. This aspect allows the use of the production possibility locus with differentiable boundaries. In general cases, this aspect cannot be assumed and the standard arguments cannot be made.[2] We shall explain what we mean more explicitly by first providing some links.

Consider then an economy with two individuals A, B, who own the scarce factors which cannot be produced L, T and the constant returns to scale technology which are used to produce two goods F, C; A, B have utility functions $U_i(x_F, x_C)$ which are continuously differentiable and strictly quasi-concave and possess stocks of the factors L_J, T_J $J = A, B$; further $y_j = \phi_j(L_j, T_j)$, $j = F$, C denote the production functions and the

---

[1] See, for instance, Bator (1957) and Jones (1965).

[2] See, for instance, Manning and Melvin (1992). In case the number of goods and factors do not match, we may not have a production possibility locus of the type we use; in fact, if there are more goods than factors there will necessarily be ruled surface (Melvin 1968). I am indebted to Tapan Mitra for advice on this matter.

amounts of L, T available are denoted by $\bar{L} = L_A + L_B$, $\bar{T} = T_A + T_B$ respectively; the functions $\phi_j(.)$ are continuously differentiable with continuous partial derivatives and we may use the standard steps to obtain the production possibility locus $G(y_F, y_C) = 0$ as the locus of full-employment outputs. With these things in place, we may define a **feasible state** as a collection $x_F^A, x_C^A, x_F^B, x_C^B, y^F, y^C, L_F.L_C, T_F, T_C$ such that

1. $x_j^A + x_j^B = y_j \; j = F, C$
2. $y_j = \phi_j(L_j, T_j) \; j = F, C$
3. $L_F + L_C = \bar{L} \; ; T_F + T_C = \bar{T}$

A **competitive equilibrium** given the initial distribution $\{L_A, T_A, L_B, T_B\}$ is a feasible state $(x_F^{A\star}, x_C^{A\star}, x_F^{B\star}, x_C^{B\star}, y^{F\star}, y^{C\star}, L_F^\star, L_C^\star, T_F^\star, T_C^\star)$ together with a price configuration $P^\star = (p_F^\star, p_C^\star = 1, w^\star, r^\star)$ such that, assuming interior maxima:

$$p_F^\star = \frac{\partial U^I(*)}{\partial x_F} \Big/ \frac{\partial U^I(*)}{\partial x_C} \; I = A, B \qquad (1.1)$$

where $*$ denotes the fact that the partial derivatives are all evaluated at the competitive equilibrium, good C being the numeraire. Relative prices match the marginal rate of substitution and utilities are maximised subject to a budget constraint.

Further,[3]

$$\phi_{jL}(*)/\phi_{jT}(*) = w^\star/r^\star \; j = F, C \qquad (1.2)$$

Thus, production is under least cost and price equals marginal cost so that we have along the production possibility locus:

$$\frac{dy_F}{dy_C} = -\frac{G_C}{G_F} = -p_F^\star \qquad (1.3)$$

And finally, an **efficient state** is a feasible state $(x_F^{A\star}, x_C^{A\star}, x_F^{B\star}, x_C^{B\star}, y^{F\star}, y^{C\star}, L_F^\star, L_C^\star, T_F^\star, T_C^\star)$ such that there is no other feasible state $x_F^A, x_C^A, x_F^B, x_C^B, y^F, y^C, L_F.L_C, T_F, T_C$ such that $U^I(x_F^I, x_C^I) \geqq U^I(x_F^{I\star}, x_C^{I\star}) \forall I$ with strict inequality for at least one.

Much of what follows will be concerned with the relationship between the states discussed. In fact, the First Fundamental Theorem of Welfare Economics is usually stated thus: A competitive equilibrium

---

[3] ϕ_{Jx} denotes the partial of the function ϕ_J with respect to x.

induces an efficient state. This is easy to see in terms of the classical marginal conditions. This is not only straightforward, but also revealing since the links that may be snapped due to one reason or another are easy to spot.

On the other hand, at an efficient state, using the definition in a straight/forward manner, and assuming that the efficient state contains positive quantities of all variables, we must have:

1. **efficiency in production,** that is, given $\bar{L}$, $\bar{T}$ it will not be possible to produce more of one good with producing less of the other or we must have

$$\frac{\phi_{FL}}{\phi_{FT}} = \frac{\phi_{CL}}{\phi_{CT}};$$

2. **efficiency in consumption,** that is, given outputs y_F, y_C, it will not be possible to redistribute the goods among the individuals so as to make one person better off without making the other worse off or we must have

$$\frac{U^A_{x_F}}{U^A_{x_C}} = \frac{U^B_{x_F}}{U^B_{x_C}};$$

3. **overall efficiency,** that is, the common value of the marginal rates of substitution must equal the absolute value of the slope of the production possibility locus or we must have

$$\frac{U^A_{x_F}}{U^A_{x_C}} = \frac{U^B_{x_F}}{U^B_{x_C}} = \frac{G_F}{G_C}.$$

To see the necessity of the last, suppose that the common marginal rate of substitution is 2 and less than the absolute value of the slope of the production possibility locus, which is, say, 1. Such a situation cannot be efficient for we can take away 2 units of good C from, say, A and reduce the output of C by 2 units; this allows the increase of F production by 2 units and may be used to more than compensate A and, thus, make A better off without affecting B.

Armed with these conditions, it is easy to see how and why a competitive equilibrium induces an efficient state. (1.1–1.3) imply that the conditions necessary at an efficient state are all satisfied and an argument to establish that these conditions are sufficient as well closes the demonstration of the fact that the competitive equilibrium induces an efficient state, that is, the First Fundamental Theorem of Welfare Economics. This result may be demonstrated under more general conditions without taking the help of the first order conditions.[4] But this argument has the advantage in that it reveals what can go wrong between the two sets of conditions since that will precisely identify what may be called the case of a market failure. Before we proceed, we need to ask whether this approach may be recast in more general situations when there are many goods and this is what we take up next.

The Linear Activity Analysis Model

We consider a model involving m individuals and n goods; some of these goods are produced, while the remaining are factors and are not produced within the system; in particular, we shall assume that goods indexed $j = 1, \cdots, r$ refer to the produced or final goods, while goods indexed $j = r + 1, \cdots, n$ refer to the primary goods or factors. We shall adopt the sign convention of using positive quantities for outputs and negative ones for inputs. The production sector will be considered as an aggregative one, satisfying constant returns to scale, with a fixed number (say m) of basic activities $\{a_{kj}\}$, $k = 1, \cdots, n$, and $j = 1, \cdots, m$. An activity is the column

$$\begin{pmatrix} a_{1j} \\ a_{2j} \\ . \\ . \\ a_{nj} \end{pmatrix}$$

There are m such basic activities at unit levels of operation; they are basic in the sense that they cannot be expressed as linear combinations of other activities; and adopting some convention, we assume that they have been scaled so that they represent unit level of operation, taking advantage of the constant returns to scale. a_{kj}, thus, denotes the usage of good k for unit level of operation of activity j. Further, $a_{kj} > 0$ implies that commodity k is an output, whereas a negative sign would imply that it is an input of activity j.[5]

The basic activities may be written as columns of a matrix $A = [a_{kj}]$, which is an $n \times m$ matrix; the first r rows of the matrix may be

---

[4] See, for example, Arrow (1951).

[5] We adopt the following sign convention for $x \in \Re^n$, $x = (x_k)$, $x \geq 0 \Rightarrow x_k \geq 0 \forall k$ and is said to be non-negative. $x \geq 0 \Rightarrow x_k \geq 0 \forall k$, $x_{k_1} > 0$ for some k_1 and is said to be semi-positive; finally $x > 0 \Rightarrow x_k > 0 \forall k$ and is said to be positive.

represented as A_F and the remaining part as A_P. Also given our sign convention, it follows that $A_P \leq 0$ since $a_{kj} \leq 0$ for $r + 1 \leq k \leq n$ and any j. We shall insist that the activity matrix satisfy, in addition, the following:

A1: $\exists z^* \geq 0$ such that $A_F.z^* > 0$.
A2: There is no $z \geq 0$ such that $A.z = 0$.
A3: There is no $z \geq 0$ such that $A.z \geq 0$.

These are standard requirements; the first ensures that all goods which are not available (the first r) can, in fact, be produced; the second ensures that that production processes are irreversible, while the last ensures that to produce outputs, some input must necessarily be required (often called more colourfully, there is no free lunch!).

There is a fixed amount of the unproduced factors available denoted by $b \in \mathfrak{R}_{++}^{n-r}$; it is the unproduced goods that are available initially with the individuals. Each individual has a real-valued utility function $U^i : \mathfrak{R}_+^n \to \mathfrak{R}$; further, each U^i is assumed to be *strictly increasing, strictly quasi-concave and continuously differentiable* over $\mathfrak{R}_{++}^n$, with the stipulation that $U^i(x) = 0$, if $x_j = 0$ for some j, for all i and $U^i(x) > 0 \forall x \in \mathfrak{R}_{++}^n.$[6] We shall specify a distribution of b among the individuals, denoted by $b^i \in \mathfrak{R}_+^{n-r}$ such that $\sum_i b^i \leq b$: these are the endowments. We note that we can write

$$\bar{W} = \begin{pmatrix} 0 \\ b \end{pmatrix}$$

where 0 refers to the first r components and b refers to the remaining, the primary goods.[7]

Let us denote the set of all feasible allocations by the set

$$\mathcal{A} = \{\{x^i\} : \exists y, \sum_i x^i \leq y + \bar{W}\}$$

and $\exists z \geq 0$ such that $A_F.z \geq 0, A_P.z \geq -b\}$;

---

[6] This is just to rule out corner maxima; otherwise we would need to state results for corner maxima separately and the presentation becomes cumbersome, to say the least.

[7] We shall write for $x \in \mathfrak{R}^n, x = (x_F, x_P)$, where x_F denotes the first r components and x_P denotes the remaining components $r + 1, \cdots, n$. Thus, $\bar{W}_F = 0, \bar{W}_P = b$.

given the endowments $\{b^i\}$, and a price situation $P = (p, q)$, where $p \in \mathfrak{R}^r_{++}, q \in \mathfrak{R}^{n-r}_{++}$, we can then proceed with defining demands $x^i(P)$ as the unique maximiser of U^i in the budget set provided by[8] $\{x : P^T.x \leq q^T.b^i\}$, where $P \in \mathfrak{R}^n_{++}, P = (p_1, \cdots, p_r, q_1, \cdots q_{n-r})$ is the price vector; in case we have a numeraire, we shall consider good r to be the numeraire and write the price vector as $P = (p, q), p_r = 1$.

Given P, profit maximisation would entail choosing y such that $P^T.y$ is maximised subject to $y \in \mathcal{A} = \{y = (y_F, y_P), y_F \in \mathfrak{R}^r_+, y_P \in \mathfrak{R}^{n-r}_- : \exists z \geqq 0, y_F \leqq A_F.z, y_P \geqq A_P.z, A_P.z \geqq -b\}$.[9] We shall denote this collection of maximisers by $Y(P)$: the $y \in Y(P)$ denotes **market supply** (although for some coordinates, namely, $y_k, r + 1 \leq k \leq n$, the factors, this will be the market demand for factors. We need to pin down some properties of the market supply. The problem being solved is

$$\max P^T.y \text{ subject to } y \in \mathcal{A}.$$

We note first of all that:

Claim 1. *If $P > 0, y \in Y(P) \Rightarrow y = A.z$ for some $z \geqq 0$.*

Proof: Since $y \in Y(P)$, there is $z \geqq 0$ such that $y_F \leqq A_F.z, y_P \geqq A_P.z$, from the definition of the collection $\mathcal{A}$; if possible, let strict inequality hold in some component; then $\exists y' \in \mathcal{A}$, either

$$y'_F \geqq y_F \text{ or } y'_P \leqq y_P \Rightarrow P^T.y' > P^T.y \Rightarrow y \notin Y(P),$$

that is, a contradiction. Hence, the claim.

Given this, we may rewrite the profit maximisation problem thus:

$$\max P^T.A.z \text{ subject to } A_F.z \geqq 0, -A_P.z \leqq b, z \geqq 0$$

This, of course, is a standard linear programming problem. We note that this problem always has a solution for any $P > 0$. To establish this fact and given the Fundamental Theorem of Linear Programming (Gale 1960), we first note that the maximum problem has the following dual minimisation problem:

$$\min \theta_F^T.0 + \theta_P^T.b \text{ subject to } -\theta_F^T.A_F - \theta_P^T.A_P \geqq P^T.A \ (\theta_F, \theta_P) \geqq 0$$

Claim 2. *The maximum and minimum problems have feasible solutions.*

---

[8] We shall use the superscript T to denote matrix transposition.
[9] There may not be a unique maximiser.

In other words,

$$\exists z \geqq 0 \text{ such that } A_F.z \geqq 0, -A_P.z \leqq b$$

and

$$\exists(\theta_F, \theta_P) \geqq 0$$

such that

$$-\theta_F^T.A_F - \theta_P^T.A_P \geqq P^T.A$$

Proof: Recall the axioms A1–A3 noted earlier. First of all, it should be pointed out that earlier A1 implies that the maximum problem has a feasible solution; since there is a $z^* \geqq 0$ such that $A_F.z^* > 0$, we can scale down z^* proportionately, if required, to satisfy the remaining constraint. Suppose then that the minimum problem has no feasible solution. In other words, suppose that there is no $\theta \geqq 0$ such that $-\theta_F^T.A_F - \theta_P^T.A_P \geqq P^T.A$ or there is no non-negative solution to $\theta_F^T.A_F + \theta_P^T.A_P \leqq -P^T.A$; by the Theorem of the Separating Hyperplane and its corollaries (Gale 1960: chapter 2), it follows that there is a non-negative solution to

$$\begin{pmatrix} A_F \\ A_P \end{pmatrix}.y \geqq 0, -P^T.A.y < 0.$$

Since the last inequality is strict, it follows that this non-negative solution y must, in fact, be semi-positive. Notice then the first set of inequalities will violate either Axiom A2 or A3. So no such solution can exist and, hence, the minimum problem must have a feasible solution.

Claim 3. *In case $P^T.A \leqq 0$, $y \in Y(P) \Rightarrow P^T.y = 0$ (zero profits).*

Proof: Consider the maximum and minimum problems defined earlier. Notice that since $P^T.A \leqq 0$, $\theta = 0$ is feasible for the minimum problem, and provides the value 0 to the objective function; no other feasible solution can provide a lower value since $b > 0$ and $\theta \geqq 0$. By the Fundamental Theorem of Linear Programming, it follows that if z solves the maximum problem, then $P^T.A.z = 0$, or, as claimed, $P^T.y = 0 \forall y \in Y(P)$.

We also note that:

Claim 4. *If z^* solves the profit maximisation problem at P, that is, the maximum problem provided earlier, and $P^T.A \leqq 0$, and for each primary factor k, $r + 1 \leqq k \leqq n$, $P_k = 0$ if $\sum_j a_{kj} z_j^* < b_k$, then z^* also* *solves the following:* $\max P_F^T.A_F.z$ *subject to* $A_F.z \geqq 0 - A_P.z \leqq b\ z \geqq 0.$[10]

Proof: The output value maximum problem has the following dual:

$$\min \theta_F^T.0 + \theta_P^T.b \text{ subject to } \left(\theta_F^T \ \theta_P^T\right). \begin{pmatrix} -A_F \\ -A_P \end{pmatrix} \geqq P_F^T.A_F$$

From the conditions given, it follows that $(0, P_P)$ is feasible for this minimum problem. In addition, note that z^* is feasible for the output maximum problem. Hence, it follows that $P_F^T.A_F.z^* \leqq P_P^T.b$; if the strict inequality holds, then since by the previous claim, we have $P_F^T.A_F.z^* = -P_P^T.A_P.z^*$, it follows that we must have $-P_P^T.A_P.z^* < P_P^T.b$, which means that there must be some unproduced factor k for which $P_k > 0$ and at the same time the $k - th$ component of $-A_P.z^* < b_k$, which contradicts the hypothesis. This establishes the claim.

Competitive Equilibrium and Efficiency

With these preliminaries in place, we are ready to show that in spite of the problems in following the route adopted in the $2 \times 2 \times 2$ situation, we can investigate the links between the competitive equilibrium state and an efficient state.

We begin with the definition of an feasible state; a configuration $\{x^I, y, z\}$ is said to be feasible if the following holds:

$$\sum_I x_F^I \leqq y_F, \ \sum_I x_P^I \leqq y_P + b, \ y_F = A_F.z \geqq 0, \ y_P = A_P.z \geqq -b, \ z \geqq 0.$$

Given the matrix A of basic activities and an allocation $\{b^I\}, b^I \geq 0 \forall I$ such that $\sum_I b^I = b$, a price vector P^* and a feasible state $\{x^{I*}, y^*, z^*\}$ constitute a competitive equilibrium (and the feasible state is called a competitive state), if the following conditions are satisfied:

1. $P^{*T}.A \leqq 0$
2. For each I, x^{I*} solves $\max U^I(x)$ subject to $P^{*T}.x \leqq P_P^{*T}.b^I$
3. $y^* = A.z^*$ where z^* solves the problem $\max P^{*T}.A.z$ subject to $A_F.z \geqq 0, -A_P.z \leqq b, z \geqq 0$

We should point out that:

Claim 5. *Given A3, $P^T.A \leqq 0$ has a semi-positive solution.*

---

[10] This problem is the maximisation of the value of the produced goods or the output value maximum problem.

Proof: Given A3, it follows that $A.z > 0$ can have no non-negative solution since that is ruled out by A3 (there can be no outputs without inputs). Now by virtue of a result in Gale (1960: chapter 2), it follows that $P^T A \leqq 0$ must have a semi-positive solution.

A feasible state $\{x^{I\circ}, y^\circ, z^\circ\}$ is said to be efficient if there is no other feasible state $\{x^I, y, z\}$ such that $U^I(x^I) \geqq U^I(x^{I\circ})$ for all I with strict inequality for one. With this definition in place, we can proceed to show that an efficient state $\{x^{I\circ}, y^\circ, z^\circ\}$ must solve the following problem for any I, say, $I = 1$:

$$\max U^1(x^1)$$

subject to

$$U^I\left(x^I\right) \geqq U^{I\circ} \forall I \neq 1,$$
$$\sum x_F^I \leqq y_F, \quad \sum x_P^I \leqq y_P + b,$$
$$y = A.z, \ A_F.z \geqq 0, -A_P.z \leqq b, z \geqq 0$$

where $U^{I\circ} = U^I(x^{I\circ})$ are the utilities at some feasible state $\{x^{I\circ}, y^\circ, z^\circ\}$. We redefine the problem using the constraints as follows:

$$\max U^1(x^1)$$

subject to

$$U'\left(x^I\right) \geqq U^{I\circ} \text{ for all } I \neq 1$$
$$\sum_I x_F^I \leqq A_F.z$$
$$\sum_I x_P^I \leqq A_P.z + b$$
$$z \geqq 0, x^I \geqq 0$$

The Lagrangean for the problem $L(\{x^I\}, z; \lambda, \mu)$ is written as:

$$U^1(x^1) + \sum_{I \neq 1} \lambda_I (U^I(x^I) - U^{I\circ}) + \sum_{i \in F} \mu_i \left(\sum_j a_{ij} z_j - \sum_I x_i^I \right)$$
$$+ \sum_{i \in P} \mu_i \left(\sum_j a_{ij} z_j + b_j - \sum_I x_i^I \right).$$

Recall that in order for $\{x^{I\circ}, z^\circ\}$ to solve the problem, *it is necessary*, provided some constraint qualification is satisfied, that there exists $\lambda^\circ, \mu^\circ \geqq 0$ such that $\{x^{I\circ}, z^\circ, \lambda^\circ, \mu^\circ\}$ form a saddle point for the

Lagrangean $L(\{x^I\}, z; \lambda, \mu)$. This, in turn, implies the following first order conditions, some times referred to as the Kuhn–Tucker conditions:[11]

$$U_j^1(x^{1\circ}) \leqq \mu_j^\circ \text{ and } \lambda_I^\circ U_j^I(x^{I\circ}) \leqq \mu_j^\circ \forall I \neq 1, \forall j = 1, \cdots, m; \quad (1.4)$$

and, further,

$$(U_j^1(x^{1\circ}) - \mu_j^\circ)x_j^{1\circ} = 0 \text{ and } (\lambda_I^\circ U_j^I(x^{I\circ}) - \mu_j^\circ).x_j^{I\circ} = 0, x_j^{I\circ} \geqq 0 \forall I, j \quad (1.5)$$

$$\sum_i \mu_i^\circ a_{i\tau} \leqq 0 \text{ and } \sum_i \mu_i^\circ a_{i\tau}.z_\tau^\circ = 0, z_\tau^\circ \geqq 0, \forall \tau = 1, \cdots, m \quad (1.6)$$

Claim 6. *The maximum problem satisfies the desired constraint qualification conditions.*

Proof: The constraint qualifications consist of the ones identified by Arrow and Enthoven (1961: 789), Theorem 2 [b]). Assume there are M individuals. First of all, note that the functions appearing in the constraint are either strictly quasi-concave or linear affine. Next note that the problem is defined given a feasible $\{x^{I\circ}, z^\circ\}$; consider therefore the array $\{x^{I\prime}\}$ defined by $x^{1\prime} = \frac{1}{4}x^{1\circ}; x^{I\prime} = x^{I\circ} + \frac{1}{4(M-1)}x^{1\circ}, \forall I \neq 1$. Notice that $\sum_I x^{I\prime} < \sum_I x^{I\circ}$ and further $U^I(x^{I\prime}) > U^I(x^{I\circ}) \forall I \neq 1$. Thus, all other inequalities are satisfied strictly as well. Consequently, we have $\{x^{I\prime}\}, z^\circ$ satisfy the inequalities strictly. In addition, note that $\nabla U^I(x) = (U_j^I(x)) \neq 0$ for all points in the constraint set and, similarly, the gradient of the remaining constraints, being linear affine, are constant and do not vanish anywhere. Hence, the constraint qualification condition is satisfied.

We note that:

Remark 1. *Whenever λ°, μ° satisfying conditions (1.4)–(1.6) exist, they must also satisfy $\mu_j^\circ > 0$. This follows from the Kuhn–Tucker Condition (1.4), since $U_j^{1\circ} > 0$.*

Before we proceed further, it is best if we note for future reference, the significance of the 'multipliers' μ. The multipliers μ correspond to the inequalities relating to the allocation of goods produced or left over after production. Thus, μ_i° is the amount by which the objective function would change, if a marginal unit of good i was allocated. Thus, the availability of an additional unit of good i, whether in the set F or P, for

---

[11] We write the partial derivative of $U^I(.)$ with respect to the variable x_j as $U_j^I(.)$.

which the maximum amount that a decision maker will be willing to pay is given by the effect on the objective function that is, $U_j^1(x^{1\circ})$; at an efficient state, this is guaranteed for all i such that $x_i^1 > 0$ by virtue of (1.4).

Moreover, notice that at an efficient state, the marginal rate of substitutions across individuals for the same pair of goods have to be identical,[12] just as in the $2 \times 2 \times 2$ case; the overall efficiency does not exactly carry over, but note that the worth to the production unit of an additional unit (μ_j°) must match the worth of this unit to consumers as well as we have remarked earlier. It is in this sense that the necessary conditions carry over. We need to understand the implications of the existence of these 'shadow prices' for the entire exercise: they must match the marginal utilities to a proportionality factor. This will become clear as we proceed.

We are now ready to show that under conditions stated:

Claim 7. *A competitive state is an efficient state.* (*The First Fundamental Theorem of Welfare Economics*)

Proof: The demonstration is based on the definition of a competitive state: at the competitive equilibrium price configuration, utility maximisation must occur; assuming an interior maximum, we must have

$$U_j^I(x^{I\star}) = \gamma^{I\star} P_j^\star \ \forall j \ \forall I$$

for some $\gamma^{I\star}$; hence, we obtain, recalling that $P_r^\star = 1$, that $U_j^I(x^{I\star}) = U_r^I(x^{I\star}).P_j^\star$ for all i and j. Thus, if we write $\mu_j^\star = P_j^\star.U_r^I(x^{1\star})$ and $\lambda^{I\star} = U_r^1(x^{1\star})/U_r^I(x^{I\star})$, then we have:

$$U_j^1(x^{1\star}) = \mu_j^\star \ \forall j \tag{1.7}$$

and

$$\lambda^{I\star} U_j^I(x^{I\star}) = \mu_j^\star \ \forall j \ \forall I \neq 1 \tag{1.8}$$

In addition, since $P^{\star T}.A \leq 0$, we have $\mu^{\star T}.A \leq 0$; we also know that $P^{\star T}.A.z^\star = 0$ (zero profits: Claim 3).

$$\mu^{\star T}.A \leq 0; \mu^{\star T}.A.z^\star = 0, z^\star \geq 0 \tag{1.9}$$

---

[12] If consumed in positive quantities.

Next consider the maximum problem

$$\max U^1(x^1)$$

subject to
$$U^I(x^I) \geq U^{I\star} \text{ for all } I \neq 1$$
$$\sum_I x_F^I \leq A_F.z, \sum_I x_P^I \leq A_P.z + b, z \geq 0, x^I \geq 0$$

where $U^{I\star} = U^I(x^{I\star})$.

Considering the (1.7)–(1.9) and comparing them with (1.4)–(1.6), corresponding to the maximum problem, we conclude that given a competitive equilibrium state $(x^{I\star}, z^\star, y^\star)$, there exists $\lambda^{I\star}, \mu^\star$ such that $\{x^{I\star}, z^\star; \lambda^{I\star}, \mu^\star\}$ satisfies the first order conditions and, hence, $\{x^{I\star}, z^\star\}$ constitutes a solution to the maximum problem defined earlier.[13] This completes the demonstration.

The demonstration also reveals where things may go wrong; basically if the various decision makers are not facing the same 'costs', the Kuhn–Tucker conditions at an efficient state will reflect this; the competitive equilibrium conditions may not reflect this and in such a situation, the demonstration constructed will fail to work; consequently, the links between the two states will be snapped.

We examine in the next section how the competitive equilibrium requirements may not alter in such situations and when the competitive equilibrium itself may either not obtain or cease to exist when the perception of the prices are different among different decision makers. These are the cases when markets are said to fail. This is also the reason why one might need outside support to ensure that this does not happen. This is also the main reason why economists and philosophers from different times have felt the need to argue that some support from outside may be required for the market to function appropriately.

THE RULE OR AN EXCEPTION?

Preliminaries
There are three types of situations which are assumed in matters discussed in the last section. The first is the matter of externalities:

---

[13] See Mukherji (1989). The Kuhn–Tucker conditions are also sufficient for a maximum; Theorem 2 specifies that $\nabla U^1(x^{1\circ}) \neq 0$ and the existence of a point in the constraint set which satisfies all inequalities strictly as being adequate to ensure the sufficiency of the first-order conditions.

where decision making is difficult because outcomes depend on not only actions chosen by oneself but also on decisions made by others. It is known that in such situations, the efficiency conditions themselves undergo a change; the competitive equilibrium requirements themselves need to be redefined due to the interdependence. As we shall show, the only applicable equilibrium notion in such situations is the one due to Nash. Investigating the conditions required for a Nash equilibrium, they turn out to be not too different from the ones required for a competitive equilibrium.

The second involves the nature of information available to decision makers, which differs across buyers and sellers. The third involves markets where some decision makers may be inclined to manipulate prices: something we rule out by fiat earlier. In fact, the last covers the list of almost all markets, and the claim made earlier that as a rule, markets will fail to attain competitive states would then be firmly in place.

We begin to examine some standard examples, for the sake of completeness. Since we have examined the efficiency–competitive allocation link in some detail, we need only point out what happens when something other than what has been assumed is introduced or taken into account.

Externalities

When the returns received by decision makers depend not only on decisions that each takes but also on decision taken by others, we have an externality. For the sake of definiteness, take the case often discussed as a standard example of externality: the case of public goods. Public goods are goods or services which can be jointly consumed and where consumers cannot be excluded from consumption by demanding that they pay a price. The standard example of a public good or service is national defence. The level of national defence made available is for all, and one person being covered by national defence does not imply that another will not be so covered; nor can the supplier say that one person is excluded from enjoying the benefits of national defence.

For the sake of definiteness, assume that one of the outputs of the activity 1, say good 1, is such a good. How does the presence of such a good change the set-up ? Notice that now it will be convenient to consider the bundle X^l as $(x_1, x^l_{\sim 1})$: the notation is to emphasise that while good 1 is available for all jointly, components of other goods $x^l_{\sim 1}$ are specific to the concerned individual. So far competitive equilibrium considerations are concerned, notice that knowing that they can enjoy the benefits of good 1 without actually having to pay for it would imply that few would agree to pay a price for this good. This would, in turn, lead to demand being small compared to what it 'should' be. In evaluating the efficiency conditions, however, the fact that this good is jointly available and is beneficial for all will have to be taken into account. To see how things get affected, consider the maximisation problem. The related Lagrangean $L(\{x^I\}, z; \lambda, \mu)$ is written as:

$$U^1(x^1) + \sum_{I \neq 1} \lambda_I (U^I(x^I) - U^{I\circ}) + \sum_{i \in F} \mu_i \left(\sum_j a_{ij} z_j - \sum_I x_i^I \right)$$

$$+ \sum_{i \in P} \mu_i \left(\sum_j a_{ij} z_j + b_j - \sum_I x_i^I \right).$$

The only difference being that in the utility functions, we need to take into account the fact that we have $U^I(x_1, x_{\sim 1}^I)$, as explained earlier. Consequently, the equation corresponding to (1.4) will reflect this and we now have:

$$U_1^1(x_1^\circ, x_{\sim 1}^{1\circ}) + \sum_{I \neq 1} \lambda^I U_1^I(x_1^\circ, x_{\sim 1}^{I\circ}) \leqq \mu_1^\circ \text{ with } = \text{ if } x_1^\circ > 0 \qquad (1.10)$$

The remaining part of (1.4), that is, the partial derivatives corresponding to the variables $x_{\sim 1}^I$ and we have, for example, for $j = r \neq 1$, exactly as before:

$$U_r^1(x_1^\circ, x_{\sim 1}^{1\circ}) = \lambda^I U_r^I(x_1^\circ, x_{\sim 1}^{I\circ}) \leqq \mu_r^\circ \text{ with } = \text{ if } x_r^{I\circ} > 0 \qquad (1.11)$$

For ease of comparison, assuming positive $x_j^{I\circ}$, (1.11) we have from (1.10), dividing throughout by $\mu_r^{\circ 14}$ that

$$\sum_I \frac{U^I(x_1^\circ, x_{\sim 1}^{I\circ})}{U_r^I(x_1^\circ, x_{\sim 1}^{I\circ})} = \frac{\mu_1^\circ}{\mu_r^\circ}$$

Notice that now it is the sum of the marginal rates of substitutions which must equal some quantity; while earlier each of the marginal rates of substitution was equal to the other,[15] the 'spirit' of the equation is the same.

---

[14] The increasing nature of the utility function ensures the positivity.

[15] This is the very well-known Samuelson condition, which is valid when the maximum occurs in the interior (Samuelson 1954). For corner maxima, the condition looks a bit different (see, for example, Mukherji 2002: chapter 5).

For the public good case, since each individual I gets to consume the total amount of good 1 produced, whether they pay for it or not, it follows that the rational thing to do is not to pay anything for it. Consequently, the demand for the public good would be small if not entirely zero and its entire provision would have to be according to the desires or wishes of an outside agency, usually the government. Clearly the situation of the public good is an extreme one. What about other examples of externalities?

Consider a situation where an individual's utility depends not only on what he consumes but also the consumption of others, thus, $U^I(x^I, x^{I\prime})$. Clearly we need to redefine the utility maximisation problem and proceed as follows: each household I maximises $U^I(x, x^{I\prime})$ taking $x^{I\prime}$ as given, subject to the usual budget constraint. The demand $x^I(P, b^I, x^{I\prime})$ depends on the usual parameters P, b^I as well as on the variables $x^{I\prime}$ over which I has no control. It is because of this that we should refer to this function not as a demand function but as a 'best-response function'. Consequently, an equilibrium is a configuration $[P^\star, x^{I\star}, y^\star, z^\star]$ such that we have that at $P^\star$, the variables $x^{I\star}, Y^\star$ are all best responses to each other and, of course, markets balance, that is, $\sum_I x^{I\star} = y^\star + \bar{W}$. This equilibrium should be called a Nash equilibrium since that is what it is. Although we have travelled a slightly different route, it follows that:

Remark 2. *The first order conditions at the Nash equilibrium described formally appear identical to the ones at a competitive equilibrium.*

This remark follows since the first order conditions are all first order derivatives, the fact that the externality inducing variables are held constant implies that they disappear from considerations; consequently, conclusions formally similar to those with no externality influences emerge in a straightforward manner.

Remark 3. *This also highlights the main reason why the link between a competitive equilibrium and efficiency may disappear. The efficiency conditions take explicit account of the externality and, hence, the conditions required for efficiency are formally different from the situation where there is no externality.*

Finally note that externality is a common phenomenon. And in the presence of all such goods and services, market failures take place. But these are not the only cases. There are some more drastic situations and we turn to these next.

Asymmetric Information

While the delinking of competitive conditions from efficiency conditions was established many years ago, the effects of asymmetric information are of relatively recent origin.[16] Any market where the quality of the product is uncertain and where the buyers have no way of determining the quality prior to purchase will fall under the paradigm of asymmetric information. The problem is simply that there is no way in which information about the product may be obtained. Consequently there is wedge in the perception of the costs associated with buying and selling. To explain, we consider an example.

Akerlof (1970) considered as 'lemons', those cars which are bad because of some manufacturing or structural defect and which may not be easily discernable. And there is no way of knowing this *a priori*. Let us say that buyers would like to buy good cars and pay a price p for it but for lemons they are not willing to pay anything. Sellers would like to sell cars at a price λp where $0 < \lambda < 1$; if somehow it could be determined whether a car was a lemon or not, then good cars would be sold for some price in the range $(\lambda p, p)$; lemons would not be sold. With information not available, the only thing buyers estimate is that a fraction μ, $0 < \mu < 1$ of cars are lemons. In this scenario, no buyer would be willing to pay more than $(1 - \mu)p$ for any car, since that is the expected valuation to him and the problem is now revealed; if $(1 - \mu) < \lambda$, the market for cars ceases to exist. Since there is no competitive market, the question of determining its efficiency does not arise.

Formally notice that what causes the problem is that quality uncertainty introduces a wedge between the prices for buyers and sellers and, as we mentioned before, the costs to the different decision makers are perceived to be different and consequently the problem surfaces.

Notice that this argument applies to any market where quality is a matter of concern and the quality cannot be determined by the buyer prior to transaction. As we shall show subsequently, this argument may be extended to cover cases where 'quality' may not be enforceable. Thus, the failure for markets to exist or generate competitive transactions become much wider than hitherto anticipated.

---

[16] Akerlof (1970) was one of the early writers pointing out the ravages which may be caused due to the presence of asymmetric information.

Manipulation

Consider[17] another reason why the competitive transactions may fail to materialise. Even if everyone else makes their competitive transactions, is it in one's best interest to go through with competitive transactions? In other words, with decision makers as players, each of them choosing quantities at the equilibrium price, consumers with utility and firms with profit as pay-off, does the competitive equilibrium also reflect a Nash equilibrium? That is, is the competitive transaction the best response to others, choice of competitive transactions? This was investigated in Mukherji (2014) and we generalise the key result presented there to make it applicable to the present set-up.

We shall show that in all competitive equilibria where there is someone buying and, hence, someone selling, all those selling have an incentive to sell less than what is expected at the competitive equilibrium.

Claim 8. *Consider a competitive equilibrium P^* such that $y_j(P^*) \neq 0$ for some j. Then there is at least one individual I who would benefit from under supplying (compared to the amount at competitive equilibrium).*

Proof: By hypothesis, $y_j^* \neq 0$ for some j; now either $j \in F$ or $j \in P$; if $j \in F$ then $y_j^* > 0$; this means that by virtue of A3, there must be some $j_1 \in P$ such that $y_{j_1}^* < 0$; in case $j \in P$, $y_j^* < 0$. Thus, in any case, there is $j \in P$ such that $y_j^* < 0$. By definition of the competitive equilibrium, we must have for this $j \in P$:

$$\sum_I x_j^{I*} \leq y_j^* + b_j \Rightarrow \sum_I (x_j^{I*} - b_j^I) \leq y_j^*$$

and, hence, for some I, $x_j^{I*} - b_j^I < 0$; by undersupplying, this I will be better off and, consequently, will do so unless forced to comply.

Thus, in any market, there would be an individual who would benefit from under-supplying and, consequently, there would be little incentive to go through with competitive transactions unless they are coerced to do so either through some taxes or peer pressure or some such external agency. We turn briefly to such activities. Competitive transactions,

---

[17] The discussion in this section is based on Mukherji (2014) and the generalisation of a result reported there.

even theoretically, cannot be justified unless there is some such outside coercion.[18]

MEASURES TO AVOID MARKET FAILURES AND THEIR CONSEQUENCES AND CONCLUDING REMARKS

There are, to reiterate, three broad classes of problems which may vitiate the properties of a competitive equilbrium. We may characterise these as cases of market failures:[19]

1. Externalities like public goods or pollution;
2. Asymmetric information, for example, the lemons problem;
3. Little incentive to carry out competitive transactions.

As should be apparent, these three cases cover all types of markets and, hence, the efficacy of competitive markets cannot be expected to be taken for granted unless there is some outside intervention. We shall briefly mention what corrective steps may be taken in each such case. At the same time, we shall indicate what the consequences of such measures are likely to be.

Taxes and Property Rights

Consider the case of externalities first. Generally speaking, externalities create two related difficulties. The first concerns the paradigm of competitive markets themselves. The second problem arises because of the manner in which we deal with the first.

We have taken for granted that different agents carry out actions to achieve their aim, maximising profits or utilities, independently of one another. In the presence of externalities, this basic ability is lost; in the presence of externalities, the agent's target, utility or profit, depends not only on their own action but also on actions chosen by others. As we have seen earlier, recalling Remarks 2 and 3, the conditions underlying competitive equilibria and efficiency may differ. Several methods have been suggested to correct for these differences.

---

[18] In Mukherji (2014), we have shown an example of penalties which are tough and credible enough and which may restore the incentives for competitive behaviour.

[19] This is a broader definition of market failure. Usually confined to the narrow case when a competitive equilibrium fails to be efficient, it should be extended to cover when the equilibrium does not exist (see, for instance, Ledyard 1987).

The classical method, attributed to Pigou, is the setting of taxes and subsidies. Clearly these cannot be set by the market and some outside agency; usually the government, is required to play a role. We shall not get into the derivation of taxes appropriate, referring the interested reader to any standard source.[20] However, we should point out that correct taxes require information of the type which is not usually available with any government. Consequently, we need to ensure that not only taxes are correctly paid, but also agencies with the correct incentives are set up to regulate activities. For instance, consider the behaviour of a polluting industry or activity; clearly the tax put on them should curb their production or they should adopt superior means of 'cleaning'; to check that these have indeed been adopted, we need agencies to check their activities.

This aspect reveals another deep-seated possibility and one which we were not concerned with when we started discussing such matters. Given the necessity for such 'regulators' to perform their task diligently, what is the incentive that these persons have for carrying out their jobs? Is it not possible that they may instead use their positions to indulge in what is sometimes called 'rent-seeking' practices?[21] Our section on manipulations, should convince people that this indeed is possible.

In fact, it is to guard against such an overwhelming government presence that Coase (1960) argued in favour of limiting the role of governments. His point was that the difficulties arise because property rights are not properly assigned. In fact, he goes on to argue that if property rights are correctly assigned and if transaction costs are zero, then efficiency property at equilibrium will be re-established in the face of externalities.[22]

Quite apart from the conditions mentioned, this method will not work unless the assigned property rights are ensured and protected. To ensure property rights we therefore need a system of courts and a judiciary which is able to correct any imbalance fairly and swiftly. Notice that, we have shifted the responsibility of maintaining the sanctity of markets from one branch to another: from the executive to the judiciary. And rent-seeking has not been affected. Maintaining the properties of markets are difficult indeed.

---

[20] For a comprehensive account of taxation to correct for externailities, see Greenwald and Stiglitz (1986).

[21] Actually the greater the number of such regulators, the more such corrupt practices flourish.

[22] For a simple exposition of this aspect, see Mukherji (2002: chapter 5).

Certifying Quality

Consider next the asymmetric information situation described. Notice that the basic problem may be overcome if some outside agency were to certify the quality of goods being purchased and sold. To carry forward the analogy of lemons, recall that the simple inequality $1 - \mu < \lambda$ was enough to rule out the market.

Recall also that $1 - \mu$ is the probability that the car is a good car; certifying agencies should be able to restore the faith of consumers in cars so that the market operates. A reputable agency should be able to convince buyers that the car is a good one and while this may raise the price of the car, this will allow the market to exist.

We notice that one must ensure that the certifying agencies work properly, that is, in the context of the lemons example, market will operate only if they certify the good cars. But, as in the case of regulators, one must examine carefully the incentives of the certifying agencies. For rent-seeking possibilities may thrive in this context too. And to ensure that the certifying agencies perform, the judiciary and the law and order mechanism need to function fairly and without tardiness.

The Executive and the Judiciary: Governance

In the last two cases, we needed the judiciary to regulate the regulators. We need to examine whether the regulators of regulators have the correct incentives to perform their jobs. For without these being in place, regulatory activities will fail to achieve the desired ends. For the last type of traders who manipulate, the need for the law and order mechanism is of course direct and central.

While we have identified what steps could be taken to restore the working of the markets, in each case, we see that the incentives of the regulators and of their regulators and their regulators (and so on) have to be ensured. A tall task indeed. So is there any set-up under which we can expect the markets to perform? Of course, as the economists over the years have pointed out, there has to be good governance, but how does one ensure this? Does this mean each one performs whatever duties and tasks each is supposed to carry out without seeking rents? This is why we expect that on the balance, the markets will fail to deliver.

Related Literature: On Widening the Scope of the First Fundamental Theorem

We mention here the attempts made to extend the scope of the First Fundamental Theorem of Welfare Economics. As we shall see, these attempts do not affect the comments made earlier. The assumptions under which the result holds may be classified thus:

1. Complete markets;
2. All decision makers (buyers and sellers) are price takers;
3. Preferences of consumers satisfy local non-satiation, and are complete, continuous, reflexive and transitive.

What we have discussed earlier may be related to the first two assumptions: markets are not complete and some decision makers will always try to manipulate prices; consequently it is not surprising that market failure takes place. Our treatment will perhaps make it easier see why these two aspects are of importance. While there has been considerable work on extending the result to cover a wider variety of preference structures, we do not have anything to add in that context.

The failure of the market to be efficient within the context of externalities has received perhaps the greatest attention. The main point made in this connection was that the inefficiency arose because there were no markets operating where the services emanating from the externalities could be bought and sold. Indeed, if there were markets of these types, the inefficiencies would disappear.[23] Attempts made by theorists to introduce fictitious commodities allowing consumers to trade in them may lead to the result but then another part of the model becomes unstuck: these commodities introduced to solve one set of problems may lead to fundamental non-convexities (Starret 1972) which may destroy the existence of equilibrium itself. The interesting construct by Conley and Smith (2005) of an externality rights model should be mentioned; in the presence of public goods, they introduce some commodities named externality rights, some privately used and others publicly held, and show how the efficiency of equilibrium may be maintained. It is important to note in this construct that not all prices are same for everyone.

We end with two quotations. The first is not from an economist but a psychologist, who answers the question, what type of goods can we expect the market to allocate correctly: 'the things we are talking about are trivial', designer jeans, compact disks, deodorant soaps, different types of breakfast cereal; on the contrary, he goes on to argue 'when things we are talking about are judged by society to be too important', things like food, housing, education, health care, transportation, jobs, the market

---

[23] For discussions involving simple examples, see Mukherji (2002: chapter 5).

would be unacceptable.[24] As we have argued, even for designer jeans, compact disks and the like, which Professor Schwartz thinks the market may allocate correctly, there would be problems.

Finally, we note that the preponderance of self-interest, sometimes attributed to Adam Smith, is supposed to be the backbone of the market mechanism. In this connection, Sen (1998: 3) writes, 'I find it amazing that so many advocates of the glory of capitalism refuse to see the moral quality of good business behaviour that has been so important in contributing to the success of capitalism: it is no less a moral success than a triumph of unconstrained greed. Stigler's praise of Adam Smith for the alleged wisdom of establishing the prevalence and sufficiency of pure self interest is thus mistaken on two grounds: it is not Smith's belief nor is it wisdom.' And we have argued why self-interest is what invariably gets us into trouble and good moral behaviour may, thus, be the only way out.

REFERENCES

Akerlof, G. 1970. 'The Market for "Lemons": Quality Uncertainty and the Market Mechanism', *Quarterly Journal of Economics*, 84(3): 488–500.

Arrow, K. J. 1951. 'An Extension of the Basic Theorems of Classical Welfare Economics', in J. Neyman (ed.), *Proceedings of the Second Berkeley Symposium on Mathematical Statistics and Probability*. Berkeley: University of California Press, pp. 507–32.

Arrow, K. J. and A. C. Enthoven. 1961. 'Quasi-concave Programming', *Econometrica*, 29(4): 779–800.

Bator, F. M. 1957. 'The Simple Analytics of Welfare Maximization', *American Economic Review*, 47(1): 22–59.

Besley, T. and T. Persson. 2011. *Pillars of Prosperity: The Political Economics of Development Clusters*. London and Oxford: Princeton University Press.

Coase, R. H. 1960. 'The Problem of Social Cost', *Journal of Law and Economics*, 3: 1–44.

Conley, J. P. and S. C. Smith. 2005. 'Coasian Equilibrium', *Journal of Mathematical Economics*, 41(6): 687–704.

Friedman, M. 1952. *Capitalism and Freedom*. Chicago: University of Chicago Press.

Gale, D. 1960. *The Theory of Linear Economic Models*. New York: McGraw Hill.

---

[24] See Schwartz (1994: 21) for the complete passage.

Greenwald, B. C. and J. E. Stiglitz. 1986. 'Externalities in Economies with Imperfect Information and Incomplete Markets', *Quarterly Journal of Economics*, 101(2): 229–64.

Jones, R. W. 1965. 'The Structure of Simple Models of General Equilibrium', *Journal of Political Economy*, 73(6): 557–72.

Ledyard, J. O. 1987. 'Market Failure', in J. Eatwell, M. Milgate and P. Newman (eds), *The New Palgrave: A Dictionary of Economics*. New York and London: Macmillan.

Manning, R. and J. R. Melvin. 1992. 'The Geometric Construction of Production Functions That Are Consistent with an Arbitrary Production Possibility Frontier, *Canadian Journal of Economics*, XXV(2): 485–92.

Melvin, J. R. 1968. 'Production and Trade with Three Goods and Two Factors', *American Economic Review*, 58(5): 1249–68.

Mukherji, A. 1989. 'Quasi-concave Optimization, Sufficient Conditions for a Maximum', *Economic Letters*, 30(4): 341–43.

———. 2002. *An Introduction to General Equilibrium Analysis*. New Delhi: Oxford University Press.

———. 2014. 'When Is Competitive Behaviour a Best Response?', in S. Marjit and M. Rajeev (eds), *Emerging Issues in Economic Development: A Contemporary Theoretical Perspective*. New Delhi: Oxford University Press.

Olson, M. 1993. 'Dictatorship, Democracy and Development', *American Political Science Review*, 87(3): 567–76.

Rangarajan, L. N. (ed.). 1992. *The Arthashastra: Kautilya*, Penguin Classics. Delhi: Penguin.

Samuelson, P. A. 1954. 'The Pure Theory of Public Expenditure', *Review of Economics and Statistics*, 36(4): 387–89.

Schwartz, B. 1994. *The Costs of Living*. New York: Norton.

Sen, A. 1998. *Reason Before Identity, The Romanes Lecture for 1998*. Oxford: Oxford University Press.

Starret, D. A. 1972. 'Fundamental Non-convexities in the Theory of Externalities', *Journal of Economic Theory*, 4(2): 180–99.

Stewart, D. 1793. 'A Lecture in 1755', quoted in *Account of the Life and Writings of Adam Smith* LL.D, available at www.adamsmith.org/sites/default/files/resources/dugald-stewart-bio.pdf (accessed on 15 July 2014).

2

Encompassing Interests, Regionalism and Public Investment

Sugato Dasgupta, Bhaskar Dutta and Kunal Sengupta

A familiar theme in the theory of resource allocation emphasises the importance of institutions which have *encompassing interests*.[1] These are institutions that represent or incorporate the interests of all individuals in society, and are, hence, capable of internalising externalities. Conversely, the absence of encompassing institutions can result in an inefficient allocation of resources.

Consider, for instance, a familiar political economy model of public spending (Persson and Tabellini 1999). A society is composed of individuals, each of whom is endowed with one unit of a private good. The individuals are partitioned into three distinct geographical locations. The political institutions of the society are stark. There is a three-seat legislature. Each geographical location is represented by its own (regional) political party and accorded a single seat in this legislature. The preferences of a regional party are fully aligned with the interests of its constituency. A government, which is a two-member coalition of regional parties, undertakes public finance decisions. It taxes the economy's endowment of private goods; the revenues are used to finance region-specific transfers and investments in a public good (for example, physical infrastructure) that benefits all individuals.

It is well known that this model generates underinvestment in the public good. The intuition is transparent. By definition, a regional party's stake in society is narrowly confined to its constituency. Hence, the stake of a government, which is a minimum winning coalition of regional parties, cannot encompass all individuals in the society. In summary, the government's political benefits from public goods investment are strictly less than the economic benefits emphasised in the traditional public finance literature (Samuelson 1954).

---

[1] This terminology is due to Olson (1991) and McGuire and Olson (1996).

By assumption, the regional parties do not have encompassing interests, and this is indeed the cause of the inefficiencies in public goods investment. This motivates our study of a *national* party. In contrast to much of the formal analysis of political parties, we do not model the national party as a unitary actor.[2] Instead, there are two groups of actors—*local leaders* who stand for election and *party bosses*—within the national party. Local leaders are solely concerned with winning elections, and so their preferences are fully aligned with the interests of their constituencies. That is, the preferences of these local leaders coincide with the preferences of regional party members. In contrast, the party bosses represent an agglomeration of disparate regional interests. We shall assume that party bosses maximise national welfare, defined here as the sum of regional utilities. Note, therefore, that the central leadership's behaviour is identical to that of a benevolent social planner.

How does the national party undertake policy decisions? Consider a legislature in which the national party has some representation. Let t denote the sum of the transfers assigned to regions with national party legislators. Given t, resources of magnitude λt are 'leaked' to the central leadership of the national party. The central leadership uses this resource to finance additional regional transfers and investments in the public good. Since λ is a measure of the power of party bosses who have a stake in the entire society, the national party becomes a more encompassing institution when λ is higher.

In order to present the results obtained here, we first define a few terms. A society will be called a *weak-party* polity if the λ-value of its national party is strictly less than a threshold level. A society is called a *strong-party* polity if λ is at least as large as the threshold value.

Our model generates the following results. First, if the rate of return to investment is sufficiently high, elected legislatures devote the entire budget to public goods. Second, if the rate of return to investment is sufficiently low, elected legislatures use the entire budget to finance regional transfers. These results are not very surprising.

However, matters are more interesting when the rate of return to investment lies in an intermediate range. Then, in a weak-party polity, the national party captures all the seats in the legislature and the government opts to invest in the public good. Note that in a polity consisting of only regional parties, the regional-party legislature does not invest

---

[2] For a survey of recent papers that also drop the 'unitary actor' assumption, the reader is referred to Dhillon (2005).

in the public good. The presence of a single national party, even with a very small encompassing interest, dramatically alters the outcome: the national party captures the legislature and the underinvestment problem is overcome.

In a strong-party polity, the composition of the legislature is not necessarily unique. A legislature where all seats are captured by the national party remains an equilibrium outcome. However, a legislature consisting entirely of regional parties or two regional parties and a national party legislator can also emerge for large λ values. In the latter event, society underinvests in the public good. This final result has an important implication. When the encompassing nature of a national party exceeds a critical threshold, the risks of regionalism and underinvestment crop up. Thus, a socially optimal national party yields limited discretion to the party bosses.

The above result may seem counter-intuitive since one's first reaction must surely be that a more encompassing institution should be more capable of internalising externalities. The explanation for this apparent paradox lies in the fact that the composition of the legislature is endogenous in our model. When the degree of encompassing interest of the national party exceeds a threshold level, then it may be in the interest of voters in each constituency to vote for the regional party. As we have mentioned earlier, this can be an equilibrium outcome in strong-party polities.

Our model of government spending is related to two distinct strands of work in political economy. Persson et al. (1997, 2000), Persson and Tabellini (1999) and Lizzeri and Persico (2001) explain government fiscal policy from a comparative politics perspective. Specifically, the authors ask how electoral rules (majoritarian versus proportional elections) and regime types (parliamentary versus presidential democracies) affect the composition of public spending. In contrast, we keep the electoral rule (majoritarian) and the regime type (parliamentary democracy) fixed; instead, we ask how the structure of political parties determines public spending.

There is also a small but growing literature that compares centralised and decentralised provision of public goods. Bolton and Roland (1997) presume that centralisation is more efficient than decentralisation; however, provision of the public good is uniform under centralisation but tailored to individual districts under decentralisation. Alesina and Spoalore (1997) explore a model wherein the extent of decentralisation involves a compromise between scale economies and preference heterogeneity. Besley and Coate (2003) study a two-region world in which local public goods have spillover effects. Under decentralisation, investments in public goods are decided by locally elected representatives, while under a centralised system, policy choices are determined by a legislature comprising elected representatives. The case for centralisation rests on the extent of taste heterogeneity, public goods spillovers and the norms underlying legislative behaviour. In our model, centralised decision making through a legislature captured by the national party weakly dominates decentralised decision making through a legislature comprising regional parties. The question we ask is whether the efficient decision-making arrangement uniquely emerges in equilibrium.

The rest of the essay is structured as follows. The second section presents our theoretical model, while the third analyses its equilibria. The last section provides a conclusion.

THE MODEL

We consider a country which has three regions, each region containing one representative citizen. Each region elects one legislator to the national legislature or parliament. In each region i, the electoral contest is between two parties, the first being a national party denoted n and the second being a regional party r_i. Hence, there are four political parties in all—the three regional parties r_1, r_2, r_3 and the national party n.

Since the parliament consists of three seats, a government must command the support of at least two legislators. So, the government is either a single-party government if party n has at least two seats, or it is a coalition government of two or more regional parties, or some regional party and the national party if the latter has one seat. We describe the process of government formation in some detail later on.

Each regional party's interests are completely aligned with those of the representative citizen from the region. So, if party r_i is part of a coalition government, then it will only promote policies which maximise welfare in region i. The objectives of the national party are more complex. The national party is made up of two distinct groups. One group consists of the party bosses, who are truly nationalistic in the sense that their objective is to maximise welfare of inhabitants in all the three regions. The second group consists of local leaders from the different regions. Their objective is identical to that of the regional parties. In particular, this means that a member of party n who is elected from region i will want to follow exactly the same policies advocated by a legislator from party r_i.

The economy has an endowment of one unit of a private good, which can be used both for consumption as well as investment in a public good. Each unit of investment gives rise to a benefit of β units of the private good per region. The elected government has to decide on the allocation of the unit of private good into transfers t_i to each region i and investment g in the public good. Thus, an allocation is a vector (t_1, t_2, t_3, g) where $t_i \geq 0$, $g \geq 0$. Notice that we rule out the possibility of a majority government consisting of representatives from two regions imposing taxes on the third region. An allocation is feasible if

$$\sum_{i=1}^{3} t_i + g = 1. \tag{2.1}$$

The representative citizen in each region only cares about her own utility. So, given any allocation (t_1, t_2, t_3, g), the utility of the representative citizen in region i is:

$$u_i(t_1, t_2, t_3, g) = t_i + \beta g. \tag{2.2}$$

Note that this will also be the utility derived by the legislator of regional party r_i.

As we have mentioned earlier, decison making in the national party depends on the parameter λ. Suppose an amount t_i has been made available to region i and the legislator is from party n. Then, a fraction λt_i becomes available to the party bosses, who can then reallocate this amount according to their own priorities.[3] The remaining part $(1 - \lambda)t_i$ is available to the legislator from party n, who uses this to maximise u_i.

We now describe the process of government formation. If the parliament contains at least two legislators from party n, then that party forms the government. Suppose, however, that the legislature contains at most one member from party n. That is, the regions have either elected three regional parties or two regional parties and one representative from the national party. Then, we assume that the head of state or president selects one of the parties (from amongst those which have representation in the legislature) at random to act as the first formateur. The formateur tries to form a government by selecting a coalition partner and proposing a feasible allocation. A majority government is formed if the coalition partner accepts the formateur's proposal. Then, the government is in office for one period, and the endowment is divided according to the agreed proposal. An election is held after one period. If the first formateur's proposal is not accepted, then the president selects one of the two

---

[3] In particular, we assume that party bosses invest λt_i entirely in the public good if $\beta \geq \frac{1}{3}$, and distribute λt_i equally amongst the three regions otherwise.

remaining parties to form the government. The process is repeated, and a government is formed if the second formateur's proposal is accepted by one of the parties. If the second formateur is also unsuccessful in forming a government, then the remaining party gets a chance to form the government. If this party is unsuccessful as well, a caretaker government forms. The caretaker government implements a default policy which gives every region a utility of *zero*. An election is held in due course one period later.

Notice that the government formation procedure conforms to the usual principle in which the *largest* party is given the first chance to form the government, the second largest party gets a chance if the largest party fails, and so on.[4] Given any legislature, we assume that the actual government which will be formed is a subgame perfect equilibrium of this process. We denote the expected payoff vector associated with such a subgame perfect equilibrium as a *legislative equilibrium*.

We illustrate the process of government formation by means of the following example.

Example: Suppose the legislature is (r_1, r_2, n).[5] Assume that $\beta < \frac{1}{3}$. Then, in this case, no party wants to invest in the public good. Suppose that party n is chosen as the first formateur. In order to make a winning proposal, party n has to calculate the expected utilities of the two regional parties if its proposal is rejected. Obviously, the last formateur can capture the entire endowment of the private good for its own region. Knowing this, the second formateur can also propose to keep the entire endowment for *its* own region since party n is indifferent between accepting and rejecting this proposal, and so must accept it in equilibrium. Noting that both regional parties have an equal chance of being the proposer, their expected payoffs if party n's proposal is rejected equals $\frac{1}{2}$. So, party n must make a proposal which gives at least one of the parties a payoff of $\frac{1}{2}$. Note that if party n proposes to keep t_3 for its own region, then the party bosses capture λt_3 and transfer $\frac{\lambda t_3}{3}$ to each of the three regions. Hence, party n will propose to keep t_3 for its own region and transfer $(1 - t_3)$ to one of the other two regions. The

---

[4] See Austen-Smith and Banks (1988) and Diermeier and Merlo (2000) for formal analyses of alternative processes of government formation.

[5] (r_1, r_2, n) denotes a legislature in which regional parties have been elected from regions 1 and 2, while the national party has been elected from region 3. Similarly, (r_1, n, n) denotes a legislature in which the regional party has been elected from region 1, and the national party from regions 2 and 3.

transfer t_3 will be chosen so that

$$\frac{\lambda t_3}{3} + (1 - t_3) = \frac{1}{2}. \tag{2.3}$$

This determines how a government is formed as well as the equilibrium proposal *provided* party n is the first formateur.[6] This happens with probability $\frac{1}{3}$. One can determine the subgame perfect equilibrium for other realisations of the order in which the formateur is chosen in an analogous manner.

The example shows that unless a single-party government is formed, an equilibrium proposal will depend upon the order in which the formateur is chosen. Given any legislature, say (r_1, r_2, n), and some subgame perfect equilibrium, let $u_{r_i}(r_1, r_2, n)\,|_n$ denote the payoff to party r_i when party n is the initial formateur, while $u_n(r_1, r_2, n)\,|_n$ is the corresponding payoff to the legislator from party n. Similarly, $u_{r_i}(r_1, r_2, n)\,|_{r_j}$ is the payoff to party r_i if party r_j is the first proposer, and so on. Then, the *ex ante* or expected payoffs to the parties corresponding to the legislature (r_1, r_2, n) and some specific equilibrium will be

$$u_{r_i}(r_1, r_2, n) = \frac{1}{3}\left[u_{r_i}(r_1, r_2, n)\,|_{r_i} + u_{r_i}(r_1, r_2, n)\,|_{r_j} + u_{r_i}(r_1, r_2, n)\,|_n\right]$$

$$u_n(r_1, r_2, n) = \frac{1}{3}\left[u_n(r_1, r_2, n)\,|_n + u_n(r_1, r_2, n)\,|_{r_1} + u_n(r_1, r_2, n)\,|_{r_2}\right]$$

$$\tag{2.4}$$

The expected payoffs corresponding to other legislatures are computed in the same manner.[7]

We now describe the voting behaviour of representative citizens. We assume that citizens choose their elected candidates simultaneously, thus determining a legislature. Citizens correctly anticipate that once a legislature is elected, some legislative equilibrium will emerge. Since we focus on the subgame perfect equilibrium of the entire process, we assume that all citizens have a common anticipation of which legislative equilibrium will be selected once a legislature is formed.

Now, consider the legislatures (r_1, r_2, n) and (r_1, n, n), and suppose $u_n(r_1, n, n) > u_{r_2}(r_1, r_2, n)$. Then, the citizen from region 2 knows that if

---

[6] Notice that since party n can choose either regional party as its coalition partner, there are multiple legislative equilibria in this example.

[7] Of course, these expected payoffs correspond to specific legislative equilibria. Strictly speaking, our notation should reflect the underlying legislative equilibrium. We ignore this in order to keep the notation simple.

other regions elect one legislator each from parties n and r_1, she is better off with party n rather than with party r_2. In this case, we will say that (r_1, r_2, n) cannot be a *voting equilibrium* since a unilateral deviation by one of the citizens gives her a strictly higher expected payoff.

We need some further notation in order to define the concept of a voting equilibrium more formally. Let $l = (l_1, l_2, l_3)$ represent a legislature where each l_i may be either r_i or n. Given l, (l_i', l_{-i}) is the legislature which differs from l in region i. Also, let $u_i(l)$ represent the expected payoff of the citizen from region i for the legislature l corresponding to the commonly anticipated legislative equilibrium corresponding to legislature l.

Definition: A legislature l is a *voting equilibrium* if $u_i(l) \geq u_i(l_i', l_{-i})$ for all $i = 1, 2, 3$ and for all l_i'.

VOTING EQUILIBRIA

In this section, we characterise the types of voting equilibria for different ranges of values of β (the proofs of all theorems are contained in the Appendix). We start with the most interesting case—where β lies in the intermediate range $(\frac{1}{3}, \frac{1}{2})$.

Theorem 1. *Suppose $\beta \in \left(\frac{1}{3}, \frac{1}{2}\right)$ and $\lambda \in (0, 1)$. Then,*

1. *For all possible legislative equilibria, (n, n, n) is always a voting equilibrium.*
2. *There exists a legislative equilibrium such that (r_1, r_2, r_3) is a voting equilibrium iff $G(\lambda, \beta) \equiv \lambda(1 - \beta)(3 - 2\lambda\beta) \geq 1$.*
3. *There exists a legislative equilibrium such that (n, r_2, r_3) and its permutations[8] are voting equilibria iff*

$$H(\lambda, \beta) \equiv \lambda \left(\frac{3}{2} - 2\beta + \frac{1}{2} \left(\frac{\beta}{1 - \beta\lambda} \right) \right) \geq 1.$$

4. *Moreover, there is no other voting equilibrium.*

What are the implications of Theorem 1? The theorem shows that given restrictions on (β, λ), there are legislative equilibria which can give rise to *regionalism* (that is, the legislature comprises only regional parties) and *partial regionalism* (that is, the national party captures just one constituency). The composition of the legislature is not without

---

[8] We abuse notation and use '(n, r_2, r_3) and its permutations' to refer to all legislatures wherein the national party captures a single constituency, that is, (n, r_2, r_3), (r_1, n, r_3) and (r_1, r_2, n).

consequence. While the unified-national-party legislature (n, n, n) fully internalises society's benefit from the public good and, therefore, invests society's entire private good endowment, regional and partially regional legislatures give rise to inefficiency since there is underinvestment in the public good. Indeed, there is no investment at all in the public good under regionalism.

Can we relate patterns of legislature composition to the degree of encompassing interest of the national party? First, holding β fixed, observe that $G(\lambda, \beta)$ and $H(\lambda, \beta)$ are strictly increasing in λ. Furthermore, $G(\lambda, \beta)$ and $H(\lambda, \beta)$ equal 0 when $\lambda = 0$, while $G(\lambda, \beta)$ and $H(\lambda, \beta)$ exceed 1 when $\lambda = 1$. Thus, regionalism and partial regionalism emerge for *large* λ values. Second, let $g(\beta) \in (0, 1)$ be such that $G(g(\beta), \beta) = 1$, and $h(\beta) \in (0, 1)$ be such that $H(h(\beta), \beta) = 1$. It is easy to check that $h(\beta)$ strictly exceeds $g(\beta)$. Holding β fixed, Theorem 1 says that (n, n, n) is the unique voting equilibrium if λ is strictly less than $g(\beta)$; pure regionalism emerges when λ is at least $g(\beta)$, while partial regionalism becomes an extra possibility when λ weakly exceeds $h(\beta)$.

To ensure that (n, n, n) is the *unique* voting equilibrium for *all* values of $\beta \in (\frac{1}{3}, \frac{1}{2})$, we need $G(\lambda, \beta) < 1$.[9] This condition is, in turn, automatically satisfied if the national party's λ is less than a threshold $\bar{\lambda} \in (0, 1)$; $\bar{\lambda}$ is the solution of

$$\frac{2\lambda(9 - 2\lambda)}{9} = 1. \tag{2.5}$$

Henceforth, we classify a society as a weak-party polity if the influence of party bosses on national party decision making is insubstantial, that is, $\lambda < \bar{\lambda}$. A society is deemed to be a strong-party polity if $\lambda \geq \bar{\lambda}$.

Theorem 1 shows that (n, n, n) is the unique voting equilibrium of a weak-party polity. The strong-party polity case is more interesting. If λ exceeds $g(\beta)$, multiple legislatures emerge as voting equilibria. Also, the investment behaviour of a strong-party polity is not uniquely determined by the exogenous parameters of the model: efficient investments are undertaken if a (n, n, n) legislature is picked, while investments dry up if regionalism emerges. Thus, social inefficiency can occur only when there is a *substantial* degree of encompassing interest.

We now provide the intuition behind Theorem 1. Why is (n, n, n) always a voting equilibrium? Note, first, that a (n, n, n) legislature

---

[9] This is because for $\beta \in (\frac{1}{3}, \frac{1}{2})$ and $\lambda \in (0, 1)$, $G(\lambda, \beta) > H(\lambda, \beta)$. So, $G(\lambda, \beta) < 1$ ensures that $H(\lambda, \beta) < 1$ as well.

implements the action of a benevolent social planner and invests the economy's entire private good endowment. Hence, each region receives a benefit of β. Suppose, for a moment, that region 3 defects and opts for regional party r_3. This defection leads to a (n, n, r_3) legislature, but the government is still formed by the national party. Since β is less than $\frac{1}{2}$, legislators from regions 1 and 2 do not desire investments in the public good; rather, they jointly *wish* to consume the economy's private good endowment. However, resources of magnitude λ are obtained by the party bosses of the national party, who invest this resource in the public good. Therefore, in a (n, n, r_3) legislature, the economy's investment in the public good drops to λ and region 3 obtains a benefit of only $\beta\lambda$. It is clear then that region 3's defection is unprofitable and (n, n, n) is a voting equilibrium.

What does it take for regionalism to emerge; that is, when is (r_1, r_2, r_3) a voting equilibrium? Consider what happens in a (r_1, r_2, r_3) legislature. A government, which is a two-member coalition of regional parties, forms and consumes the economy's private good endowment. It is easy to check that there is a legislative equilibrium in which each region is in the government with probability $\frac{1}{2}$ and obtains an expected benefit of $\frac{1}{3}$.[10] Suppose, now, that region 3 defects and opts for the national party n, thereby creating a (r_1, r_2, n) legislature. It turns out that in the government formation stage, when a regional party (say r_1) is the first formateur, it seeks a coalition with n only. Why? If r_1 forms a coalition with r_2 by offering transfers t, region 2 consumes t. On the other hand, if r_1 forms a coalition with n by offering transfers t, λt resources are leaked to party bosses, who spend λt on the public good, thereby generating direct benefits for r_1. In other words, since n has encompassing interests and places *some* weight on the welfare of all regions, while r_2 cares narrowly about the welfare of region 2 alone, n is a more desirable coalition partner.

So, by voting for n, region 3 is guaranteed to be in the government that is formed.[11] However, voting for n entails a cost as well. Party bosses of n invest some of the resources available to region 3 in the public good

---

[10] This is demonstrated in Lemma 1.

[11] Our argument regarding strategic delegation is similar to that of Chari et al. (1997) and Persson (1998). In both these papers, legislators are elected from single-member districts. Voters in each district elect legislators who excessively value local public goods. Such legislators are elected because they have a better chance of being included in the minimum winning coalition that forms.

even though voters in the region prefer consumption. Clearly, the cost of voting for n is increasing in the power of the party bosses, λ (which represents the leakage from region 3). When λ is small (weak-party polity), the cost of choosing n is small as well; hence, regionalism cannot survive in equilibrium. When λ is large (specifically exceeding $g(\beta)$ in a strong-party polity), n becomes an expensive choice and regionalism emerges in equilibrium.

The next theorem shows that regionalism breaks down when β exceeds the threshold of $\frac{1}{2}$.

Theorem 2. *Suppose $\beta \in (\frac{1}{2}, 1)$ and $\lambda \in (0, 1)$. Then, the only voting equilibria are (n, n, n), (r_1, n, n) and its permutations.*[12] *In all the voting equilibria, the economy's entire endowment of the private good is invested in the public good.*

Theorem 2 shows that when $\beta > \frac{1}{2}$, the national party plays the role of an institution with encompassing interests since it always forms a single-party majority government in every voting equilibrium. Notice that since $\beta > \frac{1}{2}$, even two legislators from the national party will agree to invest fully in the public good since this is jointly optimal for their constituencies. Hence, the payoff for each region is β.

Why does $\beta > \frac{1}{2}$ ensure that regionalism is not a voting equilibrium? Consider a (r_1, r_2, r_3) legislature and suppose that r_1 is the first formateur. As in the case of Theorem 1, the expected payoffs to the other regions if r_1's proposal is rejected is $\frac{1}{2}$. To form a government, r_1 has to win the support of one of the other regional parties. Since $\beta > \frac{1}{2}$, the optimal policy for r_1 is to offer to invest an amount $\frac{1}{2\beta}$ in the public good. Observe that while there is *some* investment in the public good even in the case of complete regionalism, its magnitude is clearly suboptimal. Suppose region 1 opts for party n instead. The equilibrium policy in the (n, r_2, r_3) legislature results in a higher level of the public good. The detailed calculations in the proof of the theorem show that region 1 is better off in the (n, r_2, r_3) legislature than in the (r_1, r_2, r_3) legislature.

Finally, we state Theorem 3, which describes voting equilibria for low values of β.

Theorem 3. *Suppose $\beta < \frac{1}{3}$ and $\lambda \in (0, 1)$. Then,*

1. (n, n, n) is always a voting equilibrium.

---

[12] We abuse notation and use '(r_1, n, n) and its permutations' to refer to all legislatures with one regional party: (r_1, n, n), (n, r_2, n) and (n, n, r_3).

2. *For some legislative equilibrium,* (r_1, r_2, r_3) *is a voting equilibrium iff* $R(\lambda) \equiv 4\lambda^2 - 18\lambda + 9 \leq 0$.

3. *For some legislative equilibrium,* (r_1, r_2, n) *and its permutations are voting equilibria iff* $P(\lambda) \equiv 5\lambda^2 - 24\lambda + 18 \leq 0$.

4. *There is no other voting equilibrium.*

When $\beta < \frac{1}{3}$, the socially optimal policy is to not invest in the public good. Indeed, public good investment will be zero in all the voting equilibria identified in Theorem 3. However, the presence of the national party in the government does have some distributional implication—the distribution of resources across regions becomes more equal when the national party is in the government.[13] So, even in this case, it is of some interest to ascertain when regionalism and partial regionalism can emerge.

For $\beta \in (0, \frac{1}{3})$, it is easy to check that $R(\lambda)$ and $P(\lambda)$ are non-positive for large λ values. In other words, regionalism and partial regionalism emerge when the national party is too encompassing in scope. The intuitive reason for this is very similar to that of Theorem 1—the higher is λ, the greater is the leakage from the region or regions that elect the national party. This raises the cost of voting for the national party and ensures that regionalism and partial regionalism become stable arrangements.

CONCLUSION

The main purpose of this essay has been to explore the effects of a country's political structure on resource allocation. We have focused on the differing nature of regional and national parties, the latter being an encompassing institution.

A regional party is concerned with the welfare of a narrow constituency of citizens. Hence, a polity comprising only regional parties inevitably experiences the following problem: any government that forms,

---

[13] Consider the legislature (r_1, r_2, r_3), which comprises only regional parties. Here, two regional parties form the government and split equally the economy's private good endowment between themselves. Now consider a legislature with partial regionalism (n, r_2, r_3). Assume that parties n and r_2 form the government: then, t_1 and t_2 are transferred to regions 1 and 2, while $t_3 = 0$. But resources λt_1 are leaked to the party bosses of the national party, who then distribute $\frac{\lambda t_1}{3}$ to each of the three regions. In contrast to what happens in the (r_1, r_2, r_3) legislature, partial regionalism ensures that all regions receive some portion of the economy's endowment.

essentially, a minimum winning coalition of regional parties, cannot have a stake in the welfare of all citizens in the polity. This lack of an encompassing interest leads to underinvestment in public goods. Surprisingly, there are clear advantages to a polity when the national party has a *small* degree of encompassing interest. In a weak-party polity, a (r_1, r_2, r_3) legislature can arise in a voting equilibrium only when it is behaviourally indistinguishable from a (n, n, n) legislature. All investment decisions are, therefore, guaranteed to be socially optimal. A strong-party polity presents the more interesting case. Here, when the rate of return to investment lies in an intermediate range, the substantial resource leakage to party bosses gives birth to a (r_1, r_2, r_3) legislature. This legislature of regional parties undertakes no investment in the public good even though it is socially optimal to do so.

APPENDIX

Lemma 1. *Let $\beta \in (0, \frac{1}{2})$. Then, the set of legislative equilibria associated with the legislature (r_1, r_2, r_3) is given by $(\frac{1}{3}, \frac{1}{3}, \frac{1}{3})$ and all permutations of $(\frac{1}{2}, \frac{1}{3}, \frac{1}{6})$.*

Proof: Let the legislature be (r_1, r_2, r_3). Without loss of generality, let the order in which parties are called upon to form the government be (r_1, r_2, r_3). If proposals of r_1 and r_2 have been turned down, then r_3 can form the government by proposing $t_3 = 1, t_1 = t_2 = 0$. Hence, the equilibrium proposal of r_2 must be $t_2 = 1, t_1 = t_3 = 0$ since r_1 will accept this proposal.

When r_1 is chosen as the first formateur, r_2 and r_3 have an equal chance of being the second formateur. Hence, if r_1 is unsuccesful in forming the government, then the expected payoffs of r_2 and r_3 are $\frac{1}{2}$ each. So, r_1 is indifferent between choosing either r_2 or r_3 as coalition partner—in either case, a transfer of $\frac{1}{2}$ must be promised.

Now, suppose that the choices of coalition partners is such that as first formateur, r_i chooses r_{i+1} as coalition partner for $i = 1, 2, 3$ with the convention that $i + 1 = 1$ when $i = 3$. Then, the expected payoff vector (that is, before choice of formateur) will be $(\frac{1}{3}, \frac{1}{3}, \frac{1}{3})$.

On the other hand, suppose both r_2 and r_3 choose r_1 as coalition partner, while r_1 chooses r_2. Then, the expected payoff vector will be $(\frac{1}{2}, \frac{1}{3}, \frac{1}{6})$. Permutations of $(\frac{1}{2}, \frac{1}{3}, \frac{1}{6})$ can be generated in an obvious way.

Proof of Theorem 1: We first derive the expected payoff of the representative citizen in each region for each possible composition of the legislature.

Case 1. Suppose the legislature is (r_1, r_2, r_3). Lemma 1 describes the set of expected payoffs in all possible legislative equilibria.

Case 2. Suppose the legislature is (n,n,n). Then, the legislators from the national party will form the government and attain the efficient outcome. So, $g = 1$, $t_i = 0$ for all i, and

$$\forall\, i, \;\; u_i(n, n, n) \;=\; \beta. \tag{2.6}$$

Case 3. Suppose the legislature is (n, n, r_3). Then, the government is formed by party n. Since $\beta < \frac{1}{2}$, legislators from regions 1 and 2 do not want any investment in the public good. So, they agree to $t_1 = t_2 = \frac{1}{2}$, $t_3 = 0$. The party bosses then get λ, which is fully invested in the public good. So,

$$u_1(n, n, r) \;=\; u_2(n, n, r) \;=\; \frac{1 - \lambda}{2} + \beta\lambda, \;\; u_3(n, n, r) \;=\; \beta\lambda. \tag{2.7}$$

Case 4. Suppose the legislature is (r_1, r_2, n).

With probability $\frac{1}{3}$, n is chosen to form the government. If n is to form a government, it must propose a feasible allocation which will be approved by at least one of the regional parties.

On the other hand, if n's proposal is rejected, then from arguments which are analogous to that in Lemma 1, the second formateur can get its proposal accepted in equilibrium even if it allocates the entire resource for its own region. Hence, r_i, $i = 1, 2$ will accept n's proposal if this gives r_i a utility of $\frac{1}{2}$. Without loss of generality, let n select r_1 and propose (t_1, t_2, t_3) with $t_1 = 1 - t_3, t_2 = 0$ such that[14]

$$(1 - t_3) + \beta\lambda t_3 = \frac{1}{2}.$$

Hence,

$$t_3 = \frac{1}{2(1 - \beta\lambda)}.$$

---

[14] That is, the legislators from the national and regional parties correctly anticipate that party bosses of n will invest λt_3 in the public good.

So, the equilibrium payoffs, conditional on n being the first formateur will be

$$u_{r_1}(r_1, r_2, n)|_n = \frac{1}{2}, u_{r_2}(r_1, r_2, n)|_n = \frac{\beta\lambda}{2(1 - \beta\lambda)},$$

$$u_n(r_1, r_2, n)|_n = \frac{1 - \lambda + \beta\lambda}{2(1 - \beta\lambda)}. \tag{2.8}$$

Each regional party is chosen to form the government with prob-
ability $\frac{1}{3}$. If r_i's proposal is rejected, (r_j, n) and (n, r_j) are the or-
ders (each with probability $\frac{1}{2}$) in which parties are called upon to
form the government. If (r_j, n) is the realisation, then r_j must propose
$t_j = 1 - \beta\lambda, t_i = \beta\lambda, t_3 = 0.$[15]

If (n, r_j) is the realisation, then n's winning proposal is
$t_3 = 1$, $t_1 = t_2 = 0$. But, since the party bosses invest λ in the
public good, region j gets utility of $\beta\lambda$ while region 3 (represented by
party n) gets utility of $1 - \lambda + \beta\lambda$.

Hence, the expected utilities from the continuation equilibrium if r_i's
proposal is rejected will be $\frac{1}{2}$ for region j and $\frac{1}{2}(1 - \lambda + \beta\lambda)$ for region 3.

So, if r_i is to make a winning proposal, then it must ensure either r_j a
utility of $\frac{1}{2}$ or party n's legislator from region 3 a utility of $\frac{1}{2}(1 - \lambda + \beta\lambda)$.
In the former case, we must have $t_j = t_i = \frac{1}{2}$, so that r_i gets utility $\frac{1}{2}$.
In the latter case, $t_3 = \frac{1}{2}$, so that $(1 - \lambda + \beta\lambda)t_3 = \frac{1}{2}(1 - \lambda + \beta\lambda)$. But,
since λt_3 is the amount invested in the public good by the party bosses
of n, region r_i prefers n as the coalition partner.

From what we have said so far,

$$u_{r_i}(r_1, r_2, n)|_{r_i} = \frac{1}{2} + \frac{\beta\lambda}{2}, u_{r_j}(r_1, r_2, n)|_{r_i} = \frac{\beta\lambda}{2},$$

$$u_n(r_1, r_2, n)|_{r_i} = \frac{1}{2}(1 - \lambda + \beta\lambda).$$

Hence,

$$u_1(r_1, r_2, n) = \frac{1}{3}\left(\frac{1}{2}\right) + \frac{1}{3}\left(\frac{1}{2} + \frac{\beta\lambda}{2}\right) + \frac{1}{3}\left(\frac{\beta\lambda}{2}\right) = \frac{1}{3}(1 + \beta\lambda),$$

$$\tag{2.9}$$

---

[15] This is because n will follow this up with $t_3' = 1$, but the party bosses will
invest λ, assuring utility of $\beta\lambda$ to r_i. So, r_j's proposal must ensure that r_i gets
utility $\beta\lambda$.

$$u_2(r_1, r_2, n) = \frac{1}{3}\left(\frac{\beta\lambda}{2(1-\beta\lambda)}\right) + \frac{1}{3}\left(\frac{1}{2} + \frac{\beta\lambda}{2}\right) + \frac{1}{3}\left(\frac{\beta\lambda}{2}\right)$$

$$= \frac{1}{6} + \frac{1}{3}\beta\lambda + \frac{1}{6}\left(\frac{\beta\lambda}{1-\beta\lambda}\right), \tag{2.10}$$

$$u_3(r_1, r_2, n) = \frac{1}{3}\left(\frac{1-\lambda+\beta\lambda}{2(1-\beta\lambda)}\right) + \frac{2}{3}\cdot\frac{1}{2}(1-\lambda+\beta\lambda)$$

$$= \frac{(1-\lambda+\beta\lambda)}{3}\left(\frac{3-2\beta\lambda}{2-2\beta\lambda}\right). \tag{2.11}$$

A comparison of expected payoffs in cases 2 and 3 shows that $u_3(n, n, n) > u_3(n, n, r_3)$. Hence, (n, n, n) is a voting equilibrium.

The inequality also shows that (n, n, r_3) is not a voting equilibrium since the representative citizen in region 3 will prefer to elect a legislator from party n.

We now show that (r_1, r_2, r_3) along with unequal expected payoffs across regions does not constitute a voting equilibrium. Without loss of generality, let $u_3(r_1, r_2, r_3) = \frac{1}{6}$. In order to prevent defection from (r_1, r_2, r_3) to (r_1, r_2, n), we need

$$\frac{1}{6} \geq u_3(r_1, r_2, n). \tag{2.12}$$

Using (2.11) and simplifying, this requires

$$V(\lambda, \beta) \equiv 2\beta(1-\beta)\lambda^2 + (2\beta - 3)\lambda + 2 \leq 0. \tag{2.13}$$

Now,

$$\frac{\partial V(\lambda, \beta)}{\partial \beta} = 2(1 - 2\beta)\lambda^2 + 2\lambda > 0.$$

So,

$$V(\lambda, \beta) > V(\lambda, \frac{1}{3}) = \frac{4}{9}\lambda^2 - \frac{7}{3}\lambda + 2.$$

Also,

$$\frac{\partial V(\lambda, \frac{1}{3})}{\partial \lambda} = \frac{8}{9}\lambda - \frac{7}{3} < 0.$$

Therefore,

$$V(\lambda, \frac{1}{3}) > V(1, \frac{1}{3}) = \frac{4}{9} - \frac{7}{3} + 2 > 0.$$

We now show that (r_1, r_2, r_3) with equal expected payoffs across regions can be a voting equilibrium under certain circumstances. Specifically, we require that a defection from say (r_1, r_2, r_3) to (r_1, r_2, n) be unprofitable; that is, we need

$$\frac{1}{3} \geq u_3(r_1, r_2, n). \tag{2.14}$$

Using (2.11) and simplifying, this implies

$$G(\lambda, \beta) \equiv \lambda(1 - \beta)(3 - 2\lambda\beta) \geq 1. \tag{2.15}$$

Finally, we show that (r_1, r_2, n) can also be a voting equilibrium given appropriate conditions. In order to prevent a defection from (r_1, r_2, n) to (r_1, r_2, r_3), suppose all citizens anticipate the legislative equilibrium in which region 3 gets a payoff of $\frac{1}{6}$ in the (r_1, r_2, r_3) legislature. Now a defection for region 3 will be strictly unprofitable since we have already shown that $u_3(r_1, r_2, n) > \frac{1}{6}$.

Hence, (r_1, r_2, n) can be sustained as a voting equilibrium if a defection from (r_1, r_2, n) to (n, r_2, n) or (r_1, n, n) can be prevented. We have assumed that region 2 has a lower payoff (compared to region 1) in the (r_1, r_2, n) legislature. So, it is sufficient to show that

$$u_2(r_1, r_2, n) \geq u_2(r_1, n, n). \tag{2.16}$$

Using (2.7), (2.10) and simplifying, we get

$$H(\lambda, \beta) \equiv \lambda \left(\frac{3}{2} - 2\beta + \frac{1}{2} \left(\frac{\beta}{1 - \beta\lambda} \right) \right) \geq 1. \tag{2.17}$$

Proof of Theorem 2: We start by deriving the expected payoffs of the representative citizen in the three regions for each composition of the legislature.

Case 1. Suppose the legislature is either (n, n, n) or (n, n, r_3). In either case, the government is formed by party n and $g = 1$. So,

$$\forall i, u_i(n, n, n) = u_i(n, n, r_3) = \beta. \tag{2.18}$$

Case 2. Suppose the legislature is (r_1, r_2, r_3). Then, the expected payoffs to the other regional parties if the first formateur's proposal is rejected is $\frac{1}{2}$. Since $\beta > \frac{1}{2}$, the first formateur will choose $g = \frac{1}{2\beta}$ and transfer $1 - g$ to its own region. So,

$$\forall i, u_i(r_1, r_2, r_3) = \frac{1}{2} + \frac{1}{3}\left(1 - \frac{1}{2\beta}\right). \qquad (2.19)$$

Case 3. Suppose the legislature is (n, r_2, r_3).

With probability $\frac{1}{3}$, party n will be chosen as the first formateur. As in case 2, the legislator from party n wants to set $g = \frac{1}{2\beta}$. Hence, t_1 will be chosen so that $\lambda t_1 + (1 - t_1) = \frac{1}{2\beta}$.[16] So,

$$\begin{aligned}
\forall i = 2, 3, u_{r_i}(n, r_2, r_3)|_n &= \tfrac{1}{2}, \\
u_n(n, r_2, r_3)|_n &= \tfrac{1}{2} + \left(1 - \tfrac{1}{2\beta}\right).
\end{aligned} \qquad (2.20)$$

Suppose r_i is the first formateur. Then, when n is the last proposer, $t_1 = 1$ and hence $g = \lambda t_1 = \lambda$. This proposal from n yields r_i a utility of $\beta\lambda$. So, r_j must also propose $g = \lambda$ (and keep the remaining resource in its own region) in order to get r_i to accept its proposal.

When r_j is the last proposer, the winning proposal from n has $t_1 = 1$ and results in $g = \lambda$ since the party bosses will invest the entire resource at their command. Hence, expected payoffs to both n and r_j if r_i's proposal is rejected is $\frac{1-\lambda}{2} + \beta\lambda$. So, r_i will set $g = \lambda + \frac{1-\lambda}{2\beta}$ and transfer $1 - g$ to its own region. Hence,

$$\begin{aligned}
\text{for } k = r_j, n, u_k(n, r_2, r_3)|_{r_i} &= \frac{1-\lambda}{2} + \beta\lambda, u_{r_i}(n, r_2, r_3)|_{r_i} \\
&= \frac{1-\lambda}{2} + \beta\lambda + \left(1 - \lambda - \frac{1-\lambda}{2\beta}\right).
\end{aligned} \qquad (2.21)$$

So,

$$\begin{aligned}
\forall i = 2, 3, u_i(n, r_2, r_3) \\
= \frac{1}{3}\cdot\frac{1}{2} + \frac{1}{3}\left(\frac{1-\lambda}{2} + \beta\lambda\right) + \frac{1}{3}\left(\frac{1-\lambda}{2} + \beta\lambda + 1 - \lambda - \frac{1-\lambda}{2\beta}\right) \\
= \frac{5}{6} - \frac{2}{3}\lambda(1 - \beta) - \frac{1-\lambda}{6\beta}.
\end{aligned} \qquad (2.22)$$

---

[16] That is, the legislator from party n correctly anticipates that the party bosses will invest λt_1 in the public good.

Similarly,

$$u_1(n, r_2, r_3) = \frac{2}{3}\left(\frac{1-\lambda}{2} + \beta\lambda\right) + \frac{1}{3}\left(\frac{3}{2} - \frac{1}{2\beta}\right). \tag{2.23}$$

From (2.19) and (2.23), we get

$$u_1(n, r_2, r_3) - u_1(r_1, r_2, r_3)$$
$$= \frac{2}{3}\left(\frac{1-\lambda}{2} + \beta\lambda\right) + \frac{1}{3}\left(\frac{3}{2} - \frac{1}{2\beta}\right) - \frac{1}{2} - \frac{1}{3}\left(1 - \frac{1}{2\beta}\right)$$
$$= \frac{\lambda}{3}(2\beta - 1) > 0 \text{ since } \beta > \frac{1}{2}.$$

This shows that complete regionalism cannot be a voting equilibrium.
From (2.18) and (2.22), we get

$$u_2(n, n, r_3) - u_2(n, r_2, r_3) = \beta - \frac{5}{6} + \frac{2}{3}\lambda(1 - \beta) + \frac{1-\lambda}{6\beta}$$
$$\equiv g(\beta).$$

Now,

$$g\left(\frac{1}{2}\right) = 0 \text{ and } g'(\beta) = 1 - \frac{2}{3}\lambda - \frac{1-\lambda}{6\beta^2}.$$

For all $\beta \in (\frac{1}{2}, 1)$, $g'(\beta)$ is minimised at $\lambda = 1$. Substituting $\lambda = 1$ in $g'(\beta)$, we get $g'(\beta) > 0$ for all $\beta \in (\frac{1}{2}, 1)$. Hence,

$$g(\beta) > 0 \text{ for all } \beta \in \left(\frac{1}{2}, 1\right).$$

This shows that (n, r_2, r_3) is not a voting equilibrium since the representative citizen in region 2 will deviate from r_2 to n. This also shows that (n, n, n) and (n, n, r_3) are voting equilibria.

Proof of Theorem 3: Again, we derive the expected payoff of the representative citizen in each region for each possible composition of the legislature.

Case 1. Lemma 1 describes the various possible legislative equilibria when the legislature is (r_1, r_2, r_3).

Case 2. Suppose that the legislature is (n, n, n). Then, since $\beta < \frac{1}{3}$, even the national party does not invest in the public good. Hence,

$$\forall i, \ u_i(n, n, n) = \frac{1}{3}. \tag{2.24}$$

Case 3. If the legislature is (n, n, r_3), then n forms the government. Legislators from regions 1 and 2 divide the unit endowment amongst themselves, but the party bosses transfer $\frac{\lambda}{3}$ to region 3. Hence,

$$\forall i = 1, 2, \quad u_i(n, n, r_3) = \frac{1}{2} - \frac{\lambda}{6}, \quad u_3(n, n, r_3) = \frac{\lambda}{3}. \tag{2.25}$$

A comparison of payoffs in cases 2 and 3 establishes that (n, n, n) is an equilibrium and that (n, n, r_3) is not an equilibrium.

Case 4. Suppose the legislature is (n, r_2, r_3). Consider first the case where one of the regional parties, say r_2, is the first formateur.

When n is the last formateur, its winning proposal will be $t_1 = 1$. Since the party bosses distribute λ equally amongst the three regions, r_2 gets $\frac{\lambda}{3}$. So, the winning proposal by r_3 must be $t_1 = 0, t_2 = \frac{\lambda}{3}, t_3 = 1 - \frac{\lambda}{3}$.

Similarly, when n is the second formateur, its winning proposal will be $t_1 = 1$. Given the action of the party bosses in n, the legislator from party n will have a final utility of $1 - 2\frac{\lambda}{3}$ and the other regions will have a final utility of $\frac{\lambda}{3}$. So, the expected payoffs to r_3 and n if r_2's proposal is rejected are $\frac{1}{2}$ and $\frac{1}{2}(1 - \frac{2\lambda}{3})$. Given the action of the party bosses in n, it is immediate that r_2 prefers n as a coalition partner. Routine calculations show that r_2's net utility will be $(\frac{1}{2} + \frac{\lambda}{6})$.

Hence,

$$u_n(n, r_2, r_3)\mid_{r_i} = \frac{1}{2}\left(1 - \frac{2\lambda}{3}\right),$$

$$u_{r_j}(n, r_2, r_3)\mid_{r_i} = \frac{\lambda}{6}, \quad u_{r_i}(n, r_2, r_3)\mid_{r_i} = \frac{1}{2} + \frac{\lambda}{6}. \tag{2.26}$$

Now, consider the case where n is the first formateur. It is simple to check that if n's offer is rejected, the expected payoff for each regional party is $\frac{1}{2}$. Party n is indifferent between which party it selects as coalition partner. Without loss of generality, assume that n selects r_3, and proposes t with $t_3 = 1 - t_1, t_2 = 0$ such that $(1 - t_1) + \frac{\lambda}{3}t_1 = \frac{1}{2}$.

Hence,

$$t_1 = \frac{3}{2(3 - \lambda)}.$$

So,

$$u_{r_3}(n, r_2, r_3)\mid_n = \frac{1}{2}, \quad u_{r_2}(n, r_2, r_3)\mid_n = \frac{\lambda}{3}t_1 = \frac{\lambda}{2(3 - \lambda)},$$

and

$$u_n(n, r_2, r_3)\,|_n \;=\; \frac{3 - 2\lambda}{2(3 - \lambda)}.$$

Given our equilibrium selection (that n selects r_3 as coalition partner), the expected payoffs of representative citizens are

$$u_3(n, r_2, r_3) = \frac{1}{3}\left(\frac{\lambda}{6}\right) + \frac{1}{3}\left(\frac{1}{2} + \frac{\lambda}{6}\right) + \frac{1}{3}\left(\frac{1}{2}\right), \qquad (2.27)$$

$$u_2(n, r_2, r_3) = \frac{1}{3}\left(\frac{\lambda}{6}\right) + \frac{1}{3}\left(\frac{1}{2} + \frac{\lambda}{6}\right) + \frac{1}{3}\left(\frac{\lambda}{2(3 - \lambda)}\right), \qquad (2.28)$$

$$\begin{aligned}
u_1(n, r_2, r_3) &= \frac{2}{3}\cdot\frac{1}{2}\left(1 - \frac{2\lambda}{3}\right) + \frac{1}{3}\cdot\left(\frac{3 - 2\lambda}{2(3 - \lambda)}\right) \\
&= \frac{1}{3}\left(1 - \frac{2\lambda}{3} + \frac{3 - 2\lambda}{2(3 - \lambda)}\right).
\end{aligned} \qquad (2.29)$$

We now show that (r_1, r_2, r_3) along with unequal expected payoffs across regions does not constitute a voting equilibrium. Without loss of generality, let $u_1(r_1, r_2, r_3) = \frac{1}{6}$. In order to prevent defection from (r_1, r_2, r_3) to (n, r_2, r_3), we need

$$\frac{1}{6} \geq u_1(n, r_2, r_3). \qquad (2.30)$$

Using (2.29), it is easy to check that $u_1(n, r_2, r_3)$ is strictly decreasing in λ. But, at $\lambda = 1$, $u_1(n, r_2, r_3) = \frac{7}{36} > \frac{1}{6}$. In other words, (2.30) cannot hold.

We now show that (r_1, r_2, r_3) with equal expected payoffs across regions can be a voting equilibrium under certain circumstances. Consider the legislative equilibrium in which $u_i(r_1, r_2, r_3) = \frac{1}{3}$ for all i. We check for

$$\frac{1}{3} \geq u_1(n, r_2, r_3). \qquad (2.31)$$

Using (2.29) and simplifying, this implies

$$R(\lambda) \equiv 4\lambda^2 - 18\lambda + 9 \leq 0. \qquad (2.32)$$

Finally, we show that (n, r_2, r_3) can also be a voting equilibrium given appropriate conditions. Consider the legislative equilibrium where

$u_1(r_1, r_2, r_3) = \frac{1}{6}$. Clearly, the citizen in region 1 will not want to deviate and elect the regional party legislator.

Hence, (n, r_2, r_3) can be sustained as a voting equilibrium if the representative citizens in region 2 or 3 do not want to defect. Given our equilibrium selection (that as first formateur, n chooses r_3 as coalition partner), it is sufficient to show that the citizen from region 2 does not want to deviate. Using (2.25), (2.28) and simplifying, we get

$$P(\lambda) \equiv 5\lambda^2 - 24\lambda + 18 \leq 0. \tag{2.33}$$

REFERENCES

Alesina, Alberto and Enrico Spaolore. 1997. 'On the Number and Size of Nations', *Quarterly Journal of Economics*, 112(4): 1027–56.

Austen-Smith, David and Jeffrey Banks. 1988. 'Elections, Coalitions and Legislative Outcomes', *American Political Science Review*, 82(2): 405–22.

Besley, Timothy and Stephen Coate. 2003. 'Centralized versus Decentralized Provision of Local Public Goods: A Political Economy Analysis', *Journal of Public Economics*, 87(12): 2611–37.

Bolton, Patrick and Gerard Roland. 1997. 'The Breakup of Nations: A Political Economy Analysis', *Quarterly Journal of Economics*, 112(4): 1057–90.

Chari, V.V., Larry Jones and Ramon Marimon. 1997. 'The Economics of Split-Ticket Voting in Representative Democracies', *American Economic Review*, 87(5): 957–76.

Dhillon, Amrita. 2005. 'Political Parties and Coalition Formation', in Gabrielle Demange and Myrna Wooders (eds), *Group Formation in Economics: Networks, Clubs, and Coalitions*. Cambridge, UK: Cambridge University Press, pp. 289–311.

Diermeier, Daniel and Antonio Merlo. 2000. 'Government Turnover in Parliamentary Democracies', *Journal of Economic Theory*, 94(1): 46–79.

Lizzeri, Alessandro and Nicola Persico. 2001. 'The Provision of Public Goods under Alternative Electoral Incentives', *American Economic Review*, 91(1): 225–39.

McGuire, Martin and Mancur Olson. 1996. 'The Economics of Autocracy and Majority Rule: The Invisible Hand and the Use of Force', *Journal of Economic Literature*, 34(1): 72–96.

Olson, Mancur. 1991. 'Autocracy, Democracy, and Prosperity', in Richard Zeckhauser (ed.), *Strategy and Choice*. Cambridge, MA: The MIT Press, pp. 131–57.

Persson, Torsten. 1998. 'Economic Policy and Special Interest Politics', *Economic Journal*, 108(447): 310–27.

Persson, Torsten, Gerard Roland and Guido Tabellini. 1997. 'Separation of Powers and Political Accountability', *Quarterly Journal of Economics*, 112(4): 1163–202.

———. 2000. 'Comparative Politics and Public Finance', *Journal of Political Economy*, 108(6): 1121–61.

Persson, Torsten and Guido Tabellini. 1999. 'The Size and Scope of Government: Comparative Politics with Rational Politicians', *European Economic Review*, 43(4–6): 699–735.

Samuelson, Paul. 1954. 'The Pure Theory of Public Expenditure', *Review of Economics and Statistics*, 36(4): 387–89.

3

Bribe Chains in a Police Administration

Amal Sanyal*

This essay is about bribe chains in police departments. A chain starts with an apprehended offender paying a bribe to a policeman.[1] If the policeman is caught, in turn, by a superior officer, he pays a bribe to get the collusion and the offence ignored. It is alleged that bribes from original offenders thus pass upwards to the top through intervening levels. Frequent occurrence of offences and bribing help form a steady pattern of sharing of the spoils among various levels of the administration. We will model such a chain and then use it to explore administrative structures that can deter them.

Bribe chains in regulating hierarchies have been previously analysed by Basu et al. (1992) and Sanyal (2000, 2002) in the context of income tax administration. Measures against tax evasion advise that expected cost of fines should be made so high as to exceed or at least equal the gains of evasion (Allingham and Sandmo 1972; Srinivasan 1973). But Sanyal (2000) has argued that if bribe chains operate in the system then raising the expected cost of wrongdoing through fines and surveillance fails to work in the long run. In this essay we first show that this claim is true for crime prevention and policing. The essay then looks for a method that can work in the long run.

Its central intuition comes from the commonplace expectation that a bribe chain can be eliminated if one link in the chain can be effectively snapped.[2] This can be achieved by establishing one layer of the supervisory hierarchy with only honest officers. In societies where corruption is deep-seated, the number of honest cadre that the

---

* I am honoured to be called upon to write in this volume. I have chosen an issue that, I think, will be of interest to Professor Jain.
[1] Offenders and police personnel are presented as male.
[2] This was also claimed by Basu et al. (1992).

administration can muster is limited. There is a general belief that the more the proportion of such officers in various levels of administration, the less would be the incidence of corruption. The essay argues against this belief. It shows that it serves no purpose to distribute this scarce resource over the levels of supervisory administration in an unplanned fashion. Nor does it help to increase the number of supervisory levels if bribe chains are operating. Increase of layers of supervision simply increases cost but brings no benefit. Instead, setting up one level that is fully impervious to corruption can completely stop bribe chains and offences.

The plan for the rest of the essay is as follows. The second section develops the intuition about bribe chains by constructing an illustrative model. In that section we also discuss the deterrent conditions based on the usual calculus of expected costs and gains. The third section shows that those conditions are likely to fail in the long run. The fourth section looks for conditions that can be effective both in the short run and the long run. We conclude the essay in the final section with a brief discussion of the features of cost-minimising hierarchical structures that can effectively deter bribe chains in the long run.

BRIBE CHAINS AND SHORT-RUN DETERRENCE

An Illustrative Chain

We will refer to an offence committed by someone outside the police administration as an original offence. Offences discussed here have a definite monetary value and are punishable with fines alone. Police personnel who would never take a bribe will be called honest. Others are assumed to take a bribe if the expected net pay-off is positive. We make the following assumptions.

1. The proportion of honest officers is k $(0 < k < 1)$ at all levels of the police hierarchy.
2. If the pay-off from a corrupt action (or original offence) and an honest action are equal, then a corrupt policeman (or original offender) chooses the latter. This assumption makes the analysis simpler without affecting its substance.
3. Economic agents are risk neutral.
4. Two sides in all bribe negotiations have equal bargaining power.

Imagine a scenario where someone has committed an original offence of monetary value V. For example, it could be stealing money, goods or services worth V; defrauding someone by an amount V; and so on. Punishment for the offence is a fine $f_1 V$. A member of the police force has detected the offence. He can book the offender or let him go after taking a bribe. If a bribe is taken, there is a positive probability that it will be detected by the supervisor of the bribe-taking policeman.

In this scenario, suppose there are m levels of policing including the ground level ($\equiv$ level 1) that directly deals with offenders. Let p_1 denote the probability that a policeman at level 1 will detect an original offence. Policemen of level 1, in turn, are supervised by level 2 officers, who can detect with probability p_2 if the lower-level policemen have colluded with an offender. In general, let p_i, $(m \geq i > 1)$ denote the probability that level i officers will catch a level $(i - 1)$ officer if the latter has colluded with a lower-level officer. Let f_{i+1} denote the fine rate for officers at level i, $i = 1, \ldots (m - 1)$, imposed on the value of the offence condoned by them. The highest policing level being m, officers of that level are not supervised and do not face fines. Instead they get a reward at the rate $r \geq 0$ on the amount of any offence that they may find out.

A bribe chain may arise in this situation extending from an original offender to officers of level m. Consider an officer at the highest level m who has caught an $(m - 1)$ level officer to have colluded with a subordinate officer. The size of the original offence is V. Either the offending officer will be booked or a bribe negotiation would start, depending on whether the m level officer is honest or not. If he is not honest then let b_m denote the rate at which a bribe is to be paid to him by the $(m - 1)$ level officer. In a successful negotiation, the gains of the two sides will be $V(b_m - r)$ and $V(f_m - b_m)$. Given symmetric bargaining, the bribe rate will maximise the product $(b_m - r)(f_m - b_m)$. So

$$b_m = \frac{f_m + r}{2}. \tag{3.1}$$

Necessary condition for this negotiation to work is $f_m > r$, implying that there is room for positive gains for both parties. Assume that this condition holds. Next consider the situation where an officer at level $(m - 1)$ has found that one at level $(m - 2)$ has colluded in an offence. In fraction k of these cases where the level $(m - 1)$ officer is honest, the offending officer will be reported straightaway. In the rest, a bribe will be negotiated at the rate b_{m-1}. While doing this negotiation, the $(m - 1)$ level officer would predict b_m as given by equation (3.1). His expected gain from the bargain is $[b_{m-1} - p_m\{(1 - k)b_m + kf_m\}]V$, and the potential gain of the lower-level officer is $(f_{m-1} - b_{m-1})V$. The equilibrium bribe rate would, therefore, be

$$b_{m-1} = \frac{f_{m-1} + p_m\{(1-k)b_m + kf_m\}}{2}.$$ (3.2)

This negotiation is possible only if $f_{m-1} > p_m\{(1-k)b_m + kf_m\}$ and we assume this to hold. Reasoning similarly, the negotiated bribe rate for the next lower level would be

$$b_{m-2} = \frac{f_{m-2} + p_{m-1}\{(1-k)b_{m-1} + kf_{m-1}\}}{2}.$$ (3.3)

In general, b_i the bribe rate to be paid to an i-level officer by an apprehended $(i-1)$ level officer is, for $i = 2, ..., (m-1)$,

$$b_i = \frac{f_i + p_{i+1}\{(1-k)b_{i+1} + kf_{i+1}\}}{2}.$$ (3.4)

Finally consider the negotiation between a level 1 policeman and an original offender. Using similar reasoning, the bribe rate will be

$$b_1 = \frac{f_1 + p_2\{(1-k)b_2 + kf_2\}}{2}.$$ (3.5)

As noted earlier, necessary conditions for these negotiations to be operative are

$$f_m > r; f_{m-1} > p_m\{(1-k)b_m + kf_m\}; ..., ...$$
$$f_i > p_{i+1}\{(1-k)b_{i+1} + kf_{i+1}\}; ...; f_1 > p_2\{(1-k)b_2 + kf_2\}.$$ (3.6)

The last inequality in equation (3.6) and equation (3.5) together imply $f_1 > b_1$, ensuring that an original offender would prefer to bribe his way out rather than pay a fine. We can write these conditions in terms of f_i's and p_i's alone by eliminating the bribe rates. Because of the iterative nature of the bribe function, $b_k = b_k(b_{k+1})$, the expressions will involve progressively higher polynomials. We will avoid that course and use inequalities (3.6) as they are while knowing that they involve only f_i's and p_i's. Finally, the condition that triggers off original offences should be added to this group. It is

$$1 > p_1 f_1.$$ (3.7)

In sum, (3.6) and (3.7) form a set of inequality conditions that are necessary for the emergence of bribe chains.

Deterrence: The Suggested Method

Literature on economic offences suggests that potential bribe negotiations can be aborted by setting f_i's and p_i's in such a way that the inequalities of (3.6) do not hold. Given assumption 2, the chain will snap if any of the following equalities hold:

$$f_m = r = b_m; f_{m-1} = p_m\{(1-k)b_m + kf_m\}; \ldots, \ldots$$
$$f_i = p_{i+1}\{(1-k)b_{i+1} + kf_{i+1}\}; \ldots; f_1 = p_2\{(1-k)b_2 + kf_2\}. \quad (3.8)$$

Any one of the equation group (3.8) is sufficient to snap the bribe chain at the level it refers to. To see this, suppose

$$f_{m-1} = p_m\{(1-k)b_m + kf_m\}.$$

The right-hand side of this equation is the expected cost of taking a bribe from below by an $(m-1)$ level officer. Hence, the officer would insist on a bribe greater than this amount. But it equals f_{m-1}, the fine rate that an $(m-2)$ officer has to pay if caught. Therefore, there cannot be a successful bribe negotiation between the $(m-1)$ and $(m-2)$ levels. If the inequalities of (3.6) continue to hold below this level, bribe chains will reach from original offenders up to level $(m-2)$ and will stop there. An apprehended $(m-2)$ officer will pay a fine and not seek to bribe his way out. Note that to set $f_{m-1} = p_m\{(1-k)b_m + kf_m\}$ involves fixing f_m, f_{m-1}, p_m since also the parameters above the $(m-1)$ level since b_m depends on them.

To root out bribe chains altogether would require to stop it at level 1. This will require setting

$$f_1 = p_2\{(1-k)b_2 + kf_2\}. \quad (3.9)$$

At the same time to prevent original offences, the condition

$$p_1 f_1 = 1 \quad (3.10)$$

needs to be ensured.[3]

k and f_1 are exogenous to the police administration. The first one is sociological, while the second is fixed by law. Police administration has to choose the other $2m$ variables: $f_2, \ldots, f_m; p_1, \ldots, p_m$; and r subject to (3.9), (3.10), (3.1) and (3.4), $i = 1, \ldots, (m-1)$. So there are adequate degrees of freedom to choose them. In fact, for all $m > 1$, there would be spare degrees of freedom to think of optimisation of suitable objective

---

[3] $p_1 f_1 = 1$ alone does not stop offences if bribing is possible and $p_1 b_1 < 1$.

functions, but we will not discuss these possibilities here. From now on, in place of f_1 we will use $\bar{f}_1$; the exogenously given value.

THE LONG RUN

We will now argue that the no-offence–no-bribe equilibria expected from configurations discussed earlier are not sustainable beyond a period. Because there are no offences in these equilibria, officials at the top-level of the hierarchy get neither bribes nor rewards. After some time, they will realise that the possibility of rewards is only notional. Corrupt ones among them would then signal their willingness to consider smaller bribes. These signals would reach all levels as well as potential original offenders. We may recall that bribe chains cannot form in these equilibria because b_2 that level 2 officers ask for is too high (equation [3.9]). As a result, level 1 officers, in turn, have to ask for bribe b_1 that primary offenders find too high. The asking rate b_2 is too high because the asking rates for bribes at higher levels are also too high. So when the top-level officers show willingness to settle for smaller bribes, it encourages bribing. Eventually the top-level bribe rate b'_m will be established at a level sufficiently low to enable bribing at all other levels. Therefore, the parameter fixing exercise discussed earlier will have little impact in the long run.

In the likely long-run equilibrium scenario, let the bribe rate at level i be denoted by b'_i. Because the top-level officers will ignore potential rewards, the bribe at that level will now be

$$b'_m = \frac{f_m}{2}. \qquad (3.11)$$

We can recursively work out b'_i for all other i using equation (3.4) and (3.11). Because $b'_m = \frac{f_m}{2} < \frac{f_m + r}{2} = b_m$, we will have $b'_i < b_i$ at all levels. Now note that in the deterrent scheme discussed earlier, f_i's and p_i's are set according to (3.8). But the values of long-run bribe rates b'_i are less than corresponding b_i in the equations of (3.8). Hence, the parameters in the long run will be characterised by

$$f_m > b'_m; f_{m-1} > p_m\{(1-k)b'_m + kf_m\}; \ldots, \ldots$$
$$f_i > p_{i+1}\{(1-k)b'_{i+1} + kf_{i+1}\}; \ldots; \bar{f}_1 > p_2\{(1-k)b'_2 + kf_2\}. \qquad (3.12)$$

These inequalities will enable bribing at all levels once again. Hence, the claim that fines and probabilities that stop the chain in the short run are not effective beyond a period.

CAN WE ELIMINATE THE OFFENDER–ADMINISTRATION NEXUS AT ALL?

A natural question is if we can at all get rid of bribe chains in the long run. We will argue that the nexus between offenders and police can be broken by a proper distribution of honest officers. If one level of the supervisory hierarchy can be entirely staffed with honest officers, then with appropriate fine rates, bribe chains can be eliminated—for both the short run and the long run.

Suppose hypothetically that the proportion of honest officers could be varied across the levels of the hierarchy. Assume that while its value continues to be k at all other levels, it is 1 at the level $(i + 1)$. In that case, an i-level officer will not be able to bribe his superior. If he is caught for wrongdoing, he will have to pay a fine. Hence, his expected cost of taking a bribe would be $p_{i+1}f_{i+1}$.

Therefore, if an officer at level i negotiates a bribe with one at level $(i - 1)$, the equilibrium rate would be $b_i = \frac{f_i + p_{i+1}f_{i+1}}{2}$. It is, however, possible to stop this negotiation from starting at all. For that we have to set $f_i = p_{i+1}f_{i+1}$. Given this condition, a level $(i - 1)$ officer would see no point in bribing a level i officer. Therefore, if he at all negotiates a bribe with someone at $(i - 2)$ level, in that negotiation he will think of his expected fine payment as the expected cost. He would, therefore, settle for a bribe rate $b_{i-1} = \frac{f_{i-1} + p_i f_i}{2}$. The negotiation for this can also be aborted—this time by setting $f_{i-1} = p_i f_i$.

We can continue with this reasoning down the levels. At each level j, it is possible to set $f_j = p_{j+1}f_{j+1}$ and, thus, eliminate the space for bribe negotiation at that level. If this is continued down to level 1, we have a situation where the bribe to be paid by an original offender to a level 1 officer would be $b_1 = \frac{\overline{f}_1 + p_2 f_2}{2}$. Let us suppose that this too is disabled by setting $\overline{f}_1 = p_2 f_2$. All the disabling restrictions starting from level i down to level 1 are

$$f_i = p_{i+1}f_{i+1}; f_{i-1} = p_i f_i; f_{i-2} = p_{i-1}f_{i-1}; \ldots, \ldots \overline{f}_1 = p_2 f_2. \quad (3.13)$$

When bribing is not possible, original offences would stop if expected fine on them is prohibitive. The condition for that is (3.10) as already noted. It ensures that committing an offence with the premeditated plan of paying fines if caught is also ruled out.

We claim that conditions (3.10) and (3.13) together with the fact that $k = 1$ at level $(i + 1)$ can stop offences and bribes not only in the short run but also in the long run. Given these conditions, original offenders and corrupt police personnel would find the bribe to be paid is no less than the fine. Further the expected fine would cost as much as the gain from a contemplated offence or taking a bribe. So the immediate effect of the set-up is to stop offences and bribe chains.

Corruptible officers at all levels (except at $(i + 1)$ where there are no corrupt officers) would of course hate this situation. Top-level officers would be getting neither bribes nor rewards. The venal among them would signal that they would consider bribes smaller than potential rewards. But this is now irrelevant. The problem is that officers at level i know that they cannot bribe their immediate superiors. Hence, they would have to pay fines if caught taking bribes from below. On the other hand, the maximum bribe that they can get from below is no greater than the expected fine cost they face. Hence, they would turn down bribes. As they turn down bribes, it affects the officers at $(i - 1)$ level who will also find that the bribe they can get from below is no greater than the expected penalty of taking those bribes. The sequence of refusing bribes would continue downward and an original offender will be unable to start a chain by bribing a first-level officer. The fact that many officers at levels above and below $(i + 1)$ look for bribes cannot start a chain even though the top-level officers are willing to ignore their rewards. The following proposition sums up this discussion.

Proposition 1.   *If all officers deployed in some level $i \geq 1$ are honest, then fine and detection probabilities can be so chosen that economic offences and bribe chains cannot exist either in the short run or in the long run.*

Further, if level i is formed entirely with honest recruits then officers at levels higher than i serve no purpose. Of course, it is true that if there were offences and collusion that remained undetected up to level i, some of them could be detected at levels higher than i. But that situation would not arise because if all officers at level i were honest, then there would be no offences and collusions below this level anyway. In fact, this is the reason why level m officers' offer of taking smaller bribes is irrelevant in this situation. This observation gives us the following proposition.

Proposition 2.   *If all officers at level i are honest and conditions (3.10) and (3.13) are satisfied, then the levels $(i + 1), (i + 2), ..., m$ are redundant for offence prevention.*

Assuming that employing extra personnel has positive cost, Proposition 2 means that if there is a level filled entirely with honest officers, then that should be the highest level in a cost-conscious structure.

Further, there should not be more than one such level since all of them except the one at the lowest level would be redundant.

The success of the strategy discussed here comes from forcing errant officers of level $(i - 1)$ to pay fines rather than bribe and making those fines too large to leave any net gain from collusion. This strategy does not require the levels below i to employ any specified number of honest officers. Even if $k = 0$ at all levels $j < i$, bribe chains cannot form and no room is left for offences. This observation is useful for mechanism building in environments where, as typically is the case where bribe chains operate, honest officers are in short supply. We write it as a corollary of Proposition 1.

Corollary 1. *If all officers at level i are honest, then fine rates can be set so that offences and bribe chains cannot exist no matter what the value of k is for levels $j \neq i$.*

Equation (3.10) and those set out in (3.13) can be used to write a set of relations among fines and probabilities:

$$\bar{f}_1 = \frac{1}{p_1}; f_2 = \frac{1}{p_1 p_2}; f_3 = \frac{1}{p_1 p_2 p_3}; ...; f_i = \frac{1}{p_1 p_2 p_3 ... p_i}. \tag{3.14}$$

Equation (3.14) implies that, in general $\frac{f_{i-1}}{f_i} = p_i$; deterrence requires fine rates to increase from one level to the next; and higher fine rates allow lower detection probabilities to suffice.

Suppose the number of honest recruits that the police department can muster is N. Let $n = n(p_i, i)$, where n is the minimum number of personnel needed to ensure the probability of detection p_i at level i. Then a deterrent structure with i levels is feasible if $N \geq n(p_i, i)$ for some i and some p_i. The structure will then consist of i levels. The fine rates and the probabilities other than p_i will be set according to (3.14).

It should be noted that a deterrent structure is never unique when it exists. First, there may be more than one level i that can be fully serviced with honest recruits for some supervision probability. Further, even when there is only one such level, it can be fitted with an infinite number of schedules of fines and probabilities.

We want to emphasise that it serves no purpose to multiply the number of supervisory levels if bribe chains operate. Distributing the limited number of honest recruits over these levels cannot break the chains but the increase of the number of supervisory levels add to cost. If N does not suffice to fully service any level of supervision, then it is better to innovate the technology of policing and supervision. With innovation it may be possible to seal one layer (generally, a sufficiently high level) of the hierarchy with given N effectively.

LEAST-COST DETERRENCE: AN EXAMPLE

We will end this essay with some discussion of cost-minimising deterrence. A deterrent structure is never unique as already noted. Hence, optimisation in some form is desired. We consider cost minimisation here.

Since the cost of policing increases with p_i, a cost-conscious mechanism should try to set detection probabilities as low as possible at all levels. They cannot be, however, set arbitrarily low as there would be some upper limit to acceptable value of fines. We will denote the exogenously given upper limit by $\overline{F}$. As fine rates have to increase with i, a cost minimising scheme will reserve $\overline{F}$ as the fine rate for the highest level that is subjected to fines. If j is the highest level, then this level has no fines. Hence, f_j, the fine rate for level $(j - 1)$, will be $\overline{F}$.

In view of Proposition 2, the highest level should consist of only honest officers. This should also be the lowest possible level that can be set-up with only honest officers. Further, the structure should minimise the sum of the hiring costs at all the levels. Hence, the number of personnel at different levels should have the property that marginal shifts from one level to another (which will require changing the p_i's) would not change the total wage bill. If deterrent structures exist, then these features provide adequate guidance to identify the minimum-cost structure. To construct analytically tractable examples, we need to ensure that deterrent structures exist. This requires some assumption about the production function. We produce the following example.

Example 1. *Let* $n(p_i, i) = va^i p_i$; $v > 1$ *and* $1 > a > 0$. *Let the unit cost of employment in level* i *be* $w_i = w_0 b^i$, $b > 1$.

Cost of a j-level hierarchy in this case will be

$$C = v. \left[\frac{w_1 a}{\overline{f}_1} + \frac{w_2 a^2 \overline{f}_1}{f_2} + \frac{w_3 a^3 f_2}{f_3} + ... + \frac{w_{j-1} a^{j-1} f_{j-2}}{f_{j-1}} + \frac{w_j a^j f_{j-1}}{\overline{F}} \right]$$
$$(3.15)$$

$(j - 2)$ parameters $f_2, f_3, ..., f_{j-1}$, and the value of j itself have to be chosen so that C is minimised. There are $(j - 2)$ first order conditions

$$\frac{\partial C}{\partial f_2} = \frac{\partial C}{\partial f_3} = ... = \frac{\partial C}{\partial f_{j-1}} = 0.$$

Manipulating them, we get

$$\frac{\bar{f}_1}{f_2} = \frac{baf_2}{f_3} = \frac{b^2 a^2 f_3}{f_4} = \dots = \frac{b^{i-2} a^{i-2} f_{i-1}}{f_i} = \dots$$
$$= \frac{b^{j-3} a^{j-3} f_{j-2}}{f_{j-1}} = \frac{b^{j-2} a^{j-2} f_{j-1}}{\bar{F}}. \qquad (3.16)$$

To determine j we note that (a) $va^i p_j \leq N$, (b) fine rates must satisfy (3.16), and (c) j is the lowest level for which (3.1) and (3.2) hold. Using these considerations we can identify j with a sequence of trials as follows.

1. If $\frac{va}{\bar{f}_1} \leq N$, then $j = 1$ and the procedure is terminated. If $\frac{va}{\bar{f}_1} > N$ then we proceed to the next step.

2. If $\frac{va^2 \bar{f}_1}{\bar{F}} \leq N$, then $j = 2$ and the procedure is terminated. Otherwise we proceed to the next step.

3. If $\frac{va^3 f_2}{\bar{F}} \leq N$, where f_2 is derived from $\frac{\bar{f}_1}{f_2} = \frac{baf_2}{\bar{F}}$, then $j = 3$ and the procedure is terminated. Otherwise we proceed to the next step, and soon.

4. If $\frac{va^4 f_3}{\bar{F}} \leq N$, where f_3 is derived from $\frac{\bar{f}_1}{f_2} = \frac{baf_2}{f_3} = \frac{b^2 a^2 f_3}{\bar{F}}$, then $j = 4$ and the procedure is terminated. Otherwise we proceed to the next step.

5. The procedure is continued till we find k such that $\frac{va^k f_{k-1}}{\bar{F}} \leq N$, where f_{k-1} is derived from $\frac{\bar{f}_1}{f_2} = \frac{baf_2}{f_3} = \frac{b^2 a^2 f_3}{f_4} = \dots = \frac{b^{k-2} a^{k-2} f_{k-1}}{\bar{F}}$, and then $j = k$.

If the procedure terminates, then we use the solution values of f_i's to calculate the p_i's using (3.14).

A sufficient condition for the procedure to terminate is $a < \frac{f_i}{f_{i+1}}$ for all i, which ensures that the terms of the sequence $\frac{va^3 f_2}{\bar{F}}, \frac{va^4 f_3}{\bar{F}}, \frac{va^5 f_4}{\bar{F}}, \dots$ fall monotonically.

REFERENCES

Allingham, M. G. and A. Sandmo. 1972. 'Income Tax Evasion: A Theoretical Analysis', *Journal of Public Economics*, 1(3–4): 323–38.

Basu, Kaushik, Sudipto Bhattacharya and Ajit Mishra. 1992. 'Notes on Bribery and the Control of Corruption', *Journal of Public Economics*, 48(3): 349–59.

Sanyal, Amal. 2000. 'Audit Hierarchy in a Corrupt Tax Administration', *Journal of Comparative Economics*, 28(2): 364–78.

————. 2002. 'Audit Hierarchy in a Corrupt Tax Administration: A Note with Qualifications and Extensions', *Journal of Comparative Economics*, 30(2): 317–24.

Srinivasan, T. N. 1973. 'Tax Evasion: A Model', *Journal of Public Economics*, 2(4): 339–46.

4

Notes towards Rationality and Institutions

Manimay Sengupta

In one of her incisive critiques of the reliance of neoclassical economic theory on individual rationality based on (expected) utility maximisation, Elinor Ostrom (1998:1) called for expanding the range of rational choice models as a foundation for the study of social dilemmas and collective action, and developing 'second-generation models of empirically grounded, boundedly rational, and moral decision making'. Ostrom (1998:5) notes the Prisoner's Dilemma as the 'best-known social dilemma in contemporary scholarship', and documents a wide variety of empirical and experimental results that shows that agents do cooperate (that is, choose actions that benefit all, provided others also take actions that jointly benefit everyone) to choose outcomes which are socially optimal in Prisoner's Dilemma–like social situations, rather than compete (that is, act non-cooperatively and rationally) and choose the suboptimal ones.

In this paper, we take some very preliminary steps towards developing a notion of rationality, and show that, under the same epistemic conditions that characterise Nash equilibria, it leads to cooperation in mutually gainful social situations, modelled as two-person Prisoner's Dilemma-like games, avoiding the suboptimal alternatives, and thus can account for the empirical and experimental findings that Ostrom cites. In simple terms, the rationality principle we put forward can be summarised as *compete, but cooperate if it is profitable, provided all others do so.* Although simple and straightforward, the principle can also provide a rationale for the 'payoff dominance' criterion of equilibrium selection put forward by Harsanyi and Selten (1988), where, if there are multiple Nash equilibria, the players play those Nash strategies that correspond to a better payoff to each player among all the equilibrium payoffs. Furthermore, application of the rationality principle in the choice of action by a player can be seen to be actuated by the principle of instrumental rationality alone. Thus, in contrast to the well-known position of institutional economists, such as North (1991,

1992) in particular, that institutions are redundant if instrumental rationality is used in explaining behaviour (as is commonly done in economics and game theory and a number of other disciplines such as sociology, political science and evolutionary biology), our result shows that instrumental rationality in some situations can alone resolve social dilemmas, provided appropriate institutions are available that promote the informational requirements under which this can be done.

The central point that our result underscores is that, if we extend the standard rationality assumption of utility maximisation by agents given their beliefs, finding appropriate modification to the rationality assumption that explains cooperation in two-person social dilemmas does not require, as Ostrom (1998) stipulates, models of either bounded rationality or moral decision making. Furthermore, under such a modification of the rationality requirement, cooperation is possible in one-shot two-person social dilemma situations—even repetition of the game is not necessary.

The objectives of this paper are, then, to suggest a modification of the standard rationality condition, and demonstrate the epistemic conditions under which cooperation could be accomplished in a class of social dilemmas with this extended rationality condition. The paper is organised as follows. In the next section, we specify the formal framework and the modified rationality principle. In the third section, we establish the result showing cooperation in social dilemmas modelled as Prisoner's Dilemma games under this principle, given the same epistemic conditions that lead to Nash equilibria. The fourth section discusses some of the implications of the result on institutional models of social and economic behaviour. The last section provides a conclusion.

THE FRAMEWORK AND THE RATIONALITY PRINCIPLE

Most social dilemmas can be modelled as n-person games.[1] Since our focus in this paper is to illustrate how the proposed rationality principle induces cooperation in Prisoner's Dilemma–like situations, we consider a complete information game in strategic form $G = (N, S, g)$, where N is the set of n players, indexed by $i = 1, 2, ..., n$; $S = S_1 \times ... \times S_n$ is the set of n-tuples of *strategies* or *actions*, called a *strategy* or an *action profile*, where S_i is the set of all (pure) strategies

---

[1] For an extensive list of different forms of social dilemmas and their appearance in various social, political and economic situations, see Ostrom (1998: pp. 1–2) and her cited references.

available to player i, $i = 1, ..., n$; and $g : S \rightarrow R^n$ is the *payoff function*, with $g_i(s)$, for $s \in S$, being the payoff to player i given s, the i-th component of the payoff vector $g(s)$. We set, for $s \in S$, $s_{-i} \equiv (s_1, ..., s_{i-1}, s_{i+1}, ..., s_n)$, the strategy $n - 1$-tuple in s with the strategy of player i deleted, and let $S_{-i} = S_1 \times ... \times S_{i-1} \times S_{i+1} \times ... \times S_n$. Let also, for any $s \in S$, $s \equiv (s_i, s_{-i})$. In this paper, we shall confine ourselves to two-person games, and consider only pure strategies for the players. Extension to mixed strategies is mostly routine, and will not be considered in this paper. We call a player *rational* if she chooses an action that maximises her expected utility given her beliefs about the environment, i.e., the constraints of her choice in the game she is faced with. For a player i, to 'know' an event means to 'ascribe probability 1' to that event.

For our purpose, we shall utilise a slightly more specific terminology for the rationality of a player. Thus, given a game $G = (N, S, g)$, we say that a player i is *rational at a strategy profile s*, or, simply, *rational at s*, if, among the actions in S_i available to her, her action s_i maximises her payoff given the actions s_{-i} of others, that is, if $g_i(s) \geq g_i(t_i, s_{-i})$ for all $t_i \in S_i$. It is clear, then, a strategy profile $s \in S$ is a *Nash equilibrium* if every player i is rational at s. We shall say that a player $i \in N$ *follows the rationality principle* if, given any $s_{-i} \in S_{-i}$, she chooses an action s_i such that i is rational at s.

We now introduce two basic results of Aumann and Brandenburger (1995) on the epistemic characterisation of Nash equilibrium in two-person games that are central to our arguments. Call (the occurrence of) an event to be *mutual knowledge* of the players if every player knows it. Note that this is distinct from, and considerably weaker than, *common knowledge* of an event, which requires that every player knows it, every player knows that every player knows it, and so on ad infinitum. Then, the following result holds:

Proposition 1. (*Aumann and Brandenburger 1995*) *Let $G = (N, S, g)$ be the game being played. Let each player be rational, know her own payoff function, and suppose the strategy choices of the players are mutual knowledge. Then the players' choice of strategies constitutes a Nash equilibrium in the game G.*

The idea of the proof of Proposition 1 is straightforward: since each player knows the strategy choices of the other, and is rational, her choice must be optimal given the strategy of the other player; so by definition, we have a Nash equilibrium.

Proposition 1 considers only pure strategies for the players. It is well known that a pure-strategy Nash equilibrium may not exist in some games. The epistemic conditions leading to a Nash equilibrium with mixed strategies are specified by the following proposition. Although in this paper we consider only pure strategies, the epistemic conditions in the proposition will be directly relevant for our purpose, since the result we shall prove will require the additional assumption of mutual knowledge of rationality introduced in the proposition. On the other hand, Proposition 1 will be used by us mainly to explicate some of our arguments.

Proposition 2. *(Aumann and Brandenburger 1995: Theorem A) Let $G = (N, S, g)$ be the game being played. Suppose the game G (that is, both payoff functions), the rationality of the players and their conjectures[2] are all mutually known. Then the players' conjectures constitute a Nash equilibrium in the game G.*

The two propositions are of significant interest, not just for game theory and related disciplines, but, as we shall argue, for all institutional analysis. The first proposition only calls for mutual knowledge of the strategy choices—that each player knows the strategy choices of the other player (including of course her own), with no need for the other player to know that she knows this (or for any higher order knowledge). In particular, it does not call for common knowledge of rationality, which was generally considered to be a basic requirement for Nash equilibrium. In the second proposition, the assumption that the game being played is mutual knowledge is automatically fulfilled in the context of complete information games that the authors (and this paper) are concerned with. Thus, the only additional assumption in Proposition 2 is the mutual knowledge of rationality of the players. Even then, as in Proposition 1, common knowledge of rationality is not needed. Notice that the epistemic conditions in Proposition 2 subsume those in Proposition 1.

In what follows, we shall assume that the Aumann–Brandenburger epistemic conditions in Proposition 2 are satisfied for the games that will be under study. Since our concern is to deal with social dilemmas in

---

[2] 'Conjectures' in this proposition refer to the mixed strategies players use. Following Harsanyi's (1973) seminal contribution, the terminology corresponds to the more recent interpretation of mixed strategies of a player as being other players' conjectures about the strategy choice of the player.

a manner that could be represented by the Prisoner's Dilemma, we shall assume further that the class of games we are considering has at least one pure-strategy Nash equilibrium, and there is also a choice of strategies for the players that can lead to a strictly Pareto-superior outcome for the players compared to their (expected) payoffs in any of the Nash equilibrium of the game. As models of social dilemmas, we shall call this class of games *social dilemma games*.[3]

The reach of the two propositions suggests that, given appropriate epistemic conditions, cooperation can well emerge in social dilemmas where the standard assumption of rationality is modified to incorporate collective rationality, without losing consonance with the standard assumption. We do this in the following definition, and call the modified notion of rationality *coherent rationality* or, simply, *C-rationality*. We define this notion, as well as the remaining ones in the sequel, in terms of pure strategies for the players, since that is what we shall be concerned with. However, they can be routinely extended to mixed-strategy Nash equilibria.

Definition 1. *Let a game $G = (N, S, g)$ be given. Assume that $NE(G)$, the set of pure-strategy Nash equilibria of the game G, is nonempty. Then, a pure strategy or an action $s_i^* \in S_i$ is a coordinating strategy (or action) for i if there exists $s_{-i} \in S_{-i}$ such that, for all $\widehat{s} \in (NE(G) \setminus \{(s_i^*, s_{-i})\})$, $g_i(s_i^*, s_{-i}) > g_i(\widehat{s})$, and for all $j \in (N \setminus \{i\})$, $g_j(s_i^*, s_{-i}) \geq g_j(\widehat{s})$.*

The set of coordinating strategies for a player i in a game G will be denoted by $CD_i(G)$.

Thus, a coordinating action by an agent is one that, given some set of actions of the others, increases the payoff of the agent relative to the payoff the agent would have received in any of the Nash equilibrium outcomes that could materialise (aside from that of the particular strategy profile under consideration if it also happens to be a Nash equilibrium), and does not make any agent worse off compared to any of these equilibrium payoffs.

Note that a coordinating action may not be available for one or more players in a game. However, for the class of social dilemma games we are concerned with, which corresponds to the Prisoner's Dilemma game, each player, by definition, has a coordinating strategy. Note also that the notion of a coordinating strategy applies to a larger set of games

---

[3] We define these games formally later.

than just the ones that correspond to the Prisoner's Dilemma. For example, if there is a number of Nash equilibria, and the payoffs in one of these equilibria are Pareto superior to the payoffs in the remaining Nash equilibria, then each player will have a coordinating strategy available, even though the game is different from a Prisoner's Dilemma.[4] Finally, since we are allowing only pure strategies for the players, the set of Nash equilibria may be empty; in this case, the definition of coordinating strategy for a player is trivial, since every strategy is trivially a coordinating strategy. It is to avoid this case that the definition of coordinating strategies assumes that the set of pure-strategy Nash equilibria in the game being played is nonempty. This does not lose generality for our purposes, since, as noted earlier, in social dilemma games, there will exist, by definition, a suboptimal pure-strategy Nash equilibrium.

We now formally introduce our rationality condition.

Definition 2. *Let $G = (N, S, g)$ be the game being played. A player $i \in N$ is coherently rational if (a) she follows the rationality principle and (b) she chooses a coordinating strategy $s_i^* \in S_i$ whenever $CD_i(G) \neq \varnothing$, if every other player selects a coordinating strategy.*

The notion of *coherent rationality*—a player adhering to (a) and (b) in Definition 2 in her choice of actions—will be abbreviated as *C-rationality*.

It is clear that the notion of C-rationality is a two-tier notion: the players are rational in the standard sense in the first place, and in the second step, they look for situations if they can improve upon the payoffs that would result where the players just follow the rationality principle, that is, given our epistemic assumptions in Proposition 2, the payoffs corresponding to the Nash equilibria of the game. The second part of coherent rationality clearly corresponds to a notion of collective rationality, so the notion can be seen to conjoin the notions of individual and collective rationality. In this sense, it is indeed a notion of meta-rationality.

As the first application of the notion of C-rationality, we provide a definition of what we call a *coordination equilibrium*.

Definition 3. *Let $G(N, S, g)$ be the game being played. Let each player be coherently rational. Then, an n-tuple of strategies $s^* = (s_1^*, ..., s_n^*) \in S$ is a coordination equilibrium if for each player $i \in N$, $s_i^* \in CD_i(G)$.*

---

[4] In the terminology of Harsanyi and Selten (1988), these games have a 'payoff dominant' Nash equilibrium. We use this notion subsequently.

The set of coordination equilibria in $G = (N, S, g)$ will be denoted $CD(G)$.

A coordinating strategy n-tuple is a coordination equilibrium precisely because we have assumed the players to be coherently rational, in the same vein that a Nash equilibrium presupposes that agents follow the rationality principle. Our reference to a coordination equilibrium will sometimes implicitly assume that players are required to be coherently rational under this notion of equilibrium. It is clear that a coordination equilibrium, where it exists, may or may not be a Nash equilibrium. For example, in social dilemma games, such as the Prisoner's Dilemma game, if players are coherently rational, a coordination equilibrium is by definition not a Nash equilibrium. On the other hand, in coordination games such as the stag-hunt game, a coordination equilibrium is one of the Nash equilibria of the game. The notion of a coordination equilibrium makes the purported aim of our work in this paper precise, that is, to demonstrate that the epistemic conditions being considered will lead agents to select such an equilibrium in Prisoner's Dilemma–like social dilemmas.

APPLICATIONS OF C-RATIONALITY

In the preceding section, we introduced the notion of C-rationality and the associated notion of coordination equilibrium in a game. In this section, we prove our main result of cooperation in the Prisoner's Dilemma games under the assumption of C-rationality of players. We first relate this notion of rationality to the payoff dominance criterion of equilibrium selection by Harsanyi and Selten (1988) in the following proposition.

Proposition 3. Let $G = (N, S, g)$ be the game being played. Let the players be coherently rational. Then, a payoff dominant Nash equilibrium of G is a coordination equilibrium of G.

Proof: Let the game $G = (N, S, g)$ be given. If a Nash equilibrium $s^* \in S$ is payoff dominant in G, then for every Nash equilibrium $s \in (NE(G) \backslash \{s^*\})$, for each $i \in N$, we have $g_i(s^*) > g_i(s)$, and for all $j \in (N \setminus \{i\})$, $g_j(s_j^*, s_{-j}^*) \geq g_j(s)$. Then, for each player i, s_i^* is a coordinating strategy, and given that the players are coherently rational, s^* is a coordination equilibrium of G.

The converse of Proposition 3 does not hold. A game may have a coordination equilibrium (for instance, the Prisoner's Dilemma) which is not a Nash equilibrium, and, therefore, not a payoff dominant Nash equilibrium.

Let $CD(G) = \prod_{i \in N} CD_i(G)$. We have $CD(G) = CD(G)$ if each player in G is C-rational. Then, we have:

Definition 4. *Let $G = (N, S, g)$ be the game being played, and assume that $NE(G) \neq \varnothing$. Then, G is a social dilemma game if $CD(G) \neq \varnothing$ and $CD(G) \cap NE(G) = \varnothing$.*

On the other hand, the class of games we shall call *coordination games* is given by:

Definition 5. *Let $G = (N, S, g)$ be a game. G is a coordination game if $CD(G) \neq \varnothing$ and $CD(G) \subset NE(G)$.*

Figure 4.1 illustrates Proposition 3, which is also a typical example of a two-person coordination game.

Player 2

		Hunt	Gather
Player 1	Hunt	(4, 4)	(0, 3)
	Gather	(3, 0)	(2, 2)

Figure 4.1 The stag-hunt game

We now turn to coordination equilibrium in a social dilemma game specified in terms of a Prisoner's Dilemma game. Given the notion of C-rationality, it is immediate that if we replace the assumption of 'each player is rational' by 'each player is C-rational' in the Aumann–Brandenburger (1995) Proposition 2, the epistemic conditions in the proposition will lead directly to a coordination equilibrium in a social dilemma game. Before we state this result formally, in order to explicate the underlying arguments in our result (Proposition 4 below), we provide an example to illustrate the more basic Proposition 1. Consider the game given in Figure 4.2.

Player 2

		L	C	R
Player 1	U	5, 2	1, 3	2, 5
	M	3, 1	2, 2	3, 1
	B	2, 5	1, 3	5, 2

Source: Based on Bernheim (1984) and Brandenburger (1999).

Figure 4.2 Illustration of mutual knowledge and Nash equilibrium

Consider what could possibly emerge as the players' selection of strategies in the game in Figure 4.2 if all we know is that each player is rational, or, more specifically, follows the rationality principle. In this case, there is nothing to prevent (U, R) as emerging the strategy choices of the players if Player 1 assesses probability 1 to Player 2 choosing L, and Player 2 assesses probability 1 to Player 1 choosing U. While this kind of situation cannot be ruled out in real life, due to the inherent uncertainty of the situation, it is nevertheless based on an incorrect calculation on the part of Player 1, and we may well consider assumptions that might eliminate such choices based on incorrect assessments by any of the players of others' strategy choices. Suppose now we introduce the assumption that the players' strategy choices are mutual knowledge. Given this assumption, can we still have (U, R) as the outcome of the game? The answer is clearly in the negative: since Player 1 will then choose B instead of U. Indeed, the only strategy pair that can be mutual knowledge is (M,C), given that both players are assumed to follow the rationality principle. Notice that this is also the only Nash equilibrium of the game, where each player's strategy is optimal given the strategy of the other player.

We now state and prove our result using the notion of coherent rationality of players to demonstrate the possibility of cooperation in a Prisoner's Dilemma game. Consider, as in Figure 4.3, a generic (symmetric) Prisoner's Dilemma game, where, for the real numbers a, b, c and d, we have $b > a > c > d$.

Player 2

Player 1	Cooperate (C)	Defect (D)
Cooperate (C)	(a, a)	(d, b)
Defect (D)	(b, d)	(c, c)

Figure 4.3 A symmetric Prisoner's Dilemma game

In this game, the coordination equilibrium is (Cooperate, Cooperate) with payoffs (a, a), and the suboptimal Nash (and dominant strategy) equilibrium is (Defect, Defect), with payoffs (c, c).

Proposition 4. Let the game $G = (N, S, g)$ being played be a two-person (symmetric) Prisoner's Dilemma game. Suppose each player is coherently rational. Suppose, moreover, that the structure of the game G (that is, the payoff functions of the players), each player's rationality and their strategy choices are mutual knowledge. Then their choice of strategies constitutes a coordination equilibrium.

Proof: Let $G = (N, S, g)$ be a symmetric two-person Prisoner's Dilemma game, with the generic form given in Figure 4.3. Let both players be coherently rational. Then, since both players are coherently rational and the players' rationality is mutual knowledge, neither of the choices of strategy pairs, (C, D) and (D, C), can be the players' mutual knowledge by requirement (*a*) in the definition of coherent rationality, nor can the choice of (D, D) be mutual knowledge by requirement (*b*) of the definition. Thus, under the assumptions in the proposition, only the strategy choice (C, C) can be mutual knowledge of the players. Since each of the strategies in (C, C) is a coordinating strategy for the respective players, (C, C) is indeed a coordination equilibrium.

Note that, just the assumption of the players being coherently rational will not lead to the coordination equilibrium without the mutual knowledge assumptions: since, as in the game in Figure 4.2, without them the assessments of the probabilities of each other's actions may be erroneous. The dynamics of the result in Proposition 4 can be outlined as follows. Each player, being cognizant of the structure of the game, first assesses the possible strategy choices of the other player as well as her own. Clearly, the players recognise that by following the rationality principle—the first stage of coherent rationality—they will find themselves with the suboptimal outcome (D, D). In the second tier of rationality, they look for coordinating strategies, and given that they are both C-rational, choose these strategies to reach the outcome (C, C). Since each player is C-rational and knows the other player to be so, each player can assess probability 1 to the choice of C as the other player's strategy, were she to choose C for herself. Neither of the players will wish to deviate to, say, strategy pair (D, D) from (C, C), as they would if they were following only the rationality principle. Notice that C-rationality of the players and their strategy choices cannot be mutual knowledge if such deviations were to arise. Since both of them are coherently rational, and each knows that the other is so, the only strategy choices by the players with mutual knowledge of their rationality and strategy choice must, therefore, lead them unambiguously to the coordination equilibrium (C, C).[5]

---

[5] A generalisation of this result, extending it to a larger class of games called 'games of common pursuit', including asymmetric *n*-person Prisoner's Dilemma games, is currently under preparation (Sengupta 2014).

SOME IMPLICATIONS OF C-RATIONALITY

In Proposition 4, we have shown that if an extended notion of rationality, which we have called C-rationality, is mutual knowledge of the agents along with the structure of the game and their strategy choices, then two-person Prisoner's Dilemma–like social dilemmas can be resolved. It is to be noted that C-rationality does not go beyond instrumental rationality, which underlies the rationality principle. Indeed, the first part of C-rationality (Definition 2) is the rationality principle itself, while the second part modifies it in the presence of a strategy choice for a player that will offer a superior payoff compared to applying the rationality principle alone. It is, thus, a principle that uses instrumental rationality for strategy choices twice over: first over the set of outcomes and the associated payoffs, then over the strategy profiles giving the Nash equilibria of the game along with those that correspond to a co-ordination equilibrium, where such an equilibrium exists.

Instrumental rationality has come under a great deal of scrutiny by economists, because of the centrality of this notion in the discipline.[6] Sen (1977), in particular, led the argument against the notion because of its extremely narrow focus, and called for a broadening of the notion of rationality in economic analysis. Myerson (1999), on the other hand, provided a defence of instrumental rationality in the context of Nash equilibrium analysis. While there is no consensus about the relevance and reach of this assumption of rationality, its limitation in terms of its restriction to only ends–means considerations is accepted generally, as much as its essential justification in terms of the argument that it permits us to build an operational model of behaviour. This latter argument essentially follows the approach of Popper (1967) in the context of the use of the principle of instrumental rationality. A similar approach to the principle is taken by Rawls (1971).

Instrumental rationality has, however, been rejected in institutional analysis. Ostrom's (1998) critique of neoclassical analysis of social dilemmas articulates such a rejection. North (1991, 1992) also rejects unequivocally any role of institutions in analyses based on instrumental rationality, and ipso facto rejects any relevance of institutions in neoclassical economics. The result we have established in this paper, however, shows that this rejection of institutions from the purview of analyses based on instrumental rationality may not be well founded. As remarked earlier, the mutual knowledge assumption is the driving force

---

[6] See, for example, Arrow (1986), Bicchieri (1993) and Sen (1977, 1993).

of the result, just as it is in the case of Nash equilibrium. Institutions play a great role in fostering this mutual knowledge, as documented in the far-reaching work of Grief (1989, 1993) on the development of Maghribi traders' contractual agreements, and that of Ostrom (1990) on the institutions of trade developed by the Turkish fishermen and the medieval English cattle-owners.[7] In particular, in the context of social dilemmas, institutions such as social norms of behaviour, social codes, mutual trust and reciprocity of the agents all lead to a greater spread of the information regarding socially desirable outcomes in such situations, and the means to achieve them. In formal terms, this is precisely what we have called mutual knowledge of rationality and choice of strategies by the agents. Given such knowledge that only appropriate institutions can induce among the agents, our result shows that instrumental rationality—one the narrowest of rationality assumptions—can, by itself, lead to social optima.

This complementarity between instrumental rationality and institutions is of importance, since instrumental rationality remains a fundamental building block in most social and as well as many physical sciences. In spite of its stringent limitations because of its narrow focus, as the development of the social and physical sciences has shown, the notion does permit testable models of behaviour, as in much of economics, and in game theory and its applications to a number of other areas, such as biology and psychology. The result that cooperation in social dilemmas can be explained without forsaking instrumental rationality is, thus, a pointer to a wider significance of institutions in rational decision making in terms of instrumental rationality alone. What might be necessary, however, as in our work here, is that the standard rationality notion in economics and game theory may need to be extended or supplemented in cases where, by itself, it fails to corroborate agents' observed behaviour.

CONCLUSION

In this paper, we have suggested a notion of rationality that extends the standard notion in economics and game theory, and have shown that mutual knowledge of this rationality of the players and their strategy

---

[7] Our result may be, thus, seen to provide a possible analytical explanation of the prevalence of the kind of institutions studied by Grief (1989, 1993) and Ostrom (1990), where, given these institutions, narrow self-interest went hand in hand with cooperative behaviour for mutual benefit.

choices will lead to the selection of the optimal, cooperative outcome in the Prisoner's Dilemma game, which typifies social dilemmas. The extended rationality principle is within the ambit of instrumental rationality, a fundamental assumption in most social and physical sciences. The mutual knowledge assumption required for the result, we have argued, can be facilitated by the availability, or, where unavailable, by the development of appropriate institutions in the economy. This can make analysis of social dilemmas based on instrumental rationality adequate enough to explain observed social behaviour of cooperation and reciprocity. Our work here highlights this basic compatibility and complementarity of institutions and instrumental rationality in dealing with social dilemmas, and, thus, permits a different perspective to their economic and decision- and game-theoretic analyses.

REFERENCES

Arrow K. J. 1986. 'Rationality of Self and Others in an Economic System', *Journal of Business*, 59(4): 385–99.

Aumann, R. J. and A. Brandenburger. 1995. 'Epistemic Conditions for Nash Equilibrium', *Econometrica*, 63(5): 1161–80.

Bernheim, D. 1984. 'Rationalizable Strategic Behavior', *Econometrica*, 52(4): 1007–28.

Bicchieri, C. 1993. *Rationality and Coordination*. Cambridge: Cambridge University Press.

Brandenburger, A. 1992. 'Knowledge and Equilibrium in Games', *Journal of Economic Perspectives*, 6(4): 83–101.

Grief, A. 1989. 'Reputation and Coalitions in Medieval Trade: Evidence on the Maghribi Traders', *Journal of Economic History*, 49(4): 857–82.

———. 1993. 'Contract Enforceability and Economic Institutions in Early Trade: The Maghribi Traders' Coalition', *American Economic Review*, 83(3): 525–48.

Harsanyi, J. C. 1973. 'Games with Randomly Disturbed Payoffs: A New Rationale for Mixed Strategy Equilibrium Points', *International Journal of Game Theory*, 2(1): 1–23.

Harsanyi, J. C. and R. Selten. 1988. *A General Theory of Equilibrium Selection in Games*. Cambridge, Mass.: MIT Press.

Myerson, R. B. 1999. 'Nash Equilibrium and the History of Economic Theory', *Journal of Economic Literature*, 37(3): 1067–82.

North, D. C. 1991. 'Institutions', *Journal of Economic Perspectives*, 5(1): 97–112.

———. 1992. 'Institutions and Economic Theory', *The American Economist*, 36(1): 3–6.

Ostrom, E. 1990. *Governing the Commons: The Evolution of Institutions for Collective Action*. New York: Cambridge University Press.

———. 1998. 'A Behavioral Approach to the Rational Choice Theory of Collective Action', *American Political Science Review*, 92(1): 1–22.

Popper, K. R. 1967 [1985]. 'The Rationality Principle', in D. Miller (ed.), *Popper Collections*. Princeton, N.J.: Princeton University Press, pp. 357–78.

Rawls, J. B. 1971. *A Theory of Justice*. Cambridge, Mass.: Harvard University Press.

Sen, A. K. 1977. 'Rational Fools: A Critique of the Behavioral Foundations of Economic Theory', *Philosophy and Public Affairs*, 6(4): 317–44.

———. 1993. 'Internal Consistency of Choice', *Econometrica*, 61(3): 495–521.

Sengupta, M. 2015. 'Social Dilemmas and Rationality', in preparation.

PART II
CHOICE AND VALUES

5

Characterisation of a Second-Best Rationalisable Choice Function with General Domain

Taposik Banerjee*

Choices made from alternatives that one faces in different situations, when described in the form of a function, provides us with a choice function. A choice function, therefore is essentially a description of observed choices. There is nothing inherent in such a description to confirm that the choices made are consistent with the behaviour that one may expect from a rational individual. Such consistency, however, is a matter of great importance to economists and philosophers as it is considered as the hallmark of a rational individual. Several axioms have been proposed in the literature of choice theory to ensure this consistency of a choice function.[1] These axioms (popularly known as *internal consistency conditions*), if satisfied by a choice function, assure us that the choices made are somewhat consistent or reasonable. The reasonableness that we are talking about here, however, is linked with the concept of rationality.

Rationality has been commonly described in the theory of individual choice or social choice as a quality of an individual that enables her to construct a ranking over alternatives she faces, so that she can choose the best one among them. It is assumed that the ranking is constructed only after taking into account all relevant considerations that may affect her choice behaviour. It is understood that with such a ranking at her disposal choosing the best element serves her interest best.

The axioms of *internal consistency* that we were talking about earlier have been designed in order to ensure that the chosen elements are all best elements. Satisfaction of those conditions ensures that the

---

* I am deeply indebted to Professor Satish K. Jain for his guidance and suggestions.
[1] See Arrow (1959), Blair et al. (1976), Plott (1973), Richter (1966), Suzumura (1977) and Uzawa (1956).

choice function is *rationalisable*, that is, such choices could be realised by choosing the best elements according to some ordering. So one may say that a rationalisable choice function represents choices that could be made by a rational individual. But what if the choice function is not rationalisable? In other words, is it necessary that choices that are not realised by choosing best elements are inconsistent and can only be made by an irrational person? The answer could be given suitably by the classic example provided by Amartya Sen (1993) where he considers the following choices:

$$C(\{x, y\}) = \{x\}$$
$$C(\{x, y, z\}) = \{y\}$$

Alternative x was chosen when y was available, whereas y was chosen when both x and z were available. Clearly the chosen elements cannot be best elements. Yet the choices are not inconsistent. Such choices would be realised if a person with preferences $zPyPx$ chooses second-best elements from the sets of alternatives. This phenomenon of choosing a second-best alternative is not unintelligible either. We would like to go back to Sen's example once again. A person who would otherwise love to have the largest piece of cake (assuming that preferences over cake pieces are determined by their size; larger the size more preferred it is) from the tray may decide not to choose the largest one and instead choose the second largest one if she does not want to be considered as greedy by others (Sen 1993). Choosing the second-best element here clearly is a purposive behaviour and by no means irrational.

The internal consistency conditions that only allow for best elements in the choice set would recommend the choice behaviour (in Sen's example) that we just described earlier as inconsistent. They would do so because in their design it was implicitly assumed that choosing a second-best element is not a rational action. As a result, a whole class of purposive behaviour has been classified as irrational behaviour. The existing internal consistency conditions that are popularly used in the social choice theory to assess a choice function, therefore, turn out to be insufficient to analyse several choice patterns. Motivated by the example provided by Sen (1993), this essay makes a modest effort to address this limitation. It would be proper to mention here that some research has already been done to overcome these limitations. Baigent and Gaertner (1996) have characterised a choice function where an individual chooses a second-best element in case there is a unique best element in the set. Gaertner and Xu (1999) have characterised choice functions where chosen elements are median elements from a preference ranking. This essay would like to characterise choice behaviours where an individual chooses a second-best element when available; otherwise, she chooses a best element. A choice function that describes such choices will be called a second-best rationalisable (alternatively 2-rationalisable) choice function. We are not imposing any restriction on the domain of the choice function which means our choice function may have any non-empty collection of non-empty subsets as its domain. We would call it a choice function with general domain. In the next section, some general definitions and notation have been introduced which are to be used in the essay. Third section describes the characterisation results.

NOTATION AND DEFINITIONS

Let X be the non-empty finite universal set of alternatives. We denote the *power set* of X (that is, the set of all subsets of X) by 2^X. Let Σ be the set of all non-empty subsets of X, that is, $\Sigma = 2^X - \{\emptyset\}$.

A *choice function* is defined as a function, $C : D \mapsto \Sigma$ such that $C(A) \subseteq A$ for all $A \in D$, where $\emptyset \neq D \subseteq \Sigma$. In other words, to every set A belonging to the domain D, which is a non-empty collection of non-empty subsets of X, we assign a set $C(A)$, which is a subset of A itself. $C(A)$ is called the *choice set* of the set A.

For any binary relation R defined over a set S, the asymmetric and symmetric parts of R, designated by P and I respectively are defined as

$$(\forall x, y \in S)[[xPy \leftrightarrow xRy \wedge \sim yRx] \wedge [xIy \leftrightarrow xRy \wedge yRx]].$$

A binary relation R is said to be an *ordering* if and only if it is reflexive, connected and transitive. A binary relation R is said to be a *quasi-ordering* if and only if it is reflexive and transitive.

For any two binary relations R_1 and R_2 on X, a *composition* thereof is defined by

$$R_1 R_2 = \{(x, y) \in X \times X \mid \exists z \in X : (x, z) \in R_1 \wedge (z, y) \in R_2\}.$$

For any binary relation R, we define the following infinite sequence of binary relations:

$$R^1 = R, R^2 = RR, R^3 = RR^2, ..., R^t = RR^{t-1}; \ t \in N - \{1\}$$

Let $T(R) = \bigcup_{n \in N} R^n$. $T(R)$ is said to be the *transitive closure* of R. A binary relation R on X is *T-consistent* iff,

$$(\forall x, y \in X)[(x, y) \in T(R) \ \rightarrow \ (x, y) \in R \ \vee \ (y, x) \notin R].$$

Let R_1 and R_2 be two binary relations defined over a set S. R_2 will be called an extension of R_1 iff,

$$[R_1 \subseteq R_2 \wedge P(R_1) \subseteq P(R_2)].$$

Let R be a binary relation defined over a set S. An element $x \in S$ is said to be a *best element* (or *first-best element*) in S with respect to R if and only if, $(\forall y \in S)(xRy)$. Let the set of all such best elements in S be $G_1(S, R)$.

We define that an element $x \in S - G_1(S, R)$ is a *second-best element* in S with respect to R if and only if, $(\forall y \in S - G_1(S, R))(xRy)$. We may say that once we remove all best elements from a set, a second-best element would be a best element of the reduced set. Let the set of all such second-best elements in S be $G_2(S, R)$.

A binary relation R is said to be a *2-rationalisation* (second-best element rationalisation) of a choice function C if and only if

$$C(S) = G_2(S, R) \qquad \text{if } G_2(S, R) \neq \emptyset$$
$$= G_1(S, R) \qquad \text{if } G_2(S, R) = \emptyset$$

for all $S \in D$. Simply put, the chosen elements are the second-best elements of a set. If a second-best element is not available, then best elements are chosen.

Necessary and Sufficient Condition for a Choice Function to be 2-Rationalisable by an Ordering

We define a set λ such that,

$$\lambda = \{S \in D \mid C(S) \neq S\}.$$

For every set in λ choice set is a proper subset of the original set. So in every set in λ there is at least one element which does not belong to the choice set. Intuitively, we can say that if the choice function is 2-rationalisable, then these should be the sets which have a second-best element.

We now define a function,

$$f : \lambda \mapsto 2^X - \{\emptyset\}$$

such that,

$$\text{for all } S \in \lambda, f(S) \subset S \wedge f(S) \cap C(S) = \emptyset.$$

The idea behind the function f is simple and intuitive. If λ is the collection of sets with second-best elements, then for any set S in λ, we would like to see $f(S)$ as the collection of best elements in S.

We define the following sets:

$$A_1 = \{(x, y) \mid (\exists S \in \lambda)(x \in f(S) \wedge y \in C(S))\}$$
$$A_2 = \{(x, y) \mid (\exists S \in \lambda)(x \in C(S) \wedge y \in S - (C(S) \cup f(S)))\}$$
$$A_3 = \{(x, y) \mid (\exists S \in D)(x, y \in C(S))\}$$
$$A_4 = \{(x, y) \mid (\exists S \in \lambda)(x, y \in f(S))\}$$

Given the interpretation of $f(S)$, it is clear that for any (x, y) that belongs to either A_1 or A_2, we need x to be strictly preferred to y. However, if (x, y) belongs to either A_3 or A_4, then we need x to be indifferent to y.

Let $A = A_1 \cup A_2 \cup A_3 \cup A_4$. Clearly A is a binary relation over X. We introduce two conditions here:

$$Condition\ 1\colon (x, y) \in A_1 \rightarrow (y, x) \notin T(A)$$
$$Condition\ 2\colon (x, y) \in A_2 \rightarrow (y, x) \notin T(A)$$

where $T(A)$ is the transitive closure of A. Condition 1 and Condition 2 ensure T-consistency of the binary relation A. It is known that a T-consistent binary relation will necessarily have a reflexive, connected and transitive extension.[2] Next we would look for such an ordering extension of A.

Clearly with these two conditions satisfied, $P(A) = A_1 \cup A_2$.

Let, $\Delta_X = \{(x, x) \mid x \in X\}$.

We define a binary relation $\overline{Q}$ such that, $\overline{Q} = \Delta_X \cup T(A)$.

It can be easily verified that $\overline{Q}$ is a quasi-ordering (that is, reflexive and transitive). Let R be an ordering extension of $\overline{Q}$.

Claim 1. $\overline{Q}$ *is an extension of* A.

Proof: It is straight forward that $(x, y) \in A$ implies $(x, y) \in \overline{Q}$. Suppose $(x, y) \in P(A)$.

$$
\begin{aligned}
(x, y) \in P(A) &\rightarrow (x, y) \in A_1 \vee (x, y) \in A_2 \\
&\rightarrow (y, x) \notin T(A) \\
&\rightarrow (x, y) \in P[T(A)] \\
&\rightarrow (x, y) \in P(\overline{Q})
\end{aligned}
$$

Hence, $\overline{Q}$ is an extension of A.

Therefore, R is an ordering extension of A.

---

[2] See Jain (2007) and Suzumura (1983).

Axiom E: *There exists a function $f : \lambda \mapsto 2^X - \{\emptyset\}$ satisfying conditions 1 and 2.*

Theorem 1. *There exists an ordering R which 2-rationalises the choice function C iff it satisfies axiom E.*

Proof: Suppose a choice function C satisfies axiom E. If $\lambda = \emptyset$, then for all $S \in D$, we have $C(S) = S$. In that case $R = X^2$ is a 2-rationalisation.

Now let $\lambda \neq \emptyset$.

Case 1. Let $C(S) = S$.

$$C(S) = S \rightarrow (\forall x, y \in S)(xAy)$$
$$\rightarrow (\forall x, y \in S)(xRy)$$
$$\rightarrow G_1(S, R) = S$$

Case 2. Let $C(S) \neq S$.

By construction, we have $f(S) \neq \emptyset$.
Let

$$x \in C(S) \wedge y \in f(S).$$

Clearly, $(y, x) \in P(A)$. As R is an extension of A, it must be $yP(R)x$. Therefore, $x \notin G_1(S, R)$.

Suppose $x \notin G_2(S, R)$. Then for some $z \in S - G_1(S, R)$, we have zPx.

$$zPx \rightarrow \sim xRz$$
$$\rightarrow z \notin C(S) \wedge z \notin S - [C(S) \cup f(S)]$$
$$\rightarrow z \in f(S)$$

$z \notin G_1(S, R)$ implies that for some w in S, we have wPz. $w \notin f(S)$, as $z \in f(S)$. Also, $w \notin C(S)$ as wPx.

Again, wPx implies $w \notin S - [C(S) \cup f(S)]$.
Therefore, $w \notin S$, which is a contradiction.

$$\therefore x \in G_2(S, R).$$

Now we prove the converse. Let $x \in G_2(S, R)$ and suppose $x \notin C(S)$. Suppose, $x \in f(S)$.

$$x \in f(S) \rightarrow x \in G_1(S, R)$$
$$\rightarrow x \notin G_2(S, R)$$

This is a contradiction. Therefore, $x \notin f(S)$.

$x \in S - [C(S) \cup f(S)]$
$\rightarrow \exists z \in f(S) \wedge \exists y \in C(S) \wedge (z, y) \in P(R) \wedge (y, x) \in P(R)$
$\rightarrow x \notin G_2(S, R)$

This is a contradiction and, hence, $x \in C(S)$.

Therefore, $C(S) \neq S$ implies that $C(S) = G_2(S, R)$.

The necessary part of the theorem is trivial and comes straight from the intuitive interpretation that was given earlier. For every set S in λ, assign $f(S)$ as the collection of best elements in S and axiom E will be satisfied.

CONCLUSION

Choosing a non-best element from a set of alternatives cannot be automatically termed as unreasonable. On certain occasions depending on the context of choice, one may reasonably choose an element that is not the best element. Internal consistency conditions of choice, therefore, cannot be applied in a context independent way. In order to see whether different parts of a choice function are consistent or not, we need to specifically consider the context of that choice. Standard consistency conditions are applicable only to cases where the chooser is interested in picking the best elements from any set. If, however, chosen elements are not best, new sets of conditions need to be applied to check for consistency of choice. This essay characterises a 2-rationalisable choice function with general domain. The characterisation result of course has a limitation as it involves a condition of existential nature. However, given the complexity of the problem, it appears that an existential condition was unavoidable. Moreover, the essay while constructing the condition also tried to throw some light on the intricate relationships between different components of a choice function and a binary relation that may 2-rationalise it. Although the essay fails to characterise a 2-rationalisable choice function without invoking an existential condition, it may not altogether be an impossible task to perform. The problem, therefore, remains open in some sense and the essay, we hope, would facilitate farther research in the area.

REFERENCES

Arrow, K. J. 1959. 'Rational Choice Functions and Orderings', *Economica*, New Series, 26(102): 121–27.

Baigent, N. and W. Gaertner. 1996. 'Never Choose the Uniquely Largest: A Characterization', *Economic Theory*, 8(2): 239–49.

Blair, D., G. Bordes, J. S. Kelly and K. Suzumura. 1976. 'Impossibility Theorems without Collective Rationality', *Journal of Economic Theory*, 13(3): 361–79.

Gaertner, W. and Y. Xu. 1999. 'On Rationalizability of Choice Functions: A Characterization of the Median', *Social Choice and Welfare*, 16(4): 629–38.

Jain, S. K. 2007. 'A Note on the Extendability of Binary Relations', unpublished paper.

Plott, C. R. 1973. 'Path Independence, Rationality, and Social Choice', *Econometrica*, 41(6): 1075–91.

Richter, M. K. 1966. 'Revealed Preference Theory', *Econometrica*, 34(3): 635–45.

Sen, A. K. 1993. 'Internal Consistency of Choice', *Econometrica*, 61(3): 495–521.

Suzumura, K. 1977. 'Houthakkers Axiom in the Theory of Rational Choice', *Journal of Economic Theory*, 14(2): 284–90.

———. 1983. *Rational Choice, Collective Decisions and Social Welfare*. Cambridge: Cambridge University Press.

Uzawa, H. 1956. 'Note on Preference and Axioms of Choice', *Annals of the Institute of Statistical Mathematics*, 8(1): 35–40.

6

Domain Conditions for
Quasi-transitive Rationalisability

Debabrata Pal*

In the literature of choice theory an important problem that has been dealt with at length is the rationalisability of choice functions. The problem investigates whether it is possible to conceive of a preference relation that would represent the choice pattern of an individual. If it is observed that an individual chooses x from $\{x, y\}$, $\{x, z\}$, $\{x, y, z\}$ and y from $\{z, y\}$, it is immediate that the preference relation xRx, yRy, xPy, xPz, yPz[1] represents such choice behaviour. The best element (x)[2] in the sets $\{x, y\}$, $\{x, z\}$, $\{x, y, z\}$ according to the aforesaid preference relation is the same as the chosen element in the sets. Similarly, y is the best as well as the chosen element in the set $\{z, y\}$. We, therefore, say that such a choice function[3] is rationalisable. In other words, a choice function is rationalisable if and only if the most preferred elements according to some preference relation are chosen from the available sets.

In general, not all choice functions are rationalisable.[4] A number of choice consistency conditions are, thus, introduced, which ensure the rationalisability of choice functions. It has been established that

---

* Assistant Professor at Indian Institute of Technology, Jodhpur (IITJ). Email: debabrata@iitj.ac.in
[1] Read xRx as 'x is at least as good as x' and xPy as 'x is preferred to y'.
[2] The definition of best element has been given in the next section.
[3] Here we use the phrases 'choice function' and 'choice pattern' interchangeably and with the same interpretation. The formal definition of choice function is given in the next section.
[4] Consider following choice function:

$$X = \{x, y, z\}, C(\{x, y\}) = \{x\}, C(\{x, z\}) = \{z\}, C(\{z, y\}) = \{y\}, C(\{x, y, z\}) = \{x\},$$

where X is the set of alternatives. This choice function is not rationalisable.

choice functions defined over the general domain[5] have ordering rationalisation if and only if they satisfy the Houthakker axiom of revealed
preference (HOA). Choice functions defined over the full domain have
ordering rationalisation if and only if they satisfy Arrow's axiom,
and have reflexive, connected quasi-transitive rationalisation, if and
only if they satisfy both the generalised conduct property and path
independence.

The nature of these choice consistency conditions is such that they
impose restrictions on the choice pattern of an individual and, in turn
characterise the partition of choice functions. On one side, there are
choice functions that have ordering rationalisation or quasi-transitive
rationalisation (as the case may be) and, on the other side, there are
choice functions that do not have ordering or quasi-transitive rationalisation. Pal (2012), however, points out that over a given domain some
choice functions are rationalisable and some are not.[6] The implications
of choice consistency conditions also change as the domain of the
choice function changes. It is, therefore, worth investigating the nature

---

[5] The general domain is a non-empty collection of non-empty subsets of the set
of alternatives. The full domain is the collection of *all* non-empty finite subsets
of the set of alternatives.

[6] Consider the following example:

$$X = \{x_1, x_2, x_3\}; D = \{\{x_1, x_2, x_3\}, \{x_2, x_3\}\},$$

where X and D denote the set of alternatives and the domain of choice functions
respectively. Now consider the following two choice functions C and $\tilde{C}$ defined
over the same domain D:

$$C(\{x_2, x_3\}) = \{x_3\}; C(\{x_1, x_2, x_3\}) = \{x_1, x_2\}$$
$$\tilde{C}(\{x_2, x_3\}) = \{x_2\}; \tilde{C}(\{x_1, x_2, x_3\}) = \{x_1, x_2\}$$

Choice function C does not have any rationalisation because of the following
reason. Alternative x_2 is chosen from the set $\{x_1, x_2, x_3\}$, any binary relation
which rationalises the choice function would necessarily entail the following
preferences: 'x_2 is at least as good as x_2', 'x_2 is at least as good as x_1' and 'x_2 is
at least as good as x_3'. Given these preferences, it is clear that x_2 belongs to the
set of best elements of the set $\{x_2, x_3\}$; but x_2 does not belong to the choice set
of $\{x_2, x_3\}$. Therefore, the choice function is not rationalisable.

Choice function $\tilde{C}$, however, does have a rationalisation. Take, for instance,
the following binary relation: $R = \{(x_1, x_1), (x_2, x_2), (x_3, x_3), (x_1, x_2), (x_1, x_3),$
$(x_2, x_1), (x_2, x_3)\}$. This binary relation rationalises the choice function $\tilde{C}$, that is
the set of best elements of a set with respect to R is same as the set of chosen
elements.

of domains in relation to the rationalisability of the choice function. The following two results have been established in Pal (2012):

1. Every choice function defined over a domain is rationalizable *iff* that domain satisfies condition C.1.[7]
2. Every choice function defined over a domain has an ordering rationalisation *iff* that domain satisfies condition C.3.[8]

This essay provides a partial characterisation of the domain over which all choice functions are rationalisable with quasi-transitive rationalisation. It has been established that if a domain satisfies conditions C.3 and C.1, then any choice function defined over such a domain has a quasi-transitive rationalisation.

This essay is divided into four sections. The second section contains the basic notations and definitions that have been used in the succeeding sections. The third section provides the characterisation result. The last section concludes the essay.

NOTATIONS AND DEFINITIONS

Let X be a non-empty finite set of alternatives and 2^X the power set of X. For a set S, $\#S$ denotes the cardinality of S. Let N denote the set of positive integers. Let D be a non-empty collection of non-empty subsets of X, $D \subseteq 2^X - \{\emptyset\}$. A choice function C is a mapping from D to $2^X - \{\emptyset\}$, $C : D \mapsto 2^X - \{\emptyset\}$ such that $C(S) \subseteq S$ for all $S \in D$. In succeeding sections, we denote D to be the domain of the choice function.

Let R be a binary relation defined over X. Let I and P denote the symmetric and asymmetric parts of R respectively. R is said to be reflexive on S *iff* $(\forall x \in S)(xRx)$:

- connected *iff* $(\forall\, x, y \in S)(x \neq y \rightarrow xRy \lor yRx)$
- transitive *iff* $(\forall\, x, y, z \in S)(xRy \land yRz \rightarrow xRz)$
- quasi-transitive *iff* $(\forall\, x, y, z \in S)(xPy \land yPz \rightarrow xPz)$

---

[7]   C1: $(\forall S \in D - D_X)[(\forall x \in S)[\sim (\forall y \in S - \{x\})(\exists S' \in D - \{S\})(\{x, y\} \subseteq S')]]$

where, D is the domain of the choice function and X is the set of alternative.

$$D_X = \{ \{x\} \mid x \in X \}.$$

[8]   C3 : $(\forall n \in N - \{1\})(\forall \text{ distinct } x_o, x_1, x_2, ..., x_n \in X)(\forall S_1, S_2, ..., S_n \in D)$
$[\sim (S_1 \neq S_n \land (\{x_o, x_1\} \subseteq S_1 \land \{x_1, x_2\} \subseteq S_2 \land ..., \land \{x_{n-1}, x_n\} \subseteq S_n)$
$\land (\exists S' \in D)(\{x_o, x_n\} \subseteq S'))],$

where, N is the set of natural numbers.

- acyclic *iff* $(\forall n \in N - \{1, 2\})(\forall x_1, x_2, ..., x_n \in S)(x_1Px_2 \wedge x_2Px_3 \wedge ... \wedge x_{n-1}Px_n \rightarrow x_1Rx_n)$ and
- asymmetric *iff* $(\forall x, y \in S)(xRy \rightarrow \sim yRx)$.

We say that R is an ordering *iff* it is reflexive, connected and transitive. Define binary relation R_c

$$R_c = \{(x, y) \in X \times X | (\exists S \in D)(x \in C(S) \wedge y \in S)\}$$
$$R_1 = \{(x, z) \in X \times X | (\exists y_1, y_2, .., y_n \in X)(xP(R_c)y_1 \wedge y_1P(R_c)y_2$$
$$\wedge ... \wedge y_nP(R_c)z) \wedge (\forall T \in D)(\{x, z\} \nsubseteq T), \text{ for some } n \in N\}$$
$$\bar{R} = R_c \cup R_1.$$

x is said to be a greatest element (best) in a set S with respect to a binary relation R *iff* $(\forall y \in S)(xRy)$.[9]

Let $G(S, R)$ denote the set of greatest elements of a set S with respect to R. We say that a choice function C is rationalisable *iff* there exists a binary relation R defined over the set of alternatives such that for every set in the domain the choice set coincides with the set of greatest elements of the set with respect to R, that is, $(\exists R \subseteq X \times X)(\forall S \in D)(C(S) = G(S, R))$.[10]

---

[9] Consider the following example:

$$\text{Let } X = \{x_o, x_1, x_2\}; S = \{x_o, x_1, x_2\}$$

and

$$R = \{(x_o, x_o), (x_2, x_2), (x_o, x_1), (x_o, x_2)\}; G(S, R) = \{x_o\}.$$

[10] Consider the following example.

$$\text{Let } X = \{x_o, x_1, x_2\}; D = \{\{x_2\}, \{x_o, x_1\}, \{x_o, x_1, x_2\}\}.$$
$$\text{Let } S_1 = \{x_2\}, S_2 = \{x_o, x_1\}, S_3 = \{x_o, x_1, x_2\}.$$

Let C be a choice function defined over D in the following way:

$$C(S_1) = \{x_2\}, C(S_2) = \{x_o\}, C(S_3) = \{x_o\}$$

Now consider the following binary relation:

$$R = \{(x_o, x_o), (x_2, x_2), (x_o, x_1), (x_o, x_2)\}.$$
$$G(S_1, R) = \{x_2\} = C(S_1); G(S_2, R) = \{x_o\} = C(S_2); G(S_3, R) = \{x_o\} = C(S_3).$$

So the choice function C is rationalisable. It may be noted that R is transitive. We, therefore, say that the choice function has a transitive rationalisation.

We say that C has an ordering rationalisation if and only if there exists an ordering over X which rationalises the choice function.

DOMAIN CONDITION FOR EVERY CHOICE FUNCTION TO HAVE QUASI-TRANSITIVE RATIONALISATION

We introduce domain condition C.2 and show that this condition along with condition C.1 is sufficient for domains over which every choice function has quasi-transitive rationalisation. Domain condition C.1 has been introduced in Pal (2012).

C.1: $(\forall S \in D - D_X)[(\forall x \in S)[\sim (\forall y \in S - \{x\})(\exists S' \in D - \{S\})(\{x, y\} \subseteq S')]]$

C.2: $(\forall n \in N - \{1\})(\forall \text{ distinct } x_o, x_1, x_2, ..., x_n \in X)(\forall \text{ distinct } S_1, S_2, ..., S_n \in D)[\sim (((\{x_o, x_1\} \subseteq S_1 \wedge \{x_1, x_2\} \subseteq S_2 \wedge ... \wedge \{x_{n-1}, x_n\} \subseteq S_n) \wedge (\exists S' \in D - \{S_1, S_2, ..., S_n\})(\{x_o, x_n\} \subseteq S'))]$

Condition C.2 requires that for distinct elements $x_o, x_1, x_2, ..., x_n$ and distinct sets $S_1, S_2, ..., S_n$ if it is the case that x_o, x_1 belong to S_1, x_1, x_2 belong to S_2, and so on, and x_{n-1}, x_n belong to S_n, then it would not be the case that there exists a set S' not belonging to $\{S_1, S_2, ..., S_n\}$ such that x_o, x_1 belong to that set. The underlying intuition of this condition is that if we have a chain like

$$\{x_o, x_1\} \subseteq S_1, \{x_1, x_2\} \subseteq S_2, ..., \{x_{n-1}, x_n\} \subseteq S_n$$

and have a choice function such that following chain is obtained

$$x_o P x_1, x_1 P x_2, x_2 P x_3, ..., x_{n-2} P x_{n-1}, x_{n-1} P x_n,$$

then existence of a set S' containing element x_o, x_n may generate $x_n R x_o$ through $x_n \in C(S')$, which is a violation of quasi-transitivity. The condition C.2 prevents this case.[11]

---

[11] Consider the following example:

$$X = \{x_1, x_2, x_3\}; \quad D = \{\{x_1, x_2\}, \{x_2, x_3\}\}.$$

In this example the domain D of the choice functions D satisfies condition C.2. In all, there are nine different choice functions that can be defined over this domain. It may be noted that the domain satisfies condition C.1, hence, owing to the results in Pal (2012), all choice functions defined over this domain are rationalisable and R_c rationalises those choice functions. Suppose for some choice

Lemma 1. *Let choice function C be defined over D. If D satisfies condition C.2, then* $(\forall n \in N - \{1\})(\forall$ *distinct* $x_o, x_1, x_2, ..., x_n \in X)$

$$[x_o P(R_c)x_1 \wedge x_1 P(R_c)x_2 \wedge x_2 P(R_c)x_3 \wedge ... \wedge x_{n-1}P(R_c)x_n$$
$$\rightarrow (\exists \text{ distinct } S_1, S_2, S_3, ..., S_n \in D)((x_o \in C(S_1)$$
$$\wedge x_1 \in S_1) \wedge (x_1 \in C(S_2) \wedge x_2 \in S_2) \wedge (x_2 \in C(S_3) \wedge x_3 \in S_3)$$
$$\wedge ... \wedge (x_{n-1} \in C(S_n) \wedge x_n \in S_n))]$$

Proof: Let choice function C be defined over D and D satisfy condition C.2. Let $x_o, x_1, x_2, ..., x_n \in X$ be distinct, for some $n \in N - \{1\}$, and

$$x_o P(R_c)x_1 \wedge x_1 P(R_c)x_2 \wedge x_2 P(R_c)x_3 \wedge ... \wedge x_{n-1}P(R_c)x_n.$$
$$x_o P(R_c)x_1 \rightarrow (\exists S_1 \in D)(x_o \in C(S_1) \wedge x_1 \in S_1)$$
$$x_1 P(R_c)x_2 \rightarrow (\exists S_2 \in D)(x_1 \in C(S_2) \wedge x_2 \in S_2)$$

$$\vdots$$

$$x_{i-1}P(R_c)x_i \rightarrow (\exists S_i \in D)(x_{i-1} \in C(S_i) \wedge x_i \in S_i)$$
$$x_i P(R_c)x_{i+1} \rightarrow (\exists S_{i+1} \in D)(x_i \in C(S_{i+1}) \wedge x_{i+1} \in S_{i+1})$$

$$\vdots$$

$$x_{n-1}P(R_c)x_n \rightarrow (\exists S_n \in D)(x_{n-1} \in C(S_n) \wedge x_n \in S_n)$$

It is clear that

$$S_{i+1}, S_{i+2} \neq S_i \text{ for } i \in \{1, 2, 3, ..., n-2\} \text{ and,}$$
$$S_{i-2}, S_{i-1} \neq S_i \text{ for } i \in \{3, ..., n\}. \tag{6.1}$$

$(6.1) \rightarrow S_1, S_2, S_3$ are distinct.
Suppose $S_1 = S_4$. This implies $x_3, x_1 \in S_1 \wedge x_1, x_2 \in S_2$ and $x_2, x_3 \in S_3$. This leads to violation of condition C.2. Hence, $S_1 \neq S_4$.
Suppose $S_1 = S_5.$[12] This implies $x_4, x_1 \in S_1 \wedge x_1, x_2 \in S_2 \wedge x_2, x_3 \in S_3$ and $x_3, x_4 \in S_4$. This leads to violation of condition C.2.

---

functions we have $x_1 P(R_c)x_2$ and $x_2 P(R_c)x_3$. Since there is no set in the domain containing x_1, x_3, it can be easily checked that the binary relation $R_c \cup \{(x_1, x_3)\}$ would rationalise the choice functions and it is quasi-transitive. Similarly, for the choice functions which generate $x_3 P(R_c)x_2$ and $x_2 P(R_c)x_1$, the binary relation $R_c \cup \{(x_3, x_1)\}$ rationalises the choice functions and it is quasi-transitive. For the rest of the cases, R_c rationalises the choice functions, and quasi-transitivity of R_c is trivially satisfied.

[12] It is easy to check with the help of preceding arguments that S_2, S_3, S_4, S_5, S_6 are distinct.

Suppose $S_1 = S_6$.[13] This implies $x_5, x_1 \in S_1 \wedge x_1, x_2 \in S_2 \wedge x_2, x_3 \in S_3 \wedge x_3, x_4 \in S_4$ and $x_4, x_5 \in S_5$. This leads to violation of condition C.2.

Suppose $S_1 = S_i$ for $i \in \{7, 8 \ldots n - 1, n\}$. Now, with similar arguments we can show that $S_1, S_2, S_3, \ldots, S_{i-1}$ are distinct. Now we have

$$x_{i-1}, x_1 \in S_1 \wedge x_1, x_2 \in S_2 \wedge x_2, x_3$$
$$\in S_3 \wedge x_3, x_4 \in S_4 \wedge \ldots, \wedge x_{i-3}, x_{i-2} \in S_{i-2}$$

and

$$x_{i-2}, x_{i-1} \in S_{i-1}.$$

This leads to violation of condition C.2. Hence, S_1 is distinct from $S_2, S_3, \ldots, S_n$. Similarly, we can show that $S_2, S_3, \ldots, S_n$ are distinct from each other.

Lemma 2. *Let choice function C be defined over D. If D satisfies condition C.2 then R_1 is asymmetric.*

Proof: Let choice function C be defined over D and D satisfy condition C.2.

Let $$x R_1 y \wedge y R_1 x \qquad (6.2)$$

$$x R_1 y \rightarrow (\exists n \in N)(\exists x_1, x_2, \ldots, x_n \in X)(x P(R_c) x_1 \wedge x_1 P(R_c) x_2$$
$$\wedge x_2 P(R_c) x_3 \wedge \ldots \wedge x_{n-1} P(R_c) x_n \wedge x_n P(R_c) y).$$
$$y R_1 x \rightarrow (\exists l \in N)(\exists v_1, v_2, \ldots, v_l \in X)(y P(R_c) v_1 \wedge v_1 P(R_c) v_2$$
$$\wedge v_2 P(R_c) v_3 \wedge \ldots \wedge v_{l-1} P(R_c) v_l \wedge v_l P(R_c) x).$$

(6.2) can be written in the following chain:

$$x P(R_c) x_1 \wedge x_1 P(R_c) x_2 \wedge x_2 P(R_c) x_3 \wedge \ldots \wedge x_{n-1} P(R_c) x_n \wedge x_n P(R_c) y$$
$$\wedge y P(R_c) v_1 \wedge v_1 P(R_c) v_2 \wedge v_2 P(R_c) v_3 \wedge \ldots \wedge v_{l-1} P(R_c) v_l$$
$$\wedge v_l P(R_c) x$$

Suppose for some $k \in N$, $x = w_0 \wedge v_l = w_k \wedge x_1 = w_1 \wedge x_2 = w_2$ and so on. Now we can write this chain in the following way:

$$w_0 P(R_c) w_1 \wedge w_1 P(R_c) w_2 \wedge w_2 P(R_c) w_3 \wedge \ldots \wedge w_{k-2} P(R_c) w_{k-1}$$
$$\wedge w_{k-1} P(R_c) w_k \wedge w_k P(R_c) w_0$$

---

[13] It is easy to check with the help of preceding arguments that S_2, S_3, S_4, S_5, S_6 are distinct.

Now,

$$w_oP(R_c)w_1 \land w_1P(R_c)w_2 \land w_2P(R_c)w_3$$
$$\land ... \land w_{k-2}P(R_c)w_{k-1} \land w_{k-1}P(R_c)w_k$$

implies that the following chain of distinct elements exists:

$$w_oP(R_c)w_1 \land w_1P(R_c)w_2 \land w_2P(R_c)w_3 \land ... \land w_{m-2}P(R_c)w_{m-1}$$
$$\land w_{m-1}P(R_c)w_m \text{ where } w_m = w_k. \qquad (6.3)$$

We, therefore, have:

$$w_oP(R_c)w_1 \land w_1P(R_c)w_2 \land w_2P(R_c)w_3 \land ... \land w_{m-2}P(R_c)w_{m-1}$$
$$\land w_{m-1}P(R_c)w_m \land w_mP(R_c)w_o.$$

$$(6.3) \rightarrow (\exists \textit{ distinct } S_1, S_2, S_3, ..., S_m \in D)((w_o \in C(S_1) \land w_1 \in S_1)$$
$$\land (w_1 \in C(S_2) \land w_2 \in S_2) \land (w_2 \in C(S_3) \land w_3 \in S_3)$$
$$\land ... \land (w_{m-1} \in C(S_m) \land w_m \in S_m))(\text{by Lemma 1})$$

and

$$w_mP(R_c)w_o \rightarrow (\exists S_{m+1} \in D)(w_m \in C(S_{m+1}) \land w_o \in S_{m+1} \backslash C(S_{m+1})).$$

Now we have:

$$w_o, w_1 \in S_1 \land w_1, w_2 \in S_2 \land w_2, w_3 \in S_3 \land ... \land w_{m-1}, w_m \in S_m$$
$$\land w_m, w_o \in S_{m+1}. \qquad (6.4)$$

Naturally $S_{m+1} \neq S_1, S_m$.
Suppose for some $i \in \{2, 3, .., m-1\}$, $S_{m+1} = S_i$; this leads to violation of condition C.2. Thus.

$$S_{m+1} \neq S_i \text{ for } i \in \{1, 2, 3, ..., m\}. \qquad (6.5)$$

$(6.4) \land (6.5)$ lead to violation of condition C.2. Hence, the lemma is established.

Theorem 1. *Any choice function defined over D has a quasi-transitive rationalisation if D satisfies conditions C.1 and C.2.*

Proof: Let D satisfy conditions C.1 and C.2 and C be any choice function defined over D. We have introduced the binary relation $\bar{R}$ which is the union of two binary relations R_c and R_1. We show that $\bar{R}$ rationalises the choice function C, that is, we show that $C(S) = G(S, \bar{R})$.

Let $x \in C(S)$

$$\rightarrow (\forall y \in S)(xR_cy)$$
$$\rightarrow x \in G(S, \bar{R}).$$

Let $x \in G(S, \bar{R})$.
Suppose $x \notin C(S)$

$$\rightarrow (\exists y \in S)(y \in C(S))$$
$$\rightarrow \{x, y\} \subseteq S.$$
$$x \in G(S, \bar{R}) \rightarrow (\forall z \in S)(x\bar{R}z).$$

Since $(\forall z \in S)(\{x, z\} \subseteq S)$

$$\rightarrow (\forall z \in S)(\sim xR_1z)$$
$$\rightarrow (\forall z \in S)(xR_cz).$$

Let $S = \{x, y, x_3, ..., x_n\}$.

$$(\forall z \in S)(xR_cz) \rightarrow (\exists S_2, S_3, S_4, ... S_n \in D)^{14}$$

$$(\{x, y\} \subseteq S_2 \wedge \{x, x_3\} \subseteq S_3 \wedge \{x, x_4\} \subseteq S_4 \wedge ... \wedge \{x, x_n\} \subseteq S_n).$$

It is clear that set S is distinct from $S_2, S_3, S_4, ... S_n$. This leads to violation of condition C.1. Therefore, $x \in C(S)$.
Now, we shall show that $\bar{R}$ is quasi-transitive.
Let $x, y, z \in X \wedge (xP(\bar{R})y \wedge yP(\bar{R})z)$. There are four cases to consider:

(a) $xP(R_c)y \wedge yP(R_c)z$;
(b) $xP(R_c)y \wedge yP(R_1)z$;
(c) $xP(R_1)y \wedge yP(R_c)z$; and
(d) $xP(R_1)y \wedge yP(R_1)z$.

Case (a): Let $x, y, z \in X \wedge (xP(R_c)y \wedge yP(R_c)z)$.
It is clear that x, y, z are distinct elements.

$$xP(R_c)y \rightarrow (\exists S_1 \in D)(x \in C(S_1) \wedge y \in S_1\backslash C(S_1))$$
$$yP(R_c)z \rightarrow (\exists S_2 \in D)(y \in C(S_2) \wedge z \in S_2\backslash C(S_2))$$

Naturally, S_1, S_2 are distinct sets.
Suppose

$$(\exists S'' \in D - \{S_1, S_2\})(\{x, z\} \subseteq S'')$$

$\rightarrow$ violation of condition C.2.

---

[14] $S_2, S_3, S_4, ... S_n$ are not necessarily distinct.

It is clear that $S'' \neq S_2$.
Suppose $S'' = S_1$.

$$\to xR_c z.$$

Now if we have $zR_c x$, this would imply

$$(\exists T \in D - \{S_1, S_2\})(\{x, z\} \subseteq T).$$

This leads to a violation of condition C.2. Therefore, $\sim zR_c x$.

$$\to xP(R_c)z,$$

and, hence, $xP(\bar{R})z$.
Let $\sim (\exists S'' \in D)(\{x, z\} \subseteq S'')$

$$\to (x, z) \in R_1.$$

Since R_1 is asymmetric by Lemma 2,
Therefore, $xP(\bar{R})z$.

Since

$$xP(R_1)y \to (\exists n \in N)(\exists m_1, m_2, ..., m_n \in X)(xP(R_c)m_1$$
$$\wedge \; m_1 P(R_c)m_2 \wedge ... \wedge m_n P(R_c)y)$$

Therefore, cases (b), (c), (d) can be written in the following general form:

$$xP(R_c)z_1 \wedge z_1 P(R_c)z_2 \wedge z_2 P(R_c)z_3 \wedge ... \wedge z_{k-2}P(R_c)z_{k-1}$$
$$\wedge \; z_{k-1}P(R_c)y. \tag{6.6}$$

(6.6) implies that the following chain of distinct elements exists:

$$xP(R_c)w_1 \wedge w_1 P(R_c)w_2 \wedge$$
$$w_2 P(R_c)w_3 \wedge ... \wedge w_{n-2}P(R_c)w_{n-1} \wedge w_{n-1}P(R_c)y.$$

Let $x = w_o \wedge y = w_n$. Now we have the following:

$$w_o P(R_c)w_1 \wedge w_1 P(R_c)w_2 \wedge w_2 P(R_c)w_3$$
$$\wedge ... \wedge w_{n-2}P(R_c)w_{n-1} \wedge w_{n-1}P(R_c)w_n. \tag{6.7}$$

(6.7) $\to (\exists \; \textit{distinct} \; S_1, S_2, S_3, ..., S_n \in D)((w_o \in C(S_1) \wedge w_1 \in S_1) \wedge (w_1 \in C(S_2) \wedge w_2 \in S_2) \wedge (w_2 \in C(S_3) \wedge w_3 \in S_3) \wedge ... \wedge (w_{n-1} \in C(S_n) \wedge w_n \in S_n))$ (by Lemma 1).
Suppose $(\exists S'' \in D - \{S_1, ..., S_n\})(\{w_o, w_n\} \subseteq S'')$
This implies violation of condition C.2.
It is clear that $S'' \neq S_2$ since we have $w_o P(R_c)w_1$.

Suppose $S'' = S_i$ for $i \in \{3, 4, ..., n\}$. This implies violation of condition C.2.

Suppose $S'' = S_1$.

If $n = 2$ that is there are only two sets S_1, S_2, then showing $w_o P(\bar{R}) w_2$ is analogous to case (a).

If $n > 2$ then $S'' = S_1$ leads to a violation of condition C.2.

Let

$$\sim (\exists S'' \in D)(\{w_o, w_n\} \subseteq S'')$$
$$\rightarrow (w_o, w_n) \in R_1.$$

Since R_1 is asymmetric by Lemma 2, therefore $w_o P(\bar{R}) w_n$ and, hence, $x P(\bar{R}) z$.

Hence, the theorem is established.

CONCLUSION

Domain conditions in the context of rationalisability of choice function are important, not only because they provide a new set of conditions for rationalisability but also because they do not tamper with the 'act of choice' or the choice behaviour of an individual. Unlike choice consistency conditions which characterise the partition between two classes of choice functions: rationalisale choice functions and non-rationalisable choice functions; domain conditions make a partition of domains. On one side, there is a class of domains over which any choice function is rationalisable and, on the other sides there is a class of domains over which not all choice functions are rationalisable. These domain conditions characterise the partition of the domains. Pal (2012) provides a full characterisation of domain for rationalisability and ordering rationalisability. This essay provides sufficient domain condition for quasi-transitive rationalisability. Full characterisations of quasi-transitive and acyclic rationalisability are yet to be obtained.

REFERENCES

Armstrong, W. E. 1939. 'The Determinateness of the Utility Function', *Economic Journal*, 49(195): 453–57.

Arrow, Kenneth J. 1959. 'Rational Choice Functions and Orderings', *Economica, New Series*, 26(102): 121–27.

———. 1963. *Social Choice and Individual Values*, 2nd edn. New York: Wiley.

Baigent, N. and W. Gaertner. 1996. 'Never Choose the Uniquely Largest: A Characterization', *Economic Theory*, 8(2): 239–49.

Blair, D. H. 1975. 'Path Independent Social Choice Functions: A Further Result', *Econometrica*, 43(1): 174–75.

Blau, Julian H. 1957. 'The Existence of Social Welfare Functions', *Econometrica*, 25(2): 302–13.

Bordes, G. 1976. 'Consistency, Rationality and Collective Choice', *Review of Economic Studies*, 43(3): 451–57.

Bossert, Walter. 2001. 'Choices, Consequences, and Rationality', *Synthese*, 129(3): 343–69.

Bossert, Walter, Yves Sprumont and Kotaro Suzumura. 2005a. 'Consistent Rationalizability', *Economica*, 72(286): 185–200.

———. 2005b. 'Maximal-Element Rationalizability', *Theory and Decision*, 58(4): 325–50.

———. 2006. 'Rationalizability of Choice Functions on General Domains without Full Transitivity', *Social Choice and Welfare*, 27(3): 435–58.

Chipman, J. S. 1960. 'The Foundations of Utility', *Econometrica*, 28(2): 193–224.

Fishburn, P. C. 1975. 'Semiorders and Choice Functions', *Econometrica*, 43(5–6): 975–76.

Gaertner, Wulf and Yongsheng Xu. 1997. 'Optimization and External Reference: A Comparison of Three Axiomatic Systems', *Economics Letters*, 57(1): 57–62.

———. 1999a. 'On Rationalizability of Choice Functions: A Characterization of the Median', *Social Choice and Welfare*, 16(4): 629–38.

———. 1999b. 'On the Structure of Choice Under External References', *Economic Theory*, 14(3): 609–20.

Hansson, B. 1968. 'Choice Structures and Preference Relations', *Synthese*, 18(4): 443–58.

Herzberger, H. G. 1973. 'Ordinal Preferences and Rational Choice', *Econometrica*, 41(2): 187–237.

Houthakker, H. S. 1950. 'Revealed Preference and the Utility Function', *Economica*, New Series, 17(66): 159–74.

Katzner, Donald W. 2000. 'Culture and the Explanation of Choice Behaviour', *Theory and Decision*, 48(3): 241–62.

Luce, R. D. 1956. 'Semiorders and a Theory of Utility Discrimination', *Econometrica*, 24(2): 178–91.

Pal, Debabrata. 2012. 'Rationalizability of Choice Functions: Domain Conditions', paper presented at the international conference '11th Meeting of Society for Social Choice and Welfare' organised by Indian Statistical Institute (ISI), Delhi, 17–20 August 2012.

Parks, R.P. 1976. 'Further Results on Path Independence, Quasi-transitivity and Social Choice', *Public Choice*, 26(1): 75–88.

Plott, Charles R. 1973. 'Path Independence, Rationality, and Social Choice', *Econometrica*, 41(6): 1075–91.

Richelson, Jeffrey. 1978. 'Some Further Results on Consistency, Rationality and Collective Choice', *Review of Economic Studies*, 45(2): 343–46.

Richter, Marcel. 1966. 'Revealed Preference Theory', *Econometrica*, 34(3): 635–45.

Samuelson, P. A. 1938. 'A Note on the Pure Theory of Consumer's Behaviour', *Economica*, New Series, 5(17): 61–71.

———. 1950. 'The Problem of Integrability in Utility Theory', *Economica*, New Series, 17(68): 355–85.

Schwartz, T. 1972. 'Rationality and the Myth of the Maximum', *Nous*, 6(2): 97–117.

———. 1976. 'Choice Functions, "Rationality" Conditions, and Variations on the Weak Axiom of Revealed Preference', *Journal of Economic Theory*, 13(3): 414–27.

Sen, A. K. 1970. *Collective Choice and Social Welfare*. San Francisco: Holden-Day.

———. 1971. 'Choice Functions and Revealed Preference', *Review of Economic Studies*, 38(3): 307–17.

———. 1977. 'Social Choice Theory: A Re-examination', *Econometrica*, 45(1): 53–88.

———. 1993. 'Internal Consistency of Choice', *Econometrica*, 61(3): 495–521.

———. 1997. 'Maximization and the Act of Choice', *Econometrica*, 65(4): 745–79.

Sugden, Robert. 1985. 'Why Be Consistent? A Critical Analysis of Consistency Requirements in Choice Theory', *Economica*, 52(206): 167–83.

Suzumura, K. 1976. 'Rational Choice and Revealed Preference', *Review of Economic Studies*, 43(1): 149–58.

———. 1976. 'Remarks on the Theory of Collective Choice', *Economica*, 43(172): 381–90.

———. 1977. 'Houthakker's Axiom in the Theory of Rational Choice', *Journal of Economic Theory*, 14(2): 284–90.

———. 1983. *Rational Choice, Collective Decisions and Social Welfare*. New York: Cambridge University Press.

Szpilrajn, E. 1930. 'Sur l'Extension de l'Ordre Partiel', *Fundamenta Mathematicae*, 16(1): 386–89.

Uzawa, H. 1957. 'Note on Preference and Axioms of Choice', *Ann Inst Stat Math*, 8(1): 35–40.

Wilson, R. B. 1970. 'The Finer Structure of Revealed Preference', *Journal of Economic Theory*, 2(4): 348–53.

PART III
LAW AND ECONOMICS

7

Existence and Efficiency of Equilibria
When Care is Multidimensional

Ram Singh

Multidimensional care is the reality of many accident contexts. Nonetheless, the economic models of liability rules generally take the care to be unidimensional.[1] True, some writings on liability rules, have modelled multidimensional care too. However, these works are based on the assumption that under every liability rule, there exists a unique equilibrium. The assumption regarding existence of equilibrium has been made without scrutinising the nature of conditions that are necessary for existence of equilibria. Moreover, the existing literature has not examined the nature of second-best liability rules.

In this essay, we model multiple dimensions of care that can be taken by the parties involved in a risky situation. Under the assumption of multidimensional care, we examine the conditions necessary for the existence of equilibrium under the standard liability rules. Besides, we examine the choices of equilibrium care levels. Moreover, we undertake the efficiency analysis of liability rules from a second-best perspective. Identification of second-best rules is important because when care is multidimensional, no liability rule can achieve the first-best outcome (Shavell 1987).

Further, we assume that while some dimensions of care are verifiable before a court, the others are not. However, the choice made by parties of verifiable as well as non-verifiable aspects of care affect the expected accident loss. For example, probability of motor-vehicle accidents depends not only on how carefully drivers drive and how much they drive but also on how much attention they pay to maintenance of the vehicles. Care taken by a driver while driving may be verifiable, but the amount of driving undertaken by a driver on a particular day is

---

[1] For example, see Calabresi (1970), Feldman and Singh (2009), Grady (1989), Jain and Singh (2002), Landes and Posner (1983, 1987), Miceli (1997), Polinsky (1989), Parisi and Singh (2010), Shavell (1987) and Singh (2007), among others.

not. As for the vehicle maintenance efforts, generally these are not even observable and, therefore, not verifiable.

Our results regarding the conditions necessary for existence of equilibria have a direct bearing on the relevant claims in the existing literature. The existing models on multidimensional care consider care to be two-dimensional; only one of the dimensions is taken to be verifiable. The verifiable aspect is called 'care level', and the non-verifiable aspect is called 'activity level'. Some of the existing works argue that when care levels as well as activity levels affect the expected accident loss, the negligence-based rules, for instance, the rule of negligence and the rule of strict liability with the defence of contributory negligence, induce equilibria in which the injurer and the victim opt for care levels that are appropriate from the view point of the first-best efficiency.[2]

In this essay, we show that this claim is not correct. In particular, we show that none of the standard liability rules, including the rule of negligence and the rule of strict liability with the defence of contributory negligence, induces an equilibrium in which both the parties opt for care levels that are appropriate from the viewpoint of the first-best efficiency.

As far the general efficiency of liability rules is concerned, Shavell (1980) showed that the first-best outcome is impossible when the activity levels as described are not verifiable. The mainstream response to the impossibility of first-best liability rule has been to restrict the analysis to the relative efficiency of the standard liability rules, which do not allow for loss sharing between non-negligent parties.[3]

We extend the analysis to allow for loss sharing between non-negligent parties. We show that the economic efficiency requires such loss sharing. In fact, depending on the context, second-best efficiency may require some loss sharing between non-negligent parties.

The second section introduces the framework of analysis that outlines the notations and assumptions made in the essay. In the third section, we identify the basic features of standard liability rules, and investigate the nature of equilibria under liability rules. In the fourth section, we extend the analysis to explore the nature of second-best liability rules. We conclude in the last section with remarks on the nature of results in the essay.

---

[2] See, for instance, Cooter and Ulen (2004: 332–33), Dari Mattiacci (2002), Miceli (1997: 29), Parisi and Fon (2004); see also Delhaye (2002).

[3] For example, see Landes and Posner (1987), Miceli (1997), and Shavell (1987).

MODEL

Basics

We consider accidents resulting from the interaction of two parties who are strangers to each other. Both parties are assumed to be rational and risk-neutral. If an accident takes place, the entire loss falls on one party to be called the victim, the other party being the injurer. For example, we can think of motor-vehicle drivers as injurers and pedestrians or bicyclists as victims. Each party decides on several aspects of care. Drivers choose, for instance, how carefully to drive as well as how much to drive. Likewise, pedestrians decide on how carefully to walk on roads and how much to walk. While some aspects of care are verifiable before a court, the others are not. The level of care exercised by either party with respect to verifiable as well as non-verifiable aspects of care affects the expected accident loss. The elements contributing to the overall social cost of the accident are the loss that is borne by the victim in the event of an the accident and the cost of care taken by the parties.

To facilitate exposition and compare our results with those in the literature, we will assume that care has only two aspects. We will call the verifiable aspect of care as the 'care level' and the non-verifiable aspect as the 'activity level'.

Following the standard notations, we denote:

x care level as well as the cost of care for the injurer as $x \in X$,
y care level as well as the cost of care for the victim as $y \in Y$,
s activity level for the injurer as $z \in Z$, and
t activity level for the victim as $t \in T$.

X, Y, S and T denote the sets of feasible level of care for the injurer, level of care for the victim, level of activity for the injurer and level of activity for the victim respectively. Further, let

u be the benefit function for the injurer,
v the benefit function for the victim,
π the probability of accident,
D the loss suffered by victim in the event of an accident, $D \geq 0$, and
$L(s, x, t, y)$ the expected accident loss.

We assume that while x and y are verifiable, s and t are not. In addition, we make the following standard assumptions: u is a function of s and x. Benefits to the injurer increase with his activity level but at a decreasing rate, that is, u is an increasing and strictly concave function of s. Care is costly to the injurer, hence u is a decreasing function of x, for all $s \in S$. Likewise, v is a function of t and y. v is an increasing and strictly concave function of the victim's activity level, t. v is a decreasing function of y, for all $t \in T$.

It is pertinent to mention that these assumptions are made only for expository convenience. In a more general model, there will be more than one type of verifiable and non-verifiable care. Moreover, the benefits to the injurer will not necessarily decrease with every verifiable aspect of care or increase with every non-verifiable aspect of care. However, our broad conclusions with respect to the verifiable and non-verifiable dimensions will hold even if we allow more than one type of verifiable and non-verifiable dimensions.

The expected accident loss L is a function of s, x, t and y. L is a decreasing function of care level of each party, and is an increasing function of both s and t, that is, a larger care by either party, given the care level of the other party, results in lesser or equal expected accident loss. Increase in activity level of either party causes an increase in the expected accident loss. $L(.) = 0$ when $s = 0$ or $t = 0$.

Social benefits from the activity of a party are fully internalised by that party. The social goal is to maximise the net social benefits from the activities of the parties; the net social benefits are the sum of the benefits to the two parties minus the total social costs of the accident. It is standard to use the following functional forms:[4]

$$u(s, x) = u(s) - sx$$
$$v(t, y) = v(t) - ty$$
$$L = stl(x, y),$$

where $l(x, y)$ is the expected accident loss, if the activity level is one for each party. Specifically,

$$l(x, y) = \pi(x, y)D(x, y)$$

Moreover, $\pi(x, y)$ and $D(x, y)$ are decreasing functions of both x and y. Therefore, $l(x, y)$ is a decreasing function of both x and y. Formally speaking, the following holds:

$$l_x(x, y) < 0, l_y(x, y) < 0, l_{xx}(x, y) > 0, l_{xx}(x, y)$$
$$> 0, l_{yy}(x, y) > 0, l_{xy}(x, y) > 0.$$

---

[4] See, for example, Landes and Posner (1987), Miceli (1997), Parisi and Fon (2004) and Shavell (1987).

Further,

$$u'(.) > 0, u''(.) < 0, v'(.) > 0,$$

and $v''(.) < 0$. It should be noted that these assumptions are standard in the literature on liability rules.[5] Next, we define the first best.

The First Best

The social optimisation problem is to maximise net social gains. So, the problem is given by:

$$\max_{(s,x,t,y) \in S \times X \times T \times Y} \{u(s) - sx + v(t) - ty - stl(x, y)\}. \tag{7.1}$$

It is standard to assume that the benefit, cost and expected loss functions are such that there is a unique tuple $((s, x), (t, y))$ that is socially optimal. We denote this tuple by $((s^*, x^*), (t^*, y^*))$. In other words, net social benefits are maximised, if the injurer chooses s^* as his activity level and x^* as his care level, and the victim simultaneously opts for t^* as his activity level and y^* as his care level. Further, $((s^*, x^*), (t^*, y^*)) >> ((0, 0), (0, 0))$, that is, social efficiency requires positive care level and activity level from each party.

Give the specification of the social objective function as in (7.1), s^*, x^*, t^* and y^* simultaneously and respectively solve the following necessary and sufficient first-order conditions:

$$u'(s) - x - tl(x, y) = 0 \tag{7.2}$$
$$1 + tl_x(x, y) = 0 \tag{7.3}$$
$$v'(t) - y - sl(x, y) = 0 \tag{7.4}$$
$$1 + sl_y(x, y) = 0 \tag{7.5}$$

That is, s^*, x^*, t^* and y^* respectively satisfy the following:

$$u'(s) = x^* + t^*l(x^*, y^*) \tag{7.6}$$
$$0 = 1 + t^*l_x(x, y^*) \tag{7.7}$$
$$v'(t) = y^* + s^*l(x^*, y^*) \tag{7.8}$$
$$0 = 1 + s^*l_y(x^*, y) \tag{7.9}$$

---

[5] See Cooter and Ulen (2004), Miceli (1997), Parisi and Fon (2004), and Shavell (1987).

Liability Rules and Individual Payoffs

Depending on the context and the care levels of the victim and the injurer, a liability rule uniquely determines the proportions in which they are to bear the accident loss. Therefore, a liability rule can be considered as a rule or a mechanism that determines the proportions, q, in which the injurer bears the accident loss, as a function of the parties' care levels. Formally, for given X and Y, a liability rule is a function

$$f : X \times Y \mapsto [0, 1]$$

such that,

$$f(x, y) = q(x, y).$$

Clearly, $1 - q$ is the proportion of D that is borne by the victim. Note that the judicial determination of liability cannot depend on the non-verifiable aspects of care. Therefore, in keeping with the reality of judicial decisionmaking, q is a taken to be a function of only the care levels and not of the activity levels. Following the literature, the legal due care standard (that is, the negligence standard) for the injurer, wherever applicable (say under the rule of negligence), is assumed to be set at x^*. Similarly, the legal negligence standard of care for the victim, wherever applicable (say under the rule of strict liability with defence) is set at y^*.

For a party, pay-off from engaging in the activity depends on its activity level, its care level as well as the proportion of accident loss the party is required to bear under the liability rule in force. Therefore, the choice of care and activity levels by a party depends on the rule in force, as well as on the choice of the care and the activity levels by the other party. Suppose, it is given that the victim has opted for some $t \in T$ as his activity level and some $y \in Y$ as his care level. Now, if the injurer opts for s as activity level and x as care level, in the event on an accident, the liability rule will require him to bear $q(x, y)D(x, y)$ out of the total accident loss $D(x, y)$; remaining loss, that is, $D(x, y) - q(x, y)D(x, y)$, will be borne by the victim. In other words, given $(t, y) \in T \times Y$ opted by the victim, if the injurer chooses a pair $(s, x) \in S \times X$, his expected liability is $q(x, y)stl(x, y)$. The injurer being rational and risk-neutral will choose a pair (s, x) that maximises his expected pay-off. Formally, given $(t, y) \in T \times Y$ opted by the victim and the liability rule in force, the problem facing the injurer is

$$\max_{(s,x) \in S \times X} \{u(s) - sx - q(x, y)stl(x, y)\}.$$

Likewise, given $(s, x) \in S \times X$ opted by the injurer, the problem facing the victim is

$$\max_{(t,y)\in T \times Y} \{v(t) - ty - (1 - q(x, y))stl(x, y)\},$$

where $q(x, y) \in [0, 1]$ and is determined by the relevant liability rule.

We assume that the optimisation problem of the injurer has a unique solution. It is similar in the case of the victim.

LIABILITY RULES AND EQUILIBRIA

In this section, we provide conditions necessary for the existence of equilibria under standard liability rules. Besides, we examine the nature of equilibria under the other possible liability rules with features common to the standard liability rules. Moreover, we examine the equilibrium choice of care levels and activity levels by the parties, as compared to the levels that are optimal from the social point of view.

To begin with, lets discuss the salient features of the standard liability rules. The liability assignment under the standard negligence-criterion based liability rules satisfy the following property: When one party is negligent and the other is not, the negligent party bears all the accident loss. Let us call this property (P1). It says that liability assignment under a liability rule is such that: A non-negligent party has no liability, if the other party is negligent, that is, whenever the injurer is negligent and the victim is not, the victim receives full compensation for the loss. If the victim is negligent and the injurer is not, the victim bears the entire loss. Formally,

Property 1. *A liability rule, f, satisfies Property (P1), if for all $x \in X$ and $y \in Y$,*

$$x \geq x^* \ \& \ y < y^* \Rightarrow q = 0$$
$$x < x^* \ \& \ y \geq y^* \Rightarrow q = 1.$$

The second property common to standard liability rules is: When both parties are non-negligent, regardless the care levels, liability shares remain constant. To formally define this property, let

$$q^* = f(x^*, y^*) = q(x^*, y^*).$$

Property 2. *A liability rule, f, satisfies Property (P2), if for all $x \in X$ and $y \in Y$,*

$$x \geq x^* \ \& \ y \geq y^* \Rightarrow f(x, y) = q^*.$$

(P2) says that when both the parties are vigilant (non-negligent), the shares in which they are required to bear the accident loss remain the same, regardless of the degrees of vigilance one of the parties. Moreover, under the standard liability rules, when both parties are non-negligent, only one of the parties bears the entire accident loss. So, the rules satisfy the following property (P3), in addition to properties (P1) and (P2).

Property 3. *A liability rule, f, satisfies property (P3), if for all $x \in X$ and $y \in Y$,*

$$x \geq x^* \ \& \ y \geq y^* \Rightarrow f(x, y) = q^* \in \{0, 1\}.$$

Remark 1. *While property (P1) is common to only negligence-criterion based rules, Properties (P2) and (P3) are satisfied by all of the standard liability rules.*

Equilibria under Property (P1)

To start with, we investigate the equilibrium choices made by parties under rules that satisfy property (P1). As discussed earlier, property (P1) puts the entire liability on the solely negligent party. We show that under a liability rule that satisfies property (P1), the parties cannot both be negligent in an N.E., no matter how the liability is assigned when both parties are negligent. In other words, in any N.E., $x < x^*$ and $y < y^*$ can never hold.

To see why, take any $((s, x), (t, y))$ such that $x < x^*$ and $y < y^*$. Suppose, the injurer opts for (s, x) and the victim for (t, y). At $((s, x), (t, y))$, let $q(x, y)$ be the injurer's share of loss, where $0 \leq q(x, y) \leq 1$. So, $1 - q(x, y)$ is share of the victim in accident loss. As a result, at $((s, x), (t, y))$, the expected pay-off of the victim is: $v(t) - ty - (1 - q(x, y))stl(x, y)$. On the other hand, given that (s, x) is opted by the injurer, if the victim instead opts for (t^*, y^*), then the injurer will be solely negligent. In that case, in view of (P1), the injurer's liability will be full and that of the victim will be none. Therefore, given that (s, x) is opted by the injurer, if the victim opts for (t^*, y^*), his pay-off will be $v(t^*) - t^*y^*$. Similarly, at $((s, x), (t, y))$ the expected pay-off of the injurer is $u(s) - sx - q(x, y) stl(x, y)$. But, given that (t, y) is opted by the victim, should the injurer instead opt for (s^*, x^*), his pay-off will be $u(s^*) - s^*x^*$. At $((s, x), (t, y))$ if $u(s^*) - s^*x^* > u(s) - sx - q(x, y) stl(x, y)$, a unilateral deviation by the injurer to (s^*, x^*) is strictly profitable. In that case, $((s, x), (t, y))$ cannot be an N.E. Thus, if $((s, x), (t, y))$ is an N.E., then a unilateral deviation by the injurer to (s^*, x^*) cannot be strictly profitable.

Therefore, assume that

$$u(s) - sx - q(x, y) \, stl(x, y) \geq u(s^*) - s^*x^*. \tag{7.10}$$

Since $((s, x), (t, y)) \neq ((s^*, x^*), (t^*, y^*))$, by assumption, we know that

$$u(s^*) - s^*x^* + v(t^*) - t^*y^* - s^*t^*l(x^*, y^*) > u(s) - sx + v(t) - ty - stl(x, y). \tag{7.11}$$

Subtracting $u(s^*) - s^*x^*$ from the LHS and $u(s) - sx - q(x, y)stl(x, y)$ from the RHS of (7.11), in view of (7.10), we get

$$v(t^*) - t^*y^* - s^*t^*l(x^*, y^*) > v(t) - ty - (1 - q(x, y))stl(x, y). \tag{7.12}$$

Now, since $s^*t^*l(x^*, y^*) \geq 0$, from (7.12) we have

$$v(t^*) - t^*y^* > v(t) - ty - (1 - q(x, y))stl(x, y).$$

So, given $(s, x < x^*)$ opted by the injurer, the pay-off of the victim is strictly greater if he chooses (t^*, y^*) rather than (t, y), that is, the victim is better off opting for (t^*, y^*) rather than (t, y). Again, $((s, x), (t, y))$ cannot be an N.E.

In other words, under a liability rule satisfying (P1), from any $((s, x), (t, y))$ such that $x < x^*$ & $y < y^*$, either the injurer finds unilaterally deviation to (s^*, x^*) profitable, or the victim finds unilaterally deviation to (t^*, y^*) profitable. Hence, if a liability rule satisfies Property (P1), then any $((s, x), (t, y))$, such that $x < x^*$ & $y < y^*$, cannot be an equilibrium. Formally, we can make the following claim.

Lemma 1. *Under a liability rule satisfying (P1),* $(\forall((s, x), (t, y)))$ *$[x < x^*$ & $y < y^* \Rightarrow ((s, x), (t, y))$ cannot be an N.E.].*

In fact, Property (P1) enables us to make further deductions about the behaviour of the parties with respect to their choice of care levels. Suppose a liability rule satisfies Property (P1). When $x \geq x^*$ and $y < y^*$, the victim is solely negligent. In such an event, due to Property (P1), the injurer has no liability. So, for given s his pay-off is $u(s) - sx$. Note that $u(s) - sx$ decreases with x. Therefore, regardless of the s opted by him whenever $x > x^*$, the injurer can increase his pay-off simply by reducing x until he reaches at x^*. This means that if the victim opts for some y such that $y < y^*$, the injurer is better off opting for x^* rather than any $x > x^*$. As a result, any tuple $((s, x), (t, y))$, such that $x > x^*$ & $y < y^*$ cannot be an N.E. Similarly, under a rule that satisfies Property (P1), a tuple $((s, x), (t, y))$, such that $x < x^*$ & $y > y^*$, cannot be an N.E. Therefore, we have the following result.

Lemma 2. *Under a liability rule satisfying (P1), for all $((s, x), (t, y))$* $[(x > x^* \, \& \, y < y^*) \, or \, (x < x^* \, \& \, y > y^*)] \Rightarrow [((s, x), (t, y)) \, cannot \, be \, an \, N.E.]$

Remark 2. *It should be noted that while establishing the claims in Lemmas 1 and 2, we have not assumed any particular functional forms. These results hold hold for any $stl(x, y)$ that satisfies the aforementioned assumptions. In particular, the results hold for continuous as well as discrete care and activity levels.*

Next, we show the following: When the injurer opts for x^*, a choice of some $y < y^*$ cannot be an optimum choice for the victim. Likewise, if the victim opts for y^*, a choice of some $x < x^*$ cannot be an optimum choice for the injurer. Let,

$s_p^* =$ the activity level that solves:

$$\max_s \{u(s) - sx^*\}.$$

$t_p^* =$ the activity level that solves:

$$\max_t \{v(t) - ty^*\}.$$

That is, s_p^* is the optimum activity level for the injurer when he simply opts for x^* as care level but does not bear the accident costs at all. Likewise, for t_p^*.

Remark 3. *When a liability rule satisfies Property (P1), in the region of $x \geq x^*$ and $y < y^*$, $u(s) - sx$ is uniquely maximised at (s_p^*, x^*). Therefore, under a liability rule that satisfies Property (P1), when $x \geq x^*$ and $y < y^*$, a tuple $((s, x), (t, y))$ can be an N.E. only if $(s, x) = (s_p^*, x^*)$. Similarly, under a rule satisfying Property (P1), when $x < x^*$ and $y \geq y^*$, a tuple $((s, x), (t, y))$ can be an N.E. only if $(t, y) = (t_p^*, y^*)$.*

Theorem 1. *Under a liability that satisfies Property (P1), for all s, x, t and y,*

$$[((\hat{s}, \hat{x}), (\hat{t}, \hat{y})) \, is \, an \, N.E.] \Rightarrow [(\hat{x} \geq x^* \& \, \hat{y} \geq y^*)].$$

Theorem 1 says that under a liability rule that satisfies Property (P1), in equilibrium no party can be negligent; both the parties will be non-negligent. For a formal proof see Appendix. For an informal argument, consider any liability rule f that satisfies Property (P1). In view of the arguments presented for Lemmas 1 and 2, a tuple $((s, x), (t, y))$ cannot be an N.E. if $x < x^*$ and $y < y^*$ or if $x > x^*$ and $y < y^*$, or if $x < x^*$ and $y > y^*$. Therefore, to prove the claim in Theorem 1, it will be sufficient if we can show that under the rule, a tuple $((s, x), (t, y))$ such that $x = x^*$ and $y < y^*$, or $x < x^*$ and $y = y^*$ cannot be an N.E. When $x = x^*$ and $y < y^*$, the victim is solely negligent. Therefore, due to Property (P1), the injurer's liability is zero. This means that the injurer has strong incentives to engage in an excessive level of activity. The excessive activity on the part of the injurer further increases the costs of accident, and it is the victim who bears the entire cost. Therefore, in order to decrease the accident costs, a solely negligent victim has incentive to increase his care level. In addition, excessive activity level of the injurer enhances the productivity of the victim's care, providing the victim with additional incentives to take even greater care.

Remark 4. *It should be noted that while proving Lemmas 1 and 2, and Theorem 1, we have used only Property (P1). Therefore, how a liability rule assigns liability when parties are either both negligent or both non-negligent has no implications for the validity of Lemmas 1 and 2, and Theorem 1.*

Let us see how the claim in Theorem 1 stands as compared to the relevant claim in literature. Note that, among other things, all of the negligence criterion-based rules discussed in the literature, for instance, the rule of negligence, the rule of negligence with the defence of contributory negligence, the rule of the comparative causation under negligence[6] and the rule of strict liability with the defence of contributory negligence, satisfy Property (P1). Therefore, as an implication of Theorem 1, we get the following corollary:

Corollary 1. *In an equilibrium neither party will be found negligent under the following rules: The rule of negligence, the rule of negligence with the defence of contributory negligence the rule of the comparative causation under negligence, and the rule of strict liability with the defence of contributory negligence.*

Corollary 1 shows that the relevant claim in Parisi and Fon (2004) is not valid, where it is suggested that under the rule of the comparative causation under negligence, in equilibrium, one or both the parties can be negligent.

---

[6] Under the rule of the comparative causation under negligence, when a party is found solely negligent, the entire loss is borne by this party. Accident loss is shared between the parties in cases where parties are either both negligent or when both are non-negligent. See Parisi and Fon (2004).

Equilibria under Properties (P1) and (P2)

In view of Theorem 1, search for the existence of an equilibrium under a liability rule can be restricted to the region where $x \geq x^*$ and $y \geq y^*$. Now, let us consider liability rules that satisfy Property (P2) in addition to Property (P1). Here, it is relevant to point out that while only negligence-criterion based rules satisfy Property (P1), Property (P2) is satisfied by all of the standard liability rules whether based on the negligence-criterion or not. Moreover, the standard negligence-based liability rules are such that $q^* = 0$ or 1. Therefore, when both the parties are non-negligent, only one party is fully liable for the accident loss; this party is the injurer if $q^* = 1$, and the victim if $q^* = 0$. For these rules, we have the following claim.

Lemma 3. *If a liability rule satisfies Properties (P1) and (P2) with*

$$q^* \in \{0, 1\},$$

then under the rule: $((s, x), (t, y))$ is an N.E.

$$\Rightarrow (x \neq x^* \text{ or } y \neq y^*).$$

Lemma 3 claims that under standard negligence-based liability rules, including the rule of negligence and the rule of the strict liability with the defence of contributory negligence a tuple $((s, x^*), (t, y^*))$ cannot be N.E. So, regardless of their choice of activity levels, in equilibrium, the injurer and the victim will not simultaneously opt for x^* and y^*.

To see why, suppose $q^* = 0$. Let the equilibrium be denoted by $((\hat{s}, \hat{x}), (\hat{t}, \hat{y}))$. Suppose, in equilibrium the injurer has opted for x^*, that is, $\hat{x} = x^*$. When $q^* = 0$ and $\hat{x} = x^*$, at equilibrium, the injurer's payoff function, $u(s) - sx^*$, attains a unique maximum at s_p^*, where s_p^* solves:

$$u'(s) = x^*.$$

So, in view of (7.4), it follows that $s_p^* > s^*$. Therefore, when $q^* = 0$ and $\hat{x} = x^*$, the $(\hat{s}, \hat{x}) = (s_p^*, x^*)$. Now, given (s_p^*, x^*) opted by the injurer, the problem facing the victim is

$$\max_{(t,y) \in T \times Y} \{v(t) - ty - s_p^* t l(x^*, y)\}.$$

Therefore, the victim will choose $\hat{y} \in Y$ that satisfies:

$$1 + s_p^* l_y(x^*, y) = 0. \tag{7.13}$$

Now in view of the fact that $s_p^* > s^*$ and that $l_{yy}(.) > 0$, a comparison of (7.7) and (7.13) implies that $\hat{y} > y^*$, that is, regardless of s and t, $((s, x^*), (t, y^*))$ cannot be N.E.

A similar argument shows that when $q^* = 1$, $((s, x^*), (t, y^*))$ cannot be N.E.

For an intuitive argument, consider a liability rule that satisfies Properties (P1) and (P2). First, assume that when the injurer opts for x^* and the victim opts for y^*, the victim bears the entire accident loss, that is, $q^* = 0$. This, in view of Properties (P1) and (P2), implies that regardless of the care level and activity level chosen by the victim, if the injurer opts for x^*, his liability is zero. Under such a rule, in order to avoid liability, the injurer will opt for x^* as care level. But, as his liability is zero, his activity level, s_p^*, is excessive. Since, the victim bears the entire cost of accident, he has incentives to increase his care and reduce his activity level. Excessive activity level of the injurer further strengthens these incentives. A similar argument applies to the case when $q^* = 1$.

Lemma 3 stands in contrast to the relevant claims in the existing literature. In Cooter and Ulen (2004: 332–33), Dari Mattiacci (2002), Miceli (1997: 29), and Parisi and Fon (2004), among others, it is argued that under the rule of negligence as well as under the rule of strict liability with the defence of contributory negligence, the injurer and the victim opt for x^* and y^* respectively. Lemma 3 shows that this claim is not valid in general. It is interesting to note that the claim has been made for the same specifications as is considered here.

Let, the pairs $(\hat{t}, \hat{y})$, $(\hat{s}, \hat{x})$ solve (7.14) and (7.15), respectively:

$$\max_{(t,y) \in T \times Y} \{v(t) - ty - s_p^* t l(x^*, y)\} \tag{7.14}$$

$$\max_{(s,x) \in S \times X} \{u(s) - sx - s t_p^* l(x, y^*)\} \tag{7.15}$$

In view of this assumption, $(\hat{t}, \hat{y})$ and $(\hat{s}, \hat{x})$ are unique solutions to (7.14) and (7.15) respectively. Moreover, suppose $(\hat{\hat{t}}, \hat{\hat{y}})$, $(\hat{\hat{s}}, \hat{\hat{x}})$ uniquely solve (7.16) and (7.17) respectively:

$$\max_{(t,y) \in T \times Y} \{v(t) - ty - \hat{s} t l(\hat{x}, y)\} \tag{7.16}$$

$$\max_{(s,x) \in S \times X} \{u(s) - sx - \hat{s} t l(x, \hat{y})\}, \tag{7.17}$$

where $(\hat{t}, \hat{y})$ and $(\hat{s}, \hat{x})$ are defined earlier.

Condition: No Downward Deviations (NDD). Functions $u(.)$, $v(.)$ and $L(.)$ are such that the following holds:

$$u(\hat{s}) - \hat{\hat{s}}\hat{x} - \hat{\hat{s}}\hat{t}l(\hat{x}, \hat{y}) < u(s_p^*) - s_p^*x^* \qquad (7.18)$$

$$v(\hat{t}) - \hat{\hat{t}}\hat{y} - \hat{\hat{s}}\hat{t}l(\hat{x}, \hat{y}) < v(t_p^*) - t_p^*y^* \qquad (7.19)$$

(7.18) says that functions $u(.)$, $v(.)$ and $L(.)$ are such that a unilateral downward deviation from $(s_p^*, x^*, \hat{t}, \hat{y})$ is unprofitable for the injurer. Similarly, (7.19) implies that that unilateral downward deviation from $(\hat{s}, \hat{x})(t_p^*, y^*)$ is unprofitable for the victim.

Theorem 2. *Suppose a liability rule satisfies Properties (P1)–(P3). There exists an N.E. under the rule, iff $u(.)$, $v(.)$ and $L(.)$ satisfy the condition NDD. Moreover, the N.E. is unique.*

Theorem 2 guarantees existence of a unique N.E. under a liability rule that satisfies Properties (P1)–(P3), as long as functions $u(.)$, $v(.)$ and $L(.)$ satisfy the condition NDD. For a formal proof, see Appendix. Specifically, the proof shows that if $q^* = 0$, then there exists a pair (t, y) such that $y > y^*$, $t < t^*$ and $((s_p^*, x^*), (t, y))$ is an N.E. And, if $q^* = 1$, then there exists a pair (s, x) such that $x > x^*$, $s < s^*$ and $((s, t), (t_p^*, y^*))$ is an N.E.

Informally put, this means that if a non-negligent injurer has no liability—such as under the rule of negligence—in equilibrium, the injurer will choose a socially optimum care level, but his activity level will be excessive. As far as the victim is concerned, he will choose excessive care level and less than optimum activity level. The incentive structure induced by a rule under which the injurer has full liability is just the opposite, for example, under the rule of strict liability with defence of contributory negligence. As an implication, we get the following corollary.

Corollary 2. *Suppose, $u(.)$, $v(.)$ and $L(.)$ satisfy the condition NDD. $((s_p^*, x^*), (t, y))$ is a unique N.E. under the following rules: the rule of negligence, the rule of negligence with defence of contributory negligence and the rule of comparative negligence. $((s, t), (t_p^*, y^*))$ is a unique N.E. under the rule of strict liability with defence of contributory negligence. Moreover, the equilibrium exists only if NDD condition is met with.*

SECOND-BEST LIABILITY RULES

In this section, we explore the nature of second-best liability rules. Again, we restrict our analysis to the standard liability rules. However, we will relax condition imposed by Property (P3). Further, we assume that the condition NDD holds.

For the set of liability rules satisfying Properties (P1)–(P3), then in view of Theorem 2, the outcome is a unique N.E.—it is $((s_p^*, x^*), (\hat{t}, \hat{y}))$ if $q^* = 0$, and $((\hat{s}, \hat{x}), (t_p^*, y^*))$ if $q^* = 1$. Therefore, the total social welfare, W, is a function of q^*; $W = W(q^*)$. Further,

$$W(q^* = 0) = u(s_p^*) + v(\hat{t}) - s_p^* x^* - \hat{t}\hat{y} - s_p^* \hat{t} l(x^*, \hat{y}).$$
$$W(q^* = 1) = u(\hat{s}) + v(t_p^*) - \hat{s}\hat{x} - t_p^* y^* - \hat{s} t_p^* l(\hat{x}, y^*).$$

In any given accident context, a liability rule with $q^* = 0$ is more efficient than the rule with $q^* = 1$ *iff* $W(q^* = 0) > W(q^* = 1)$ and vice-versa. Suppose, in a given context, it turns out that $W(q^* = 0) > W(q^* = 1)$ and, therefore the liability rules with $q^* = 0$ are more efficient than those with $q^* = 1$. The question is: Can we achieve better outcome by relaxing condition imposed by Property (P3)? It turns out that the answer is: Yes.

Let us remove the constraints imposed by Property (P3). Note that due to Property (P2), we have: for all $x \geq x^*$, and $y \geq y^*$

$$q^* \in [0, 1].$$

So, now we allow for sharing of liability between the non-negligent parties. However, such sharing of liability raises questions about the existence of equilibria under a liability rule. We cannot be sure of the existence or uniqueness of equilibrium under a liability rule that satisfies Properties (P1) and (P2). This issue requires further research.

As of now, we will assume that under every liability rule satisfying Properties (P1) and (P2), there exists a unique N.E. Equipped with this assumption, we get the following theorem that shows that the second-best efficiency requires loss sharing between the parties, when both the parties are non-negligent.

Theorem 3. *Suppose a liability rule satisfies properties (P1) and (P2). The second-best q is such that $(\forall x \geq x^*)(\forall y \geq y^*)[q(x, y) \in (0, 1)]$.*

Theorem 3 says that if the legal standards for the injurer and the victim are at x^* and y^* respectively and if the rule satisfies the condition of negligence liability, then the second-best efficiency requires loss sharing whenever parties are non-negligent. For a formal proof, see Appendix. The informal argument is as follows. Consider a liability rule that satisfies the condition of negligence liability. Due to (P2), for all $x \geq x^*$ and $y \geq y^*$, $q(x, y) = q(x^*, y^*)$. If $q(x^*, y^*) = 0$, as under the rule of negligence, then by Lemma 3 $((s_p^*, x^*), (t, y))$, where $t < t^*$ and $y > y^*$, is a unique N.E., that is, the injurer's care level is x^*, but his activity level, is excessive at s_p^*. On the other hand, the victim takes too much care and opts for too little activity level, as compared to the first-best levels. Now, if the non-negligent injurer is required to bear a very small fraction of the accident loss, it will leave his care level at x^*, but will reduce his activity level, making it closer to the first-best level, s^*. Sharing of liability means that the victim's care will come down and his activity level will go up little bit. As the proof shows, the net result of these changes is an increase in the social welfare. Likewise, it can be shown that $q(x^*, y^*) = 1$ is not the second-best.

The optimum q^* depends on the context at hand. However, the theorem shows that an appropriate sharing of liability improves incentives related to the non-verifiable aspects of care without diluting those related to verifiable aspects. This argument is true for a context broader than what we have formally captured. For instance, we have assumed that benefits to injurers increase with the non-verifiable aspect of care. This and the other simplifications are not necessary for the validity of Theorem 3. To illustrate the point, suppose the care taken by drivers has three aspects: driving speed, regular checking of brake oil, and the amount of driving. Assume that while the speed is verifiable care, quality of brake oil and the level of driving are not. Note that the benefits to a driver decrease with one of the non-verifiable aspects of care (namely, quality of oil), and increases with the other. Under negligence liability, drivers will invest too little in the non-verifiable aspects of care. Theorem 3 says that the sharing of liability when both driver and pedestrian are non-negligent induces the drivers to better maintain the quality of brake oil and drive less.

Note that under every standard liability rule, whether based on negligence criterion or not, when both the parties are non-negligent, only one party bears the accident loss, that is, either $q = 0$ or $q = 1$. However, Theorem 3 shows that social welfare can be increased by loss sharing between non-negligent parties. Therefore, it follows that none of the standard liability rules is efficient even from a second-best perspective.

CONCLUSION

Contrary to some of the claims in the existing literature, we have shown that none of the standard liability rules induces equilibrium in which parties exercise care appropriate from a first-best perspective. Within the confines of the law of torts, we have shown that each of the standard liability rules fails to be efficient even from a second-best perspective.

Under these standard liability rules, one party takes too little care with respect to the non-verifiable aspects of care, while other takes too much of care. Theorem 3 shows that the second-best efficiency requires some loss sharing between the non-negligent parties. Such sharing of liability improves parties' incentives with respect to the non-verifiable aspects of care. The result is an improvement in social welfare.

Our analysis has some limitations too. In the previous section, while exploring the nature of second-best liability rules, we have assumed that under a liability rule, equilibrium exists and is unique. It should be noted that the sharing of liability between non-negligent parties opens up the possibility of there being no equilibrium or there being multiple equilibria. Though the possibility of multiple equilibria as such does not undermine the argument that *some* sharing of liability between non-negligent parties may be desirable, it does introduce complications have not been fully explored here. These issue needs to be analysed further.

As a matter of practice, liability is determined only on the basis of the verifiable aspects of care levels of the parties. Therefore, a liability rule can have direct control only over the verifiable aspects of care; the non-verifiable aspects cannot be controlled directly. At the same time, there are two policy tools available under a liability rule, namely, the due care levels in terms of the verifiable aspects, and the liability assignment as a function of verifiable care levels. In this essay, we have considered the implications of the second tool only. However, at least in theory, the analysis of the nature of second-best liability rules can be extended beyond what has been done here.

APPENDIX

Proof of Theorem 1. Take any liability rule f that satisfies Property (P1). In view of Lemmas 1 and 2, it will be sufficient to show that under the rule, a tuple $((\hat{s}, \hat{x}), (\hat{t}, \hat{y}))$ such that $\hat{x} = x^*$ and $\hat{y} < y^*$, or $\hat{x} < x^*$ and $\hat{y} = y^*$ cannot be an N.E. Suppose there is an N.E., say $((\hat{s}, \hat{x}), (\hat{t}, \hat{y}))$, in which $\hat{x} = x^*$ and $\hat{y} < y^*$. Since $\hat{x} = x^*$ and $\hat{y} < y^*$, it means $q(x^*, \hat{y}) = 0$. So, the injurer's pay-off is given by $u(s) - sx^*$, which attains a unique maximum at (s_p^*, x^*), where s_p^* solves

$$u'(s) = x^*.$$

In view of (7.4), $s_p^* > s^*$. Therefore, when

$$\hat{x} = x^* \text{ and } \hat{y} < y^*, (\hat{s}, \hat{x}) = (s_p^*, x^*).$$

Now, given $(\hat{s}, \hat{x})$, that is, (s_p^*, x^*) opted by the injurer, the problem facing the victim is

$$\max_{(t,y)\in T\times Y} \{v(t) - ty - s_p^* tl(x^*, y)\}.$$

Therefore, the victim will choose $\hat{t} \in T$ and $\hat{y} \in Y$ that simultaneously satisfy

$$v'^* t = y + s_p^* l(x^*, y) \tag{7.20}$$

$$1 + s_p^* l_y(x^*, y) = 0. \tag{7.21}$$

Now in view of $s_p^* > s^*$ and $l_{yy}(.) > 0$, equations (7.3) and (7.21) imply that $\hat{y} > y^*$, which is a contradiction. An analogous argument shows that $\hat{x} < x^*$ and $\hat{y} = y^*$ cannot be an N.E.

Proof of Theorem 2. First consider the case when $q^* = 0$. Suppose the injurer has opted the pair (s_p^*, x^*). Now, given (s_p^*, x^*) opted by the injurer, the problem facing the victim is

$$\max_{(t,y)\in T\times Y} \{v(t) - ty - s_p^* tl(x^*, y)\}.$$

Therefore, the victim will choose $\hat{t} \in T$ and $\hat{y} \in Y$ that simultaneously satisfy:

$$v'(t) = y + s_p^* l(x^*, y) \tag{7.22}$$

$$1 + s_p^* l_y(x^*, y) = 0. \tag{7.23}$$

We have already seen $\hat{y} > y^*$ will hold. Moreover, by assumption, $((s^*, x^*)(t^*, y^*))$ uniquely solves the social optimisation problem. This means that (t^*, y^*) uniquely solves the following optimisation problem:

$$\max_{(t,y)\in T\times Y} \{v(t) + u(s^*) - ty - s^* x^* - s^* tl(x^*, y)\},$$

i.e.,

$$\max_{(t,y)\in T\times Y} \{v(t) - ty - s^* tl(x^*, y)\}.$$

This further implies that y^* uniquely solves:

$$\max_{y}\{v(t^*) - t^* y - s^* t^* l(x^*, y)\}.$$

So, y^* uniquely solves $\min_y\{t^*[y + s^* l(x^*, y)]\}$, that is,

$$\min_{y}\{y + s^* l(x^*, y)\}.$$

Therefore, we conclude that

$$(\forall y \in Y)[y + s^*l(x^*, y) \geq y^* + s^*l(x^*, y^*)].$$

Moreover, since $s_p^* > s^*$, we have

$$(\forall y \in Y)[y + s_p^*l(x^*, y) > y + s^*l(x^*, y)].$$

Hence, the following holds:

$$(\forall y \in Y)[y + s_p^*l(x^*, y) > y^* + s^*l(x^*, y^*)]. \tag{7.24}$$

Recall, t^* solves

$$v'(t) = y^* + s^*l(x^*, y^*) \tag{7.25}$$

but, equilibrium choice $\hat{t}$ solves (7.22). A comparison of (A.3) and (7.25), in view of (7.24), gives us $\hat{t} < t^*$. Therefore, given (s_p^*, x^*) opted by the injurer, there exists $(\hat{t}, \hat{y})$, such that $\hat{t} < t^*$, $\hat{y} > y^*$ and $(\hat{t}, \hat{y})$ is a best response for the victim.

Next, suppose $(\hat{t}, \hat{y})$ is opted by the victim. Since $q^* = 0$, in the region $x \geq x^*$, the injurer's pay-off function, $u(s) - sx^*$, attains a unique maximum at (s_p^*, x^*). However, if the injurer opts for some pair (s, x) such that $x < x^*$, he will be fully liable and his pay-off will be $u(s) - sx - s\hat{t}l(x, \hat{y})$. However, in view of condition NDD, that is, (7.20), we have, for all s and $x < x^*$,

$$u(s) - sx - s\hat{t}l(x, \hat{y}) < u(s_p^*) - s_p^*x^*.$$

Therefore, injurer's best response to $(\hat{t}, \hat{y})$ is (s_p^*, x^*). As a result, $((s_p^*, x^*), (\hat{t}, \hat{y}))$ is an N.E. under the rule. To see uniqueness, notice that in view of Theorem 2, equilibrium is possible only in the region $x \geq x^*$ and $y \geq y^*$. In this region, there cannot be an N.E. in which injurer opts for $x > x^*$. However, if $x = x^*$, then $((s_p^*, x^*), (\hat{t}, \hat{y}))$ is the only possible N.E.

Finally note that if condition NDD is violated, then $((s_p^*, x^*), (\hat{t}, \hat{y}))$ cannot be an N.E. No other N.E. is possible anyway. The case when $q^* = 1$ is similar.

Proof of Theorem 3. Take any liability rule f that satisfies properties (P1) and (P2). Due to (P2), for all $x \geq x^*$ and $y \geq y^*$, $q(x, y) = q^* \in [0, 1]$. Suppose $((s, x), (t, y))$ is a unique N.E. under f. In view of Theorem 1, $x \geq x^*$ & $y \geq y^*$.

Recall, in the region $x \geq x^*$ & $y \geq y^*$, the objectives of the injurer and the victim are given by

$$\max_{(s,x)\in S\times X} \{u(s) - sx - q^*stl(x, y)\}$$

and

$$\max_{(t,y)\in T\times Y} \{v(t) - ty - (1 - q^*)stl(x, y)\}$$

respectively. Therefore, the equilibrium activity levels of the injurer and the victim satisfy the following equations respectively:

$$v'(s) = xq^*tl(x, y) \tag{7.26}$$

$$v'(t) = y + (1 - q^*)sl(x, y) \tag{7.27}$$

From (7.26), we see that s is a function of q^*, along with t, x, y, that is, we can write $s = s(q^*, t, x, y)$. From (7.27), we get $t = t(q^*, t, x, y)$. Similarly, it can be seen that the equilibrium care level, x, in general is a function of q^*, along with s, t, y, that is, $x = x(q^*, s, y, t)$. Moreover, in equilibrium, if $x > x^*$, then x solves:

$$1 + qtl_x(x, y) = 0. \tag{7.28}$$

Likewise for the equilibrium level of y, that is,

$$y = y(q^*, s, x, t).$$

If $y > y^*$, then y solves:

$$1 + (1 - q)sl_y(x, y) = 0. \tag{7.29}$$

From these first-order conditions, it is clear that at the equilibrium $((s, x), (t, y))$, the following holds: $\partial s/\partial q^* < 0$; $\partial t/\partial q^* > 0$; $\partial x/\partial q^* \geq 0$; and $\partial y/\partial q^* \leq 0$.

Moreover, the equilibrium $((s, x), (t, y))$ is a function of q^*. Therefore, the total social welfare, W, as also a function of q^*:

$$W(q^*) = u(s(q^*)) + v(t(q^*)) - s(q^*)x(q^*) - t(q^*)y(q^*)$$
$$-s(q^*)t(q^*)l(x(q^*), y(q^*)).$$

Consider the case when $q^* = 0$. When $q^* = 0$, from Theorem 2, equilibrium $(s(q^*), x(q^*)), (t(q^*), y(q^*))|_{q^*=0}$ is unique and is such that $s(q^*)|_{q^*=0} = s_p^* > s^*$; $x(q^*)|_{q^*=0} = x^*$; $y(q^*)|_{q^*=0} > y^*$; & $t(q^*)|_{q^*=0} < t^*$.

Furthermore, at $q^* = 0$, $s(q^*)$, $t(q^*)$ and $y(q^*)$ satisfy the following first-order conditions respectively:

$$u'^*(s(q^*) - x(q^*) = 0, \qquad (7.30)$$
$$vu'(t(q*)) - y(q^*) - s(q^*)l(x(q^*), y(q^*)) = 0, \qquad (7.31)$$
$$1 + s(q^*)l_y(x(q^*), y(q^*)) = 0, \qquad (7.32)$$

Besides, when q^* is positive but very small, regardless of s, t, and y, for all $x > x^*$, $\| qtl_x(x, y) \| < 1$. Therefore, when q^* increases slightly from 0, for the injurer, the optimal x remains at x^*, that is,

$$\frac{dx(q^*)}{dq^*} = 0.$$

Also, given that

$$\frac{dx(q^*)}{dq^*} = 0,$$

the only implication of an increase in q^* from 0 is that s is determined by $u'(s) = x^* + q^*tl(x, y)$, where $q^*tl(x, y)$ is positive. In fact, it can be seen that

$$\frac{dx(q^*)}{dq^*}\Big|_{q^*=0} = 0; \quad \frac{ds(q^*)}{dq}\Big|_{q^*=0} < 0.$$

Now, differentiating $W(q^*)$ with respect to q^* yields:

$$\frac{dW(q^*)}{dq^*} = u'(s(q^*))\frac{ds(q^*)}{dq^*} + v'(t(q^*))\frac{dt(q^*)}{dq^*} - x(q^*)\frac{ds(q^*)}{dq^*} - s(q^*)\frac{dx(q^*)}{dq^*}$$
$$- y(q^*)\frac{dt(q^*)}{dq^*} - t(q^*)\frac{dy(q^*)}{dq^*} - t(q^*)l(x(q^*), y(q^*))\frac{ds(q^*)}{dq^*}$$
$$- s(q^*)l(x(q^*), y(q^*))\frac{dt(q^*)}{dq^*} - s(q^*)t(q^*)l_x(x(q^*), y(q^*))\frac{dx(q^*)}{dq^*}$$
$$- s(q^*)t(q^*)l_y(x(q^*), y(q^*))\frac{dy(q^*)}{dq^*}. \qquad (7.33)$$

In view of equations (7.30)–(7.32), (7.33) yields

$$\frac{dW(q^*)}{dq}\Big|_{q^*=0} = -t(q^*)l(x(q^*), y(q^*))\frac{ds(q^*)}{dq^*}\Big|_{q^*=0}.$$

Since

$$\frac{ds(q^*)}{dq^*}\Big|_{q^*=0} < 0,$$

therefore,

$$\frac{dW(q^*)}{dq^*}|_{q^*=0} > 0.$$

Similarly, it can be shown that

$$\frac{dW(1)}{dq^*}|_{q=1} < 0.$$

Furthermore, assuming that s, x, t and y are continuous functions of q^*, W is a continuous function of q^* on a compact domain $[0, 1]$. Therefore, there exists $q \in (0, 1)$ that maximises the social welfare.

REFERENCES

Calabresi, Guido. 1970. *The Costs of Accidents: A Legal and Economic Analysis*. New Haven: Yale University Press.

Cooter, R. D. and T. S. Ulen. 2004. *Law and Economics*, 4th edn. New York: Addison-Wesley.

Dari Mattiacci, G. 2002. 'Tort Law and Economics', in A. Hatzis (ed.), *Economics Analysis of Law: A European Perspective*. Cheltenham, UK: Edward Elgar.

Delhaye, Eef. 2002. 'Accident Analysis: The Role of Liability Rules', www.econ.kuleuven.be/ete/downloads/delhaye 2002liab:pdf (accessed on 13 March 2013).

Feldman, Allan and Ram Singh. 2009. 'Comparative Vigilance', *American Law and Economics Review*, 11: 134–61.

Grady, Mark F. 1989. 'Untaken Precautions', *Journal of Legal Studies*, 18: 139–56.

Jain, Satish K. and Ram Singh. 2002. 'Efficient Liability Rules: Complete Characterization', *Journal of Economics*, 75(2): 105–24.

Landes, William M. and R. A. Posner. 1983. 'Causation in Tort Law: An Economic Approach', *Journal of Legal Studies*, 12: 109–34.

———. 1987. *The Economic Structure of Tort Law*. Cambridge (MA): Harvard University Press.

Miceli, Thomas J. 1997. *Economics of the Law: Torts, Contracts, Property, Litigation*. Oxford: Oxford University Press.

Parisi, Francesco and Vincy Fon. 2004. 'Comparative Causation', *American Law and Economics Review*, 6: 345–68.

Parisi, Francesco and Ram Singh. 2010. 'The Efficiency of Comparative Causation', *Review of Law and Economics*, 6(2): 219–45.

Polinsky, A. Mitchell. 1989. *An Introduction to Law and Economics*, 2nd edn. Boston: Little,Brown and Co.

Shavell, S. 1987. *Economic Analysis of Accident Law*. Cambridge, MA: Harvard University Press.

Singh, Ram. 2007. 'Causation-Consistent Liability, Economic Efficiency and the Law of Torts', *International Review of Law and Economics*, 27(2): 179–203.

8

Efficiency of (1, 2)-Incremental Liability Rules:
Some Results

Rajendra P. Kundu*

In economic analysis of tort law,[1] the formal notion of a liability rule is used to analyse questions relating to efficient apportionment of accident losses among parties involved in harmful interactions. In the context of interactions involving two parties[2] a liability rule apportions the loss, for instance, in case of an accident, between the parties on the basis of their levels of nonnegligence.[3] The central result in the extensive literature on the efficiency of liability rules[4] states that

---

* I would like to thank Papiya Ghosh, Debabrata Pal and Sugata Bag for helpful comments and suggestions.

[1] Courts from across the world are routinely called upon to decide on matters relating to apportionment of losses resulting from accidents. A variety of rules are used by courts for the apportionment of such losses. Which of these rules provide efficient incentives to parties involved is the key question addressed in the economic analysis of the law of torts.

[2] In the framework which is now standard in this literature, the analysis is usually done in the context of interactions between two risk-neutral parties who are strangers to one another. It is assumed that the loss in case of an accident, falls on one of the parties called the victim. The other party is referred to as the injurer. The probability of accident and the actual loss in case of accident is assumed to depend on the care levels of the two parties. It is also assumed that the social objective is to minimise the total social costs, which are defined as the sum of costs of care of the parties involved and the expected accident losses.

[3] Depending on the liability rule a due level of care may be legally specified for each of the two parties. If there is a legally specified due care for a party and the party chooses a care level that is less than the due care specified for the party then the party is called negligent; otherwise the party is nonnegligent. The level of nonnegligence of a party is either 1 or the ratio of his actual level of care to the due care level legally specified for him, whichever is lower.

[4] See Calabresi (1961, 1965, 1970), Coase (1960), Brown (1973), Diamond (1974), Jain and Singh (2002), Landes and Posner (1987), Miceli (1997) Posner

a liability rule is efficient[5] iff it ensures that whenever one party is negligent and the other is not, the negligent party is made to bear the entire loss.[6]

Although use of the notion of a liability rule is almost universal in this literature, questions have been raised as to how well this formal construct corresponds to the rules of apportionment applied by courts. According to Kahan (1989), when courts hold a negligent injurer liable, they do not usually hold the injurer liable for the entire loss but only for that part of the loss that could be attributed to the negligence of the injurer. He shows that the negligence rule is efficient even when the apportionment of accidental loss is done along these lines. Jain (2009) introduces the concept of incremental liability rule to formalise the idea put forward by Kahan and provides a complete characterisation of efficient incremental liability rules.[7] An incremental liability rule has been defined as a rule which specifies, as a function of proportions of nonnegligence of the two parties (i) which of the two parties, the victim or the injurer, is to be the non-residual liability holder; and (ii) the proportion of the incremental loss, for which the non-residual party can be held responsible, to be borne by the non-residual liability holder. He shows that an incremental liability rule is efficient iff its structure is such that (a) if the party which is the residual liability holder when both are non-negligent is negligent and the other party is non-negligent, then the negligent party must remain the residual liability holder; and (b) if the party which is the non-residual liability holder when both are non-negligent is negligent and the other party is non-negligent, then the negligent party must become the residual liability holder or liability of the negligent party must be equal to the entire incremental loss which can be ascribed to the negligence of the party.

(1972, 1973), and Shavell (1980, 1987). Brown was the first to present a formal analysis of many of the important liability rules. The subsequent literature is built upon Brown's formal model. A complete characterisation of efficient liability rules was provided by Jain and Singh (2002).

[5] A liability rule is said to be efficient iff it induces the victim and the injurer to take total social cost minimising levels of care.

[6] From this result, which is due to Jain and Singh (2002), it follows that while the rules of negligence, negligence with the defence of contributory negligence and strict liability with the defence of contributory negligence are efficient, no liability and strict liability are inefficient.

[7] For an analysis of the incremental version of the negligence rule, see Jain (2010).

This essay investigates the question of efficient apportionment of accident losses resulting from harmful interaction involving one victim and two injurers.[8] The notion of a $(1, 2)$-incremental liability rule is introduced and complete characterisations of efficient rules belonging to two important classes of $(1, 2)$-incremental liability rules are provided.

A $(1, 2)$-incremental liability rule is a rule which specifies, as proportions of non-negligence of the parties, (i) the set of non-residual liability holders, (ii) the proportions of the incremental loss to be borne by each of the non-residual liability holders and (iii) the proportions of the residual loss to be borne by each of the residual liability holders. The incremental loss is the difference between the actual loss and the adjusted value of the loss that would have resulted in case of accident if, given the care levels of the residual liability holders, the non-residual liability holders had taken their due care levels whenever this difference is positive and it is zero otherwise.[9] The residual loss is that portion of the actual loss which is in excess of the the loss collectively borne by the non-residual liability holders.

In this essay, we consider two classes of $(1, 2)$-incremental liability rules: (i) $\mathcal{F}_{\{1,2\}}$, the class of all $(1, 2)$-incremental liability rules which are such that the set of non-residual liability holders is always the set of injurers and they always collectively bear the entire loss that is attributable to their negligence, and (ii) $\mathcal{F}_{\{0\}}$, the class of all $(1, 2)$-incremental liability rules which are such that the victim alone is always the non-residual liability holder and he bears the entire loss that is attributable to his negligence. A rule in $\mathcal{F}_{\{1,2\}}$ is efficient iff whenever one of the injurers is negligent and the other is not then the negligent injurer bears the entire incremental loss. A rule in $\mathcal{F}_{\{0\}}$ is efficient iff whenever one of the

---

[8] Efficiency properties of liability rules in the context of accidents involving one victim and multiple injurers have been analysed by Landes and Posner (1980), Tietenberg (1989), Kornhauser and Revesz (1989), Miceli and Segerson (1991) and Jain and Kundu (2006). The main result that has emerged in this context is that while all versions of the negligence rule are efficient, not all variants of the rule of strict liability with the defence of contributory negligence are efficient.

[9] The value of the loss which would have resulted in case of an accident if, given the care levels of the residual liability holders, the non-residual liability holders had taken their due care levels is suitably adjusted to take into account differing probabilities of accident with different care levels. The notion of incremental loss is formally defined in the second section.

injurers is negligent and the other is not then the negligent injurer bears the entire residual loss. The results obtained in the essay show that the efficiency requirements for the rules of apportionment of accident losses in the context of interactions between one victim and two injurers are different from the efficiency requirements for the rules of apportionment of accident losses in the context of interactions between one victim and one injurer.

The essay is organised as follows. The framework of analysis is laid out in the second section. All definitions and assumptions are introduced in this section along with some illustrative examples. The main results of the essay are contained in the following two sections. The third section presents a complete characterisation of efficient (1, 2)-incremental liability rules in $\mathcal{F}_{\{1,2\}}$ and the fourth section presents a complete characterisation of efficient (1, 2)-incremental liability rules in $\mathcal{F}_{\{0\}}$. This is followed by the conclusion.

DEFINITIONS AND ASSUMPTIONS

We consider accidents involving one victim (individual 0) and two injurers (individuals 1 and 2). Let $N = \{0, 1, 2\}$. Let $a_i \geq 0, i \in N$, is the index of the level of care taken by individual i. Let $A_i = \{a_i \mid a_i \geq 0$ be the index of some feasible level of care that can be taken by individual $i\}, i \in N$.

We assume that $0 \in A_i$ for all $i \in N$. (A1)

We denote by $c_i(a_i)$ the cost to the individual i of care level a_i. Let $C_i = \{c_i(a_i) \mid a_i \in A_i\}$.

We assume $c_i(0) = 0$ for all $i \in N$. (A2)

We also assume that for all $i \in N$, c_i is strictly increasing function of a_i. (A3)

In view of (A2) and (A3), it follows that $(\forall i \in N)(\forall c_i \in C_i)(c_i \geq 0)$.

A consequence of (A3) is that c_i itself can be taken to be an index of the level of care taken by individual i, $i \in N$.

Let π denote the probability of occurrence of accident and $H \geq 0$ the loss in case of occurrence of accident. Both π and H will be assumed to be functions of (c_0, c_1, c_2); $\pi = \pi(c_0, c_1, c_2), H = H(c_0, c_1, c_2)$. Let $L = \pi H$. L is, thus, the expected loss due to accident.

We will often denote (c_0, c_1, c_2) by c, (c'_0, c'_1, c'_2) by c' and (c_0^*, c_1^*, c_2^*) by c^*. In addition, we will also use the notation $(c_B^*, c_{\overline{B}})$ to denote the configuration of costs of care in which everyone in $B \subset N$ chooses care level c_i^* and everyone in $\overline{B} = N - B$ chooses c_i and the notation $(c_i, c_{\sim i}^*)$

to denote the configuration of costs of care in which individual $i \in N$ chooses care level c_i and everyone in $N - \{i\}$ chooses c_i^*. $C_0 \times C_1 \times C_2$ will be denoted by C.

We assume:

$$(\forall c, c' \in C)(\forall j \in N)[(\forall i \in N)(i \neq j \to c_i = c_i') \land c_j > c_j' \to L(c) \leq L(c')].$$
$$\text{(A4)}$$

That is to say, it is assumed that greater care by an individual, given the levels of care of all other individuals, results in lesser or equal expected accident loss. The decrease in expected loss can take place because of decrease in the probability of occurrence of accident or because of decrease in the magnitude of loss in case of occurrence of accident.

Total social costs (TSC) are defined to be the sum of costs of care of all the individuals and the expected loss due to accident; TSC $= c_0 + c_1 + c_2 + L(c_0, c_1, c_2) = T(c)$. Total social costs are, thus, a function of (c_0, c_1, c_2).

Let $M = \{c' \in C \mid (\forall c \in C)[c_0' + c_1' + c_2' + L(c') \leq c_0 + c_1 + c_2 + L(c)]\}$. Thus, M is the set of all costs of care profiles c' which are total social cost minimising. It will be assumed that:

C_0, C_1, C_2, and L are such that M is non-empty. $\qquad$ (A5)

Negligence. Let $c^* \in M$. Given c_0^*, c_1^*, c_2^*, we define for each $i \in N$, function $p_i, p_i : C_i \mapsto [0, 1]$, as follows:

$$p_i(c_i) = \frac{c_i}{c_i^*} \text{ if } c_i < c_i^*$$
$$= 1 \text{ otherwise}$$

If there is a legally specified due care level for individual $i \in N$, then c_i^* used in the definition of p_i would be taken to be identical with the legally specified due care level. If no due care level is legally specified for individual i, then c_i^* used in the definition of p_i can be taken to be any $c_i^* \in C_i$ subject to the requirement that $c^* \in M$. Thus in all cases, for each individual i, c_i^* would denote the legally binding due care level for individual i whenever the idea of legally binding due care level for individual i is applicable.[10]

$p_i(c_i)$ would be interpreted as the proportion of non-negligence of individual i. $p_i(c_i) = 1$ would mean that individual i is taking at least the due care and $p_i(c_i) < 1$ as meaning that individual i is taking less

---

[10] Thus, implicitly it is being assumed that the legally specified due care levels are in all cases consistent with the objective of total social cost minimisation.

than due care. If $p_i(c_i) = 1$, individual i would be called nonnegligent; and if $p_i(c_i) < 1$, individual i would be called negligent.

Incremental Loss. For $B \subset N$ define function G_B as follows:

$$G_B(c) = H(c) - H(c_B^*, c_{\overline{B}}) \frac{\pi(c_B^*, c_{\overline{B}})}{\pi(c)} \quad \text{if } \pi(c) \neq 0 \wedge H(c) > H(c_B^*, c_{\overline{B}}) \frac{\pi(c_B^*, c_{\overline{B}})}{\pi(c)}$$

$$= 0 \qquad \qquad \text{otherwise.}$$

Let $S_B(c) = \pi(c) G_B(c)$. In other words

$$S_B(c) = L(c) - L(c_B^*, c_{\overline{B}}) \quad \text{if } \pi(c) \neq 0 \wedge L(c) > L(c_B^*, c_{\overline{B}})$$

$$= 0 \qquad \qquad \text{otherwise.}$$

Thus $G_B(c) = \max\{0, H(c) - H(c_B^*, c_{\overline{B}}) \frac{\pi(c_B^*, c_{\overline{B}})}{\pi(c)}\}$; where $\pi(c) \neq 0$ and $S_B(c) = \max\{0, L(c_B^*, c_{\overline{B}})\}$.[11] $G_B(c)$ will be called the incremental loss attributable to the negligence of individuals in B and $S_B(c)$ will be called expected value of the incremental loss attributable to the negligence of individuals in B. Individuals in B will be called non-residual liability holders. The loss over and above the portion of incremental loss borne collectively by the non-residual liability holders will be called the residual loss and will be denoted by $F_B(c)$. We shall denote the expected value of the residual loss by $R_B(c)$. Individuals in $N - B$ will be called the residual liability holders.

Example 1. Let $C_0 = C_1 = C_2 = \{0, 1\}$. Let $L(c)$ be specified as follows:

(c_0, c_1, c_2)	$L(c)$
$(0, 0, 0)$	10
$(0, 0, 1)$	9.25
$(0, 1, 0)$	8.25
$(0, 1, 1)$	7.5
$(1, 0, 0)$	8.5
$(1, 0, 1)$	7.75
$(1, 1, 0)$	6.75
$(1, 1, 1)$	6

---

[11] Note that for all $(c_B', c_{\overline{B}}) \in C$, if $c_i' \geq c_i^*$ for all $i \in B$ then $S_B(c_B', c_{\overline{B}}) = 0$, where $(c_B', c_{\overline{B}})$ denotes the configuration of costs of care in which everyone in $B \subset N$ chooses care level c_i' and everyone in $\overline{B} = N - B$ chooses c_i.

Total social costs are as given in the following table:

(c_0, c_1, c_2)	$TSC(c)$
$(0, 0, 0)$	10
$(0, 0, 1)$	10.25
$(0, 1, 0)$	9.25
$(0, 1, 1)$	9.5
$(1, 0, 0)$	9.5
$(1, 0, 1)$	9.75
$(1, 1, 0)$	8.75
$(1, 1, 1)$	9

Thus, $M = \{(1, 1, 0)\}$. Let $c^* = (1, 1, 0)$. $S_{\{0\}}(c)$ and $S_{\{1,2\}}(c)$ are as follows:

(c_0, c_1, c_2)	$S_{\{0\}}(c)$	$S_{\{1,2\}}(c)$
$(0, 0, 0)$	1.5	1.75
$(0, 0, 1)$	1.5	1
$(0, 1, 0)$	1.5	0
$(0, 1, 1)$	1.5	0
$(1, 0, 0)$	0	1.75
$(1, 0, 1)$	0	1
$(1, 1, 0)$	0	0
$(1, 1, 1)$	0	0

(1, 2)-Incremental Liability Rule. Let I denote the closed interval $[0, 1]$ and let $K = 2^N - \{N\}$. A $(1, 2)$-incremental liability rule is a rule which specifies, for every possible configuration of levels of non-negligence of the three parties,

(i) the set of non-residual liability holders,
(ii) the proportions of the incremental loss to be borne by each of the non-residual liability holders, and
(iii) the proportions of the residual loss to be borne by each of the residual liability holders.

Formally, a $(1, 2)$-incremental liability rule is a function f from I^3 to $K \times I^3$, $f : I^3 \mapsto K \times I^3$, such that: $f(p_0, p_1, p_2) = f(p) = f[p_0(c_0), p_1(c_1), p_2(c_2)] = (B, (x_0, x_1, x_2)) = (B, x) = (B(p), (x_0(p), x_1(p), x_2(p)))$, where

$x_i(p)$ is a share of the incremental loss if $i \in B(p)$ and $x_i(p)$ is a share of the residual loss if $i \in N - B(p)$ with $\sum_{i \in B} x_i \leq 1$ and $\sum_{i \in \bar{B}} x_i = 1$.[12] Given (1, 2)-incremental liability rule f, $F_{B(p)}(c) = H(c) - \sum_{i \in B(p)} x_i(p)G_{B(p)}(c)$ and $R_{B(p)}(c) = L(c) - \sum_{i \in B(p)} x_i(p)S_{B(p)}(c)$. Individual i's expected liability is given by: $x_i(p)S_{B(p)}(c)$ if $i \in B(p)$, and $x_i(p)R_{B(p)}(c)$ if $i \in N - B(p)$. The expected costs of individual i, EC_i, are the sum of his cost of care and his expected liability. Thus, the individual i's expected costs EC_i are given as follows:

$$EC_i(c) = c_i + x_i(p)S_{B(p)}(c) \quad \text{if } i \in B(p)$$
$$= c_i + x_i(p)R_{B(p)}(c) \quad \text{if } i \in N - B(p).$$

It would be assumed that every individual considers an outcome O_1 to be at least as good as another outcome O_2 iff expected costs for the individual under O_1 are less than or equal to expected costs under O_2.

Efficiency. A specification of C_0, C_1, C_2, L and $c^* \in M$ satisfying (A1)–(A5) will be called an application. A (1, 2)-incremental liability rule f is defined to be efficient for a particular application given by C_0, C_1, C_2, L and $c^* \in M$ satisfying (A1)–(A5) iff $(\forall \bar{c} \in C)[\bar{c}$ is a Nash equilibrium $\rightarrow \bar{c} \in M] \wedge (\exists \bar{c} \in C)[\bar{c}$ is a Nash equilibrium].[13] A (1, 2)-incremental liability rule f is defined to be efficient iff it is efficient for every possible specification of C_0, C_1, C_2, L and $c^* \in M$ satisfying (A1)–(A5).

In other words, a (1, 2)-incremental liability rule f is defined to be efficient for a given application iff (i) every Nash equilibrium is total social cost minimising and (ii) there exists at least one Nash equilibrium. A (1, 2)-incremental liability rule is efficient iff it is efficient for every possible application.

Remark 1. *It should be noted that if (A5) is not satisfied then no (1, 2)-incremental liability rule can be efficient.*

Example 2. Consider the (1, 2)-incremental liability rule f defined as follows:

$$f(p) = \left(\{1, 2\}, \left(1, \frac{1}{2}, \frac{1}{2} \right) \right) \quad \text{for all } p \in I^3.$$

---

[12] Throughout the essay, $x_0(p(c^*))$, $x_1(p(c^*))$ and $x_2(p(c^*))$ will be denoted by x_0^1, x_1^1, x_2^1 respectively.

[13] Only pure-strategy Nash equilibria are considered in this essay.

Let C_0, C_1, C_2, L and c^* be as in Example 1.[14] We obtain $R_{\{1,2\}}(c)$ as follows:

(c_0, c_1, c_2)	$R_{\{1,2\}}(c)$
$(0, 0, 0)$	8.25
$(0, 0, 1)$	8.25
$(0, 1, 0)$	8.25
$(0, 1, 1)$	7.5
$(1, 0, 0)$	6.75
$(1, 0, 1)$	6.75
$(1, 1, 0)$	6.75
$(1, 1, 1)$	6

Accordingly, $EC_0(c)$, $EC_1(c)$ and $EC_2(c)$ are as given below:

(c_0, c_1, c_2)	$EC_0(c)$	$EC_1(c)$	$EC_2(c)$
$(0, 0, 0)$	8.25	.875	.875
$(0, 0, 1)$	8.25	.5	1.5
$(0, 1, 0)$	8.25	1	0
$(0, 1, 1)$	7.5	1	1
$(1, 0, 0)$	7.75	.875	.875
$(1, 0, 1)$	7.75	.5	1.5
$(1, 1, 0)$	7.75	1	0
$(1, 1, 1)$	7	1	1

Note that $EC_1(1, 0, 0) < EC_1(1, 1, 0)$. Therefore the unique TSC-minimising configuration of costs of care $(1, 1, 0)$, is not a Nash equilibrium. Hence, the given rule is inefficient.

Example 3. Consider the incremental liability rule f defined as follows:

$$f(p) = (\{0\}, (1, 0, 1)) \quad \text{if } p_1 = 1 \wedge p_2 < 1$$
$$= (\{0\}, (1, 1, 0)) \quad \text{otherwise.}$$

Let C_0, C_1, C_2, L and c^* be as in Example 1. We obtain $R_{\{0\}}(c)$ as follows:

---

[14] Note that C_0, C_1, C_2, L and c^* given in Example 1 satisfy assumptions (A1)–(A5).

(c_0, c_1, c_2)	$R_{\{0\}}(c)$
$(0, 0, 0)$	8.5
$(0, 0, 1)$	7.75
$(0, 1, 0)$	6.75
$(0, 1, 1)$	6
$(1, 0, 0)$	8.5
$(1, 0, 1)$	7.75
$(1, 1, 0)$	6.75
$(1, 1, 1)$	6

Accordingly, $EC_0(c)$, $EC_1(c)$ and $EC_2(c)$ are as given below:

(c_0, c_1, c_2)	$EC_0(c)$	$EC_1(c)$	$EC_2(c)$
$(0, 0, 0)$	1.5	8.5	0
$(0, 0, 1)$	1.5	7.75	1
$(0, 1, 0)$	1.5	7.75	0
$(0, 1, 1)$	1.5	7	1
$(1, 0, 0)$	1	8.5	0
$(1, 0, 1)$	1	7.75	1
$(1, 1, 0)$	1	7.75	0
$(1, 1, 1)$	1	7	1

Note that $(\forall c_1, c_2 \in \{0, 1\})[EC_0(1, c_1, c_2) < EC_0(0, c_1, c_2)]$, $(\forall c_0, c_2 \in \{0, 1\})[EC_1(c_0, 1, c_2) < EC_1(c_0, 0, c_2)]$ and $(\forall c_0, c_1 \in \{0, 1\})[EC_2(c_0, c_1, 0) < EC_2(c_0, c_1, 1)]$. Therefore the unique TSC-minimising configuration of costs of care, $(1, 1, 0)$, is also the unique Nash equilibrium. Hence, the given rule is efficient for the application under consideration.[15]

Classes of (1, 2)-Incremental Liability Rules. Let f be a (1, 2)-incremental liability rule. For any $p \in I^3$ the set of non-residual liability holders is $B(p)$ and the incremental loss is given by $G_{B(p)}$. In general, it is not necessary that the non-residual liability holders collectively bear the entire incremental loss. However, as the incremental loss is that portion of the actual loss which can be ascribed to the negligence of the individuals in $B(p)$, rules which make these individuals liable for the entire incremental loss are of particular interest.

---

[15] The given rule is efficient. The efficiency of the rule follows from Theorem 2.

Let $\mathcal{F}$ be the class of $(1, 2)$-incremental liability rules which are such that the entire incremental loss is always borne collectively by the non-residual liability holders. Consider the following subclasses of $\mathcal{F}$:

(i) $\mathcal{F}_{\{1,2\}} = \{f \in \mathcal{F} \mid (\forall p \in I^3)[B(p) = \{1, 2\}]\}$ and
(ii) $\mathcal{F}_{\{0\}} = \{f \in \mathcal{F} \mid (\forall p \in I^3)[B(p) = \{0\}]\}$.

$\mathcal{F}_{\{1,2\}}$ is the class of all $(1, 2)$-incremental liability rules under which the injurers are always the non-residual liability holders and they collectively bear the entire incremental loss. $\mathcal{F}_{\{0\}}$ is the class of all $(1, 2)$-incremental liability rules under which the victim is always the non-residual liability holder and the victim bears the entire incremental loss. Thus, $\mathcal{F}_{\{1,2\}} = \{f \mid (\forall p \in I^3)[B(p) = \{1, 2\} \wedge x_1(p) + x_2(p) = 1]\}$ and $\mathcal{F}_{\{0\}} = \{f \mid (\forall p \in I^3)[B(p) = \{0\} \wedge x_0(p) = 1]\}$.

Example 4. Note that the $(1, 2)$-incremental liability rule given in Example 2 belongs to $\mathcal{F}_{\{1,2\}}$ and that in Example 3 belongs to $\mathcal{F}_{\{0\}}$.

Condition $\mathcal{N}$. A $(1, 2)$-incremental liability rule f satisfies condition $\mathcal{N}$ iff $(\forall p \in I^3)[(p_1 < 1 \wedge p_2 = 1 \rightarrow x_1(p) = 1) \wedge (p_1 = 1 \wedge p_2 < 1 \rightarrow x_2(p) = 1)]$.

Thus, if f belongs to $\mathcal{F}_{\{0\}}$, then f satisfies condition $\mathcal{N}$ iff whenever one of the injurers is negligent and the other is not then the negligent injurer bears the entire residual loss. On the other hand, if f belongs to $\mathcal{F}_{\{1,2\}}$, then f satisfies condition $\mathcal{N}$ iff whenever one of the injurers is negligent and the other is not then the negligent injurer bears the entire incremental loss.

Example 5. Note that while the $(1, 2)$-incremental liability rule in Example 2 violates condition $\mathcal{N}$, the one in Example 3 satisfies condition $\mathcal{N}$.

EFFICIENT $(1, 2)$-INCREMENTAL LIABILITY RULES IN $\mathcal{F}_{\{1,2\}}$

Proposition 1. If $f \in \mathcal{F}_{\{1,2\}}$ satisfies condition $\mathcal{N}$ then for every application satisfying assumptions (A1)–(A5), c^* is a Nash equilibrium.

Proof: Let $f \in \mathcal{F}_{\{1,2\}}$ satisfy condition $\mathcal{N}$. Consider any application of f. Suppose c^* is not a Nash equilibrium. This implies

$$(\exists i \in N)(\exists c_i \in C_i)[EC_i(c_i, c^*_{\sim i}) < EC_i(c^*)].$$

Suppose $EC_0(c_0, c_1^*, c_2^*) < EC_0(c^*)$.

$EC_0(c_0, c_1^*, c_2^*) < EC_0(c^*)$
$\rightarrow c_0 + R_{\{1,2\}}(c_0, c_1^*, c_2^*) < c_0^* + R_{\{1,2\}}(c^*)$
$\rightarrow c_0 + L(c_0, c_1^*, c_2^*) < c_0^* + L(c^*)$
$\rightarrow c_0 + c_1^* + c_2^* + L(c_0, c_1^*, c_2^*) < c_0^* + c_1^* + c_2^* + L(c^*)$.

This contradicts the fact that $c^* \in M$.

Therefore, $EC_0(c_0, c_1^*, c_2^*) < EC_0(c^*)$ cannot hold. (8.1)

Suppose $EC_1(c_0^*, c_1, c_2^*) < EC_1(c^*)$.
$EC_1(c_0^*, c_1, c_2^*) < EC_1(c^*)$
$\rightarrow c_1 + x_1(1, p_1(c_1), 1)S_{\{1,2\}}(c_0^*, c_1, c_2^*) < c_1^* + x_1^1 S_{\{1,2\}}(c^*)$
$\rightarrow c_1 + x_1(1, p_1(c_1), 1)S_{\{1,2\}}(c_0^*, c_1, c_2^*) < c_1^*$ (8.2)

Suppose $c_1 < c_1^*$.

$c_1 < c_1^* \rightarrow S_{\{1,2\}}(c_0^*, c_1, c_2^*) = L(c_0^*, c_1, c_2^*) - L(c^*)$.
$c_1 < c_1^*$ also implies $x_1(1, p_1(c_1), 1) = 1$ by condition $\mathcal{N}$.

Therefore, (8.2) implies $c_1 + L(c_0^*, c_1, c_2^*) - L(c^*) < c_1^*$

$\rightarrow c_1 + L(c_0^*, c_1, c_2^*) < c_1^* + L(c^*)$
$\rightarrow c_0^* + c_1 + c_2^* + L(c_0^*, c_1, c_2^*) < c_0^* + c_1^* + c_2^* + L(c^*)$.

This contradicts the fact that $c^* \in M$.
Therefore, $c_1 < c_1^* \rightarrow EC_1(c_0^*, c_1, c_2^*) < EC_1(c^*)$ cannot hold. (8.3)
Suppose $c_1 > c_1^*$.

$c_1 > c_1^* \rightarrow S_{\{1,2\}}(c_0^*, c_1, c_2^*) = 0$

Therefore, (8.2) $\rightarrow c_1 < c_1^*$.
This contradicts the supposition $c_1 > c_1^*$.
Therefore, $c_1 > c_1^* \rightarrow EC_1(c_0^*, c_1, c_2^*) < EC_1(c^*)$ cannot hold. (8.4)
(8.3) and (8.4) imply that $EC_1(c_0^*, c_1, c_2^*) < EC_1(c^*)$ cannot hold. (8.5)
A similar argument establishes that $EC_2(c_0^*, c_1^*, c_2) < EC_2(c^*)$ cannot hold. (8.6)

(8.1), (8.5) and (8.6) imply that $\sim (\exists i \in N)(\exists c_i \in C_i)[EC_i(c_i, c_{\sim i}^*) < EC_i(c^*)]$.
Therefore, c^* is a Nash equilibrium.

Proposition 2. *If $f \in \mathcal{F}_{\{1,2\}}$ satisfies condition $\mathcal{N}$, then for every application satisfying assumptions (A1)–(A5), $\bar{c}$ is a Nash equilibrium implies $\bar{c} \in M$.*

Proof: Let $f \in \mathcal{F}_{\{1,2\}}$ satisfy condition $\mathcal{N}$. Consider any application of f. Suppose $\bar{c}$ is a Nash equilibrium. This implies

$$(\forall c_0 \in C_0)[EC_0(\bar{c}) \le EC_0(c_0, \bar{c}_1, \bar{c}_2)] \tag{8.7}$$
$$\wedge (\forall c_1 \in C_1)[EC_1(\bar{c}) \le EC_1(\bar{c}_0, c_1, \bar{c}_2)] \tag{8.8}$$
$$\wedge (\forall c_2 \in C_2)[EC_2(\bar{c}) \le EC_2(\bar{c}_0, \bar{c}_1, c_2)] \tag{8.9}$$

$$(8.7) \to EC_0(\bar{c}) \le EC_0(c_0^*, \bar{c}_1, \bar{c}_2) \tag{8.10}$$
$$(8.8) \to EC_1(\bar{c}) \le EC_1(\bar{c}_0, c_1^*, \bar{c}_2) \tag{8.11}$$
$$(8.9) \to EC_2(\bar{c}) \le EC_2(\bar{c}_0, \bar{c}_1, c_2^*) \tag{8.12}$$

Adding (8.10), (8.11) and (8.12) we obtain

$T(\bar{c}) \le EC_0(c_0^*, \bar{c}_1, \bar{c}_2) + EC_1(\bar{c}_0, c_1^*, \bar{c}_2) + EC_2(\bar{c}_0, \bar{c}_1, c_2^*)$, which implies

$$T(\bar{c}) \le c_0^* + c_1^* + c_2^* + R_{\{1,2\}}(c_0^*, \bar{c}_1, \bar{c}_2) + x_1(p_0(\bar{c}_0), p_1(c_1^*), p_2(\bar{c}_2))S_{\{1,2\}}$$
$$(\bar{c}_0, c_1^*, \bar{c}_2) + x_2(p_0(\bar{c}_0), p_1(\bar{c}_1), p_2(c_2^*))S_{\{1,2\}}(\bar{c}_0, \bar{c}_1, c_2^*) \tag{8.13}$$

$\bar{c}_1 < c_1^* \to x_2(p_0(\bar{c}_0), p_1(\bar{c}_1), p_2(c_2^*)) = 0$ and $\bar{c}_2 < c_2^* \to x_1(p_0(\bar{c}_0), p_1(c_1^*), p_2(\bar{c}_2)) = 0$.
$\bar{c}_1 \ge c_1^* \to S_{\{1,2\}}(\bar{c}_0, \bar{c}_1, c_2^*) = 0$ and $\bar{c}_2 \ge c_2^* \to S_{\{1,2\}}(\bar{c}_0, c_1^*, \bar{c}_2) = 0$.
$\bar{c}_1 < c_1^* \vee \bar{c}_2 < c_2^* \to R_{\{1,2\}}(c_0^*, \bar{c}_1, \bar{c}_2) \le L(c^*)$.
$\bar{c}_1 \ge c_1^* \wedge \bar{c}_2 \ge c_2^* \to R_{\{1,2\}}(c_0^*, \bar{c}_1, \bar{c}_2) = L(c_0^*, \bar{c}_1, \bar{c}_2) \le L(c^*)$.

Thus, $x_1(p_0(\bar{c}_0), p_1(c_1^*), p_2(\bar{c}_2))S_{\{1,2\}}(\bar{c}_0, c_1^*, \bar{c}_2) = x_2(p_0(\bar{c}_0), p_1(\bar{c}_1), p_2(c_2^*))$
$S_{\{1,2\}}(\bar{c}_0, \bar{c}_1, c_2^*) = 0$ and $R_{\{1,2\}}(c_0^*, \bar{c}_1, \bar{c}_2) \le L(c^*)$ for all $\bar{c} \in C$.
Therefore, (8.13) implies $T(\bar{c}) \le c_0^* + c_1^* + c_2^* + L(c^*)$.
This, in view of the fact that $c^* \in M$, implies $\bar{c} \in M$.

Proposition 3. *If $f \in \mathcal{F}_{\{1,2\}}$ is efficient for every application satisfying assumptions (A1)–(A5), then f satisfies condition $\mathcal{N}$.*

Proof: Let f be a (1, 2)-incremental liability rule in $\mathcal{F}_{\{1,2\}}$. Suppose f violates $\mathcal{N}$. Then $(\exists(p_0, p_1, p_2) \in [0, 1]^3)[p_1 < 1 \wedge p_2 = 1 \wedge x_1(p_0, p_1, p_2) \ne 1] \vee (\exists(p_0, p_1, p_2) \in [0, 1]^3)[p_1 = 1 \wedge p_2 < 1 \wedge x_2(p_0, p_1, p_2) \ne 1]$.

Suppose $(\exists(p_0, p_1, p_2) \in [0, 1]^3)[p_1 < 1 \wedge p_2 = 1 \wedge x_1(p_0, p_1, p_2) \ne 1]$.
Let $P = \{(p_0, p_1, p_2) \in [0, 1]^3 \mid p_1 < 1 \wedge p_2 = 1 \wedge x_1(p_0, p_1, p_2) \ne 1\}$. Choose $(\delta, \theta, 1) \in P$ such that $\theta < \theta'$ for all $(\delta, \theta', 1) \in P$. Let k be a positive number. $0 \le x_1(\delta, \theta, 1)k < k$. Choose t such that $x_1(\delta, \theta, 1)k < t < k$.

Let $v = \frac{t}{1-\theta}$. Also choose numbers u, w and ε such that $u > 0, \varepsilon < 0$ and $w + \varepsilon > k$. Let $C_0 = \{0, \delta u, u\}$, $C_1 = \{0, \theta v, v\}$ and $C_2 = \{0, w\}$. Let L be specified as follows:

(c_0, c_1, c_2)	$L(c_0, c_1, c_2)$
$(0, 0, 0)$	$u + \theta v + k + w + \varepsilon$
$(0, 0, w)$	$u + \theta v + k$
$(0, \theta v, 0)$	$u + k + w + \varepsilon$
$(0, \theta v, w)$	$u + k$
$(0, v, 0)$	$u + w + \varepsilon$
$(0, v, w)$	u
$(\delta u, 0, 0)$	$(1 - \delta)u + \theta v + k + w + \varepsilon$
$(\delta u, 0, w)$	$(1 - \delta)u + \theta v + k$
$(\delta u, \theta v, 0)$	$(1 - \delta)u + k + w + \varepsilon$
$(\delta u, \theta v, w)$	$(1 - \delta)u + k$
$(\delta u, v, 0)$	$(1 - \delta)u + w + \varepsilon$
$(\delta u, v, w)$	$(1 - \delta)u$
$(u, 0, 0)$	$\theta v + k + w + \varepsilon$
$(u, 0, w)$	$\theta v + k$
$(u, \theta v, 0)$	$k + w + \varepsilon$
$(u, \theta v, w)$	k
$(u, v, 0)$	$w + \varepsilon$
(u, v, w)	0

Note that $k > t = v(1 - \theta)$ and $\varepsilon < 0$ imply $M = \{(0, v, 0), (\delta u, v, 0), (u, v, 0)\}$. Let $(c_0^*, c_1^*, c_2^*) = (u, v, 0)$.

Note that the application satisfies assumptions (A1)–(A5).

$EC_0(\delta u, \theta v, 0) = \delta u + R_{\{1,2\}}(\delta u, \theta v, 0) = \delta u + L(\delta u, v, 0) = \delta u + (1 - \delta)u + w + \varepsilon = u + w + \varepsilon$;
$EC_0(0, \theta v, 0) = R_{\{1,2\}}(0, \theta v, 0) = L(0, v, 0) = u + w + \varepsilon$;
$EC_0(u, \theta v, 0) = u + R_{\{1,2\}}(u, \theta v, 0) = u + L(u, v, 0) = u + w + \varepsilon$.
Therefore $EC_0(\delta u, \theta v, 0) = EC_0(u, \theta v, 0) = EC_0(0, \theta v, 0)$. $\qquad$ (8.14)

$EC_1(\delta u, \theta v, 0) = \theta v + x_1(\delta, \theta, 1)S_{\{1,2\}}(\delta u, \theta v, 0) = \theta v + x_1(\delta, \theta, 1)$
$[L(\delta u, \theta v, 0) - L(\delta u, v, 0)] = \theta v + x_1(\delta, \theta, 1)[(1 - \delta)u + k + w + \varepsilon - (1 - \delta)u - w - \varepsilon] = \theta v + x_1(\delta, \theta, 1)k$;
$EC_1(\delta u, 0, 0) = x_1(\delta, 0, 1)S_{\{1,2\}}(\delta u, 0, 0) = [L(\delta u, 0, 0) - L(\delta u, v, 0)]$
$= [(1 - \delta)u + \theta v + k + w + \varepsilon - (1 - \delta)u - w - \varepsilon] = \theta v + k$;
$EC_1(\delta u, v, 0) = v + x_1(\delta, 1, 1)S_{\{1,2\}}(\delta u, v, 0) = v$.
$EC_1(\delta u, v, 0) - EC_1(\delta u, \theta v, 0) = (1 - \theta)v - x_1(\delta, \theta, 1)k$
$= t - x_1(\delta, \theta, 1)k > 0$.

$EC_1(\delta u, 0, 0) - EC_1(\delta u, \theta v, 0) = \theta v + k - \theta v - x_1(\delta, \theta, 1)k > 0.$
Therefore, $EC_1(\delta u, \theta v, 0) < EC_1(\delta u, v, 0), EC_1(\delta u, 0, 0).$ $\hspace{1cm}$ (8.15)

$EC_2(\delta u, \theta v, 0) = x_2(\delta, \theta, 1)S_{\{1,2\}}(\delta u, \theta v, 0) = x_2(\delta, \theta, 1)[L(\delta u, \theta v, 0)$
$- L(\delta u, v, 0)] = x_2(\delta, \theta, 1)[(1 - \delta)u + k + w + \varepsilon - (1 - \delta)u - w - \varepsilon]$
$= x_2(\delta, \theta, 1)k;$
$EC_2(\delta u, \theta v, w) = w + x_2(\delta, \theta, 1)S_{\{1,2\}}(\delta u, \theta v, w) = w.$
$EC_2(\delta u, \theta v, w) - EC_2(\delta u, \theta v, 0) = w - x_2(\delta, \theta, 1)k > 0.$
Therefore, $EC_2(\delta u, \theta v, 0) < EC_2(\delta u, \theta v, w).$ $\hspace{1cm}$ (8.16)

(8.14), (8.15) and (8.16) imply that $(\delta u, \theta v, 0)$ is a Nash equilibrium. This, in view of the fact that $(\delta u, \theta v, 0)$ does not minimize the total social costs, imply that if $(\exists (p_0, p_1, p_2) \in [0, 1]^3)[p_1 < 1 \wedge p_2 = 1 \wedge x_1(p_0, p_1, p_2) \neq 1]$ then f is not efficient. $\hspace{1cm}$ (8.17)

An analogous argument establishes that if $(\exists (p_0, p_1, p_2) \in [0, 1]^3)[p_1 = 1 \wedge p_2 < 1 \wedge x_2(p_0, p_1, p_2) \neq 1]$ then f is not efficient. $\hspace{1cm}$ (8.18)

(8.17) and (8.18) imply that if f is efficient then f satisfies $\mathcal{N}$.

Theorem 1. $f \in \mathcal{F}_{\{1,2\}}$ *is efficient for every application satisfying assumptions (A1)–(A5) iff it satisfies condition* $\mathcal{N}$.

Proof. Immediate from Propositions 1, 2 and 3.

EFFICIENT $(1, 2)$-INCREMENTAL LIABILITY RULES IN $\mathcal{F}_{\{0\}}$

Proposition 4. *If* $f \in \mathcal{F}_{\{0\}}$ *satisfies condition* $\mathcal{N}$, *then for every application satisfying assumptions (A1)–(A5),* c^* *is a Nash equilibrium.*

Proof: Let $f \in \mathcal{F}_{\{0\}}$ satisfy condition $\mathcal{N}$. Consider any application of f. Suppose c^* is not a Nash equilibrium. This implies

$(\exists i \in N)(\exists c_i \in C_i)[EC_i(c_i, c^*_{\sim i}) < EC_i(c^*)].$

Suppose $EC_0(c_0, c_1^*, c_2^*) < EC_0(c^*).$

$EC_0(c_0, c_1^*, c_2^*) < EC_0(c^*) \rightarrow c_0 + S_{\{0\}}(c_0, c_1^*, c_2^*) < c_0^* + S_{\{0\}}(c^*)$ $\hspace{0.5cm}$ (8.19)

Suppose $c_0 < c_0^*.$
Then (8.19)$\rightarrow c_0 + L(c_0, c_1^*, c_2^*) - L(c^*) < c_0^*$
$\rightarrow c_0 + L(c_0, c_1^*, c_2^*) < c_0^* + L(c^*)$
$\rightarrow c_0 + c_1^* + c_2^* + L(c_0, c_1^*, c_2^*) < c_0^* + c_1^* + c_2^* + L(c^*).$

This contradicts the fact that $c^* \in M.$
Therefore, $c_0 < c_0^* \rightarrow EC_0(c_0, c_1^*, c_2^*) < EC_0(c^*)$ cannot hold. $\hspace{0.5cm}$ (8.20)

Suppose $c_0 > c_0^*$.

$$c_0 > c_0^* \rightarrow S_{\{0\}}(c_0, c_1^*, c_2^*) = 0$$

Therefore, $(8.19) \rightarrow c_0 < c_0^*$.
This contradicts the supposition $c_0 > c_0^*$.
Therefore, $c_0 > c_0^* \rightarrow EC_0(c_0, c_1^*, c_2^*) < EC_0(c^*)$ cannot hold. $\qquad$ (8.21)
(8.20) and (8.21) imply that $EC_0(c_0, c_1^*, c_2^*) < EC_0(c^*)$ cannot hold. $\qquad$ (8.22)
Suppose $EC_1(c_0^*, c_1, c_2^*) < EC_1(c^*)$.

$$EC_1(c_0^*, c_1, c_2^*) < EC_1(c^*)$$
$$\rightarrow c_1 + x_1(1, p_1(c_1), 1)R_{\{0\}}(c_0^*, c_1, c_2^*) < c_1^* + x_1^1 R_{\{0\}}(c^*)$$
$$\rightarrow c_1 + x_1(1, p_1(c_1), 1)[L(c_0^*, c_1, c_2^*) - S_{\{0\}}(c_0^*, c_1, c_2^*)] < c_1^* + x_1^1$$
$$[L(c^*) - S_{\{0\}}(c^*)]$$
$$\rightarrow c_1 + x_1(1, p_1(c_1), 1)L(c_0^*, c_1, c_2^*) < c_1^* + x_1^1 L(c^*) \qquad (8.23)$$

Suppose $c_1 < c_1^*$.
$c_1 < c_1^* \rightarrow x_1(1, p_1(c_1), 1) = 1$ by condition $\mathcal{N}$; and $x_1^1 \leq 1$ by definition. Therefore, (8.23) implies $c_1 + L(c_0^*, c_1, c_2^*) < c_1^* + L(c^*)$
$\rightarrow c_0^* + c_1 + c_2^* + L(c_0^*, c_1, c_2^*) < c_0^* + c_1^* + c_2^* + L(c^*)$.
This contradicts the fact that $c^* \in M$.
Therefore, $c_1 < c_1^*$ implies that $EC_1(c_0^*, c_1, c_2^*) < EC_1(c^*)$ cannot hold. $\qquad$ (8.24)
Suppose $c_1 > c_1^*$.
$c_1 > c_1^* \rightarrow x_1(1, p_1(c_1), 1) = x_1^1$ by definition of $p_1(c_1)$.
Therefore, (8.23) implies
$$c_1 + x_1^1 L(c_0^*, c_1, c_2^*) < c_1^* + x_1^1 L(c^*). \qquad (8.25)$$
$c_1 > c_1^*$ also implies $L(c_0^*, c_1, c_2^*) \leq L(c^*)$ by assumption (A4) and this in view of the fact that $x_1^1 \leq 1$ implies

$$(1 - x_1^1)L(c_0^*, c_1, c_2^*) \leq (1 - x_1^1)L(c^*). \qquad (8.26)$$

Adding (8.25) and (8.26) and then adding $c_0^* + c_2^*$ to both sides of the resulting inequality we obtain $c_0^* + c_1 + c_2^* + L(c_0^*, c_1, c_2^*) < c_0^* + c_1^* + c_2^* + L(c^*)$.
This contradicts the fact that $c^* \in M$.
Therefore, $c_1 > c_1^*$ implies that $EC_1(c_0^*, c_1, c_2^*) < EC_1(c^*)$ cannot hold. $\qquad$ (8.27)
(8.24) and (8.27), imply that $EC_1(c_0^*, c_1, c_2^*) < EC_1(c^*)$ cannot hold. $\qquad$ (8.28)

A similar argument establishes that $EC_2(c_0^*, c_1^*, c_2) < EC_2(c^*)$ cannot hold. $\qquad$ (8.29)

(8.22), (8.28) and (8.29) imply that $\sim (\exists i \in N)(\exists c_i \in C_i)[EC_i(c_i, c^*_{\sim i}) < EC_i(c^*)]$.
Therefore, c^* is a Nash equilibrium.

Proposition 5. *If $f \in \mathcal{F}_{\{0\}}$ satisfies condition $\mathcal{N}$ then for every application satisfying assumptions (A1)–(A5), $\bar{c}$ is a Nash equilibrium implies $\bar{c} \in M$.*

Proof: Let $f \in \mathcal{F}_{\{0\}}$ satisfy condition $\mathcal{N}$. Consider any application of f. Suppose $\bar{c}$ is a Nash equilibrium.

$\bar{c}$ is a Nash equilibrium implies

$$(\forall c_0 \in C_0)[EC_0(\bar{c}) \le EC_0(c_0, \bar{c}_1, \bar{c}_2)] \tag{8.30}$$
$$\wedge(\forall c_1 \in C_1)[EC_1(\bar{c}) \le EC_1(\bar{c}_0, c_1, \bar{c}_2)] \tag{8.31}$$
$$\wedge(\forall c_2 \in C_2)[EC_2(\bar{c}) \le EC_2(\bar{c}_0, \bar{c}_1, c_2)] \tag{8.32}$$

$$(8.30) \to EC_0(\bar{c}) \le EC_0(c^*_0, \bar{c}_1, \bar{c}_2) \tag{8.33}$$
$$(8.31) \to EC_1(\bar{c}) \le EC_1(\bar{c}_0, c^*_1, \bar{c}_2) \tag{8.34}$$
$$(8.32) \to EC_2(\bar{c}) \le EC_2(\bar{c}_0, \bar{c}_1, c^*_2) \tag{8.35}$$

Adding (8.33), (8.34) and (8.35) we obtain

$$T(\bar{c}) \le EC_0(c^*_0, \bar{c}_1, \bar{c}_2) + EC_1(\bar{c}_0, c^*_1, \bar{c}_2) + EC_2(\bar{c}_0, \bar{c}_1, c^*_2) \tag{8.36}$$

$$(8.36) \to T(\bar{c}) \le c^*_0 + c^*_1 + c^*_2 + S_{\{0\}}(c^*_0, \bar{c}_1, \bar{c}_2) + x_1(p_0(\bar{c}_0), 1, p_2(\bar{c}_2))$$
$$R_{\{0\}}(\bar{c}_0, c^*_1, \bar{c}_2) + x_2(p_0(\bar{c}_0), p_1(\bar{c}_1), 1)R_{\{0\}}(\bar{c}_0, \bar{c}_1, c^*_2) \tag{8.37}$$

$\bar{c}_1 < c^*_1 \to x_2(p_0(\bar{c}_0), p_1(\bar{c}_1), 1) = 0$ and $\bar{c}_2 < c^*_2 \to x_1(p_0(\bar{c}_0), 1, p_2(\bar{c}_2)) = 0$.

$\bar{c}_0 < c^*_0 \wedge \bar{c}_1 \ge c^*_1 \to R_{\{0\}}(\bar{c}_0, \bar{c}_1, c^*_2) = L(\bar{c}_0, \bar{c}_1, c^*_2) - S_{\{0\}}(\bar{c}_0, \bar{c}_1, c^*_2)$
$= L(c^*_0, \bar{c}_1, c^*_2) \le L(c^*)$.

$\bar{c}_0 < c^*_0 \wedge \bar{c}_2 \ge c^*_2 \to R_{\{0\}}(\bar{c}_0, c^*_1, \bar{c}_2) = L(\bar{c}_0, c^*_1, \bar{c}_2) - S_{\{0\}}(\bar{c}_0, c^*_1, \bar{c}_2)$
$= L(c^*_0, c^*_1, \bar{c}_2) \le L(c^*)$.

$\bar{c}_0 \ge c^*_0 \wedge \bar{c}_1 \ge c^*_1 \to R_{\{0\}}(\bar{c}_0, \bar{c}_1, c^*_2) = L(\bar{c}_0, \bar{c}_1, c^*_2) \le L(c^*)$.

$\bar{c}_0 \ge c^*_0 \wedge \bar{c}_2 \ge c^*_2 \to R_{\{0\}}(\bar{c}_0, c^*_1, \bar{c}_2) = L(\bar{c}_0, c^*_1, \bar{c}_2) \le L(c^*)$.

$S_{\{0\}}(c^*_0, \bar{c}_1, \bar{c}_2) = 0$.

If $\bar{c}_1 < c^*_1 \wedge \bar{c}_2 < c^*_2$ then (8.37) implies
$T(\bar{c}) \le c^*_0 + c^*_1 + c^*_2 \le c^*_0 + c^*_1 + c^*_2 + L(c^*)$.

If $\bar{c}_1 < c^*_1 \wedge \bar{c}_2 \ge c^*_2$ then (8.37) implies
$T(\bar{c}) \le c^*_0 + c^*_1 + c^*_2 + x_1(p_0(\bar{c}_0), 1, 1)L(c^*) \le c^*_0 + c^*_1 + c^*_2 + L(c^*)$.

If $\bar{c}_1 \ge c^*_1 \wedge \bar{c}_2 < c^*_2$ then (8.37) implies
$T(\bar{c}) \le c^*_0 + c^*_1 + c^*_2 + x_2(p_0(\bar{c}_0), 1, 1)L(c^*) \le c^*_0 + c^*_1 + c^*_2 + L(c^*)$.

If $\bar{c}_1 \ge c^*_1 \wedge \bar{c}_2 \ge c^*_2$ then (8.37) implies

$$T(\overline{c}) \leq c_0^* + c_1^* + c_2^* + x_1(p_0(\overline{c}_0), 1, 1)L(c^*) + x_2(p_0(\overline{c}_0), 1, 1)L(c^*)$$
$$\leq c_0^* + c_1^* + c_2^* + L(c^*).$$

Therefore, (8.37) implies $T(\overline{c}) \leq c_0^* + c_1^* + c_2^* + L(c^*)$.
This, in view of the fact that $c^* \in M$, implies $\overline{c} \in M$.

Proposition 6. *If $f \in \mathcal{F}_{\{0\}}$ is efficient for every application satisfying assumptions (A1)–(A5), then f satisfies condition $\mathcal{N}$.*

Proof: Let f be a $(1, 2)$-incremental liability rule in $\mathcal{F}_{\{0\}}$. Suppose f violates $\mathcal{N}$. Then $(\exists(p_0, p_1, p_2) \in [0, 1]^3)[p_1 < 1 \wedge p_2 = 1 \wedge x_1(p_0, p_1, p_2) \neq 1] \vee (\exists(p_0, p_1, p_2) \in [0, 1]^3)[p_1 = 1 \wedge p_2 < 1 \wedge x_2(p_0, p_1, p_2) \neq 1]$.

Suppose $(\exists(p_0, p_1, p_2) \in [0, 1]^3)[p_1 < 1 \wedge p_2 = 1 \wedge x_1(p_0, p_1, p_2) \neq 1]$. Let $P = \{(p_0, p_1, p_2) \in [0, 1]^3 \mid p_1 < 1 \wedge p_2 = 1 \wedge x_1(p_0, p_1, p_2) \neq 1\}$. Choose $(\delta, \theta, 1) \in P$ such that $\theta < \theta'$ for all $(\delta, \theta', 1) \in P$.

Choose numbers k, w and ε such that $k > 0$, $\varepsilon < 0$, $w + \varepsilon > 0$ and $x_1(\delta, \theta, 1)[k + w + \varepsilon] < k$. Choose t such that $x_1(\delta, \theta, 1)[k + w + \varepsilon] < t < k$. Let $v = \frac{t}{1-\theta}$. Also choose $u > 0$.
Let $C_0 = \{0, \delta u, u\}$, $C_1 = \{0, \theta v, v\}$ and $C_2 = \{0, w\}$. Let L be specified as follows:

(c_0, c_1, c_2)	$L(c_0, c_1, c_2)$
$(0, 0, 0)$	$u + \theta v + k + w + \varepsilon$
$(0, 0, w)$	$u + \theta v + k$
$(0, \theta v, 0)$	$u + k + w + \varepsilon$
$(0, \theta v, w)$	$u + k$
$(0, v, 0)$	$u + w + \varepsilon$
$(0, v, w)$	u
$(\delta u, 0, 0)$	$(1 - \delta)u + \theta v + k + w + \varepsilon$
$(\delta u, 0, w)$	$(1 - \delta)u + \theta v + k$
$(\delta u, \theta v, 0)$	$(1 - \delta)u + k + w + \varepsilon$
$(\delta u, \theta v, w)$	$(1 - \delta)u + k$
$(\delta u, v, 0)$	$(1 - \delta)u + w + \varepsilon$
$(\delta u, v, w)$	$(1 - \delta)u$
$(u, 0, 0)$	$\theta v + k + w + \varepsilon$
$(u, 0, w)$	$\theta v + k$
$(u, \theta v, 0)$	$k + w + \varepsilon$
$(u, \theta v, w)$	k
$(u, v, 0)$	$w + \varepsilon$
(u, v, w)	0

Note that $k > t = v(1 - \theta)$ and $\varepsilon < 0$ imply $M = \{(0, v, 0), (\delta u, v, 0), (u, v, 0)\}$. Let $(c_0^*, c_1^*, c_2^*) = (u, v, 0)$.

Note that the application satisfies assumptions (A1)–(A5).

$EC_0(\delta u, \theta v, 0) = \delta u + S_{\{0\}}(\delta u, \theta v, 0) = \delta u + L(\delta u, \theta v, 0) - L(u, \theta v, 0)$
$= \delta u + (1 - \delta)u + k + w + \varepsilon - k - w - \varepsilon = u;$
$EC_0(0, \theta v, 0) = S_{\{0\}}(0, \theta v, 0) = L(0, \theta v, 0) - L(u, \theta v, 0) = u + k + w$
$+ \varepsilon - k - w - \varepsilon = u;$
$EC_0(u, \theta v, 0) = u + S_{\{0\}}(u, \theta v, 0) = u.$
Therefore $EC_0(\delta u, \theta v, 0) = EC_0(u, \theta v, 0) = EC_0(0, \theta v, 0).$ \hfill (8.38)

$EC_1(\delta u, \theta v, 0) = \theta v + x_1(\delta, \theta, 1)R_{\{0\}}(\delta u, \theta v, 0) = \theta v + x_1(\delta, \theta, 1)$
$L(u, \theta v, 0) = \theta v + x_1(\delta, \theta, 1)[k + w + \varepsilon];$
$EC_1(\delta u, 0, 0) = x_1(\delta, 0, 1)R_{\{0\}}(\delta u, 0, 0) = L(u, 0, 0) = \theta v + k + w + \varepsilon;$
$EC_1(\delta u, v, 0) = v + x_1(\delta, 1, 1)R_{\{0\}}(\delta u, v, 0) = v + x_1(\delta, 1, 1)L(u, v, 0) =$
$v + x_1(\delta, 1, 1)[w + \varepsilon].$
$EC_1(\delta u, v, 0) - EC_1(\delta u, \theta v, 0) = v + x_1(\delta, 1, 1)[w + \varepsilon] - \theta v - x_1(\delta, \theta, 1)$
$[k + w + \varepsilon] = (1 - \theta)v - x_1(\delta, \theta, 1)[k + w + \varepsilon] + x_1(\delta, 1, 1)[w + \varepsilon] =$
$t - x_1(\delta, \theta, 1)[k + w + \varepsilon] + x_1(\delta, 1, 1)[w + \varepsilon] > 0.$
$EC_1(\delta u, 0, 0) - EC_1(\delta u, \theta v, 0) = \theta v + k + w + \varepsilon - \theta v - x_1(\delta, \theta, 1)$
$[k + w + \varepsilon] = [1 - x_1(\delta, \theta, 1)][k + w + \varepsilon] > 0.$
Therefore $EC_1(\delta u, \theta v, 0) < EC_1(\delta u, v, 0), EC_1(\delta u, 0, 0).$ \hfill (8.39)

$EC_2(\delta u, \theta v, 0) = x_2(\delta, \theta, 1)R_{\{0\}}(\delta u, \theta v, 0) = x_2(\delta, \theta, 1)L(u, \theta v, 0)$
$= x_2(\delta, \theta, 1)[k + w + \varepsilon];$
$EC_2(\delta u, \theta v, w) = w + x_2(\delta, \theta, 1)R_{\{0\}}(\delta u, \theta v, w) = w + x_2(\delta, \theta, 1)$
$L(u, \theta v, w) = w + x_2(\delta, \theta, 1)k.$
$EC_2(\delta u, \theta v, w) - EC_2(\delta u, \theta v, 0) = w + x_2(\delta, \theta, 1)k - x_2(\delta, \theta, 1)$
$[k + w + \varepsilon] = w - x_2(\delta, \theta, 1)[w + \varepsilon] > 0.$
Therefore $EC_2(\delta u, \theta v, 0) < EC_2(\delta u, \theta v, w).$ \hfill (8.40)

(8.38), (8.39) and (8.40) imply that $(\delta u, \theta v, 0)$ is a Nash equilibrium. This, in view of the fact that $(\delta u, \theta v, 0)$ does not minimize the total social costs, imply that if $(\exists(p_0, p_1, p_2) \in [0, 1]^3)[p_1 < 1 \wedge p_2 = 1 \wedge x_1(p_0, p_1, p_2) \neq 1]$ then f is not efficient. \hfill (8.41)
An analogous argument establishes that if $(\exists(p_0, p_1, p_2) \in [0, 1]^3)[p_1 = 1 \wedge p_2 < 1 \wedge x_2(p_0, p_1, p_2) \neq 1]$ then f is not efficient. \hfill (8.42)

(8.41) and (8.42) imply that if f is efficient then f satisfies $\mathcal{N}$.

Theorem 2. $f \in \mathcal{F}_{\{0\}}$ *is efficient for every application satisfying assumptions (A1)–(A5) iff it satisfies condition $\mathcal{N}$.*

Proof. Immediate from Propositions 4, 5 and 6.

CONCLUSION

This essay focuses on two specific classes of (1, 2)-incremental liability rules and provides necessary and sufficient conditions for efficient rules belonging to each of these classes. Rules in both these classes have the property that the same individuals always constitute the set of non-residual liability holders and they collectively bear the entire incremental loss that is attributable to their negligence. From the results obtained in the essay it is clear that not all rules under which the non-residual liability holders are always the same and are collectively liable for the entire incremental loss are efficient. This stands in contrast to the efficiency properties of incremental liability rules in the context of two-party interactions. From the characterisation of efficient incremental liability rules obtained in Jain (2009), it follows that every incremental liability rule which always designates the same individual as the non-residual liability holder and makes him bear the entire incremental loss due to his negligence is efficient. This divergence arises from the fact that unlike the two-party context, here the set of non-residual liability holders or the set of residual liability holders may have more than one individual. Consequently, depending upon the number of individuals in these sets, the apportionment of the incremental loss between the non-residual liability holders or the apportionment of the residual loss between the residual liability holders turns out to be crucial for efficiency.

REFERENCES

Brown, John Prather. 1973. 'Toward an Economic Theory of Liability', *Journal of Legal Studies*, 2: 323–50.

Calabresi, Guido. 1961. 'Some Thoughts on Risk Distribution and the Law of Torts', *Yale Law Journal*, 70: 499–553.

———. 1965. 'The Decision for Accidents: An Approach to Non-fault Allocation of Costs', *Harvard Law Review*, 78: 713–45.

———. 1970. *The Costs of Accidents: A Legal and Economic Analysis*. New Haven: Yale University Press.

Coase, Ronald H. 1960. 'The Problem of Social Cost', *Journal of Law and Economics*, 3: 386–405.

Diamond, Peter A. 1974. 'Accident Law and Resource Allocation', *Bell Journal of Economics*, 5(2): 366–405.

Jain, Satish K. 2009. 'The Structure of Incremental Liability Rules', *Review of Law and Economics*, 5(1): 373–98.

———. 2010. 'On the Efficiency of the Negligence Rule', *Journal of Economic Policy Reform*, 13(4): 343–59.

Jain, Satish K. and Rajendra P. Kundu. 2006. 'Characterization of Efficient Simple Liability Rules with Multiple Tortfeasors', *International Review of Law and Economics*, 26(3): 410–27.

Jain, Satish K. and Ram Singh. 2002. 'Efficient Liability Rules: Complete Characterization', *Journal of Economics (Zeitschrift für Nationalökonomie)*, 75: 105–24.

Kahan, M. 1989. 'Causation and Incentives to Take Care under the Negligence Rule', *Journal of Legal Studies*, 18(2): 427–47.

Kornhauser, Lewis A. and Richard L. Revesz. 1989. 'Sharing Damages among Multiple Tortfeasors', *Yale Law Journal*, 98(5): 831–84.

Landes, William M. and Richard A. Posner. 1980. 'Joint and Multiple Tortfeasors: An Economic Analysis', *Journal of Legal Studies*, 9(3):517–55.

———. 1987. *The Economic Structure of Tort Law*. Cambridge (MA): Harvard University Press.

Miceli, Thomas J. 1997. *Economics of the Law: Torts, Contracts, Property, Litigation*. New York: Oxford University Press.

Miceli, Thomas J. and Kathleen Segerson. 1991. 'Joint Liability in Torts: Marginal and Infra-marginal Efficiency', *International Review of Law and Economics*, 11(3): 235–49.

Posner, Richard A. 1972. 'A Theory of Negligence', *Journal of Legal Studies*, 1: 28–96.

———. 1973. 'Strict Liability: A Comment', *Journal of Legal Studies*, 2: 205–21.

Shavell, Steven. 1980. 'Strict Liability versus Negligence', *Journal of Legal Studies*, 9(1): 1–25.

———. 1987. *Economic Analysis of Accident Law*. Cambridge (MA): Harvard University Press.

Tietenberg, Tom H. 1989. 'Indivisible Toxic Torts: The Economics of Joint and Several Liability', *Land Economics*, 65(4): 305–19.

9

On Breach Remedies
*Contracting with Bilateral Selfish Investment and Two-sided Private Information**

Sugata Bag

INTRODUCTION

In this essay, we shall be presenting a model involving two-sided informational asymmetry and bilateral selfish investments. To introduce the analysis, suppose that two risk-neutral parties come together to exchange a specific commodity in the future. Both the parties invest in their respective valuations and costs, which enhance the social surplus when they trade. At the beginning, the parties know their respective distributions from which the values of the relevant parameters related to their valuations will be drawn. The parties individually learn the respective true valuations only after they invest; but these values are neither observable to the other party nor verifiable to the court and are, thus, private information. The parties will then continue their venture if the market favours the commodity, that is, if they can produce it at a particular cost and exchange it at a particular (predefined) price. Otherwise, disputes arise and they settle it in a court.

The essay deals with the question of whether the first-best outcome is possible (with or without the support of legal remedies), when investments undertaken in reliance by both the parties are unobservable and the good's value and cost are also private information (ex post). This problem is not trivial. Two distinct cases are identified. First, when there is a 'gap' between the supports of the seller's cost and the buyer's valuation. Second, when there is 'no gap' between the supports. In the 'gap' case, trade is always feasible. When it is common knowledge

* Based on a chapter of my doctoral thesis at JNU under the supervision of Prof. Satish Jain. It is my honour to contribute this essay for this book. I highly solicit suggestions from Priyodorshi Banerjee, ISI-Calcutta, and Abhijit Banerjee, DSE. All errors are mine.

between the parties that gains from trade exist, contract theory says that efficiency is attained quite trivially by a single-price mechanism: trade for sure at a price belongs to the gap. This is *incentive compatible*, since the outcome does not depend on the report. It also is *individually rational* (*IR*), since each party receives a non-negative pay-off in every realisation.[1] We thus concentrate on the non-trivial case where there is 'no gap'. The bargaining does not conclude with probability one after any finite number of periods. One basic question is whether the private information prevents the bargainers from reaping all possible gains from trade.

Myerson and Satterthwaite (1983) find that if there is a positive probability of gains from trade, but if it is not common knowledge that gains from trade exist, then no incentive compatible, individually rational, budget-balanced mechanism can be ex post efficient. In the *Groves–Clarke mechanism* (similar to Vickrey's [1961] second-price auction mechanism), both the parties have the incentive to truthfully announce their valuations to the court. Indeed, this is the only scheme where truth-telling is implementable as a dominant strategy (Green and Laffont 1979). Despite this very attractive feature, the Groves–Clarke mechanisms are problematic because they do not provide a *balanced budget* (*BB*). The 'basic' Groves mechanism generates an expected deficit. In other words, the 'basic' Groves mechanism satisfies *IR*, but violates *BB* whenever the expected gains from trade are positive. More general Groves mechanisms can try to finance the deficit by taxing the agents, but *IR* limits the magnitude of those taxes.

Whenever there is some uncertainty about whether trade is desirable, ex post efficient trade is impossible. For this reason, private information is a compelling explanation for the frequent occurrence of bargaining breakdowns or costly delays. Inefficiencies are a necessary consequence of the strong incentives for misrepresentation between the bargainers, each holding certain private information.

However, it is by now well known that ex post efficiency can be achieved in such a problem with quasi-linear utilities, if the parties can write a comprehensive contract ex ante, that is, before they privately learn their types.[2] It has been shown by Hermalin and Katz (1993), Konakayama et al. (1986) and Rogerson (1992) that comprehensive

---

[1] See, Ausubel et al. (March, 2001).
[2] See Arrow (1979) and D'Aspremont and Gérard-Varet (1979).

contracts can implement the first-best even if the parties' valuations are private information and reliance investments are of selfish types.

While optimal contracts that induce first-best trading under bilateral asymmetry are often quite complicated, real-world contracts seem to be rather simple. Most often the parties come up with fixed-price incomplete contracts, which are generally renegotiated later (if not prohibited by court). Hence, it is an interesting question to ask whether it is also possible to achieve the first-best in this case. Taking this route Schmitz (2002), using a mechanism design approach, demonstrates that voluntary bargaining over a collective decision under asymmetric information may well lead to ex post allocative efficiency as well as ex ante efficient reliance if the default decision is non-trivial (and the parties' valuations are symmetrically distributed). In a non-trivial default decision, he argues, the parties merely specify an unconditional level of trade, $q^o \in [0, 1]$, that is the default decision is an interior choice. His work was motivated by the solutions to hold-up problems using simple contracts that just specify a threatpoint for future negotiations, given that the parties are symmetrically informed.[3] However, all these elements of the literature are based on the premise that renegotiation can always exploit any inefficiency remaining after a contract has been written under a complete information setting. This assumption, unfortunately, does not seem compelling in an incomplete information setting. Any efficient renegotiation process must be *interim individually rational*, that is, having observed his/her private information, each party must always expect to become at least as well off from participating in the renegotiation process as from not participating and enforcing the existing contract. Otherwise, in some instances, efficient breach opportunities will be lost. Accordingly, we can directly apply the theorem of *MS* and state the impossibility of efficient renegotiation. As a consequence, ex post efficiency is still under question.

In the light of the preceding discussion, instead of renegotiation, this essay considers standard breach mechanisms (that specify a fixed compensation paid by the contract breacher) following the usual *subgame perfect Nash equilibrium method*. Under asymmetric information, when valuation problems are extreme, the legal proceedings (under common law and civil law countries) may either turn to assess the expectancy

---

[3] See Aghion et al. (1990, 1994), Chung (1991), Edlin (1996), Edlin and Reichelstein (1996) and Nöldeke and Schmidt (1995, 1998).

of the victim of breach or allow opting for reliance damages by the victim of breach. Generally, courts adopt two methods to establish the expectation interest of the victim—an objective method and a subjective method. Objective damage measures are based on prudent or reasonable investment behaviour and/or on the average type of a fictitious agent. By construction, these measures differ from subjective expectation damages that were required to compensate the promisee for her loss. We try to examine the efficacy of such practices and analyse whether these solutions to the valuation problem alleviate or exacerbate opportunistic behaviour by the parties. It begins with a standard analysis of the behavioural effects of restitution and reliance damages. It then proceeds to the application of expectation damage measures in a world where the courts are not perfectly informed about the parties' valuations of the contract.

In this essay, we find some interesting results: (*a*) as opposed to the conventional under-investment result under the Restitution (no-damage) remedy the restitution here both the parties tend to over-invest; (*b*) reliance damage remedy leads to conventional over-investment; (*c*) analysis of subjective valuation and objective valuation (expected expectation damage or EED)—two court-adopted methods of establishing the breach victim's expectation interest under asymmetric information—draws the conclusion that the EED is superior to the others but still falls short of what party-designed liquidated damage could achieve; (*d*) however, first-best is generally not achievable. We further establish two important but competing facts. First, the parties may deliberately use a high penalty as a liquidated damage to induce efficient relation–specific investment, which, however, may not induce ex post efficiency or augment social welfare. Second, the optimal rule that can be chosen ex post by the court under bilateral incomplete information corresponds to the EED rule that maximises social welfare but induces inefficient incentive to invest. These results complement the existing literature on the issue of optimal breach remedies, which has been mostly concerned with the ex ante efficiency issue, that is, inducing a correct level of relationship-specific investment when information is complete (and hence renegotiation is assumed to make the ex post outcome always efficient).[4]

---

[4] See Chung (1991), Edlin and Reichelstein (1996), Rogerson (1984, 1992), Shavell (1980) and Spier and Whinston (1995).

Related Literature

There are three types of literature that are closely related to the present analysis: the literature that addresses the efficiency of various contract remedies, the literature that compares the different information disclosure effects of these remedies, and finally the literature on the optimal accuracy of damages assessment.

Among the first type, there is a large volume of literature on the comparative advantage of various contract damages measures. For example, Barton (1972), Birmingham (1970), Goetz and Scott (1980), Miceli (2004) and Shavell (1980, 1984), among many others, have studied various damage measures for breach of contract and compared their efficiency. Edlin and Schwartz (2003) provide an excellent survey of this literature. Almost without exception these studies assume that the non-breaching party will always pursue a remedy for the contract breach regardless of her post-breach valuation. As a result, these studies ignore the endogenous option of the non-breaching party to not litigate the case if her post-breach valuation is smaller than the contracted price. In contrast, our model incorporates the embedded option to rationally acquiesce to a breach and demonstrates that this has important efficiency implications.

The second type of literature analyses the incentives to disclose private information that the various remedies provide.[5] Bebchuk–Shavell exhibited that awarding EED by the court induces better information disclosure at the contracting stage from the privately informed party and thus makes the estimation of expectation damage more accurate, leading to a more efficient breach decisions. As against this, we deal with a framework where the parties to the contract have no private information at the contracting stage; thus no information disclosure incentives need to be dealt with at that stage. However, the advantage of EED over actual expectation damages in our model emerges because: first, it maximises expected social pay-off; second, the breacher has distorted incentives to breach under actual damages as the non-breaching party may not file a lawsuit.

The final type of related literature deals with the accuracy of the appraisal of damages and its incentive effects on parties' primary behaviour.[6] These studies analyse the incentive effect of the accuracy of a court's assessment of damages on the victim's reliance,

---

[5] See Adler (1999), Ayres and Gertner (1989) and Bebchuk and Shavell (1991).

[6] See Kaplow and Shavell (1996); Spier (1994).

information acquisition and evidence production. These analyses focus on a unilateral-care tort model, where, under the most reasonable conditions (and ignoring litigation costs), the victim would always sue for damages. Conversely, in our contract-based model, the victim might choose not to pay the contracted price in return for actual damages when her post-breach valuation is low. As a result, the breaching party's performance incentives are again distorted. Friehe (2005) extends Kaplow and Shavell (1996) to a bilateral-care model and finds that the courts should utilise the information available to assess accurate damages. He also proposes using payments as an incentive to screen different types of victims and reduce the burden of assessment by inducing self-selection. However, even Friehe ignores the option of not sueing and assumes that the filing of a lawsuit is exogenously given.

Certain Issues Related to the Applicability of Damages

From a social point of view, private information is a barrier to mutually beneficial exchange; it is a type of transaction cost that may prevent parties from capturing a potential surplus or may lead them to enter into inefficient transactions. In the real world, the parties' private interest in keeping information private makes the goal of full information revelation within a particular market unattainable. Rather than revealing such information, parties will—often driven by a *secrecy interest*—prefer to forego suit in the event of breach, change their patterns of contracting and/or important aspects of the terms on which they deal, or forego the transaction entirely. As opposed to secrecy interest, there is a *compensatory interest* by the parties, which will compensate their expectation loss in the event of breach.

Thus the secrecy interest and the compensatory interest are often in direct conflict, and they cannot be reconciled simply by elevating one over the other ex post. When the secrecy interest is sufficiently strong, the cost of revealing the underlying private information may well exceed the aggrieved party's expected recovery from trial. As a consequence, the aggrieved party may not file suit and may, therefore, receive no compensation. As the breacher may be informed about the existence of the victim's secrecy interest, she may breach too often. On the other hand, if the victim of breach brings a suit and asks for expectation damage guided by compensatory interest, she will overstate her valuation, which is a pure rent-seeking motive.

Thus, from a policy perspective, the challenge is to structure legal rules in general, and damage remedies in particular, to achieve 'second-best' outcomes in transactional contexts that will always be characterised by asymmetric information.[7] In particular, damage measures like fully compensatory expectation damages that give efficient breach or perform incentives in an ideal world need to be replaced or supplemented by the measures that take into account the 'secrecy interest' of the aggrieved party and the type of discovery that will be available.

THE MODEL SETTING

To formalise the model, let two risk-neutral parties—a seller and a buyer—meet at Time 1 to consider a project. A specific commodity is to be supplied by the seller under this contract, which would be further used as an intermediary input by the buyer to manufacture a final good whose uncertain demand is yet to be seen in the market. The project will certainly fail unless both the parties invest in it, though it may still fail even if both invest. If the parties do not reach an agreement and thereby do no trade, then the investments undertaken by them are wasted, that is, their investments are fully of the relation-specific and selfish type. We consider a procurement contract between a seller and a buyer in a situation when after contracting, neither party can find any other buyer or seller in the market for the specific commodity, but some unforeseen contingencies may induce breach after an agreement has been reached. Thus it is a thin market, and investments are agent specific. The parties recognise this possibility, but may have the oppotunity to write a fixed-price contract. This price, essentially a device to divide the ex post surplus, depends on the relative bargaining strength of the parties. So, in the contract formation stage, they bargain over an ex ante price and may specify a damage remedy, which the breacher agrees to pay the victim in the event of not honouring the contractual obligations. Some

---

[7] The ex post revelation of information that is required by subjective damage measures and the rules of discovery may also reduce parties' incentives to either deliberately acquire certain types of information or to invest in the types of innovations and activities whose profitability is dependent on keeping information private. Consider a manufacturer, who invents a low cost production process for a product. If she brings a suit for damages against a supplier of a component, she will have to reveal her cost of production, which will induce her competitors to try to obtain information about her production process. First, protecting this type of information from revelation in such a suit would have the beneficial effect of preserving or enhancing parties' incentive to devise such innovations. Second, there are many contracting contexts in which protecting private information ex post is likely to create more efficient ex ante incentives to gather and use information.

of our discussion of breach remedies will be couched as if the remedy selection were made by courts.

Now let us describe the ex ante uncertainty features of the model. The first source derives from the seller's cost of production. And the second one comes from the buyer's valuation of the contract due to future fluctuations in the market prices of the products the buyer ultimately manufactures and sells. We assume here that the court cannot observe both the buyer's true valuation and the exact cost of performance by the seller; however, the court is able to fashion a noisy estimate of both valuation and cost out of the information provided by the buyer and the seller during the trial (upon breach). What is clear, however, is that by the time the parties' dispute is deliberated in the courts, both the parties will have learned the new market prices. The seller will know her costs and the buyer his valuation respectively at the individual level, but neither party is able to verify these valuations in the court. These therefore, private information of the individual parties. So, remain in the present model, there is two-dimensional ex post asymmetric information between the parties themselves and the court. When a dispute arises, this creates a problem for the court in terms of choosing a damage measure as the judge cannot credibly ascertain the expectation interest of the promisee.

The court can observe the written contract (which clearly specifies the good(s) to be delivered and the price to be paid) and can verify whether the good has been delivered and the price has been paid. Clearly, the courts can determine efficient remedies if they have sufficient information about the valuations of the parties. However, being unable to verify the buyer's value and the seller's cost in actual terms, the court is limited in its ability to remedy the dispute efficiently and thus often employs damages incorrectly, which leads to an inefficient outcome. We focus on the ex ante design of the contract in light of new information expected in future (and thus assume no renegotiation)[8] despite the fact

---

[8] Most literature that used fixed-price contracts required the assumption of costless renegotiation to be able to achieve the first-best outcome, an outcome which the contingent-contract literature was able to achieve without assuming costless renegotiation. A renegotiation game is, in reality, never costless ex post and hard to design ex ante. It is thus questionable whether writing a fixed-term contract and designing a renegotiation game (which itself should be renegotiation proof) is indeed simpler than writing a contingent contract (Schmitz 2002). It is, therefore, also questionable whether costless renegotiation is a more

that the specific investments by the parties increase their risk and pave a way for renegotiation.

Technical Assumption

It is assumed that the buyer's valuation of the good and the seller's cost of performance are dependent on respective transaction-specific reliance investments incurred by them at the individual level, as well as the respective private information they may hold ex post.

Thus the buyer's valuation is denoted by:

$$v = V(r^b) + \phi,$$

where, $\qquad E(v) = V(r^b), V'(r^b) > 0, V''(r^b) < 0, \forall r^b,$

further, $\qquad E(\phi) = 0, Var(\phi) = \sigma_\phi^2 \quad$ and $\quad r^b \in [0, r^{b\,max}].$

And the seller's cost of performance is denoted by:

$$c = C(r^s) + \theta,$$

where, $\qquad E(c) = C(r^s), C'(r^s) < 0, C''(r^s) > 0, \forall r^s$

further, $\qquad E(\theta) = 0, Var(\theta) = \sigma_\theta^2 \quad$ and $\quad r^s \in [0, r^{s\,max}].$

---

plausible assumption to make than the one we make here. Besides throughout the analysis, it is our maintained assumption that the parties' valuation(s) are not observable even at the stage when parties decide to perform or breach, thus under this kind of asymmetric participation, the renegotiation is probably more costly than when parties' valuations are observable. Indeed, models which account for renegotiation typically assume that parties' valuations at the trade-or-renegotiate stage are observable. Although making renegotiation less costly, the observability assumption (which we do not make) is quite restrictive (see Chung 1992, Edlin and Reichelstein 1996, Hart and Moore 1999, Spier and Whinston 1995). Third, some have argued that the parties may find ways to commit not to renegotiate or at least find ways to significantly raise the costs of renegotiation. Maskin and Tirole (1999) analyse several ways by which the parties can commit not to renegotiate (but see Hart and Moore 1999). Thus, our model also captures situations where the parties were able to commit to not renegotiate. As Hart and Moore (1999) have noted, the degree of the parties' ability to commit not to renegotiate 'is something about which reasonable people can disagree'. Thus, they argue, both the cases where the parties can and cannot commit not to renegotiate are worthy of study. Lastly, even if renegotiation were simple and costless, our forthcoming result shows that there is no room for it under two-sided asymmetry.

Here θ and ϕ represent the information parameters held respectively by the seller and the buyer. Each of these information parameters is a random variable and can be thought of as the agents' type; once realised by one particular agent, it is not observed by the other agent and thus is not contractible. So a contract cannot directly depend upon it. Let $f(.)$ and $F(.)$ respectively be the probability density function and the corresponding distribution function of the seller's uncertainty component θ, while $g(.)$ and $G(.)$ represent the same for the buyer. We assume that $f(.)$ and $g(.)$ are continuous and positive on their respective domains and are independent that is, the seller's private information does not affect the buyer's valuation for the object and vice versa. The distributions $f(.)$ and $g(.)$ are common knowledge between the parties and follow the monotone hazard property. Figure 9.1 provides a stylised representation of the agents' value and cost.

In the figure 9.1, the buyer's expected valuation $E(v) = V(r^b)$ is continuously increasing in r^b up till $r^b max$; whereas the seller's expected cost $E(c) = C(r^s)$ is decreasing in r^s. There is a starting gap between the expected value and cost of the agents, which diverges further as the parties invest more. However, there can be "no-gap" between the supports of the seller's cost and the buyer's valuation in some contingencies depending upon the particular realisation of θ and ϕ (like the one shown), say $[C(r^s) + \theta_1 =:]c_I > v_I[:= V(r^b) + \phi_1]$.

In the face of two-sided ex post private information, ex ante trading opportunity between the parties arises whenever $E(v) \geq E(c)$, that is, whenever the buyer's expected valuation is larger than the seller's

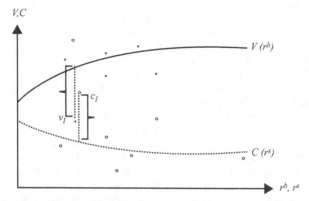

Figure 9.1 A stylised representation of the agents' value and cost

expected cost in Time 1, they may find the contracting worthwhile. Without any loss of generality, we assume here that the buyer holds the entire bargaining power and thereby she sets a very low price P in such a way (so close to $E(c)$, with very little surplus from the contract) that only the seller faces the option to breach unilaterally. Note here, in this particular kind of set-up, that either party can contemplate breaching the contract whenever the cost of performance is higher than the value. But we shall restrict our analysis to unilateral breach by the seller; this does not affect any other aspect. The analysis of breach by the buyer is just similar to that of the seller.

Proposition 1. The First-Best. *The optimum level of reliance investments under two-sided informational asymmetry must not only be lower when compared to the social optimum under complete information but also less than the optimum levels of reliance under one-sided informational asymmetry.*

Proof: We provide the proof in three simple steps.

Step 1: The first best is achieved if the ex ante investment decision and the ex post trade decision are efficiently made. Therefore, following the convention, before the realisation of c and v, the probability of efficient performance under two-sided informational asymmetry is:

$$
\begin{aligned}
&\Pr[\text{efficient performance}] \\
&= \Pr[c \le v] = \Pr[C(r^s) + \theta \le V(r^b) + \phi] \\
&= \Pr[\theta - \phi \le V(r^b) - C(r^s)] = \Pr[\xi \le V(r^b) - C(r^s)] \\
&= H[V(r^b) - C(r^s)],
\end{aligned}
\tag{9.1}
$$

where $\xi = (\theta - \phi) \backsim h(0, \sigma_\theta^2 + \sigma_\phi^2)$, therefore, θ and ϕ are independent. And,

$$
\Pr[\text{efficient breach}] = 1 - H[V(r^b) - C(r^s)]
\tag{9.2}
$$

This completes the analysis of the efficient breach decision. Given the efficient breach decision, the other issue is to determine the efficient amount of reliance. Given the efficient probability of breach, the socially efficient reliance investment by the buyer is that which maximises the joint expected value of the contract. The expected joint value is defined as:

$$EPJ = [1 - H[V(r^b) - C(r^s)]].(0 - r^b - r^s)$$
$$+ H[V(r^b) - C(r^s)].\{[E(v) - r^b - P] + [P - r^s - E(c|c \le v]\}$$
$$= H[V(r^b) - C(r^s)].[V(r^b) - \{E(C(r^s) + \theta|C(r^s)$$
$$+ \theta \le V(r^b) + \phi\}] - r^b - r^s \qquad (9.3)$$

For the Kaldor–Hicks efficient level of investments that maximise this joint value, we deduce the first-order conditions as follows:

For the buyer,

$$EPJ'(r^b) = h(.).V'(r^b).V(r^b) - h(.).V'(r^b).V(r^b) + H(.).V'(r^b) - 1 = 0.$$

Thus at the efficient level of investment for the buyer, we have:

$$V'(r^{b**}) = \frac{1}{H[V(r^{b**}) - C(r^{s**})]} > 1, \text{ [since } H(.) < 1]. \qquad (9.4)$$

Now for the seller,

$$EPJ'(r^s) = 0$$
$$\Rightarrow h(.).[-C'(r^s)].V(r^b) - h(.).[-C'(r^s)].V(r^b) + H(.).C'(r^s) - 1 = 0$$
$$\Rightarrow H[V(r^b) - C(r^s)].C'(r^s) = -1.$$

Therefore, at the efficient level of investment for the seller, we have:

$$-C'(r^{s**}) = \frac{1}{H[V(r^{b**}) - C(r^{s**})]} > 1, \text{ [since } H(.) < 1]. \qquad (9.5)$$

This means that the amount of investment under dual-sided uncertainty must be less than the amount without uncertainty since $C'(r^s) < 0, C''(r^s) > 0$.

For the purposes of comparison, let us now derive the efficient levels of investment respectively under one-sided private information and complete information.

Step 2: Without any loss of generality, now consider that only one of the two parties holds ex post private information. Let the seller hold the private information θ, so that her cost is $c = C(r^s) + \theta$; and the buyer's valuation be $v = V(r^b)$ as she does not have any information.

Thus in an ex post sense (ignoring the 'sunk costs' of investments), contract breach is efficient iff: $v < c$; otherwise performance is efficient.

Thus,

$$Pr[\text{performance}] = Pr[c \leq V(r^b)] = Pr[C(r^s) + \theta \leq V(r^b)]$$
$$= Pr[\theta \leq V(r^b) - C(r^s)] = F[V(r^b) - C(r^s)].$$

Thus the expected joint pay-off would be:

$$EPJ = F(.).[\{V(r^b) - r^b - p\} + \{p - E(c|c \leq V(r^b)) - r^s\}$$
$$+ \{1 - F(.)\}.\{0 + 0 - r^b - r^s\}$$
$$= F[V(r^b) - C(r^s)].\{V(r^b) - E(c|C(r^s) + \theta \leq V(r^b))\} - r^b - r^s.$$

To check the investment incentives for the contracting parties, we differentiate the previous expression and obtain the following expressions.

For the buyer,

$$EPJ'(r^b) = f(.).V'(r^b).V(r^b) + F(.).V'(r^b) - f(.).V'(r^b).V(r^b) - 1 = 0$$

$$\Rightarrow \quad V'(r^{b*}) = \frac{1}{F[V(r^{b*}) - C(r^{s*})]} > 1, \tag{9.6}$$

since $V'(r^b) > 0$, $V''(r^b) < 0$.

For the seller,

$$EPJ'(r^s) = f(.).(-C'(r^s)).V(r^b) - f(.).(-C'(r^s)).V(r^b)$$
$$+ F(.).(-C'(r^s)) - 1 = 0$$

$$\Rightarrow \quad -C'(r^{s*}) = \frac{1}{F[V(r^{b*}) - C(r^{s*})]} > 1, \tag{9.7}$$

since $C'(r^s) < 0$, $C''(r^s) > 0$.

Step 3: Now coming to a set-up without any uncertainty (or private information), the efficient amounts of reliance investment simply solves the following: The buyer solves

$$\max_{r^b} V(r^b) - r^b; \text{ let } r^b = r_c^b$$

that satisfy the first-order condition (FOC):

$$V'(r_c^b) = 1 \tag{9.8}$$

and the seller solves

$$\max_{r^s} C(r^s) - r^s; \text{ let } r^s = r_c^s$$

that satisfy the FOC:

$$V'(r_c^s) = 1. \tag{9.9}$$

So, at this point, we are in a position to weigh the levels of reliances for different dimensions of asymmetry. Since $V'(r^{b*}) > 1 = V'(r_c^b)$, this means that, since $V'(r^b) > 0$ and $V''(r^b) < 0$, the amount of reliance investment under one-sided uncertainty must be less than the amount without uncertainty. We can construct a similar argument for the seller's investment.

Comparing the expressions (9.6) with (9.4) and (9.7) with (9.5), we infer that under two-sided uncertainty, the efficient levels of investments by the parties would be even less vis-à-vis under one-sided uncertainty (since $H(x) < F(x)$ for all $x[:= V(r^b) - C(r^s)] > 0$ except at the extreme, see Figure 9.2). The reason is that uncertainties at double margin (about the buyer's valuation as well as the seller's cost), coupled with the possibility of breach, undermine the value of reliance for the parties when compared to the one-sided uncertainty case.

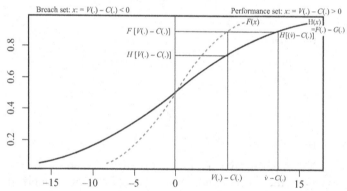

Note: The horizontal axis represents x that in turn represents $[V(.) - C(.)]$. Vertical axis represents the values of distribution functions based on x. As $[V(.) - C(.)] \lessgtr 0$, so can be x. The broken curve represents the $F(.)$ distribution, and the thick continuous curve $H(.)$ distribution, discussed above. As per the construction, $F(x)$ follows a normal distribution with variance 25 and mean 0 [corresponding to θ], whereas $H(x)$ follows a normal distribution function with variance 100 and mean 0 [corresponding to ξ]. The area on the left of the horizontal mark 0, according to our assumption, represents the breach set $[x := V(.) - C(.) < 0]$ i.e. no contract is feasible since the argument takes negative value. Thus the relevant performance set of the contract is the RHS of $x = 0$ mark. In this zone $F(.) > H(.)$, so $x > 0$.

Figure 9.2 Comparison of distribution functions H and F

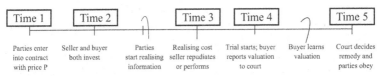

Figure 9.3 Periodic structure for the contracting model

COURT-IMPOSED DAMAGES

The Setting

To formalise the model, the buyer offers the seller in Time 1 (see Figure 9.3) a take-it-or-leave-it contract (with price P) for exchanging one unit of an indivisible specific good. The price will be paid when the seller performs. Once the contract is signed, it becomes binding and no further alteration is allowed.

At Time 2, both the parties invest in their respective cost and valuation. At the end of this phase, all uncertainties relating to cost and valuation start getting resolved in the sense that all new information—unknown at the time of contracting—is now revealed. At Time 3, once the seller realises her exact cost of performance, she decides whether to perform the contract or to repudiate. It is useful to highlight the situation here, when the seller contemplating breach does not know the actual loss it will cause to the buyer—a paradigmatic case of asymmetric information. Thus in deciding whether or not to breach, the promisor will attempt to estimate the expected value of the damages she will be ordered to pay if a suit is brought (a suit may not be even brought).[9] So she decides on the basis of two factors—first, the pre-decided price P and, second, the forthcoming default legal damages regime a court will adopt and apply at Time 5 if the seller does not deliver at Time 3 and a lawsuit is filed by the buyer at Time 4.[10]

In case the seller chooses to repudiate (that is, she delays her delivery), then the buyer reasonably suspects that the seller will not perform at Time 4, as was promised. The buyer's suspicions could be based on a message that she received from the seller (such as a letter saying she would not perform in time) or due to some exogenous information that

---

[9] Think of a situation when the value to the buyer is less than the agreed price.
[10] Also they may take into account that the price and incentives to breach reflect the anticipated ex post costs of verifying a buyer's valuation, as well as whether the English rule of the loser pays or the American rule of shared costs applies.

has arrived (for example, the seller has filed for bankruptcy). The buyer files a suit. At Time 4, the trial starts; since the goods have no readily available market price, the court hears evidence about the damages that the breach of the promise to deliver has caused to the buyer and consequently determines the amount of damages the seller needs to pay the buyer. We further assume that at Time 5, when the court makes its decisions, both the seller's cost of performance and the buyer's valuation are not observable to the other party and not verifiable to the court.[11]

This creates a moral hazard problem as well as gives vent for opportunistic behaviour by the parties. We demonstrate the impact of restitution and reliance damages first. We then move to the case of expectation damage. When it comes to the court to fix the buyer's expectation damages, the competence and the rationality of the court becomes quite important. At Time 4, when the buyer presents evidence to the court about his valuation, contract incompleteness coupled with asymmetry of information in between the parties and the court may create some room for the buyer to customise the evidence. We shall consider three distinct cases as to the court's behaviour in this scenario.

Restitution Damages

Restitution damages are defined as the amount of money that restores the buyer to the position he was in before the breach was made. This means that if the buyer prepays the price P before delivery of the good, restitution damages will be $D_s = P$. On the other hand, if, as we are assuming here, there is no prepayment of the price, $D_s = 0$. In this case, restitution damages are the same as no damages. The seller performs if

$$P - c \geq 0, \text{ or if, } c \leq P;$$

otherwise she chooses to breach.

Since $P \in \{[\bar{V}, \bar{V}] \cap [\bar{c}, \bar{c}]\}$ and $c \leq V \leq \bar{c} \leq \bar{V}$, we cannot say conclusively that the seller breaches too often when compared to the

---

[11] This is a substantial departure from notions immanent in the existing models in the literature that deal with incomplete contracts. At Time 1, the parties only observe each other's distributions and their estimates, and do not even know their individual (ex post) valuations. Thus, in this sense, they are symmetrically uninformed ex ante. This is the only similarity with other models in the literature. Hidden action exists in the form of self-investments by each party. At Time 3, asymmetry of information is introduced. A party learns her individual valuation, but still cannot observe (and definitely cannot verify) the other's valuation, and the court knows nothing but the estimates.

first-best level of efficient breach, as was the case in earlier models in the literature (Shavell 1980). In fact, since the buyer's valuation is private information (moreover, the seller cannot observe it), in some contingencies such as $v \leq P$, the seller cannot breach. Thus, the breach set is actually smaller.

Therefore,

$$\Pr[\text{performance}] = \Pr \left[c \leq P \right] = \Pr \left[C(r^s) + \theta \leq P \right]$$
$$= \Pr \left[\theta \leq P - C(r^s) \right] = F[P - C(r^s)].$$

Now the buyer's expected pay-off would be:

$$EPB = F[P - C(r^s)].[V(r^b) - r^b - P] + \{1 - F[P - C(r^s)]\}.\{0 - r^b\}.$$

The first-order condition for the buyer's pay-off maximisation can be derived as:

$$EPB'(r^b) = F[P - C(r^s)].V'(r^b) - 1 = 0$$

$$\Rightarrow V'(r_S^b) = \frac{1}{F[P - C(r_S^s)]} \lessgtr \frac{1}{H[V(r^{b**}) - C(r^{s**})]}$$

$\Rightarrow$ The buyer makes over-investment if

$$F[P - C(r_S^s)] > H[V(r^{b**}) - C(r^{s**})],$$

and if

$$F[P - C(r_S^s)] < H[V(r^{b**}) - C(r^{s**})],$$

then he would under-invest.

$\Rightarrow$ Buyer's investment incentive cannot be determined conclusively. Most likely, he over-invests. Investment incentive is highly dependent on the initial choice of contracted price P as also on the seller's investment structure and the particular shape of the two distribution functions $F(.)$ and $H(.)$. If P is chosen sufficiently low, then efficient investment or even under-investment is possible (see Figure 9.2).

Similarly, the seller's expected pay-off would be:

$$EPS = F[P - C(r^s)].[P - r^s - E(c|c \leq P)] + \{1 - F[P - C(r^s)]\}.(0 - r^s).$$

The first-order condition for the seller's pay-off maximisation can be derived as:

$$EPS'(r^s) = F[P - C(r^s)].[-C'(r^s)] - 1 = 0$$

$$\Rightarrow -C'(r_S^s) = \frac{1}{F[P - C(r_S^s)]} \lessgtr \frac{1}{H[V(r^{b**}) - C(r^{s**})]}.$$

$\Rightarrow$ Most likely, the seller would also over-invest in reliance. See the argument provided in the buyer's case.

Remark 1. *These over-investment results are in stark contrast to the under-investment results obtained under single-dimensional asymmetry.*

Intuition: As the buyer's valuation is his private information, she, in some contingencies, receives some free performance by the seller (though this is inefficient from the economic point of view as $v \leq c$). Thus she still gets some private return on the specific investment, even when the separation of the parties is efficient and the investment has no social return. This is the *insurance motive*. Since the buyer does not need to fully internalise all social costs of breach, her incentive to invest is 'not' held up here (when compared to a model with one-sided private information of the seller, see equations (9.6) and (9.7)). Besides, if the contracted price is not so high, the seller anticipating this phenomenon increases her investment, with a precautionary motive, to the point that she has to perform under restitution damage.

Reliance Damages

Reliance damages are defined as the amount of money that puts the buyer in the same position as she would be if the contract was not signed. The buyer's position if the contract was never signed is zero, while her position in the event of breach is $\{-r^b\}$. Reliance damages are computed as the difference between these two, that is, $D_r = r^b$.

Now the seller's pay-off when the contract is honoured is $\{P - c\}$; when she breaches her wealth, it is $\{-D_r\}$. Thus the seller chooses to perform when $P - c \geq -D_r$, that is, $P + r^b \geq c$ otherwise she breaches.

Therefore,

$$\Pr[\text{performance}] = \Pr[c < P + r^b] = \Pr[C(r^s) + \theta \leq P + r^b]$$
$$= \Pr[\theta \leq P + r^b - C(r^s)] = F[P + r^b - C(r^s)].$$

Now the buyer's expected pay-off would be:

$$EPB = F(.).[V(r^b) - r^b - P] + \{1 - F(.)\}.\{r^b - r^b\}.$$

The first-order condition for the buyer's pay-off maximisation can be derived as:

$$EPB'(r^b) = f(.).[V(r^b) - P - r^b] + F(.).V'(r^b) - 1 = 0.$$

Thus at the efficient level of reliance by the buyer, we get the following:

$$V'(r_R^b) = 1 - [V(r_R^b) - P - r_R^b].\frac{f[P + r_R^b - C(r_R^s)]}{F[P + r_R^b - C(r_R^s)]}$$

$$\leq 1 < \frac{1}{H[V(r^{b**}) - C(r^{s**})]} \tag{9.10}$$

$\Rightarrow$ Thus the buyer will over-invest as compared to the first-best. Similarly, the seller's expected pay-off would be:

$$EPS = F(.).[P - r^s - E(c|c \leq P + r^b)] + \{1 - F(.)\}.[-r^b - r^s].$$

The first-order condition for the seller's pay-off maximisation can be derived as:

$$EPS'(r^s) = F(.).[-C'(r^s)] - 1 = 0,$$

that is,

$$-C'(r_R^b) = \frac{1}{F[P + r_R^b - C(r_R^s)]} < \frac{1}{H[V(r^{b**}) - C(r^{s**})]} \qquad (9.11)$$

$\Rightarrow$ The seller will also be investing more relative to the first-best.

Remark 2. *The buyer is as usual investing excessively under reliance damage because of the separation prevention motive. But over-investment by the seller here stands in surprising contrast to the case of single-dimensional asymmetry. This again happens because of the precautionary motive adopted by the seller, similar to the case of restitution damage.*

Notice here that the seller's equilibrium investment incentive condition (9.11) in this case is essentially the same as the condition in the one-sided asymmetry case. So naturally the question of, how to get this over-investment result arises. The reason is that the first-best levels are different for different dimensions of asymmetry. The first-best optimum level of reliance under two-sided private information is lower than that under one-sided private information (see Proposition 1). Thus when the reliance damage is the remedy concerned, even if the seller undertakes the same amount of investment in both cases, her investment stands higher under two-sided asymmetry, whereas it falls below under one-sided asymmetry (compared to the respective first-best levels).

Analysis of Expectation Damage

Whenever it is efficient for the seller, she pays the court-imposed expectation damages in Time 3 and exits the contract. So, the seller's gain on performance is $(P - c)$ and on failure to honour the contract, it is $(-D_E)$, where D_E is the expectation damage measure. Therefore, the seller will perform whenever $P - c > -D_E$, otherwise she will breach.

In the face of breach, the buyer will most likely misguide the court about her actual valuation of performance of the contract so that her ex post pay-off increases. At this juncture, it is worth commenting on how her expected pay-off may vary depending upon how the court reacts to her claim on valuation. There could be different level of strictness (competence) attached to different courts. Following Avraham and Zhiyong (2006), there are three possible cases:

(a) the court is naive and simply believes in the evidence produced by the promisee regarding her (inflated) valuation and grants expectation on the basis of that,

(b) the court is very strict and refutes the evidence and only accepts the ex ante expected level of the promisee's valuation, and

(c) the court at its discretion chooses a value in between the expected valuation and the evidential (inflated) valuation by the promisee.

We have sought to focus on these cases because of the interest in contributing to the legal debates on expectation liability for reliance. When expectation interest is not properly verifiable in the court either because of uncertainty in valuations or because of hidden information or both, the liability for such a reliance is highly debated in the literature. The legal debate is thus relevant to those cases in which liability could in principle be imposed by the courts, and the question is whether it should be imposed and to what extent. Let us now try to show, one by one, what happens in the aforementioned three different situations.

Case 1.   The Court is Naive

In this case, the court adopts *subjective measures* of damage that either require the revelation or permit the discovery of firm-specific information. The court accepts the evidence put before it by the promisee (buyer) and grants her to recover a D_E, the expectation damage measure based on the buyer's reported valuation, $\hat{V}$, to the court. Thus $D_E = \hat{V} - P$. Therefore, the seller will breach whenever $c > \hat{V}$, and will perform otherwise. Thus we calculate the probabilities of performance and breach as follows:

$$\Pr\,(\text{performance}) = \Pr\,[c \le \hat{V}] = \Pr\,[C(r^s) + \theta \le \hat{V}]$$
$$= \Pr\,[\theta \le \hat{V} - C(r^s)] = F[\hat{V} - C(r^s)]$$

Therefore, the buyer's expected pay-off would be:

$$EPB_E = F[\hat{V} - C(r^s)].[E(v) - P - r^b] + [1 - F(\hat{V} - C(r^s))].[D_E - r^b]$$
$$= F[\hat{V} - C(r^s)].[V(r^b) - P - r^b] + [1 - F(\hat{V} - C(r^s))].[\hat{V} - P - r^b]$$
$$= F[\hat{V} - C(r^s)].V(r^b) + \hat{V} - F[\hat{V} - C(r^s)].\hat{V} - P - r^b. \qquad (9.12)$$

Similarly, the seller's expected pay-off is:

$$EPS_E = F[\hat{V} - C(r^s)].[P - r^s - E(c|c \leq \hat{V})]$$
$$+ [1 - F[\hat{V} - C(r^s)]].[-D_E - r^s]$$
$$= P - r^s - F[.].E[C(r^s) + \theta|C(r^s) + \theta \leq \hat{V}] - \hat{V}$$
$$+ \{1 - F[.]\}.\hat{V}. \tag{9.13}$$

To check the parties' investment incentives, we derive following lemma.

Lemma 1. *To check whether the buyer and the seller make efficient investment or not, we now, one by one, maximise the buyer's expected pay-off in equation (9.12) with respect to r^b and the seller's expected pay-off in equation (9.13) with respect to r^s.*

$$EPB'_E(r^b) = F[\hat{V} - C(r^s)].V'(r^b) - 1 = 0$$
$$\Rightarrow F[\hat{V} - C(r^s)].V'(r^b) = 1$$

Therefore,

$$V'(r^b_E) = \frac{1}{F[\hat{V} - C(r^s_E)]} \underset{>}{\overset{\leq}{\gtrless}} \frac{1}{H[V(r^{b**}) - C(r^{s**})]} = V'(r^{b**}). \tag{9.14}$$

Thus, from the previous expression, we cannot conclusively comment upon whether the buyer would make over-investment or efficient investment in reliance compared to the first-best level in this case; we need further evidence on $\hat{V}$ to be able to compare the values of $F(.)$ and $H(.)$ in the expression (9.14).

The seller's expected pay-off maximisation gives us the following:

$$EPS'_E(r^s) = -1 - f[\hat{V} - C(r^s)].[-C'(r^s)].\hat{V}$$
$$- F[\hat{V} - C(r^s)].C'(r^s) + f[\hat{V} - C(r^s)].[-C'(r^s)] = 0$$
$$\Rightarrow F[\hat{V} - C(r^s)].C'(r^s) = -1$$

Therefore,

$$-C'(r^s_E) = \frac{1}{F[\hat{V} - C(r^s_E)]} \underset{>}{\overset{\leq}{\gtrless}} \frac{1}{H[V(r^{b**}) - C(r^{s**})]} = -C'(r^{s**}). \tag{9.15}$$

Again we cannot say anything conclusive about over/under/efficient level of investment by the seller compared to first-best. Comment 7 following the subsequent lemma will conclusively state the equilibrium outcome.

Now, when the buyer tries to maximise his expected pay-off by choosing $\hat{V}$, we get the following condition and eventually derive the lemma next:

$$f[\hat{V} - C(r^s)].1.V(r^b) + 1 - f[\hat{V} - C(r^s)].\hat{V} - F[\hat{V} - C(r^s)].1 = 0 \tag{9.16}$$

Lemma 2.

$$\hat{V}^E = E(v) + \frac{1 - F[\hat{V} - C(r_E^s)]}{f[\hat{V} - C(r_E^s)]} \tag{9.17}$$

where

$$E(v) = V(r^b)$$

$$P^E = E(c|c \le \hat{V}^E) + \{1 - F[\hat{V}^E - C(r_E^s)]\}.\hat{V}^E$$

$$D_E = F[\hat{V}^E - C(r_E^s)].\hat{V}^E - E(c|c \le \hat{V}^E).$$

Proof: $\hat{V}^E$ is directly derived from equation (9.16). This $\hat{V}^E$, as we shall call, is the agent's 'virtual valuation under expectation damage'.[12] The other conditions are calculated by substituting FOC values in the relevant places.

Observations:

1. Observe that FOC implies that $\hat{V}^E \ge E(v)$.
2. From equation (9.13), we can see that the buyer tends to inflate her valuation by the amount

$$\left\{ \frac{1 - F[\hat{V} - C(r_E^s)]}{f[\hat{V} - C(r_E^s)]} \right\}.$$

This evidence confirms our suspicion that the buyer would try to fetch more than her expected valuation during the litigation by misguiding the court.

---

[12] The 'virtual valuation cost' (see Myerson 1981) appears in many related models where agents have private information about their willingness to pay. See Bulow and Roberts (1989) for an interesting economic interpretation of 'virtual valuations' and 'virtual costs'.

3. As the buyer's $E(v)$ increases, the buyer's reported value $\hat{V}^E$ also increases, but the exaggeration factor, that is,

$$\frac{1 - F[\hat{V} - C(r^s_E)]}{f[\hat{V} - C(r^s_E)]}$$

decreases. This can be directly derived from the monotone hazard property we ascribed to $f(.)$.

4. Observe that the buyer faces an ambivalence in terms of (mis)reporting her anticipated value to the court: if the buyer inflates her valuation and the seller's cost is even higher with the probability,

$$[1 - F(\hat{V} - C(r^s))],$$

then the seller will breach and the buyer wins higher damages. However, a higher reported valuation, and hence a higher damage payment, will discourage the seller from breaching, in which case the buyer only gets $E(v)$ instead of a higher $\hat{V}$. She will balance these two countervailing incentives when choosing her evidence.

5. Note that in this case we assumed that the buyer's uncertainty has not realised fully when the breach occurs and so she has reported an anticipated valuation. However, even if her valuation is fully realised, it is her dominant strategy under trial to report such a valuation so long as her actual valuation $v < \hat{V}^E$. Also to be noted here is that in case the buyer's actual valuation $v > \hat{V}^E$, then she may even ask for a 'specific performance' remedy in the court.

6. Note here that the seller breaches whenever $c > \hat{V}^E$ ($\neq v$). Therefore, importantly, there is inefficient breach from the ex ante and ex post perspectives. Clearly, there is under-breach if $v < \hat{V}^E$ and there is over-breach whenever $v > \hat{V}^E$.

7. Therefore, in the light of the previous point, we can now conclusively say that in the expressions (9.14) and (9.15), only strict inequality hold good (since $F(.) > H(.)$, refer to Figure 9.2), and thus both the buyer and the seller will over-invest in reliance compared to the individual first-best levels under this case.

Intuition. When a naive court accepts the buyer's reported value in establishing the expectation compensation, knowing this, the buyer then does not stretch her reliance too much; rather she tries to customise her report to maximise her gain. We mean to say that while the insurance motive is still present in the mind of the buyer, the separation prevention motive is absent here (as against Case II, see the intuition of remark 3 following (Lemma 4).

Remark 3. *Note that, in a special case when* $F[\hat{V} - C(r^s)] = H[V(r^b) - C(r^s)]$, *then both the buyer and the seller would undertake efficient levels of investment as under the first best. This is striking and has an important bearing on court decisions to uphold efficiency (at least in terms of efficient reliance when ex post efficient breach is very unlikely). In case the parties foresee this particular possibility, they may at the time of contracting (under the provision of liquidated damage) fix a high-penalty, according to* $F(.) = H(.)$, *as a default option in the case of a dispute, which will effectively ensure the efficient reliance for both the parties. Also note that this penalty may often be higher than the* actual expectation damage *(in case verified, it could be lower as well; but certainly higher than the* expected expectation damage *(vide equation [9.17]) at the time of dispute settlement depending upon the realisation of the buyer's valuation. Note that this finding stands in stark contrast to the result by Stole (1991), which suggests that liquidated damages cannot be higher than the buyer's expected valuation. In fact, his analysis was motivated by the social welfare maximisation, whereas our result arises from the parties' interest to induce the efficient reliance when the efficient breach is difficult to detect. But it is noted in the literature that the courts routinely refute these stipulated penalties in case of disputes and only allow non-penalty liquidated damages.*

What is surprising here is the following: When the promisee's expectation interest is difficult to monetise and the contract is silent regarding remedies, the court, at its will, may threaten the promisor with a large penalty (actually this is the specific performance remedy) in order to induce the promisor either to perform or to make a supra-compensatory payment to the promisee. However, when the promisee's expectation is difficult to monetise, the parties themselves cannot threaten the promisor with a large penalty in order to induce the promisor either to perform or to make a supra-compensatory payment to the promisee. Why can the courts do what the parties cannot? Without questioning the welfare impacts of the penalties, from the logical point of view, we advocate that the court (which itself suffers from a lack of competence in the face of parties' private information) should drop its bias towards this issue and allow the parties to set the contractual terms freely (under mutual assent).

Case 2. The Court is Strict

When the court is strict, it adopts measures that neither require the aggrieved party to reveal nor permit the breaching party to discover firm-specific information. It completely overlooks all the evidences produced by the promisee regarding his ex post valuation and only accepts $E(v)$, which is observable and easier to calculate and may be due to the seller's refutal. This is thus an 'objective damage' measure. We call this as 'expected expectation damage'. The court thereby sets expectation damage $D_e = E(v) - P$ and allows the breach victim to recover this amount when trade is inefficient. Thus, the seller performs iff

$$P - c \geq -D_e = -\{E(v) - P\} \text{ or if, } c \leq E(v);$$

otherwise she breaches.

Therefore,

$$\Pr[\text{Performance}] = \Pr[c \leq E(v)] = \Pr[C(r^s) + \theta \leq E(v)]$$
$$= \Pr[\theta \leq E(v) - C(r^s)] = F[V(r^b) - C(r^s)]. \quad (9.18)$$

Now the expected pay-off for the buyer would be:

$$EPB_e = F[V(r^b) - C(r^s)].\{E(v) - P - r^b\}$$
$$+\{1 - F[V(r^b) - C(r^s)]\}.\{D_e - r^b\} = V(r^b) - P - r^b. \quad (9.19)$$

And the expected pay-off for the seller would be:

$$EPS_e = F[V(r^b) - C(r^s)].\{P - r^s - E(c|c \leq E(v))\}$$
$$+\{1 - F[V(r^b) - C(r^s)]\}.\{-D_e - r^b\}$$
$$= P - r^s - F[V(r^b) - C(r^s)].E(C(r^s) + \theta|C(r^s) + \theta \leq V(r^b))$$
$$-V(r^b) + F[V(r^b) - C(r^s)].V(r^b). \quad (9.20)$$

Lemma 3. Investment Incentives to check whether the buyer and the seller make efficient investment or not, we maximise the buyer's expected pay-off in equation (9.19) with respect to r^b and the seller's expected pay-off in equation (9.20) with respect to r^s:

$$EPB'_e(r^b) = 0 \Rightarrow V'(r^b_e) = 1 < \frac{1}{H[V(r^{b**}) - C(r^{s**})]} = V'(r^{b**}) \quad (9.21)$$

$\Rightarrow$ The buyer severely over-invests in reliance as compared to the first-best level.

Again,

$$EPS'_e(r^s) = -1 - f[V(r^b) - C(r^s)].[-C'(r^s)].V(r^b) - F[V(r^b) - C(r^s)].C'(r^s)$$
$$+ f[V(r^b) - C(r^s)].[-C'(r^s)].V(r^b) = 0$$
$$\Rightarrow -C'(r^s_e) = \frac{1}{F[V(r^b_e) - C(r^s_e)]} < \frac{1}{H[V(r^{b**}) - C(r^{s**})]}.$$

(9.22)

⇒ The seller also over-invests in reliance compared to the first-best level.

Remark 4.

1. Note that the level of reliance investments by both the parties in this case is equivalent to that in the case where there is only one-sided uncertainty pertinent to the seller's cost of performance. This result is not very surprising as the breach decision is unilateral in both cases and is exercised by the seller.

2. Note that the breach condition here is different from efficient breach; we observe that the seller breaches whenever $c > E(v)$. This is inefficient in some states of the world when $E(v) > v$. Therefore, importantly, there is over-breach from the ex ante perspective. Also worth noting, from the ex post perspective, there is under-breach whenever $E(v) > v$, otherwise over-breach if $E(v) < v$.

3. Comparing the expressions (9.21) with (9.14), we can conclude that the investment incentives to the buyer under Case 2 are far higher than under Case 1. The reason is twofold: first, an insurance motive (which is a common argument for expectation damages); second, here the separation prevention motive also works (in contrast to the view of Sloof et al. [2006], where they say that this motive only works under reliance damage measure) as the buyer's expected valuation is directly dependent on her investment choice (by construction, in our model). Since in this case the buyer is better off when the parties trade than when they efficiently separate, she may, therefore, have an incentive to invest at least so much such that the valuation within the relationship reaches the highest possible valuation.

4. Now for the seller, comparing the expressions (9.22) with (9.15), we can infer that the investment incentives to the seller under Case 2 are somewhat higher than under Case 1. The reason being that when the buyer invests far in excess due to the separation

prevention motive and forces the seller to perform, the seller, in order to cope with this extra burden of performance, also has to be induced to undertake excess investment that will further reduce her cost of performance. This is just the precautionary/insurance motive.

In case the court imposes a measure of damages that is equal to the breacher's estimate of the aggrieved party's loss (and does not condition it on the aggrieved party's subjective loss), then the seller's breach-or-perform decisions under this 'flat' measure of damages would be the same as they would be if the law provided for the recovery of fully compensatory expectation damages. As has been recognised in the tort literature, accuracy in the assessment of damages is socially beneficial only if it can improve incentives ex ante, that is, only if the party contemplating an action has access to the more accurate information at a reasonable cost at the time she is deciding how to act.

Case 3. The Court's Nature and Behaviour are Uncertain

Different courts will have different levels of naivety. To capture this point, we assume that courts will determine the expectation damages in such a way that they will lie somewhere in between thresholds of the aforementioned two cases. Thus, the court is assumed to hear the buyer's report and, knowing that the buyer has an incentive to misreport the loss, the judge will also use her discretion to make some (downward) adjustments. Specifically, we assume that the damages will be a linear combination of the buyer's report ($\hat{V}$) and the buyer's (observed/expressed) expected value $E(v)$, that is, the new measure of damage will be

$$d_n = \gamma.D_e + (1 - \gamma).D_E$$
$$= \gamma.[E(v) - P] + (1 - \gamma).[\hat{V} - P] = \hat{V} - P + \gamma.[E(v) - \hat{V}],$$

where $0 \leq \gamma \leq 1$ is a parameter representing the court's level of 'strictness'. We assume that the buyer does not know in advance the level of strictness of the court, and, therefore, cannot adapt its report to the specific court in which the trial takes place. Instead, we assume that the buyer can observe only $E[\gamma]$, the average level of strictness of the court, when it decides whether and by how much to inflate her loss. At Time 4, based on the evidence that the buyer presented to the court, the court decides the amount of expectation damages that the breach caused. Then, after the trial, but before Time 5, the buyer learns her realised valuation.

We suppress the calculations here as that will proceed in the same way as in Case 1 and the results will be similar. The only difference that arises here is that the buyer would be less aggressive in exaggerating her reported value.

A Case of Buyer's Ex Post Verifiable Valuation to Court
It was assumed that the seller's costs and the buyer's valuation are private information and non-observable to the other party throughout the entire transaction. Now, for expository purposes, we can argue that the buyer's damages are verifiable ex post (only) in court through discovery, and not while the seller is making a decision on performance or breach. We assume that there are no costs associated with the verification of the buyer's ex post valuation (or there could be some reasonable cost for verification; under common laws this cost is borne by the seller, whereas under US laws this cost goes to the buyer). As the buyer's valuation is verifiable by the court, the court is capable of awarding actual damages. But there is a catch—the buyer in this case would only file a lawsuit when her ex post actual valuation is larger than the contracted price; otherwise the buyer might end up paying damages. Thus, the seller does not, in fact, face the entire distribution of the buyer's valuations under actual damages remedy. Instead, she faces a truncated distribution which has a higher mean than the ex ante expectation damages she would pay under the fixed ex ante expectation damages remedy. As a result, the seller breaches too little. Therefore, joint welfare in an actual damages award regime is reduced relative to a fixed expected expectation damages regime. We suppress the analysis of incentive to investment as it is more or less expected to be inefficient.

SOCIAL WELFARE AND THE DAMAGE MEASURES
Let us now try to find the optimal value of D, that is, the value of D that maximises the total ex post surplus. In this regard, we assume a unilateral breach by the seller so that the seller will pay the amount D and free herself of the contract iff:

$$P - c < -D \text{ or, } P + D < c.$$

Therefore,

$$\Pr[\text{Performance}] = \Pr[P + D \geq c] = \Pr[\theta \leq P + D - C(r^s)]$$
$$= F[P + D - C(r^s)].$$

Given any damage D, let the expected total surplus $EPJ(D)$ be a function of D:

$$
\begin{aligned}
EPJ(D) &= F[P+D-C(r^s)].\{[E(v) - P - r^b] + [P - r^s - E(c|c \leq P + D)]\} \\
&\quad +\{1 - F[P + D - C(r^s)]\}.\{[D - r^b] + [-D - r^s]\} \\
&= F[P + D - C(r^s)].\{E(v) - E[C(r^s) + \theta|C(r^s) + \theta \leq P + D]\} \\
&\quad -r^b - r^s
\end{aligned}
$$

We want to maximise this with respect to D bounded in the region $[0; P - C]$. The upper bound comes from the fact that if D is too high, it would never be paid by the breacher or else too high, a D would be treated as specific performance.

Let us define $D^* = \arg\max EP(D)$. The solution to the previous equation gives us a situation that entails the optimal mechanism is the expectation damage.

Proposition 2. $D^* = \min[E(v) - P, P - C]$.

Proof: The FOC for EPJ(D) maximisation gives us:

$$
\begin{aligned}
EPJ'(D) &= f[P + D - C(r^s)].1.V(r^b) - f[P + D - C(r^s)].1.\{P + D\} \\
&= f[P + D - C(r^s)].\{V(r^b) - P - D\}.
\end{aligned}
$$

And the second-order condition gives us:

$$
EPJ''(D) = f'[P + D - C(r^s)].1.\{V(r^b) - P - D\} - f[P + D - C(r^s)].1.
$$

Therefore, setting $D^* = V(r^b) - P$ gives us the unique global maximum since

$$
EPJ'[V(r^b) - P] = 0
$$

and

$$
EPJ''[V(r^b) - P] = -f[V(r^b) - P] < 0.
$$

Note here that by setting

$$
f[P - C(r^s) + D^*] = 0
$$

instead, we cannot get another solution since $f(.)$ is strictly positive. Also worth noting is that

$$
P + D - C(r^s) > 0
$$

by assumption (we assumed unilateral breach by the seller), thus,

$$D^* = E(v) - P \text{ or, } P - C,$$

depending upon the parameters in the claim.

Our observations from the three cases are summarised through following claim:

Claim 1. *Under a fixed price incomplete contract that has bilateral investments and two-dimensional asymmetry, any variant of expectation damage remedy results neither in ex ante efficient relation–specific investment nor in ex post inefficient breach; although* expected expectation damage *(Case 2) optimises expected social welfare and* high expectation damage *(Case 1) may induce efficient reliance.*

PARTY-DESIGNED LIQUIDATED DAMAGES

In the light of the preceding analysis, the parties can agree to keep a provision for a breach of contract by including a liquidated damage clause in their contract agreement. There could be three different contracting scenarios to provide a diverse range of environments for analysis. First, the buyer may propose the contract to the seller, and the seller may accept or reject it. Second, the seller may propose the contract, and the buyer may accept or reject it. Finally, an uninformed broker may design a contract that maximises the joint surplus from trade between the parties. We take the usual route here: as is familiar in the contract theory literature, the buyer designs the contract. We now study the impact of this remedy.

The Sequence of Events

Two parties at Time 1 sign a contract and specify the fixed delivery price p and the liquidated damage payment, $D_L \rightarrow$ in the interim of Time 1 and Time 2, both the buyer and the seller make reliance investments of $r^b, r^s > 0$, given p and $D_L \rightarrow$ at Time 2, the seller observes her cost of production $\rightarrow$ given p and D_L, the seller decides whether to perform the contract or breach the contract $\rightarrow$ If the seller breaches, the buyer files a suit and the court awards her with the liquidated damages D_L at Time 3.

The seller's breach decision is subjected to cost, p, and D_L. The seller will perform, only when $p - c \geq -D_L$ or if $c \leq p + D_L$.

Let's define T as the sum of the price and the liquidated damage clause, that is, $T \equiv p + D_L$. We will refer to T as the promisor's *total breach cost* when leaving the existing contract consisting of her opportunity costs p and the damage D_L.

Thus, the probability of efficient performance by the seller is:

$$\Pr[C(r^s)+\theta \le p + D_L] = \Pr[\theta \le p + D_L - C(r^s)] = F[p + D_L - C(r^s)].$$

Given the probability of performance, the buyer's expected pay-off is:

$$EP_L^b = F[p + D_L - C(r^s)]$$
$$\times [V(r^b) - p] + \{1 - F[p + D_L - C(r^s)]\}.D_L - r^b.$$

And the seller's expected pay-off is:

$$EP_L^s = F[p + D_L - C(r^s)][p - E(c|c \le p + D_L)]$$
$$+\{1 - F[p + D_L - C(r^s)]\}.(-D_L) - r^s$$
$$= F[.].(p + D_L) - F[.].E(c|c \le p + D_L) - D_L - r^s.$$

Therefore,

$$EP_L^b + EP_L^s = F(.)\{V(r^b) - E(c|c \le p + D_L)\} - r^b - r^s.$$

We obtain the following lemma.

Lemma 4. For any given $T \equiv p + D_L$ and $p > 0$, *the buyer can always be made strictly better off by increasing D_L and decreasing p by the same amount, thereby keeping T constant.*

Proof: Simply note that the buyer's pay-off:

$$EP_L^b = F[p + D_L - C(r^s)].[V(r^b) - p] + \{1 - F[p + D_L - C(r^s)]\}.D_L - r^b$$

can also be written as

$$EP_L^b = F[T - C(r^s)].V(r^b) + D_L - F[T - C(r^s)]\}.T - r^b,$$

which is strictly increasing in D_L. The lemma implies that, for T given, buyer prefers to offer a price p as low as possible to the seller. Although p and D_L are prefect substitutes from the standpoint of contract performance, the buyer prefers to obtain a higher damage payment D_L rather than paying a higher price p. Clearly, there is a limit in lowering p due to the non-negativity constraint and the seller's participation requirement.

Since the buyer determines p and D_L to maximise her expected pay-off under asymmetric information, the principal cannot observe the agent's effort. Thus the buyer's programme is then to offer the seller a contract (p, D_L) that will maximise her expected pay-off subject to the IC and the IR of the seller, so that the seller receives a non-negative utility. We assume that the buyer has all the bargaining power in contracting, that is, she makes a take-it-or-leave-it offer to the seller. The seller can accept or reject the contract. If the seller rejects, the outcome is $(q, p) = (0, 0)$. This is the seller's reservation bundle. The seller's reservation utility is, therefore, $c = 0$ as there is no market alternative.

Thus we have the following optimisation problem:

$$\max_{p, D_L, r^b, r^s} EP_L^b(p, D_L, r^b)$$

s.t. (i) $EP_L^s \geq 0[\text{IR}]$,

(ii) $\max_{r^s} EP_L^s[\text{IC}]$.

The seller's maximisation problem gives us the following FOC:

$$f(.).[-C'(r^s).(p + D_L) - f(.).[-C'(r^s).(p + D_L) + F(.).[-C'(r^s)] = 1$$
$$=> \quad F(.).C'(r^s) = -1.$$

Replacing this into the buyer's maximisation problem, we rewrite the buyer's problem as follows:

$$\max_{p, D_L, r^b, r^s} EP_L^b(p, D_L, r^b)$$

s.t (i) $EP_L^s \geq 0[\text{IR}]$,

(ii) $F(.).C'(r^s) = -1$ $[\text{IC}]$.

The buyer, by assumption, has the entire bargaining power and thus extracts the entire ex ante surplus, which entails that the participation constraint is binding in the light of Lemma 6. We derive the following lemmata:

Lemma 5.

$$p^* + D_L^* = V(r^{b*})$$
$$D_L^* = F(V(r^{b*}))\{V(r^{b*}) - E(c|c \leq V(r^{b*}))\} - r^{s*}$$
$$p^* = [1 - F(V(r^{b*})]V(r^{b*}) + F(V(r^{b*})).E(c|c \leq V(r^{b*})) + r^{s*}$$
$$EP_L^b = D_L^* - r^{b*}$$
$$EP_L^s = 0$$

Lemma 6. *Both the seller (promisor) and the buyer (promisee) make efficient investment vis-á-vis the socially desired level of investments under liquidated damage remedy when one-sided private information (pertinent to the promisor) is present. But those investment levels are higher when there is two-sided information asymmetry.*

Proof of Lemma 7 and 8: We provide a joint proof of the lemmata as they are interlinked with each other.

Substituting IR into the objective function we get:

$$F(.)V(r^b) - F(.)E[C(r^s) + \theta|C(r^s) + \theta \le p + D_L] - r^b - r^s.$$

Now replacing IC into the previous expression, we get:

$$\frac{1}{C'(r^s)}.V(r^b) - .E[C(r^s) + \theta|C(r^s) + \theta \le p + D_L] - r^b - r^s.$$

Maximising the preceding expression w.r.t. r^b and r^s gives us the following:

$$\frac{1}{C'(r^s)}.V'(r^b) = -1 \qquad \text{or,} \qquad V'(r^{b*}) = -C'(r^{s*}) \qquad (9.23)$$

$\Rightarrow$ Marginal returns from reliance investments by the parties are equal. And,

$$f(.).[-C'(r^s)].V(r^b) - f(.).[-C'(r^s)].(p + D_L) - F(.).[-C'(r^s)] - 1 = 0$$
$$\Rightarrow f(.).C'(r^s).[V(r^b)-(p+D_L)]=0, \text{ [since from (IC), } F(.).C'(r^s) = -1]$$
$$\Rightarrow V(r^{b*}) = (p^* + D_L^*) \qquad \text{[since } f(p + D_L) \ne 0]. \qquad (9.24)$$

$\Rightarrow$ The optimum total breach cost is equal to the optimum valuation of contract by the buyer, that is,

$$r^{b*} = V^{-1}(p^* + D_L^*).$$

Putting p^* and D_L^* into the seller's pay-off function, we get her equilibrium pay-off:

$$EP_L^{s*} = F(p^* + D_L^*)[p^*-E(c|c \le V(r^b))]+[1-F(p^*+D_L^*)](-D_L^*) - r^s$$
$$= F(V(r^b)).[p^*-E(c|c \le V(r^b))]+[1 - F(V(r^b))].(p^* - V(r^b)) - r^s,$$
$$= p^* - F(V(r^b)).E(c|c \le V(r^b)) - [1 - F(V(r^b))]V(r^b) - r^s \quad (9.25)$$

When we set $EP_L^{s*} = 0$, then

$$p^* = [1 - F(V(r^b)].V(r^b) + F(V(r^b)).E(c|c \le V(r^b)) + r^s.$$

Thus,

$$D_L^* = F(V(r^b)).\{V(r^b) - E(c|c \le V(r^b))\} - r^s.$$

Therefore, the buyer's equilibrium pay-off:

$$EP_L^{b*} = F(p^* + D_L^*)[V(r^b) - p^*] + [1 - F(p^* + D_L^*)]D_L^* - r^b$$
$$= F(p^* + D_L^*)[p^* + D_L^* - p^*] + [1 - F(p^* + D_L^*)]D_L^* - r^b$$
$$= D_L^* - r^b \qquad (9.26)$$

Observations and Remarks:

1. Note that under liquidated damage $p + D_L = V(r^b) = E(v)$. This is just the same condition that induces efficient breach under expectation damage in the one-sided uncertainty model.
2. Further, under liquidated measure $p + D_L = V(r^b) = E(v)$ means that this damage is equal to the EED (Case 2) when the court is strict.
3. Under liquidated damage measure, we observe that the reliance levels undertaken by the two parties are as follows: for the buyer, $V'(r^b) = 1/F(p + D_L)$, and for the seller, $C'(r^s) = -1/F(p + D_L)$.

   Thus levels of investment undertaken by the said parties are still inefficient compared to the first-best level (the buyer over-invests and the seller under-invests), but the buyer invests less and the seller invests less and that is exactly equal to the level in Case 2.
4. Note from the ex ante perspective that there is efficient breach but ex post there could be inefficient breach whenever $c > E(v)$. To put it starkly, inefficiency arises in both the cases when $v > c > E(v)$ and when $v < c < E(v)$.

From our analysis it is quite evident that in the presence of ex post dual-sided asymmetry when parties employ a fixed price contract, none of the expectation measures awarded by the court nor even party-designed liquidated damage can achieve the first best. However, among all the considered measures, the liquidated damage measure performs better than the court imposed ones.

CONCLUSION

The earlier literature on the analysis of contract remedies for breach does not account for the non-breaching party's option to not sue for damages upon breach. They typically start the efficiency analysis of various contract remedies assuming, as given, that there will be litigation for breach of the contract. However, we have identified that the victim of breach might choose not to sue for remedy if the expected pay-off from the lawsuit is negative, given the contractual terms and her private information about her loss from breach. Our analysis has shown that this option of acquiescing to a breach as well as the non-observability of the parties' valuations and reliances together have important implications for incentives to both breach and reliance and the efficiencies of various contract remedies. Specifically, we have also pointed out that when actual expectation damages of the victim (although not directly observable to the breacher) can be verified later (at a cost) in the court, it will induce under-breach from the ex ante perspective. Lastly, we have also investigated the court's optimal choice of damages under the case of non-verifiable damages, where the parties engage in a strategic signalling game trying to present evidence strategically to influence the court's damages award. And our results have a twofold implication: first, when the parties do not specify any particular damage measure in their initial contract, the courts should adopt the *expected expectation damage* as this will augment the social surplus and to some extent curb the strategic behaviour of the parties, although this does not lead to efficient investments by the parties; second, in case the parties come up with some mutually agreed upon liquidated damage provision in their contract, the court should implement the same unequivocally, as the parties might be designing this damage provision either from the perspective of maximising the joint pay-off or from the perspective of implementing efficient levels of bilateral reliance investments.

REFERENCES

Adler, B. 1999. 'The Questionable Ascent of Hadley v. Baxendale', *Stanford Law Review*, 51: 1547–90.

Aghion, P., M. Dewatripont and P. Rey. 1990. 'On Renegotiation Design', *European Economic Review*, 34: 322–29.

———. 1994. 'Renegotiation Design with Unverifiable Information', *Econometrica*, 62: 257–82.

Anderlini, Luca, Leonardo Felli and Andrew Postlewaite. 2004. 'Should Courts Always Enforce What Contracting Parties Write?', CPER Working Paper No. 4197.

Arrow, K. J. 1979. 'The Property Rights Doctrine and Demand Revelation under Incomplete Information', in M. J. Boskin (ed.), *Economics and Human Welfare: Essays in Honor of Tibor Scitovsky*. New York: Academic Press, pp. 23–39.

Ausubel, L. M., P. Crampton, P. and R. J. Deneckere. 2001. 'Bargaining with Incomplete Information', in Aumann and Hart (eds), *Handbook of Game Theory*, Vol. 3, Amsterdam: Elsevier Science B.V., chapter 50, 2002, pp. 1897–945.

Avraham, R. and L. Zhiyong. 2006. 'Incomplete Contracts with Asymmetric Information: Exclusive versus Optional Remedies', *American Law and Economics Review*, 8(3): 523–61.

Ayers, I. and R. Gertner. 1989. 'Filling Gaps in Incomplete Contracts: An Economic Theory of Default Rules', *Yale Law Journal*, 99(1): 87–130.

Bag, S. 2010. 'Whither Contract Damages: Contracts with Bilateral Reliance, One-Sided Private Information', *Journal of Law, Economics and Regulation*, 6: 17–48.

Barton, J. 1972. 'The Economic Basis of Damages for Breach of Contract', *Journal of Legal Studies*, 1: 277–304.

Bebchuk, L. A. and S. Shavell. 1991. 'Information and the Scope of Liability for Breach of Contract: The Rule of Hadley v. Baxendale', *Journal of Law, Economics and Organization*, 7: 284–312.

Birmingham, R. L. 1970. 'Breach of Contract, Damage Measures, and Economic Efficiency', *Rutgers Law Review*, 24: 273–92.

Bulow, J. and J. Roberts. 1989. 'The Simple Economics of Optimal Auctions', *Journal of Political Economy*, 97: 1060–90.

Che, Y. K. and T. Y. Chung. 1999. 'Cooperative Investments and the Value of Contracting', *American Economic Review*, 4(1): 84–105.

Chung, T. Y. 1991. 'Incomplete Contracts, Specific Investments, and Risk Sharing', *Review of Economic Studies*, 58: 1031–42.

D'Aspremont, C. and L. A. Gérard-Varet. 1979. 'Incentives and Incomplete Information', *Journal of Public Economics*, 11(1): 25–45.

Edlin, A. S. 1996. 'Cadillac Contracts and Up-Front Payments: Efficient Investment under Expectation Damages', *Journal of Law, Economics, and Organization*, 12: 98–118.

Edlin, A. S. and S. Reichelstein. 1996. 'Holdups, Standard Breach Remedies and Optimal Investment', *American Economic Review*, 86: 478–501.

Edlin, A. S. and A. Schwartz. 2003. 'Optimal Penalties in Contracts', *Chicago-Kent Law Review*, 78: 33–54.

Friehe, T. 2005. 'Damage Heterogeneity and Accuracy in Tort Law', Working Paper, Johannes-Gutenberg University.

Goetz, C. J. and R. E. Scott. 1980. 'Enforcing Promises: An Examination of the Basis of Contract', *Yale Law Journal*, 89: 1261–322.

Green, J. and J. J. Laffont. 1979. *Incentives in Public Decision Making*. Amsterdam: North-Holland.

Hart, O. and J. Moore. 1999. 'Foundations of Incomplete Contracts', *Review of Economic Studies*, 66: 115–38.

Hermalin, B. E. and M. L. Katz. 1993. 'Judicial Modification of Contracts between Sophisticated Parties: A More Complete View of Incomplete Contracts and Their Breach', *Journal of Law, Economics and Organization*, 9(2): 230–355.

Kaplow, L. and S. Shavell. 1996. 'Accuracy in the Assessment of Damages', *Journal of Law and Economics*, 39(1): 191–210.

Konakayama, A., T. Mitsui and S. Watanabe. 1986. 'Efficient Contracting with Reliance and a Damage Measure', *The RAND Journal of Economics*, 17: 450–57.

Miceli, T. 2004. *The Economic Approach to Law*, Stanford University Press.

Myerson, R. B. 1981. 'Optimal Auction Design', *Mathematics of Operations Research*, 6(1): 58–73.

Myerson, R. B. and M. A. Satterthwaite. 1983. 'Efficient Mechanisms for Bilateral Trading', *Journal of Economic Theory*, 28: 265–81.

Nöldeke, G. and K. M. Schmidt. 1995. 'Option Contracts and Renegotiation: A Solution to the Hold-Up Problem', *The RAND Journal of Economics*, 26: 163–79.

———. 1998. 'Sequential Investments and Options to Own', *The RAND Journal of Economics*, 29: 633–53.

Rogerson, W. 1984. 'Efficient Reliance and Damage Measure for Breach of Contract', *The RAND Journal of Economics*, 15: 39–53.

———. 1992. 'Contractual Solutions to the Hold-Up Problem', *Review of Economic Studies*, 59: 774–94.

Schmitz, P. W. 2002. 'Simple Contracts, Renegotiation under Asymmetric Information, and the Hold-Up Problem', *European Economic Review*, 46(1): 169–88.

Shavell, S. 1980. 'Damage Measures for Breach of Contract', *Bell Journal of Economics*, 11: 466–90.

———. 1984. 'The Design of Contracts and Remedies for Breach', *Quarterly Journal of Economics*, 99(1): 121–48.

Spier, K., 1994. 'Settlement Bargaining and the Design of Damage Awards', *Journal of Law, Economics, & Organization*, 10: 84–95.

Spier, K. and M. Whinston. 1995. 'On the Efficiency of Privately Stipulated Damages for Breach of Contract: Entry Barriers, Reliance, and Renegotiation', *The RAND Journal of Economics*, 26: 180–202.

Stole, L. 1991. 'Mechanism Design under Common Agency', Mimeo, University of Chicago, Graduate School of Business.

Vickrey, William. 1961. 'Counterspeculation, Auctions, and Competitive Sealed Tenders', *The Journal of Finance*, 16(1): 8–37.

PART IV
STRATEGEMS AND PRIVATE GAINS

10
Auctions with Ceilings*

Priyodorshi Banerjee and Archishman Chakraborty

Should a profit-maximising seller allow unrestricted competitive bidding by potential buyers or should she specify an upper limit on allowable bids? When placing a talented player with a sports club, can the player and his agent gain by specifying a cap on the acceptable salary? When outsourcing a public works contract, can a government agency lower expected costs by announcing a minimum price guarantee for the suppliers? In general, can one gain by putting limits on the share of the pie that one is willing to receive? We consider these questions in the context of a common value auction for a single object.

In common value environments, a bidder fears overpaying precisely when her bid is the highest and she wins the auction—the act of winning contains unfavourable information. This winner's curse problem becomes acute when, at the bidding stage, some bidders have poorer information than others. In such cases, a poorly informed bidder can win only when not outbid by a better informed bidder. Anticipating such an acute winner's curse, rational but poorly informed bidders bid cautiously in equilibrium. This adversely affects the incentives to bid aggressively for all types of bidders and lowers the seller's expected revenues.

We show that in such situations, the seller can often benefit by imposing a *ceiling* or upper limit on allowable bids. By imposing a ceiling, the seller restrains competitive bidding by better informed bidders. Any poorly informed bidder when winning at the ceiling then attaches positive probability to the joint event such that (*a*) the true value of the good is higher than the ceiling and (*b*) she is tied with a bidder with superior information. This reduces the fear of

---

* This essay has benefitted from presentations at INSEAD Fontainebleau, ISI New Delhi, and the 2005 Econometric Society World Congress, London. We thank Alessandro Citanna, Parikshit Ghosh, Faruk Gul, Rick Harbaugh, Hsueh-Ling Huynh and Bilge Yilmaz for helpful comments.

being outbid by poorly informed bidders and encourages them to bid aggressively. Aggressive bidding by poorly informed bidders enables the seller to extract more information rents from better informed bidders. Consequently, compared to a standard auction without a ceiling, the seller earns higher revenues on an average.

A bid ceiling is not costless. By imposing a ceiling, the seller rules out the possibility of receiving a price higher than the ceiling. When considering the relative merits of an auction with a ceiling and an auction without one, the seller has to trade off the expected benefit of increased bidding below the ceiling with the expected cost of not allowing bids higher than the ceiling. For a fixed number of bidders, we show that imposing a ceiling is profitable for the seller if and only if the expected proportion of better informed bidders is low enough. Imposing a ceiling is also better for the seller if the total number of bidders is large enough.

A bid ceiling in effect raises the expected demand for the seller's object at prices below the ceiling. To see this, note that for a standard auction, the seller obtains a price for which demand equals supply in every state of the world. By exploiting competitive bidding among buyers, with a standard auction, the seller is able to (imperfectly) price discriminate across different states of bidder valuations. With a price ceiling, the seller commits to no price discrimination in states where the better informed bidders have high demand. This, however, increases total demand. By alleviating the winner's curse it shifts outwards the demand from poorly informed bidders at every price below the ceiling. Consequently, the seller is able to generate more competition and obtain a higher market clearing price in states where better informed demand is not so high. When most bidders are likely to be poorly informed, the seller's expected cost from ruling out prices higher than the ceiling is low, while the expected benefit via a higher demand from poorly informed bidders is high. As a result, the seller does better from imposing a ceiling as compared to a standard auction. When there are many bidders, each poorly informed bidder bidding at the ceiling attaches a large probability to the presence of favourable information among at least some other bidders. As a result, the seller is able to set a relatively high ceiling, but still generates high demand from poorly informed bidders, lowering the cost and raising the benefit from imposing a ceiling.[1]

---

[1] The idea that a price ceiling imposed by a seller may improve demand under conditions of incomplete/imperfect information is well-known in other non-auction contexts. Stiglitz and Weiss (1981) show that in credit markets with

In initial public offers that are held via auctions, ceilings on allowable bids are often specified. The Google's initial public offering (IPO) is one example, where acceptable bids had to lie in the range USD 85 to US\$ 95. Such ceilings have been justified on the grounds of providing a 'level playing field' or a 'bidding guide' or an 'anchor price' for small investors.[2] In our symmetric auction of an indivisible object, all bidders are ex ante identical. Nonetheless, the logic of our results extends to an IPO context and a bid ceiling act can be interpreted as a bidding guide for bidders who are poorly informed at the bidding stage. In 'reverse' auctions that are held in government procurement contexts, a bid ceiling takes the form of a minimum price guarantee. Although such practices are vulnerable to accusations of being 'sweetheart deals', our results provide one defense of why they may not be so. By reducing the winner's curse faced by potential suppliers, a minimum price guarantee may in fact lower the government's outsourcing costs.

Auctions with ceiling also have important advantages over posted price mechanisms where the seller offers the object at a fixed price, randomly allocating the object when faced with excess demand. A posted price has one virtue in common with an auction that has a ceiling—it also reduces the fear of being outbid by poorly informed bidders. As Bulow and Klemperer (2002) and Campbell and Levin (2006) show, a posted price may in fact dominate a standard auction in expected revenues.[3] In our setting, however, a posted price introduces the bidders to a winner's curse problem on the 'downside', that is, to winning the good and paying the posted price in states where better informed bidders do not bid. Such a downside winner's curse is mitigated in an auction with a ceiling since poorly informed bidders typically pay lower prices when better informed bidders do not bid at the ceiling. By holding an auction with a ceiling, the seller combines the benefits of an auction and a posted price mechanism and does better than either an auction or a posted price.

---

adverse selection, an interest rate ceiling can benefit a lender by improving the quality of demand. Shapiro and Stiglitz (1984) show that in labour markets with a moral hazard, a wage floor can improve productivity. In our model, we emphasise a distinct force. A price ceiling alleviates the winner's curse and so increases the quantity demanded.

[2] See http://www.wrhambrecht.com/, the website of the lead investment bank for the Google IPO for further details (accessed on 15 June 2013).

[3] Wang (1993) makes the same point, but in an independent private values model where auctioning may be costly.

An auction with a ceiling has similarities with offering an object for sale at a negotiable posted price (equivalently, at a fixed price or the best offer). In such situations, it is clear that the seller is willing to accept a lower market clearing price in the event that sufficient demand is not forthcoming at the fixed price. If the posted price is thought of as an upper limit on allowable bids, then an auction with a ceiling is a description of a simple negotiation procedure between the buyers and the sellers, corresponding to a negotiable posted price mechanism. In many housing markets (in the UK and France, for instance), the seller often posts a price and it is against the law for the seller to accept a bid above this price. The seller, however, often accepts negotiated bids below the posted price.[4]

In private value auctions, a seller may benefit from undertaking inefficient amount of trades by imposing a reserve or floor price (that is, a lowest allowable bid.[5] In common value contexts, the gains from a reserve price are less pronounced, especially for a large number of bidders.[6] We also provide an analysis of reserve prices in our model and show that for a sufficiently large number of bidders, the optimal reserve price is zero. In contrast, imposing a non-trivial ceiling results in a disproportionate fall in information rents when the number of bidders are large enough. In common value environments such as ours, imposing a ceiling can benefit the seller more than imposing a floor. We do not consider the optimal direct mechanism in this essay. It is well known that with correlated signals, an auction (with or without a ceiling) is not optimal.[7] We justify our focus on ceilings as a simple change in the rules of a standard auction, which is itself a commonly observed mechanism.

In a preliminary note, Chakraborty (2002) provides a numerical example of a sealed-bid auction with three bidders where imposition of a ceiling can improve revenue. This essay generalises and extends the analysis and situates it in context. Che and Gale (1998) as well as Gavious et al. (2002) show that imposition of bid ceilings may increase the seller's revenue in private value *all-pay* auctions, thus, providing insights on the value of imposing caps on contributions by political

---

[4] The original intention behind such laws may have been to prevent the seller from discriminating against particular groups. As we show, such laws may also raise the expected proceeds from the sale in certain natural circumstances.

[5] See, for example, Myerson (1981).

[6] See, for example, Levin and Smith (1996).

[7] Cremer and Maclean (1988) and McAfee and Reny (1992) show that in such settings (near) full extraction of surplus is possible with interim incentive compatible and individually rational mechanisms.

lobbies. In Che and Gale (1998), the results are driven by ex ante asymmetry between publicly known bidder valuations, while Gavious et al. (2002) show that if bidders are ex ante symmetric, a bid ceiling may be optimal, but only if the total cost to a bidder is strictly convex in her bid.[8] In private value all-pay auctions, a ceiling encourages bidding by lowering a bidder's expected costs in the event that she *does not* win the auction. In contrast, in our common value winner-pays auction, a ceiling encourages bidding by lowering a bidder's expected winner's curse, in the event that she *does* win the auction.[9]

Chen and Rosenthal (1996a, 1996b) show that if buyers arrive randomly and sequentially, and incur inspection costs of discovering their own true valuations, a seller may benefit from imposing a price ceiling.[10] By imposing a ceiling, the seller makes it worthwhile for buyers who turn up early to pay the cost, thereby avoiding inefficiencies arising out of too many bidders paying the cost. In contrast, we show that even when information acquisition is not costly and all prospective buyers can be easily attracted to the venue of the auction, a ceiling may still be beneficial since it mitigates the winner's curse.

The rest of the essay proceeds as follows. In the second section, we introduce our model, characterise the equilibrium of the standard auction and compare it with auctions that have a reserve price as well as with posted price mechanisms. In the third section, we introduce a ceiling and show when it dominates a standard auction and a posted price mechanism. The last section concludes, while the two appendices contain proofs of some of the ancillary results as well as some robustness exercises.

THE STANDARD AUCTION

A seller wants to sell an indivisible object to one of $n \geq 2$ bidders in the set $N = \{1, ..., n\}$. The value of the object to the seller equals 0, whereas the common value of the object to all the buyers is denoted by a random variable V that is distributed according to a continuous increasing distribution function F with density f that is positive on

---

[8] In a recent essay, Sahuguet (2006) extends these results to an asymmetric environment. See also Szech (2012) for a consideration of alternative tie-break provisions.

[9] See Roy Chowdhury (2008) for an analysis of a private value winner-pay second-price auction, where she argues that ceilings and reserves may benefit the seller by reducing collusion.

[10] See also Milgrom (2004) for a model with a similar flavour.

$V = [0, 1]$. We denote by v a realisation of V and let $\bar{v}$ be the expected value of V. Let $\phi(v) = \frac{f(v)}{1-F(v)}$ denote the hazard rate associated with F that we assume is monotone increasing. The pay-off to a buyer from obtaining the object of value v at price p is $v - p$ and the pay-off from not obtaining the object is zero. The pay-off to the seller is the price that she receives in the event of making a sale; it is zero otherwise.

The realised value of V is not common knowledge, although each bidder may have private information about it. We impose the cleanest possible information structure on the bidders that allows us to make our points. Each bidder $i \in N$ knows the realisation v of V with probability $\alpha \in (0, 1)$; otherwise, she receives no additional information and only knows the prior. The probability that any one bidder is informed is independent across bidders and independent of V. Each bidder knows whether or not he is informed, but does not know how many other bidders are informed. For $0 \leq k \leq K \leq n$, let $\pi(k, K) = \binom{K}{k}\alpha^k(1 - \alpha)^{K-k}$ be the probability that k out of K bidders are informed. The seller is uninformed. We denote by $\theta_i \in \Theta = V \cup \{u\}$ the type of bidder i, where $\theta_i = u$ denotes that bidder i is uninformed while $\theta_i = v$ denotes that bidder i is informed that $V = v$.

This information structure is a simple formulation of the idea that bidders who are ex ante identical may be ordered (in the sense of Black-well 1953), in the quality of their information at the interim bidding stage. For instance, bidders may try to obtain information about the value of the object, but, with positive probability, the technology used by the bidders may fail to provide any conclusive evidence. The lack of conclusive evidence does not automatically preclude any bidder from participating in the auction. The key feature of this information structure that we exploit is that the degree of ex post asymmetry among bidders is not common knowledge—while each bidder privately knows whether or not she has precise information, she does not know how many other bidders possess such information.[11]

---

[11] The fact that bidders are either perfectly informed or perfectly uninformed is not important for our results. Our qualitative results also obtain when each bidder may either obtain a noisy superior signal or a more noisy inferior signal, as well in cases with some private value component in bidder estimates. See Piccione and Tan (1996) for a model of an auction with a similar information structure. Engelbrecht-Wiggans et al. (1983) and Hendricks et al. (1994) are some of the other essays that consider bidders who differ in the quality of their information, although such asymmetries are common knowledge in these essays. None of these essays consider bid ceilings.

We suppose that the seller sells the object in a continuous ascending clock English (or Japanese) auction.[12] We allow the seller to set a reserve or floor price r (that is, a minimum allowable bid) or a ceiling price c (that is, a maximum allowable bid) with $0 \leq r \leq c \leq 1$. A clock (signifying the price p) rises continuously starting at r and continuing till c. At each point $p \in [r, c]$, each bidder has one of two actions: to remain active or to quit upon observing bidding activity at all $p' < p$. Quits are final.

Let $A(p)$ be the set of bidders who are active when the clock is at $p \in [r, c]$. Since quits are final, for $p > p'$, $A(p) \subset A(p')$. For $p > r$, let $Q(p) = \cap_{p':p'<p}A(p') - A(p)$ be the set of bidders who quit at p and let $Q(r) = N - A(r)$. Let $B(p) = \cup_{p':p'>p}A(p)$ be the set of bidders who are active beyond p with $B(c) = \varnothing$. Let $|X|$ denote the cardinality of any set X. Since there are a finite number of bidders, the non-increasing function $|A(p)|$ can have only a finite number of discontinuities and further, $|B(p)| \leq |A(p)|$ for all p, with strict inequality only at their common points of discontinuity. Furthermore, $|B(p)|$ is a non-increasing right-continuous function of p.

The auction assigns a winner and the price that she pays as follows: If $|A(r)| = 0$, then no bidder is ever active and the good is not sold. In all other cases, the auction stops at a price $P = \inf\{p \in [r, c] : |B(p)| \leq 1\}$. The set is non-empty since $|B(c)| = 0$. The price P is the lowest price beyond which at most one bidder is active and it is equal to the price that the winner pays.[13] The winner is determined as follows: Since $|B(p)|$ is right continuous in p we must have $|B(P)| \leq 1$. If $|B(P)| = 1$, then there is only one bidder active beyond P and the winner is this bidder, the only element of $B(P)$. If $|B(P)| = 0$ but $|A(P)| > 0$, then more than one bidder is active at P, but none of them are active beyond P. The winner is then decided by uniform randomisation among the bidder(s) in $A(P)$. Similarly, if $|B(P)| = |A(P)| = 0$, all bidders active at $p < P$ simultaneously quit at P and so $|Q(P)| > 0$. In this case, the winner is decided by uniform randomisation among the bidders in $Q(P)$. This completes the description of the rules of the auction with a reserve and ceiling pair $\{r, c\}$. The standard auction is a special case of the auction where

---

[12] All qualitative results extend to the case where the seller instead holds a sealed-bid second-price auction. Recall in this respect from Milgrom and Weber (1982) that an ascending auction dominates all other standard auction formats in general symmetric environments of which ours is a special case.

[13] If one lets $A(p) = \varnothing$ for $p > c$, P can also be taken to equal $\inf\{p \in [r, c]| |A(p)| \leq 1\}$.

$r = 0$ and $c = 1$. A posted price mechanism is another special case where $r = c$.

In any auction defined by the pair $\{r, c\}$, a strategy for any bidder is to choose a probability of staying active at every point $p \in [r, c]$ upon observing the past history of activity $A(p')$ for all $p' < p$, given also the bidder's type. Formally, for any $p \in [r, c]$, let the collection $h_p = \{A(p')\}_{p' < p}$ denote the history of bidding activity prior to p. We say that h_p is a 'history of no quits' if $|A(p')| = n$ for all $p' < p$ and specify that the null history h_r is such a history. Further, let H_p be the set of possible histories prior to $p \in [r, c]$ with $H = \cup_{p \in [r,c]} H_p$ and let $H^n \subset H$ be the set of histories with no prior quits, of arbitrary length. A (behaviour) strategy for bidder i is a function $\sigma_i : \Theta \times H \to [0, 1]$ that maps the type of the bidder θ_i and the history of bidding activity h_p into a probability $\sigma_i(\theta_i, h_p)$ of staying active at p, for each $p \in [r, c]$, conditional on having being active at all $p' < p$. Let $\sigma = (\sigma_1, ..., \sigma_n)$. For $i, j \in N, i \neq j$, let $\mu_{i,j} : \Theta \times H \to \Delta(\Theta)$ be the belief of bidder i about bidder j's types given her own type θ_i and the observed history h_p. Let $\mu_i = \{\mu_{i,j}\}_{j \neq i}$ and let $\mu = (\mu_1, ..., \mu_n)$. A perfect Bayesian equilibrium of the auction is a pair (σ, μ) such that σ is sequentially rational given μ and μ is derived from σ (and the priors) via Bayes' rule if possible.

Due to the symmetry of the model, it is natural to look for an equilibrium in symmetric bidding strategies, that is, where σ_i does not depend on i. Our objective is to characterise the reserve and ceiling combination $\{r, c\}$ that maximises the seller's ex ante expected revenues, given that bidders play a symmetric equilibrium. For notational convenience, whenever we characterise a symmetric equilibrium in what follows, we will only specify the strategy profile σ and omit the belief profile μ, as it will cause no confusion.

We begin by deriving the symmetric equilibrium for the standard auction. In order to do so, it is convenient to define the function $S:[0, 1] \to \mathbb{R}_+$ as follows:

$$S(x) = (1 - F(x)) [E(V|V > x) - x] = \int_x^1 [1 - F(u)] \, du \qquad (10.1)$$

It may be useful to think of $1 - F(x)$ as a 'demand curve' written as a function of the price x. With such an interpretation, $S(x)$ is the 'consumer's surplus', that is, the area above the price x and under the demand curve $1 - F(x)$. Our first result shows that, in the symmetric equilibrium of the standard auction, any informed bidder stays active till the price p reaches the value v of the object. In contrast, any uninformed bidder stays active at a price p as long as p is below $\bar{v}$ and she has observed no prior quits. Otherwise, an uninformed bidder quits at p.

Given such equilibrium behaviour, $S(\bar{v})$ is the expected information rent an informed bidder earns when she is competing only against uninformed bidders and wins at a price $\bar{v}$. To state the result concisely, let $\mathbf{1}_{\{\bullet\}}$ denote the indicator function and for $i = 1, ..., n$ and for $p \in [0, 1]$, let $A_{-i}(p)$ and $Q_{-i}(p)$ be the set of bidders other than i who are active at and quit at p, respectively, defined in a manner identical to the sets $A(p)$ and $Q(p)$

Proposition 1. *The following is a symmetric equilibrium of the standard auction: for all $i = 1, ..., n$,*

$$\sigma_i(\theta_i, h_p) = \begin{cases} \mathbf{1}_{\{p < v\}} & \text{all } h_p, \text{ if } \theta_i = v \in V \\ \mathbf{1}_{\{p < \bar{v}\}} \mathbf{1}_{\{h_p \in H^n\}} & \text{if } \theta_i = u. \end{cases} \quad (10.2)$$

The seller's equilibrium ex ante expected revenue is given by:

$$R_s = \bar{v} - n\alpha(1 - \alpha)^{n-1} S(\bar{v}). \quad (10.3)$$

Proof: We prove a stronger result. In Step 1 we show that the strategy $\sigma_i(v, \bullet)$ is sequentially rational for an informed bidder i (when $\theta_i = v \in V$) for *every* strategy profile σ'_{-i} of the other bidders. In Step 2 we show that, given informed bidders use the profile $\{\sigma_{-i}(v, \bullet)\}_{v \in V}$, the strategy profile $\sigma_i(u, \bullet)$ is sequentially rational for bidder $i = 1, ..., n$ when $\theta_i = u$, for *every* symmetric pure strategy profile $\sigma'_{-i}(u, \bullet)$ used by other uninformed bidders.

Step 1: For $p \in [0, 1]$ and an arbitrary history of bidding activity h_p with $A_{-i}(p') \neq \varnothing$ for all $p' < p$, consider bidder i when $\theta_i = v \in V$ who has been active at all $p' < p$. Fix σ'_{-i}. Let $\mu_i[A_{-i}(p) = \varnothing | v, h_p]$ be the probability attached by i to all other previously active bidders quitting simultaneously at p given her type $\theta_i = v$ and the history h_p. Then

$$\mu_i[A_{-i}(p) = \varnothing | v, h_p] = \prod_{j \in \cap_{p':p' < p} A_{-i}(p')}$$

$$\times \left[(1 - \sigma'_j(v, h_p))(1 - \mu_{i,j}(u|v, h_p)) + (1 - \sigma'_j(u, h_p))\mu_{i,j}(u|v, h_p) \right]$$

where $\mu_{i,j}(u|v, h_p)$ is the probability i attaches to j being uninformed given $\theta_i = v$ and h_p.

Suppose first that $p \geq v$. If bidder i quits at p, she wins the object only when (a) all other bidders also quit at p, that is, when $A_{-i}(p) = \varnothing = A(p) = B(p)$ and so $Q_{-i}(p)$ equals $\cap_{p' < p} A_{-i}(p')$ if $p > 0$ and equals

$N - \{i\}$ otherwise; and (*b*) *i* is chosen as the winner after uniform ran-
domisation among the $|Q_{-i}(p)| + 1$ bidders who quit, for an expected
pay-off equal to

$$\frac{\mu_i[A_{-i}(p) = \varnothing | v, h_p]}{|Q_{-i}(p)| + 1}[v - p] \leq 0.$$

On the other hand, if bidder *i* continues at *p*, she wins with probability 1 and pays *p* when all other bidders quit at *p* since in this case
$B(p) \subseteq A(p) = \{i\}$. Furthermore, if she subsequently wins the auction at
a price $p' \geq p \geq v$, she earns non-positive pay-offs conditional on winning. Therefore, the expected pay-off from continuing at *p* is at most as
high as

$$\mu_i[A_{-i}(p) = \varnothing | v, h_p][v - p] \leq \frac{\mu_i[A_{-i}(p) = \varnothing | v, h_p]}{|Q_{-i}(p)| + 1}[v - p],$$

since $p \geq v$. Therefore, it is a weak best response of bidder *i* of type
$\theta_i = v$ to quit at all $p \geq v$ regardless of h_p.

Next, suppose that $p < v$. Once again, if bidder *i* quits at *p*, she
wins the object only if all other bidders quit at *p* and she wins the
randomisation for an expected pay-off of

$$\frac{\mu_i[A_{-i}(p) = \varnothing | v, h_p]}{|Q_{-i}(p)| + 1}[v - p] \geq 0.$$

However, if she continues at *p* and quits only when the price reaches *v*
regardless of the history (that is, plays according to $\sigma_i(v, \bullet)$), she wins
with Probability 1 when all other bidders quit at *p* and earns $v - p$ conditional on winning. Furthermore, if she subsequently wins the auction
at a price $p' \geq p$ with $p' \leq v$, she makes non-negative expected profits. Finally, she cannot win the auction at any price $p'' > v$. It follows
that her expected pay-off from playing according to $\sigma_i(v, \bullet)$ is at least
$\mu_i[A_{-i}(p) = \varnothing | v, h_p][v - p]$. Comparing with the expected pay-off from
quitting at *p*, we see that it is a weak best response for bidder *i* of type
$\theta_i = v$ to continue at $p < v$ and quit only at *v*, regardless of h_p. This
completes Step 1.

Step 2: Fix a symmetric pure strategy profile $\sigma'_{-i}(u, \bullet)$ for uninformed
bidders and the profile $\{\sigma_{-i}(v, \bullet)\}_{v \in V}$ for informed bidders and with $p \in$
[0, 1] and an arbitrary history of bidding activity h_p with $A_{-i}(p') \neq \varnothing$
for all $p' < p$, consider bidder *i* with $\theta_i = u$ who has been active at all
$p' < p$.

Consider first the case $h_p \in H^n$ and notice first that such a history is always consistent with the strategy profile used by the other bidders since, in particular, all other bidder may be informed and playing according to $\sigma_{-i}(v, \bullet)$ with $v \geq p$.

Suppose first that $p \geq \bar{v}$. If bidder i quits at p then she wins the object only when all other bidders also quit and i is chosen as the winner after uniform randomisation among the bidders. Conditional on winning and conditional on every other bidder being uninformed, the expected pay-off to i from quitting is $\bar{v} - p \leq 0$. The same is true if she continues at p and she wins the auction with Probability 1 when all other bidders quit at p. Furthermore, if all other bidders do not quit at p and she subsequently wins the auction at a price $p' \geq p \geq \bar{v}$, she earns non-positive pay-offs conditional on winning and conditional on every other bidder being uninformed. Thus, behaving according to $\sigma_i(u, \bullet)$ and quitting at $p \geq \bar{v}$ is a weak best response to $\sigma'_{-i}(u, \bullet)$ conditional on every other bidder being uninformed. Further, given the behaviour of informed bidders, uninformed bidder i can earn at most zero profits when every other bidder is not uninformed, that is, there is a bidder $j \in A_{-i}(p')$ all $p' < p$, with $\theta_j = v \geq p$. In this case, however, bidder i also earns zero profits by quitting at p. Hence, behaving according to $\sigma_i(u, \bullet)$ is a weak best response conditional on the state where all other bidders are uninformed as well as on the state where at least one other bidder is informed, and so a best response overall, for any $h_p \in H^n$, $p \geq \bar{v}$.

Suppose next $h_p \in H^n$ but $p < \bar{v}$. As before, if bidder i quits at p then she wins the object only when all other bidders also quit and i wins the subsequent uniform randomisation. Conditional on winning and conditional on every other bidder being uninformed, the expected pay-off to i from quitting is $\bar{v} - p$. However, if she continues at p and plays according to $\sigma_i(u, \bullet)$, she wins with Probability 1 when all other bidders quit at p and earns $\bar{v} - p$ conditional on winning and on every other bidder being uninformed. Furthermore, if she subsequently wins the auction at a price $p' \geq p$ with $p' \leq \bar{v}$, she makes non-negative expected profits conditional on winning and on every other bidder being uninformed. Finally, she cannot win the auction at any price $p'' > \bar{v}$. Thus, behaving according to $\sigma_i(u, \bullet)$ and continuing at $p < v$ is a weak best response conditional on every other bidder being uninformed. Further, recall that given the behaviour of informed bidders and given $h_p \in H^n$, uninformed bidder i can earn at most zero profits when there is a bidder $j \neq i$, active at all $p' < p$ with $\theta_j = v \geq p$. In such a case, however, by continuing at p and playing according to $\sigma_i(u, \bullet)$ bidder i will also earn zero profits. Thus, behaving according to $\sigma_i(u, \bullet)$ is a weak best response, whether or not all other bidders are uninformed, for any $h_p \in H^n$, $p < \bar{v}$. This establishes the result for all $h_p \in H^n$, $p \in [0, 1]$.

To complete the proof, consider first the case where $h_p \notin H^n$ but quits have occurred at exactly one $p' < p$. Since $\sigma'_{-i}(u, \bullet)$ is a symmetric pure strategy profile and since $A_{-i}(p') \neq \varnothing$ for all $p' < p$, uninformed bidder i must conclude at h_p that all bidders who quit at p' must be informed and that $v = p'$, provided subsequent bidding behaviour for $p'' \in (p', p)$ in the history h_p is consistent with $\sigma'_{-i}(u, \bullet)$. In such a case, regardless of the behaviour of the other bidders, who i must believe are all uninformed; it is a weak best response for this bidder to quit at all $p'' > p$, since otherwise she only ends up paying a higher price for an object worth p' conditional on winning. In case the history h_p is inconsistent with $\sigma'_{-i}(u, \bullet)$ (or if there have been multiple quits before p, a history necessarily inconsistent with the symmetric pure strategy profile $\sigma'_{-i}(u, \bullet)$ and $\{\sigma_{-i}(v, \bullet)\}_{v \in V}$, the beliefs of bidder i cannot be derived by Bayes' rule. We suppose that after such histories, bidder i attaches Probability 1 to the event that $v = p'$ where p' is the lowest price at which quits occurred, so that it is a best response for bidder i to quit at all $p'' > p'$, given her beliefs. This shows that $\sigma_i(u, \bullet)$ is sequentially rational when informed bidders behave according to $\{\sigma_{-i}(v, \bullet)\}_{v \in V}$ and all other uninformed bidders behave according to the arbitrary symmetric pure strategy profile $\sigma'_{-i}(u, \bullet)$ and so this completes Step 2.

Observe finally that since the object is always sold in equilibrium, the sum of the ex ante expected pay-offs of all bidders and the seller must equal the ex ante expected value of the object $\bar{v}$. Since a bidder makes positive profits in equilibrium only when she is the only informed bidder and $v > \bar{v}$, and since there are n bidders, we immediately obtain (10.3) as the expression for expected revenues.

We make the following remarks. The equilibrium of Proposition 1 is not the unique symmetric equilibrium, even though the steps in the proof are suggestive of an iterated dominance argument. There are other symmetric pure strategy equilibria that differ in behaviour at knife-edge points, that is, where a bidder of type v differs in her behaviour at $p = v$, or a bidder of type u differs at $p = \bar{v}$. Such differences will not affect the seller's ex ante expected revenues. We have been unable to find other symmetric equilibria, pure or mixed, where the seller obtains ex ante revenues that are different from (10.3). Notice also in this respect that the equilibrium characterised by Proposition 1 is similar to separating symmetric equilibria characterised by Milgrom and Weber (1982) and Bikhchandani et al. (2002) in more general models. The latter paper, in particular, demonstrates the existence of multiple symmetric equilibria that are identical from the perspective of seller revenues in continuous, irrevocable exit English auctions under common values.

With the standard auction in place as our benchmark mechanism we turn next to the question of imposing a reserve price $r > 0$, but no ceiling (that is, $c = 1$). Levin and Smith (1996) show that the benefits from a reserve price asymptotically approach zero as the number of bidders increases. We confirm this finding in our context with our next result which shows that there is no benefit from imposing a reserve price for finite n. In order to do this, for each α we let n_α be the smallest value of n satisfying:

$$\frac{\bar{v}f(\bar{v})}{1 - F(\bar{v})} \geq \frac{\pi(1, n)}{1 - \pi(0, n)}. \tag{10.4}$$

Proposition 2. *For each α, if $n \geq n_\alpha$, then the expected revenues of the seller from the standard auction is higher than the expected revenue from any auction with a positive reserve price.*

Proof: In Appendix A.

For any positive reserve price r, informed bidder behaviour will remain unchanged from the standard auction when $v \geq r$ (with no participation when $v < r$). However, for any positive reserve price, uninformed bidders will not participate with strictly positive probability, and will not participate at all for a sufficiently high reserve, for instance, when $r > \bar{v}$. In the Appendix, we show that it does not pay the seller to set such a high reserve price that excludes uninformed bidders completely and lowers the probability of making a sale, provided there are sufficiently many bidders (that is, when (10.4) holds).[14]

For a sufficiently low reserve price, uninformed bidders will participate with positive probability. However, they will bid less aggressively than in the standard auction, typically quitting below $\bar{v}$. As a result, informed bidders will make higher profits in comparison to the standard auction. Since uninformed bidders make zero profits and the object is not sold with positive probability, the seller is strictly worse off from such a low reserve price relative to the standard auction, regardless of n.

We end this section with a consideration of posted price mechanisms where the seller offers the object at a fixed price. Bulow and Klemperer

---

[14] Since $\bar{v} = E[\frac{1}{h(V)}]$, note from (10.4) that for all distributions where the inverse of the hazard rate $\frac{1}{h(V)}$ is a convex function, such a high reserve price is not optimal for all $n \geq 2$. The uniform distribution is one example of such a distribution.

(2002) as well as Campbell and Levin (2006) demonstrate that posted price mechanisms can be attractive to a seller in comparison to the standard auction because the rent transferred to bidders when the true value of the object is higher than the posted price mitigates the winner's curse and encourages aggressive bidding. In our model, however, a posted price mechanism is not without its costs as an uninformed bidder may end up winning the object with a greater chance when informed bidders know the value of the object is below the posted price and so do not bid. As we show next, this 'upside' benefit of reducing the winner's curse that a posted price has may not be enough to swamp its 'downside' risk, so that the standard auction will yield the seller higher expected revenues compared to any posted price mechanism, at least for n large enough.

Proposition 3.   *For each α, there exists n'_α such that if $n \geq n'_\alpha$, the expected revenues of the seller from the standard auction is higher than the expected revenue from any posted price mechanism.*

Proof: In Appendix A.

The intuition for this result is similar to that for the last one. For any fixed price p, informed bidders participate if and only if $v > p$. For a high enough p (for instance, $p \geq \bar{v}$), uninformed bidders will not participate. In such a case, the seller can obviously do better by instead holding an auction with a reserve price equal to p. From Proposition 2, however, such an auction is dominated by the standard auction when n is large enough.

For a sufficiently low posted price, uninformed bidders will participate with positive probability. However, conditional on winning at the low posted price $p < \bar{v}$, informed bidders will make higher profits compared to winning at a price $\bar{v}$ in the standard auction. Furthermore, an informed bidder will make positive profits from winning not only when she is the only informed bidder (as in the standard auction), but also when there is more than one competing informed bidder present. Since the probability of being the only informed bidder becomes vanishingly small when there are many bidders, any posted price mechanism is dominated by the standard auction for n large enough.

CEILINGS

We turn now to a consideration of auctions with ceilings. Like a posted price mechanism (but unlike a standard auction), a ceiling on allowable bids reduces the fear of uninformed bidders from being outbid precisely when the object is worth bidding for. Unlike a posted price mechanism (but like the standard auction), by holding an auction at prices below the ceiling, the seller reduces the downside winner's curse problem for uninformed bidders as they typically pay a price lower than the ceiling when the value of the good is low. In this section, we identify conditions under which an auction with a ceiling dominates the standard auction.

Let $c^* \in (\bar{v}, 1)$ be a candidate ceiling price that solves the following equation:

$$\pi(0, n - 1)[\bar{v} - c^*] + (1 - \pi(0, n - 1))S(c^*) = 0 \qquad (10.5)$$

It is straightforward to verify the existence of a unique c^* that solves (10.5). In Proposition 4, we characterise the symmetric equilibrium of the auction with a ceiling c^* (and $r = 0$, henceforth referred to as the c^*-auction). In symmetric equilibrium, informed bidders stay in till the true value or the ceiling c^*, whichever is lower, while uninformed bidders bid till the ceiling, dropping out before as soon as any one else drops out. Equation (10.5) states that an uninformed bidder earns zero expected profits conditional on bidding at the ceiling, given that no quits have occurred before. The first term is her probability weighted expected pay-off from winning in the event that all other bidders are uninformed and have bid till the ceiling, while the second term is her probability weighted expected pay-off from winning in the event that at least one other bidder is informed and $V > c^*$.[15] Of course, the bidder earns zero profits when she does not win. Finally, if the true value of the good $V < c^*$ and at least one informed bidder is present, the latter drops out at V, triggering dropouts by all uninformed bidders immediately after so that uninformed bidders earn zero expected profits overall. Observe that c^* is increasing in n. When n becomes large, an uninformed bidder attaches a large probability to at least one other bidder being informed and so is willing to bid till a high ceiling.[16]

With the ceiling c^*, a bidder earns profits only when both the following conditions are satisfied: (a) she is informed and (b) the value of the good is greater than c^*. We, therefore, obtain expression (10.6) for the

---

[15] Note that in both cases, the bidder will be tied with n other bidders when winning, and so will win with probability $\frac{1}{n}$, which, thus, cancels out from the zero-profit condition (10.5). Furthermore, the probabilities in expression (10.5) should both be conditional probabilities. But since this only has the effect of dividing the expression by a constant, it is harmless to drop it.

[16] We show in Appendix B that c^* is the highest possible ceiling consistent with the uninformed bidders bidding up to the ceiling with Probability 1 and that with two bidders, c^* is the optimal non-trivial ceiling.

seller's ex ante expected revenues. Note than in contrast to the standard auction (but like a posted price mechanism), an informed bidder may earn strictly positive profits even when other bidders are informed.

Proposition 4. *Symmetric equilibrium strategies in the* c^**-auction are as follows. Any informed bidder who knows* $V = v$*, quits only when* $p > v$ *if* $v < c^*$*, staying in till* c^* *otherwise, regardless of the history of quits, while any uninformed bidder quits whenever anyone else quits, but otherwise does not quit at any* $p \in [0, c^*]$*. The ex ante expected revenue for the seller equals*

$$R(c^*) = \bar{v} - \alpha S(c^*). \tag{10.6}$$

Proof: Fix the ceiling c^* defined by (10.5). It is straightforward to show, by using arguments identical to those used previously, that it is essentially a weakly dominant strategy for an informed bidder to stay in the auction till the true value, or the ceiling, whichever is lower.

Consider next uninformed bidders. Due to arguments identical to those contained in the proof of Proposition 1, it follows that uninformed bidders will not drop out at any price strictly less than $\bar{v}$ conditional on having observed no dropouts in a symmetric equilibrium.

Let $\sigma_{\bar{v}} \in [0, 1]$ be the probability with which uninformed bidders continue at $p = \bar{v}$, given no prior dropouts. Observe first that by dropping out at $\bar{v}$, an uninformed bidder earns zero expected pay-offs, and this is true regardless of how other uninformed bidders behave. Observe next that $\sigma_{\bar{v}} > 0$ in a symmetric equilibrium. For if not, then by continuing at $\bar{v}$ till c^*, dropping out immediately after a dropout, an uninformed bidder competes only against informed bidders and so makes strictly positive expected pay-offs when she wins at the ceiling and zero pay-offs otherwise.

We show next that, in fact, $\sigma_{\bar{v}} = 1$. Suppose an uninformed bidder is indifferent between continuing and dropping out at $\bar{v}$. Let $k' = 0, ..., n$ be the number of bidders who continue at $\bar{v}$. Then, conditional on observing $k' \geq 2$ bidders continuing at $\bar{v}$, any uninformed bidder who continues at $\bar{v}$ must continue with Probability 1 at each $p \in (\bar{v}, c^*]$, given no further dropouts. For suppose to the contrary that for some such k' uninformed bidders continue with probability $\sigma_p < 1$ at some $p > \bar{v}$. The expected pay-offs from dropping out at p conditional on having reached it is equal to $(\bar{v} - p) < 0$ times the probability of winning the object upon dropping out at p, an event that occurs with positive probability only when all other bidders are uninformed. Observe that since $\sigma_p < 1$, this is equal to the expected pay-offs overall from following this strategy of continuing at p with probability σ_p. However, for any such k' and p, by dropping out earlier, at some $p' = \bar{v} + \varepsilon < p$, any such uninformed bidder can earn strictly higher expected pay-offs, for ε small enough, a contradiction establishing that uninformed bidders must continue till c^*, for each $k' \geq 2$, after continuing at $\bar{v}$, given no further dropouts. It follows from this that, for each k', an uninformed bidder must make zero expected pay-offs given that she continues at $\bar{v}$ and observes that k' bidders are continuing. For if from continuing at $\bar{v}$ and observing k', an uninformed bidder earns negative expected pay-offs from continuing till c^*, for some k', then it is better for her to dropout immediately and earn zero expected pay-offs. Given this, if an uninformed bidder earns strictly positive pay-offs after continuing at $\bar{v}$ and observing k', for some k', it is strictly better for her to continue at $\bar{v}$ rather than dropout with positive probability, a contradiction with the supposition that she is indifferent between dropping out and continuing at $\bar{v}$. However, the expected pay-offs from continuing at $\bar{v}$, observing k' and then continuing till c^*, in the case that $k' = n$, is equal to (ignoring multiplicative constants),

$$\pi(0, n-1)\xi_{\bar{v}}(n-1, n-1)[\bar{v} - c^*]$$
$$+ \sum_{k=1}^{n-1} \pi(k, n-1)\xi_{\bar{v}}(n-1-k, n-1-k)S(c^*), \qquad (10.7)$$

where $\xi_{\bar{v}}(k, K) = \binom{K}{k}\sigma_{\bar{v}}^k(1 - \sigma_{\bar{v}})^{K-k}$ is the probability that k out of K uninformed bidders continue at $\bar{v}$. Since $\sigma_{\bar{v}} \in (0, 1)$, from the definition of c^* in (10.5) it is easily seen that the expression in (10.7) is strictly positive—a contradiction with the fact established earlier that the expected pay-offs from continuing at $\bar{v}$ and observing $k' = n$ is zero. Thus, $\sigma_{\bar{v}} = 1$.

Given that uninformed bidders continue with Probability 1 at $p = \bar{v}$, it follows that they must continue with Probability 1 at any $p \in (\bar{v}, c^*]$, given no dropouts—for if not, they make strictly negative profits from dropping out at any price $p > \bar{v}$ and zero profits from dropping out at $\bar{v}$. Finally, given these strategies of informed and uninformed bidders, it is a best response for uninformed bidders to dropout upon observing a dropout at any $p < c^*$ since such a dropout can come only from an informed bidder.

In equilibrium, from (10.5), it follows that uninformed bidders earn zero expected pay-off, while informed bidders obtain a positive pay-off equal to $S(c^*)$ only when the true value of the object is at least c^* and she wins with probability $1/n$. Since the good is always sold and there are n ex ante identical bidders, the ex ante expected revenue for the seller equals

$$R(c^*) = \bar{v} - \alpha S(c^*).$$

This concludes the proof.

How does the seller do in the c^*-auction compared to the standard auction? Although by imposing a ceiling the seller gives up on high bids from better informed bidders, in Proposition 5, we show that the added participation that a ceiling generates from poorly informed bidders more than compensates the seller when there are many bidders or when most bidders are likely to be poorly informed.

Proposition 5. *For each $n \geq 2$, there exists $\alpha_n^* \in (0, 1]$ such that the c^*-auction earns the seller higher revenues than the standard auction iff $\alpha < \alpha_n^*$. Furthermore, for $n \geq n^* = \frac{1-\bar{v}}{S(\bar{v})}$, the c^*-auction earns the seller higher revenues than the standard auction regardless of $\alpha \in (0, 1)$.*

Proof: From the expressions for expected revenue obtained above, we see that the c^*-auction dominates the standard auction iff

$$n(1 - \alpha)^{n-1} S(\bar{v}) > S(c^*) \tag{10.8}$$

For $x \in [0, 1]$ define

$$U(x) \equiv \pi(0, n - 1)[\bar{v} - x] + (1 - \pi(0, n - 1))S(x) \tag{10.9}$$

and observe from the definition of c^* in (10.5) that $U(c^*) = 0$. Using this last fact in (10.8), we obtain the following necessary and sufficient condition for the ceiling to dominate the standard auction:

$$c^* < \bar{v} + n\left(1 - (1 - \alpha)^{n-1}\right) S(\bar{v}).$$

Since $U(x)$ is easily checked to be a decreasing function, we conclude that a necessary and sufficient condition for the last inequality to hold is that

$$U(\bar{v} + n(1 - (1 - \alpha)^{n-1})S(\bar{v})) < 0,$$

which in turn yields,

$$-(1 - \alpha)^{n-1} n S(\bar{v}) + S[\bar{v} + n\left(1 - (1 - \alpha)^{n-1}\right) S(\bar{v})] < 0 \tag{10.10}$$

as our necessary and sufficient condition for the c^*-auction to dominate the standard auction in expected revenues.

For fixed n, using the fact that the derivative of $S(.)$ is limited below by -1, it is easy to verify that the left–hand side of (10.10) is negative at $\alpha = 0$ and continuous and strictly increasing in $\alpha \in [0, 1)$. Furthermore, if n is such that $\bar{v} + nS(\bar{v}) < 1$, then this expression is positive at $\alpha = 1$, establishing the existence of $\alpha_n^* \in (0, 1)$ such that the c^*-auction dominates the standard auction iff $\alpha < \alpha_n^*$. On the other hand, if n is such that $\bar{v} + nS(\bar{v}) \geq 1$, then the left-hand side of (10.10) is equal to 0 at $\alpha = 1$. By the monotonicity of the expression in α, it follows that for such n the c^*-auction dominates the standard auction for all $\alpha < \alpha_n^* = 1$, establishing the first of the proposition and also the second part for

$$n > n^* \equiv \frac{1 - \bar{v}}{S(\bar{v})}.$$

In the standard auction, the seller leaves rents for bidders when only one of the bidders is informed and the true value of the object is at least the uninformed bidders' maximum possible bid $\bar{v}$. With a ceiling c^*, however, since uninformed bidders bid till c^*, the seller gains in states where there is only one informed bidder and the value of the good $V > \bar{v}$, as she receives a price higher than $\bar{v}$ in these states. The seller also gains in states where all bidders present are uninformed when she receives a price c^* that is higher than $\bar{v}$. However, a ceiling has some costs as the seller loses in states where multiple informed bidders are present and $V > c^*$. When $\alpha < \alpha_n^*$, the seller's expected loss in the last case is swamped by her gains from increased bidding by uninformed bidders. In such cases, the seller earns higher revenues by imposing a ceiling.

To gain intuition for the second part of the result, note first that for a large number of bidders, there are almost always two informed bidders present. Thus, the seller almost always loses from a ceiling, whenever $V > c^*$. However, in order to guarantee participation from uninformed bidders till the ceiling, the expected loss to an uninformed bidder from winning at the ceiling when all other bidders are uninformed must balance out her expected gains from winning at the ceiling against at least one informed bidder. With a large number of bidders, each uninformed bidder knows that at least a few of the other bidders are likely to be informed and so is willing to bid till a high ceiling. In other words, as n grows, c^* grows as well so that the probability that $V > c^*$ times the expected loss to the seller from a ceiling in that event becomes small. However, the seller still gains below the ceiling and, hence, overall, since uninformed bidders bid up to $c^* > \bar{v}$ in the c^*-auction. For uniformly distributed V, $n^* = \frac{1-\bar{v}}{S(\bar{v})} = 4$ so that a ceiling raises expected revenues whenever there are four or more bidders. In general, one can exploit the zero-profit condition (10.5) to show that the ratio of information rents in the c^*-auction to that in the standard auction converges to zero as n becomes large. From Propositions 2 and 3, it then follows that the c^*-auction also dominates any auction with a reserve price as well as any posted price mechanism for n large enough.

A ceiling is beneficial in our model exactly because it encourages uninformed bidders to bid beyond $\bar{v}$, the ex ante expected value of the object, in return for the positive probability of winning at the ceiling against an informed bidder and making positive profits when $V > c^*$. In contrast, in the standard auction, even though conditional on reaching $\bar{v}$ with no dropouts, an uninformed bidder may attach (for large n) a large probability to the event that $V > \bar{v}$; such a bidder will always be outbid by an informed bidder if she competes further and so is unwilling to do so. In a sense then, by banning price discrimination via competitive bidding above the ceiling, the seller provides a bidding guide or anchor price for uninformed bidders. This allows her to more effectively price discriminate below the ceiling.

Example 1. Suppose that V follows the uniform distribution on $[0, 1]$ so that $\bar{v} = \frac{1}{2}$ and

$$S(x) = \frac{1}{2}(1 - x)^2.$$

The expected revenue in a standard auction equals

$$R_s = \frac{1}{2} - n\alpha(1 - \alpha)^{n-1}\frac{1}{8}.$$

Note that for the uniform distribution condition (10.4) holds for all $n \geq 2$, so that from Proposition 2, a standard auction dominates any auction with a positive reserve price. Furthermore, note from Proposition 3 that any posted price $p \geq \bar{v}$ is dominated by an auction with the same reserve price which, by the previous remark, is dominated by the standard auction for all n. Finally, it is easily seen that a posted price $p < \bar{v} < c^*$ is dominated by the c^*-auction for all n. To see this, observe that for such a posted price, an informed bidder makes profits equal to $S(p)$ conditional on winning, and wins with probability at least $1/n$ (when all other bidders bid with her) for a total ex ante expected profits for all bidders that is at least $\alpha S(p)$ (since uninformed bidders also make non-negative profits). But since $p < c^*$, $\alpha S(p) > \alpha S(c^*)$, the total ex ante expected profits for all bidders in the c^*-auction.[17] Thus, either the standard auction or the c^*-auction dominate all other mechanisms

---

[17] While we do not state this as a proposition, this last argument clearly does not depend on the distributional assumptions made in this example.

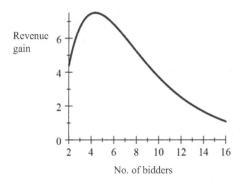

Figure 10.1 Percentage gain in revenue

that we have considered so far. Consequently, we will focus on these two mechanisms for the rest of this example.

For the uniform distribution, exploiting (10.5), it can be seen that

$$c^* = \frac{1}{1 + \sqrt{(1 - \alpha)^{n-1}}}.$$

For $n = 2$, the cut-off value $\alpha_2^* = 0.828$ below which the c^*-auction dominates the standard auction. Furthermore, for $n \geq n^* = 4$, the c^*-auction dominates the standard auction for all $\alpha \in (0, 1)$. Figure 10.1 depicts the percentage gain in revenue from the c^*-auction over the standard auction, as a function of n, when $\alpha = 0.25$. The percentage revenue gain is the highest at $n = 4$, when $c^* = 0.60624$, $R(c^*) = 0.48062$ and $R_s = 0.44727$ for an expected gain in revenue of 7.46 per cent and a reduction in rents by 63.25 per cent.

Bulow and Klemperer (1996) show that standard auctions, even when they are not optimal, frequently do quite well compared to the optimal mechanism. In their model, an auction with a last minute reserve may be optimal, but the seller's revenues from such a mechanism with n bidders is lower than that from the standard auction with just one more bidder.[18] This is a compelling argument for devoting resources to expanding the size of the bidder pool rather than to performing the

---

[18] In an auction with a last minute reserve, the seller holds an auction, but instead of transferring the good to the highest bidder at the going price, the seller offers the good to the highest bidder at a take-it-or-leave-it fixed price. It is important that the seller commits ex ante to such a menu of fixed prices, depending on the history of bidding. (See footnote 22 in Bulow and Klemperer (1996).)

evaluations necessary for a last minute reserve, from the perspective of the seller. However, in our framework, with hierarchically informed bidders, such a limit does not obtain and a simple ceiling yields significant gains over the standard auction. For instance, with $\alpha = 0.25$, the seller needs to have 11 bidders in the standard auction to have revenues higher than what she would earn in the c^*-auction with four bidders. Therefore, when expanding her market is not especially easy, the seller may be well advised to impose a ceiling. While a ceiling imposes greater informational requirements on the seller in terms of estimating the market parameters compared to a standard auction, these requirements are no more onerous than those involving reserve prices or standard monopoly pricing.

We do not consider the optimal mechanism in this essay (see, however, Appendix B for a characterisation of the optimal ceiling and reserve combination). Mechanisms involving an auction followed by negotiation or bargaining between the seller and all or some of the bidders, of the sort considered by Bulow and Klemperer (1996) and Lopomo (2001), dominate an auction with or without a ceiling.[19] Instead, we justify our focus on auctions with ceilings as a simple change in the rules of a commonly observed mechanism that should be easy to understand for the bidders.

CONCLUSION

In common value environments with ex post hierarchically informed bidders, a bid ceiling may significantly raise seller revenues. In particular, such a ceiling mechanism may dominate auctions with reserve prices as well as posted price mechanisms. While a bid ceiling prevents the seller from obtaining bids higher than the ceiling, it benefits the seller by alleviating the winner's curse problem for poorly informed bidders, and so, by increasing competition and demand below the ceiling. These results provide insight into the prevalence of fixed price or best offer mechanisms that make explicit the possibility of negotiations. More broadly interpreted, our results suggest that it may be beneficial to impose an upper limit on the share of the pie one is willing

---

[19] Bulow and Klemperer (1996) demonstrate optimality under independent signals or private values. Lopomo (2001) extends this result to correlated signals, but in a smaller class of mechanisms that satisfy a posterior implementability or no-regret condition. With interim implementability and correlated signals, Lopomo shows the optimality of mechanisms with both auction- and bargaining-like features.

to receive in multi-agent bargaining environments. An investigation of such questions outside the context of auctions is, therefore, also of interest.

APPENDIX A: PROOFS

Proof of Proposition 2. We first define some basic objects in order to characterise the symmetric equilibrium of an auction with a reserve price $r > 0$. For $x \in [0, 1]$, define

$$G(x) = F(x)\,[E[V|V < x] - x] = -\int_0^x F(u)du. \tag{10.11}$$

and observe that it is a negative, decreasing and concave function. Let r^* be defined as the solution to

$$\pi(0, n - 1)[\bar{v} - r^*] + (1 - \pi(0, n - 1))G(r^*) = 0. \tag{10.12}$$

Note from the definition of $G(.)$ that such an $r^* \in (0, \bar{v})$ exists and is unique. The next lemma characterises symmetric equilibrium in the auction with a reserve price $r > 0$. We will say that a bidder is present at the open whenever she belongs to the set $A(r)$ and say that she participates in the auction (with positive probability) if she is present at the open (with positive probability).

Lemma 1. *Fix $r > 0$. Then symmetric equilibrium strategies are as follows. Any informed bidder who knows $V = v$ participates in the auction if and only if $v \geq r$, and given that she participates, quits only at $p > v$, staying in otherwise, regardless of the history of quits. Furthermore,*

1. *if $r \geq r^*$ then uninformed bidders participate in the auction with probability 0;*
2. *while if $r < r^*$, then uninformed bidders participate in the auction with probability $\sigma_r \in (0, 1)$ given by the solution to*

$$\pi(0, n - 1)\,[1 - \sigma_r]^{n-1}\,[\bar{v} - r]$$
$$+ \sum_{k'=1}^{n-1} \pi(k', n - 1)\,[1 - \sigma_r]^{n-1-k'}\,G(r) = 0 \tag{10.13}$$

and upon participation, an uninformed bidder quits as soon as anyone quits and otherwise quits only at $p > \bar{v}_k$, where $\bar{v}_k$ is the *expected value of the object given all k bidders present at the open are uninformed, for $k \in \{1, ..., n\}$.*

Proof of Lemma. The optimality of the behaviour of informed bidders immediately follows using arguments analogous to the proof of Proposition 1. Given this, consider the behaviour of uninformed bidders in a symmetric equilibrium.

Fix $r > 0$ and let $\sigma_r \in [0, 1]$ be the probability with which an uninformed bidder participates in the auction. Let $k \in \{0, 1, ..., n\}$ be the total number of bidders present at the open.

Observe first that given the behaviour of informed bidders and conditional on participation and observing that $k > 1$, an uninformed bidder makes at most zero expected profits whenever at least one other bidder present at the open is informed. On the other hand, conditional on the event $k > 1$ and all other bidders present at the open are uninformed, an uninformed bidder must earn zero expected profits, in any symmetric equilibrium, at least whenever such an event has positive probability (that is, $\sigma_r > 0$).

To see this, let $\bar{v}_k$ denote the expected value of the object given that all k bidders present at the open are uninformed (where we suppress the dependence of $\bar{v}_k$ on σ_r). If an uninformed bidder makes positive profits conditional on winning, given $k > 1$ and all other bidders are uninformed, then all uninformed bidders must quit with strictly positive probability at some price $p < \bar{v}_k$, conditional on a history of no quits. In such a case, the uninformed bidder wins the object with probability $\frac{1}{k}$ (for strictly positive profits $\bar{v}_k - p$) by quitting at p, when all other bidders are uninformed and also quit at p, and does not win the object in any other state (ignoring the zero probability case that $V = p$). If instead she continues at p and drops out immediately after, then she wins the object with higher probability compared to quitting at p, and earns the same expected profits in all other cases—a contradiction with equilibrium. Similarly, if an uninformed bidder earns negative profits conditional on $k > 1$ and all other bidders present are uninformed, all uninformed bidders must remain active with positive probability at some $p > \bar{v}_k$, conditional on a history with no quits. It is easy to see that by quitting with Probability 1 at such a p an uninformed bidder strictly increases her expected profits. It follows that an uninformed bidder must earn zero expected profits conditional on being present at the open and observing $k > 1$, whenever $\sigma_r > 0$.

Consider next the profits of the uninformed bidder, conditional on being the only bidder present at the open (that is, $k = 1$) and so winning at the reserve r. Letting $D = \sum_{k'=0}^{n-1} \pi(k', n-1)[1 - \sigma_r]^{n-1-k'}$, this is given by

$$\frac{1}{D}\left[\pi(0, n-1)[1 - \sigma_r]^{n-1}[\bar{v} - r] + \sum_{k'=1}^{n-1} \pi(k', n-1)[1 - \sigma_r]^{n-1-k'} G(r)\right].$$

$$(10.14)$$

The first term reflects the probability that all other bidders are uninformed and not present at the open multiplied by the expected profits from winning in this case. Each term in the sum reflects the probability that all k' informed bidders as well as all uninformed bidders are not present at the open multiplied by the expected profits from winning in this case.

Observe first that $\sigma_r < 1$. For if $\sigma_r = 1$, then the expression in (10.14) reduces to $G(r) < 0$, so that an uninformed bidder will be strictly better off from not participating in the auction at all. Next notice that if $r \geq r^*$, then $\sigma_r = 0$. For if not, the expression in brackets in (10.14) is strictly less than

$$\pi(0, n-1)[\bar{v} - r] + \sum_{k'=1}^{n-1} \pi(k', n-1)G(r) \leq 0$$

since $r \geq r^*$. Conversely, if $r < r^*$, then we must have $\sigma_r > 0$. For if not, an uninformed bidder will strictly prefer to participate in the auction with Probability 1 and quit immediately after r. It follows that when $r < r^*$, σ_r is chosen so that the expression in (10.14) exactly equals zero, that is, σ_r is the solution to (10.13).

Furthermore, since conditional on participating and observing k, an uninformed bidder must always earn zero expected profits, she cannot do better than by quitting as soon as she observes a quit and quitting above $\bar{v}_k$ otherwise, where for $k \in \{1, ..., n\}$, $\bar{v}_k$ is defined as the solution to the zero expected profit condition conditional on winning at $\bar{v}_k$ and all k bidders are uninformed:

$$\pi(0, n-1)\xi_r(k-1, n-1)[\bar{v} - \bar{v}_k]$$

$$+ \sum_{k'=1}^{n-k} \pi(k', n-1)\xi_r(k-1, n-k'-1)F(r)[E[V|V < r] - \bar{v}_k] = 0$$

where for

$$0 \leq k \leq K \leq n, \quad \xi_r(k, K) = \binom{K}{k}\sigma_r^k(1 - \sigma_r)^{K-k}$$

is the probability that k out of K uninformed bidders are present at the open. Observe that $\bar{v}(1) = r$ and $\bar{v}_k \leq \bar{v}_n = \bar{v}$. This concludes the proof of the lemma.

For the proof of the proposition, recall first that in the standard auction a bidder makes positive profits when she is the only informed bidder and $V > \bar{v}$, in which case she pays a price equal to $\bar{v}$. Using Lemma 1 observe next that when the seller imposes a reserve price $r \in (0, \bar{v})$, such a bidder makes weakly higher expected profits as with positive probability, she wins the object at a price weakly less than $\bar{v}$. Furthermore, an informed bidder with a realised value $v \in (r, \bar{v}]$ makes strictly positive profits when she is the only informed bidder, whereas in the standard auction such a bidder makes zero profits. Since uninformed bidders make zero profits in both auctions, it follows that each bidder makes weakly higher ex ante expected profits in the auction with a reserve price $r \leq \bar{v}$. Since the object is not sold with strictly positive probability, it follows that the seller is strictly worse off from imposing a reserve price $r \in (0, \bar{v}]$, compared to the standard auction.

Consider next $r > \bar{v} > r^*$. Since uninformed bidders do not participate by Lemma 1, the seller's expected revenue is

$$\pi(1, n)(1 - F(r))r + (1 - \pi(0, n) - \pi(1, n))(1 - F(r))E[V|V > r].$$

Using the monotone hazard rate condition, observe that for the optimal choice of r to be greater than $\bar{v}$, the derivative of the last expression must be positive at $r = \bar{v}$. This yields

$$\frac{\bar{v}f(\bar{v})}{1 - F(\bar{v})} < \frac{\pi(1, n)}{1 - \pi(0, n)} = \frac{n\alpha(1 - \alpha)^{n-1}}{1 - (1 - \alpha)^n}.$$

For n large enough, this inequality is violated so that the optimal choice of a reserve r cannot be greater than $\bar{v}$. This completes the proof.

Proof of Proposition 3

For any posted price $p \in [0, 1]$, an informed bidder will participate only if $v \geq p$. Let $\sigma_p \in [0, 1]$ be the probability with which an uninformed bidder participates in a symmetric equilibrium. For $0 \leq k \leq K \leq n$, let $\xi_p(k, K) = \binom{K}{k}\sigma_p^k(1 - \sigma_p)^{K-k}$ be the probability that k out of K uninformed bidders participate. Consider the expected profits of an uninformed bidder from bidding at the posted price p. This is given by

$$\pi(0, n-1) \sum_{k'=0}^{n-1} \xi_p(k', n-1) \frac{1}{k'+1} [\bar{v} - p]$$

$$+ \sum_{k=1}^{n-1} \pi(k, n-1) \sum_{k'=0}^{n-1-k} \xi_p(k', n-1-k)$$

$$\times [\frac{1}{k'+1} G(p) + \frac{1}{k+k'+1} S(p)] \qquad (10.15)$$

where the functions S and G have been defined in (10.1) and (10.11) respectively. The first term is the probability that all other bidders are uninformed multiplied by the expected probability of winning and the expected pay-off conditional on winning in such a case. The second term has the same interpretation, but in the case where at least one bidder is informed. The bidder makes zero profits when she is not the winner.

A symmetric equilibrium exists for all p. To see this observe that if the expression in (10.15) is non-positive for $\sigma_p = 0$, then it is an equilibrium for uninformed bidders not to participate. On the other hand, if the expression in (10.15) is positive for $\sigma_p = 0$, but negative for $\sigma_p = 1$, then by continuity, there exists $\sigma_p \in (0, 1)$ for which the expression in (10.15) is exactly equal to 0 and uninformed bidders are willing to participate with positive probability. Finally, if the expression in (10.15) is non-negative for $\sigma_p = 1$, then it is an equilibrium for uninformed bidders to participate with Probability 1.

Note next that from the definitions of S and G, for all $x \in [0, 1]$

$$S(x) + G(x) = \bar{v} - x. \qquad (10.16)$$

Using this in (10.15), we can rewrite an uninformed bidders expected profits from participating as

$$\sum_{k=0}^{n-1} \pi(k, n-1) \sum_{k'=0}^{n-1-k} \xi_p(k', n-1-k)$$

$$\times \left[\frac{1}{k'+1} (\bar{v} - p) + \frac{k}{(k+k'+1)(k'+1)} G(p) \right]. \qquad (10.17)$$

Suppose first that $p > \bar{v}$. Then the expression (10.17) is negative for any $\sigma_p > 0$ and so we must have $\sigma_p = 0$. From Lemma 1, if the seller holds an auction with a reserve price equal to p, then uninformed bidders will still not participate, but informed bidders will bid and pay a price above p whenever $v > p$ and at least two bidders are informed. As a result, the seller will earn higher revenues from such an auction with a reserve price p compared to offering up the object at a fixed price p. However, from Proposition 2, for $n \geq n_\alpha$, the seller earns even higher revenues from the standard auction compared to the revenues from the auction with a reserve price of p so that the standard auction dominates all such posted prices $p \geq \bar{v}$ for $n \geq n_\alpha$.

Next consider $p \leq \bar{v}$. Conditional on winning, an informed bidder's expected profit is given by $S(p)$. Furthermore, an informed bidder wins with probability at least $1/n$ when she bids at p. Since uninformed bidders earn non-negative profits, it follows that the sum of the expected profits of all bidders is at least $\alpha S(p)$. Recall that the analogous expression for the standard auction is $n\alpha(1 - \alpha)^{n-1}S(\bar{v})$. Since S is a decreasing function and $p \leq \bar{v}$, it follows that the seller is strictly better off from the standard auction compared to any posted price $p \leq \bar{v}$, for any n large enough satisfying $n(1 - \alpha)^{n-1} < 1$.

APPENDIX B: OPTIMAL CEILING AND RESERVE PRICES

In this section, we characterise the optimal reserve and ceiling combination $\{r, c\} \in Z = \{r, c | 0 \leq r \leq c \leq 1\}$ for the case of $n = 2$ bidders, under commitment. The restriction to 2 bidders is to minimise the number of cases to consider. We also assume that condition (10.4) holds for the case of two bidders. We then have the following result.

Proposition 6. *Suppose $n = 2$ and that (10.4) holds. Then the optimal reserve is $r = 0$ and the optimal ceiling $c \in \{c^*, 1\}$.*

Proof: We proceed in steps. In Step 1 we characterise the symmetric equilibrium with two bidders for every reserve and ceiling combination in the set Z. In Step 2, we show that a positive reserve price is not optimal. In Step 3, we show that either the simple ceiling c^* is optimal or a ceiling is not optimal at all.

Step 1: We begin by defining a few objects. For $\{r, c\} \in Z$, let

$$U_1(r, c) \equiv (1 - \alpha)\frac{1}{2}[\bar{v} - c] + \alpha[G(r) + \frac{1}{2}S(c)]$$

and

$$U_0(r, c) \equiv (1 - \alpha)[\bar{v} - r] + \alpha[G(r) + \frac{1}{2}S(c)]$$

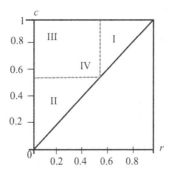

Figure 10.2 Equilibrium zones

and

$$W(r, c) \equiv (1 - \alpha)[1 + \frac{\alpha G(r)}{(1 - \alpha)[\bar{v} - r]}][\bar{v} - c] + \alpha S(c).$$

Using (10.16), notice that since $r \leq c$, whenever $U_1(r, c) \geq 0$, we have $U_0(r, c) > U_1(r, c)$. We will show below that symmetric equilibria have the following structure. Informed bidders participate iff $v \geq r$ and continue till $\min[v, c]$ regardless of dropouts. Uninformed bidders participate with probability $\sigma_r \in [0, 1]$, continuing till $\bar{v}$ with Probability 1, continuing at $\bar{v}$ with probability $\sigma_{\bar{v}} \in [0, 1]$, and continuing beyond till c with Probability 1, quitting at any point immediately after observing a quit.

We show now that for $\{r, c\}$ such that $U_0(r, c) \leq 0$, $\sigma_r = 0$. This is represented by zone I in Figure 10.2. Further, for $\{r, c\}$ such that $U_1(r, c) \geq 0$, $\sigma_r = 1 = \sigma_{\bar{v}}$ (zone II in the figure), while for $\{r, c\}$ such that $U_1(r, c) < 0 < U_0(r, c)$, $\sigma_r \in (0, 1)$ with $\sigma_r < 1$ if $r > 0$ (zones III and IV). In the last case, $\sigma_{\bar{v}} \in [0, 1]$ with $\sigma_{\bar{v}} > 0$ iff $c < 1$ and $\sigma_{\bar{v}} < 1$ if $W(r, c) < 0$ (zone III), while $\sigma_{\bar{v}} = 1$ if $W(r, c) \geq 0$ (zone IV).

The behaviour of informed bidders is immediate, for every $\{r, c\}$. As for uninformed bidders, conditional on participating and observing that both bidders are present, uninformed bidders must continue with Probability 1 for all $p \in [r, c]$, with $p \neq \bar{v}$. For if they dropout with positive probability at any $p < \bar{v}$, then by continuing at p and dropping out immediately after such a bidder makes strictly higher expected profits than from dropping out at p. On the other hand, if they dropout with positive probability at any $p > \bar{v}$, then the expected pay-off is negative, whereas by dropping out at $\bar{v}$, such a bidder can guarantee zero expected profits. It follows that uninformed bidders must dropout anytime they observe a dropout at a $p \neq \bar{v}$.

Observe next from Propositions 1 and 2 that symmetric equilibrium behaviour is as specified in the case $c = 1$. As a result, in what follows, we focus on the case where $c < 1$. Note that whenever $c < 1$, we must have $\sigma_{\bar{v}} > 0$—for if not, an uninformed bidder by continuing till c competes only against an informed bidder and makes strictly positive profits, whereas she makes zero profits from dropping out at $\bar{v}$.

Consider first a symmetric equilibrium where $\sigma_r = 0$. Since no uninformed bidder wants to participate, we must have that the expected profits from participating be non-positive, or $U_0(r, c) \leq 0$. It is straightforward to check that the specified behaviour is an equilibrium in this zone.

Consider next a symmetric equilibrium where $\sigma_r = 1 = \sigma_{\bar{v}}$. Since uninformed bidders must earn non-negative expected profits, we must have $U_1(r, c) \geq 0$. It is straightforward to check that the specified behaviour is an equilibrium in this zone.

Next suppose that in a symmetric equilibrium $\sigma_r = 1$ but $\sigma_{\bar{v}} \in (0, 1)$. Conditional on reaching $\bar{v}$ and dropping out, an uninformed bidder must make zero expected profits and since $\sigma_{\bar{v}} \in (0, 1)$ must also make zero expected profits from continuing till c. This implies that $\sigma_{\bar{v}}$ must solve:

$$(1 - \alpha)\sigma_{\bar{v}}\frac{1}{2}[\bar{v} - c] + \alpha\frac{1}{2}S(c) = 0. \tag{10.18}$$

It follows that $c > c^*$. Notice next that the ex ante expected profits of an uninformed bidder is equal to a weighted sum of her expected profits when she is the only bidder present at the open and her expected profits when both bidders are present at the open. Due to arguments used to establish (10.18), the second expected value is equal to zero, while since $\sigma_r = 1$, the first expected value is negative if $r > 0$ and zero otherwise. It follows that $r = 0$. It is straightforward to check that the specified behaviour is an equilibrium in this zone and furthermore that $U_1(r, c) < 0 < U_0(r, c)$.

Consider now a symmetric equilibrium where $\sigma_r \in (0, 1)$ and $\sigma_{\bar{v}} \in (0, 1)$. Using arguments similar to those used in establishing (10.18), we must have that uninformed bidders must earn zero profits so that (given σ_r), $\sigma_{\bar{v}}$ must solve

$$(1 - \alpha)\sigma_r\sigma_{\bar{v}}\frac{1}{2}[\bar{v} - c] + \alpha\frac{1}{2}S(c) = 0. \tag{10.19}$$

It follows that $c > \bar{v}$. Furthermore, since $\sigma_r \in (0, 1)$, uninformed bidders must earn zero profits from participating, that is, σ_r must solve

$$(1 - \alpha)(1 - \sigma_r)[\bar{v} - r] + \alpha G(r) = 0. \tag{10.20}$$

It follows that $r \in (0, \bar{v})$. Furthermore, using the solution for σ_r obtained in (10.20) in (10.19), we obtain

$$(1 - \alpha)[1 + \frac{\alpha G(r)}{(1 - \alpha)[\bar{v} - r]}]\sigma_{\bar{v}}[\bar{v} - c] + \alpha[S(c)] = 0.$$

Since $c > \bar{v}$ and $r \in (0, \bar{v})$, we must then have $W(r, c) < 0$ and, using (10.19), $U_1(r, c) < 0$ and furthermore, using (10.20), $U_0(r, c) > 0$. It is straightforward to check that the specified behaviour is an equilibrium in this zone.

Finally, consider a symmetric equilibrium where $\sigma_r \in (0, 1)$ but $\sigma_{\bar{v}} = 1$. Since uninformed bidders randomise participation, we must have that the ex ante expected profits of an uninformed bidder equals zero, that is,

$$(1 - \alpha)[(1 - \sigma_r)(\bar{v} - r) + \sigma_r \frac{1}{2}(\bar{v} - c)] + \alpha[G(r) + \frac{1}{2}S(c)] = 0. \tag{10.21}$$

It follows that $r < \bar{v}$. For if not, since $c \geq r$ and by (10.16), $G(r) + \frac{1}{2}S(c) \leq \frac{1}{2}G(r) + \frac{1}{2}(\bar{v} - r) < 0$, we obtain a contradiction with (10.21). Furthermore, the expression in (10.21) is monotonically decreasing in σ_r. It follows that it is strictly less than $U_0(r, c)$ and strictly greater than $U_1(r, c)$, yielding $U_1(r, c) < 0 < U_0(r, c)$. Furthermore, uninformed bidders must make non-negative profits conditional on reaching $\bar{v}$ and continuing, that is,

$$(1 - \alpha)\sigma_r[\bar{v} - c] + \alpha[S(c)] \geq 0$$

From (10.21) it follows that

$$\sigma_r \geq 1 + \frac{\alpha G(r)}{(1 - \alpha)[\bar{v} - r]} \tag{10.22}$$

so that, substituting the term on the right-hand side of the last expression for σ_r in the left-hand side of (10.21) and using the monotonicity of the expression in (10.21), we obtain $W(r, c) \geq 0$. It is straightforward to check that the specified behaviour is an equilibrium in this zone. This completes the description for symmetric equilibria for all $\{r, c\} \in Z$.

Step 2: We will show that each auction $\{r, c\} \in Z$ with a reserve price $r > 0$ is strictly dominated in expected revenues by some auction $\{0, c'\} \in Z$, that has no reserve.

Consider first the expected revenues of the seller for the auction with reserve and ceiling pair $\{r, c\} \in Z$ such that $r \geq \bar{v}$. From Step 1, using (10.16) observe that then $U_0(r, c) < 0$ so that $\sigma_r = 0$. Given the behaviour of informed bidders it follows immediately that the seller will do better by instead holding the auction $\{r, 1\}$, which by the assumed conditions of the proposition is dominated by the standard auction $\{0, 1\}$. The same logic also eliminates all auctions $\{r, c\}$ where $U_0(r, c) \leq 0$, allowing us to focus throughout what follows on the case where $U_0(r, c) > 0$ so that $\sigma_r > 0$.

Next consider the auction $\{r, c\}$ with $0 < r < \bar{v}$ and $c^* < c < 1$ and $U_0(r, c) > 0$. From Step 1, we must have $\sigma_r \in (0, 1)$ and $\sigma_{\bar{v}} \in (0, 1]$, as in such a case $U_1(r, c) < 0$. We compare the expected revenues from such an auction with that from the auction $\{0, c\}$ that has the same ceiling but no reserve. From Step 1, in the auction $\{0, c\}$, uninformed bidders participate with Probability 1 and continue at $\bar{v}$ with probability $\sigma'_{\bar{v}} \in (0, 1)$. In either auction an informed bidder makes positive profits only when she is the only informed bidder or when $V > c$, while uninformed bidders make zero expected profits. Furthermore, the object is sold with Probability 1 in the auction $\{0, c\}$, while it is not sold with positive probability in the auction $\{r, c\}$. It, thus, suffices to show that informed bidders earn higher expected profits in the auction $\{r, c\}$ as compared to the auction $\{0, c\}$. Suppose first that $\{r, c\}$ is such that $W(r, c) \geq 0$. Then $\sigma_{\bar{v}} = 1$ in the auction $\{r, c\}$. Furthermore, letting $\Pi(r, c|v)$ denote the expected profits of a bidder conditional on being informed and conditional on the realised value of $V = v$, it is seen that

$$\Pi(r, c|v) = \begin{cases} 0 & \text{when } v < r \\ (1 - \alpha)(1 - \sigma_r)[v - r] & \text{when } r \leq v < c \\ (1 - \alpha)(1 - \sigma_r)[v - r] + ((1 - \alpha)\sigma_r + \alpha)\frac{1}{2}[v - c] & \text{when } v \geq c \end{cases}$$

(10.23)

In contrast, in the auction $\{0, c\}$, conditional on being an informed bidder and the realised value of v of V, the expected profits of an informed bidder is

$$\Pi(0, c|v) = \begin{cases} 0 & \text{when } v < \bar{v} \\ (1 - \alpha)(1 - \sigma'_{\bar{v}})[v - \bar{v}] & \text{when } \bar{v} \leq v < c \\ (1 - \alpha)(1 - \sigma'_{\bar{v}})[v - \bar{v}] + ((1 - \alpha)\sigma'_{\bar{v}} + \alpha)\frac{1}{2}[v - c] & \text{when } v > c \end{cases}$$

(10.24)

Comparing state by state, we see that the $\{0, c\}$ auction dominates the $\{r, c\}$ auction if $\sigma_r \leq \sigma'_{\bar{v}}$. But, from Step 1, $\sigma'_{\bar{v}}$ solves (10.18). Since $c > c^* > \bar{v}$, the expression in (10.18) is decreasing in $\sigma_{\bar{v}}$, so that if $\sigma_r > \sigma'_{\bar{v}}$, then the expression in (10.18) is negative if we replace $\sigma_{\bar{v}}$ with σ_r in it. Since, again from Step 1, σ_r solves (10.21), it follows that σ_r must satisfy

$$(1 - \alpha)(1 - \sigma_r)(\bar{v} - r) + \alpha G(r) > 0$$

which, since $r < \bar{v}$, yields the desired contradiction with (10.22).

Suppose next that $\{r, c\}$ is such that $W(r, c) < 0$. Then $\sigma_{\bar{v}} \in (0, 1)$ in the auction $\{r, c\}$ and solves (10.19), whereas, $\sigma'_{\bar{v}}$ (corresponding to the $\{0, c\}$ auction) solves (10.18) so that we obtain $\sigma_r \sigma_{\bar{v}} = \sigma'_{\bar{v}}$. Furthermore, conditional on being an informed bidder and the realised value v of V, the expected profits of an informed bidder in the $\{r, c\}$ auction is equal to 0 when $v < r$, equal to $(1 - \alpha)(1 - \sigma_r)[v - r]$ when $r \le v < \bar{v}$, equal to

$$(1 - \alpha)[(1 - \sigma_r)(v - r) + \sigma_r(1 - \sigma_{\bar{v}})(v - \bar{v})]$$

when $\bar{v} \le v < c$ and equal to

$$(1 - \alpha)[(1 - \sigma_r)(v - r) + \sigma_r(1 - \sigma_{\bar{v}})(v - \bar{v})] + [(1 - \alpha)\sigma_r\sigma_{\bar{v}} + \alpha]\frac{1}{2}S(c)$$

when $v \ge c$. Since $\sigma_r\sigma_{\bar{v}} = \sigma'_{\bar{v}}$, comparing state by state with the expression for $\Pi(0, c|v)$, it follows that the $\{0, c\}$ auction strictly dominates the $\{r, c\}$ auction.

Next, consider the auction $\{r, c\}$ with $0 < r < \bar{v}$ and $r \le c \le c^*$ and $U_0(r, c) > 0 > U_1(r, c)$. It is immediate from Step 1 then that $W(r, c) \ge 0$ so that $\sigma_r \in (0, 1)$ and $\sigma_{\bar{v}} = 1$. We compare such an auction with the c^*-auction $\{0, c^*\}$. Conditional on being an informed bidder and the realised value v of V, the expected profits of an informed bidder in the $\{0, c^*\}$ auction is equal to $\frac{1}{2}(v - c^*)$ when $v \ge c^*$ and 0 otherwise. Since $c^* \ge c$, comparing with the expression for $\Pi(r, c|v)$ in (10.23), we see that informed bidders earn strictly higher profits in the $\{r, c\}$ auction compared to the $\{0, c^*\}$ auction. Since uninformed bidders earn zero expected profits in both auctions and the object is sold with Probability 1 in the $\{0, c^*\}$ auction, but not in the $\{r, c\}$ auction, it follows that the former strictly dominates the latter in expected revenues.

It remains to consider auctions with $\{r, c\}$ such that $0 < r < \bar{v}$ and $r \le c \le c^*$ and $U_1(r, c) \ge 0$. From Step 1, $\sigma_r = \sigma_{\bar{v}} = 1$ so that conditional on being informed and the realised value v of V, the profits of an informed bidder equals $\frac{1}{2}[v - c]$ when $v \ge c$ and 0 otherwise. This is higher than the corresponding expression in the $\{0, c^*\}$ auction, state by state. Uninformed bidders earn non-negative expected profits in the $\{r, c\}$ auction and zero expected profits in the $\{0, c^*\}$ auction. Furthermore, since $r > 0$, the object is not sold with positive probability in the $\{r, c\}$ auction, but sold with Probability 1 in the $\{0, c^*\}$ auction. It follows that the latter strictly dominates the former in expected revenues. This completes Step 2.

Step 3 : From Step 2, it follows that the revenue maximising choice of a reserve and ceiling pair $\{r, c\}$ must satisfy $r = 0$. Then, the object is always sold with Probability 1, for any c. Furthermore, it is easy to see that the optimal ceiling c is at least c^*—from Step 1, compared to an auction $\{0, c\}$ with $c < c^*$, both informed and uninformed bidders earn lower profits in the auction $\{0, c^*\}$.

Let $\Pi(0, c)$ be the unconditional expected information rents that the buyers earn in any auction with $r = 0$ and $c \in [c^*, 1]$. Since all these auctions are efficient (from Step 1), in order to compare revenues across these auctions, it suffices to compare $\Pi(0, c)$ for different values of c. Observe first that for $c \in [c^*, 1]$,

$$\Pi(0, c) = \alpha[(\alpha + (1 - \alpha)\sigma_{\bar{v}})\frac{1}{2}S(c) + (1 - \alpha)(1 - \sigma_{\bar{v}})S(\bar{v})].$$

Using the solution (10.18) for $\sigma_{\bar{v}}$, let

$$\Delta(c) \equiv \Pi(0, c) - \Pi(0, 1) = \frac{1}{2}\frac{\alpha S(c)}{c - \bar{v}}[c + S(c) - \bar{v} - 2S(\bar{v})]. \quad (10.25)$$

Note that $\Delta(c) \leq 0$ iff

$$c + S(c) \leq \bar{v} + 2S(\bar{v}). \quad (10.26)$$

The left-hand side of (10.26) is monotone increasing in c, implying that if the standard auction dominates the c^*-auction (that is, if (10.26) is violated for $c = c^*$), then it also dominates all ceilings $c < 1$. Conversely, for c such that (10.26) holds, the derivative with respect to c of $\Delta(c)$ is

$$\Delta'(c) = [c + S(c) - \bar{v} - 2S(\bar{v})]\frac{d}{dc}[\frac{\alpha S(c)}{c - \bar{v}}] + \frac{\alpha S(c)}{c - \bar{v}}[1 + S'(c)] > 0.$$

implying that when the c^*-auction dominates the standard auction, it also dominates all ceilings $c > c^*$. This completes the proof.

REFERENCES

Bikhchandani, S., P. Haile and J. Riley. 2002. 'Symmetric Separating Equilibria in English Auctions', *Games and Economic Behavior*, 38(1): 19–27.

Blackwell, D. 1953. 'Equivalent Comparisons of Experiments', *The Annals of Mathematical Statistics*, 24(2): 265–72.

Bulow, J. and P. Klemperer. 1996. 'Auctions versus Negotiations', *American Economic Review*, 86(1): 180–94.

———. 2002. 'Prices and the Winner's Curse', *The RAND Journal of Economics*, 33(1): 1–21.

Campbell, C. M. and D. Levin. 2006. 'When and Why Not to Auction', *Economic Theory*, 27(3): 583–96.

Chakraborty, A. 2002. 'Optimal Price Ceilings in a Common Value Auction', *Economics Bulletin*, 3(7): 1–7.

Che, Y. and I. Gale. 1998. 'Caps on Political Lobbying', *American Economic Review*, 88(3): 643–51.

Chen, Y. and R. W. Rosenthal. 1996a. 'Asking Prices as Commitment Devices', *International Economic Review*, 37(1): 129–55.

———. 1996b. 'On the Use of Ceiling-Price Commitments by Monopolists', *The RAND Journal of Economics*, 27(2): 207–20.

Cremer, J. and R. Maclean. 1988. 'Full Extraction of the Surplus in Bayesian and Dominant Strategy Auctions', *Econometrica*, 56(6): 1247–57.

Engelbrecht-Wiggans, R., P. Milgrom and R. Weber. 1983. 'Competitive Bidding and Proprietary Information', *Journal of Mathematical Economics*, 11(2): 161–69.

Gavious, A., B. Moldovanu and A. Sela. 2002. 'Bid Costs and Endogenous Bid Caps', *The RAND Journal of Economics*, 33(4): 709–22.

Hendricks, K., R. Porter and C. Wilson. 1994. 'Auctions for Oil and Gas Leases with an Informed Bidder and a Random Reservation Price', *Econometrica*, 62(6): 1415–44.

Levin, D. and J. L. Smith. 1996. 'Optimal Reservation Prices in Auctions', *Economic Journal*, 106(438): 1271–83.

Lopomo, G. 2001. 'Optimality and Robustness of the English Auction', *Games and Economic Behavior*, 36(2): 219–40.

McAfee, R. P. and P. Reny. 1992. 'Correlated Information and Mechanism Design', *Econometrica*, 60(2): 395–421.

Milgrom, P. R. 2004. *Putting Auction Theory to Work*. Cambridge: Cambridge University Press.

Milgrom, P. R. and R. J. Weber. 1982. 'A Theory of Auctions and Competitive Bidding', *Econometrica*, 50(5): 1089–122.

Myerson, R. B. 1981. 'Optimal Auction Design', *Mathematics of Operations Research*, 6(1): 58–63.

Piccione, M. and G. Tan. 1996. 'A Simple Model of Expert and Non-expert Bidding in First Price Auctions', *Journal of Economic Theory*, 70(2): 501–15.

Porter, R. H. 1995. 'The Role of Information in U.S. Offshore Oil and Gas Lease Auctions', *Econometrica*, 63(1): 1–27.

Roy Chowdhury, P. 2008. 'Controlling Collusion in Auctions: The Role of Ceilings and Reserve Prices', *Economics Letters*, 98(3): 240–466.

Sahuguet, N. 2006. 'Caps in Asymmetric All-Pay Auctions with Incomplete Information', *Economics Bulletin*, 3(9): 1–8.

Shapiro, C. and J. Stiglitz. 1984. 'Equilibrium Unemployment as a Worker Discipline Device', *American Economic Review*, 74(3): 433–44.

Stiglitz, J. and A. Weiss. 1981. 'Credit Rationing in Markets with Imperfect Information', *American Economic Review*, 71(3): 393–410.

Szech, N. 2012. 'Tie-Breaks and Bid-Caps in All-Pay Auctions', mimeo, University of Bonn.

Wang, R. 1993. 'Auctions versus Posted-Price Selling', *American Economic Review*, 83(4): 838–51.

11

Corruption in Union Leadership

Sarbajit Chaudhuri and Krishnendu Ghosh Dastidar*

The phenomenon of corruption has existed for ages. Over the last few decades, it has become all-pervasive, especially in many developing countries, and is widely believed to be the single-most important obstacle to development. Widespread corruption across organisations, both public and private, surely goes a long way in explaining the poor performance of developing countries.

In this short essay, we deal with a specific form of corruption, viz., the effects of the presence of a corrupt union leader in an unionised industry. The presence of such forms of corruption often contribute to perpetuation of low wages among workers, especially in emerging economies. We try to explore this issue here.

We develop a model about determination of unionised wage in the presence of a corrupt leader who acts as an intermediary between the workers and management of a firm. Being the representative of all the workers, he bargains with the management for setting the workers' wages. Since he is corrupt (which is often the case in emerging economies), he receives a bribe from the management of the firm for keeping wages as close as possible to the workers' reservation wage. However, workers are aware that their leader may be taking a bribe and, hence, the leader has to be careful. In case he settles for a very low wage (which is very close to the reservation wage), the workers will realise that he has taken a bribe and, consequently, they may throw him out. We model this story as a two-stage game and analyse the equilibrium levels of unionised wage, employment and bribe.

There are a large number of papers dealing with corruption within a hierarchical administrative architecture. We concentrate on a few such papers directly related to our exercise. Following Becker and Stigler

* The authors are deeply honoured to be able to contribute to this volume of essays dedicated to Professor Satish Jain, who is one of the finest minds in our country.

(1974), most of the theoretical papers[1] focus on the principal–agent framework of corruption. These models deal with the relationship between the principal, that is, the top-level government official and the agent, that is, a lower-level official who takes a bribe from private individuals interested in some government-produced goods. These studies examine different ways of controlling corruption. Cadot (1987) has analysed bribery in a model with a hierarchical administration. Basu et al. (1992) have also considered a hierarchical administrative system. In a very different context, Shleifer and Vishny (1992) show that since the planners—meaning bureaucrats in the ministries and managers of firms—cannot keep the official profits that public sector firms earn, it is in their interest to create shortages of output and to collect bribes from consumers. In another related paper, Shleifer and Vishny (1993) demonstrate that the structure of government institutions and of the political process are very important determinants of the level of corruption.

We now proceed to provide the model of our exercise.

THE MODEL

Consider a scenario where there is a corrupt union leader who intermediates between the workers and a firm in a unionised competitive industry. The reservation wage of the workers is $\underline{W}$ (informal wage). The union leader does all the bargaining with the firm as the sole representative of the workers. He receives a bribe Z from the firm for keeping W as close as possible to $\underline{W}$. Production requires only labour (L). The labour market facing the industry is unionised. Each firm in the industry has a separate trade union. Such a scenario is very common in emerging economies. In such a framework, we analyse the equilibrium levels of unionised wage W, employment L and bribe Z.

We model this as a two-stage game. In stage 1, the corrupt leader and the firm play a Nash bargaining game and determine the unionised wage, W, and the amount of bribe, Z. In stage 2, the firm takes W and Z as given and chooses the level of employment L.

Second Stage

The firm's pay-off (profit) is given by $\pi = PQ(L) - WL(1 + r) - Z$. The firm can sell any amount at price P. It essentially acts as a competitive firm in the output market. $Q(L)$ is the amount of output produced

---

[1] See, for example, Banfield (1975), Klitgaard (1988, 1991), and Rose-Ackerman (1975, 1978).

when the firm employs L units of labour. We assume that for all $L > 0$, $Q'(L) > 0$ and $Q''(L) < 0$. This simply means that the marginal product of labour is positive and this marginal product diminishes with increases in output. This assumption is justified when the firm has a fixed stock of physical capital. The wage payment, W, is made in advance which can be regarded as working capital. This means the firm has to incur $W(1 + r)$ amount of cost where r is the interest rate.

Note that W and Z are determined in the first stage. Given this, the firm chooses L to maximise π. The first and second order conditions are as follows.

$$\frac{\partial \pi}{\partial L} = PQ'(L) - W(1 + r) = 0 \tag{11.1a}$$

$$\frac{\partial^2 \pi}{\partial L^2} = PQ''(L) < 0 \tag{11.1b}$$

From (11.1a), we get that the profit-maximising amount of employment is given by $L^*(W, P, r)$. Clearly

$$L^*(W, P, r) = Q'^{-1}\left(\frac{W(1 + r)}{P}\right). \tag{11.1c}$$

Routine computations yield the following.

$$L_W^* = \frac{\partial L^*}{\partial W} = \frac{1 + r}{PQ''(L^*)} < 0 \tag{11.2a}$$

$$L_P^* = \frac{\partial L^*}{\partial P} = \frac{-Q'(L)}{PQ''(L^*)} > 0 \tag{11.2b}$$

$$L_r^* = \frac{\partial L^*}{\partial r} = \frac{w}{PQ''(L^*)} < 0 \tag{11.2c}$$

Let us define $\Pi = PQ(L^*) - WL^*(1 + r) - Z$. Note that Π gives the maximum profit accruing to the firm when it employs the optimum amount of labour (L^*). Using the envelope theorem, we get the following.

$$\Pi_W = \frac{\partial \Pi}{\partial W} = -L^*(1 + r) < 0 \tag{11.3a}$$

$$\Pi_Z = \frac{\partial \Pi}{\partial Z} = -1 \tag{11.3b}$$

$$\Pi_P = \frac{\partial \Pi}{\partial P} = Q(L^*) > 0 \tag{11.3c}$$

$$\Pi_r = \frac{\partial \Pi}{\partial r} = -WL^* < 0 \tag{11.3d}$$

From 11.3a–11.3d, we also get the following.

$$\Pi_{WW} = \frac{\partial^2 \Pi}{\partial W^2} = -(1+r)L_W^* > 0 \qquad (11.4a)$$

$$\Pi_{rW} = \frac{\partial^2 \Pi}{\partial r \partial W} = -WL_W^* - L^* \qquad (11.4b)$$

$$\Pi_{WP} = \frac{\partial^2 \Pi}{\partial W \partial P} = -L_P^*(1+r) < 0 \qquad (11.4c)$$

$$\Pi_{ZZ} = \Pi_{ZW} = \Pi_{Zr} = 0 \qquad (11.4d)$$

We now proceed to solve the first stage of the game.

First Stage

In the first stage, the firm and the corrupt union leader play a cooperative game and determine W and Z jointly through a Nash bargaining process. Let $p(W)$ be the probability that the union leader will be detected by other workers for his unethical practice and be removed from his post.[2]

Note that $W \geq \underline{W}$. We assume the following.

$$p(.) : [\underline{W}, \infty] \longrightarrow [0, 1]$$
$$p'(W) < 0, \ p''(W) \leq 0 \text{ and } p(\underline{W}) = 1$$

These properties of the $p(.)$ function are obvious in our context. If the leader (along with the firm) sets a wage equal to $\underline{W}$, then the workers will clearly realise that there has been a deal struck between the firm and the leader (with kickbacks being paid), and in this case, the leader will be removed from his post with certainty. If the chosen W is strictly higher than $\underline{W}$, then the workers are not certain whether such a deal has taken place or not and, consequently, the probability that the leader will be caught is less than one. The higher the chosen wage W, the lower will be the probability of getting caught since with higher wages the workers become less suspicious. If the union leader is detected in resorting to bribe-taking, he will be summarily removed from his post and will lose his formal-sector job. In this case, he has to fall back upon an informal-sector job where the wage rate is $\underline{W}$. The union leader is

---

[2] Typically in emerging economies such as India, the workers (or a substantial fraction of them) revolts against such a leader and he is removed forcibly.

risk neutral and his expected income is, therefore, given by

$$Y = (1 - p\,(W))\,(W + Z) + p\,(W)\,\underline{W} = W + Z - p\,(W)\,(W + Z - \underline{W}).$$

$$(11.5)$$

The following may be noted.

$$Y_W = \frac{\partial Y}{\partial W} = 1 - p'\,(W)\,(W + Z - \underline{W}) - p\,(W) > 0 \qquad (11.5a)$$

$$Y_Z = \frac{\partial Y}{\partial W} = 1 - p\,(W) \geq 0 \qquad\qquad\qquad (11.5b)$$

$$Y_{WW} = \frac{\partial^2 Y}{\partial W^2} = -p''\,(W)\,(W + Z - \underline{W}) - 2p'\,(W) > 0 \quad (11.5c)$$

$$Y_{ZW} = -p'\,(W) > 0 \qquad\qquad\qquad (11.5d)$$

$$Y_{ZZ} = 0 \qquad\qquad\qquad (11.5e)$$

The union leader has a reservation income, $\underline{Y}$ (say from directly joining politics). He will not be engaged in union leadership unless $Y \geq \underline{Y}$.

The firm's pay-off is $\Pi = PQ\,(L^*) - WL^*\,(1 + r) - Z$. We assume that if the bargaining process breaks down, no production will take place and, consequently, the firm's profit in this case would be zero. The disagreement pay-off vector is thus $(\underline{Y}, 0)$.

The Nash Bargaining Solution
To arrive at the Nash bargaining solution, we maximise $B = (Y - \underline{Y})\,\Pi$ w.r.t. W and Z.

The first-order conditions are given as follows.

$$B_W = \Pi Y_W + (Y - \underline{Y})\,\Pi_W = 0 \qquad\qquad (11.6a)$$

$$B_Z = \Pi Y_Z + (Y - \underline{Y})\,\Pi_Z = 0 \qquad\qquad (11.6b)$$

Note that from (11.6a) and (11.6b), the equilibrium levels of wage and bribe, W^* and Z^*, can be obtained as functions of r, P and $\underline{Y}$.

We now write (11.6a) and (11.6b) as implicit functions in the following way.

$$F^1\,(W, Z; r, P, \underline{Y}) = 0$$

$$F^2\,(W, Z; r, P, \underline{Y}) = 0$$

Just note that $F^1\,(.) = B_W$ and $F^2\,(.) = B_z$. We now report the following computations.

$$F_W^1 = \frac{\partial F^1}{\partial W} = \Pi Y_{WW} + 2\Pi_W Y_W + (Y - \underline{Y})\Pi_{WW} \tag{11.7a}$$

$$F_Z^1 = \frac{\partial F^1}{\partial Z} = \Pi Y_{WZ} + \Pi_W Y_Z + Y_W \Pi_Z \tag{11.7b}$$

$$F_W^2 = \frac{\partial F^2}{\partial W} = \Pi Y_{WZ} + \Pi_W Y_Z + Y_W \Pi_Z \tag{11.7c}$$

$$F_Z^2 = \frac{\partial F^2}{\partial Z} = 2Y_Z \Pi_Z \tag{11.7d}$$

Note that since $Y_{WW} > 0$ (11.5c), $\Pi_{WW} > 0$ (11.4a), $\Pi_W < 0$ (11.5a), and $Y_W > 0$ (11.5a), we cannot sign F_W^1. But if Π is high enough, then $F_W^1 > 0$. In fact, we will assume this throughout our exercise. Note that Π will be high if P (the price that the firm faces in the market) is very high. Note that from (11.7b) and (11.7c) we have $F_Z^1 = F_W^2$. By a similar logic, when Π is high enough, since $Y_{WZ} > 0$ (11.5d), we get that $F_Z^1 = F_W^2 > 0$. Since $Y_Z \geq 0$ (11.5b), and $\Pi_Z = -1$ (11.3b), we have $F_Z^2 \leq 0$.

We now provide some reasons as to why Π can be high enough. Consider the case where the firm is an exporting one. Then it can receive a very high price (P) for its product in the international market vis-à-vis the domestic market where demand for the product might be lacking. If the income elasticity for such a product is very high in the international market, P can indeed be very high. On the other hand, since the firm operates in the formal sector, it can receive loans from the organised credit market at a low and competitive interest rate. Besides, exporting firms often receive export subsidies from the government as part of export promotional measures, which makes the credit cost even lower and this can also push up Π.

We, summarise our findings now.

Lemma 1. *If in equilibrium, the firm's profit, Π, is high enough then $F_W^1 > 0$, $F_Z^1 = F_W^2 > 0$ and $F_Z^2 \leq 0$.*

$$\text{Let } D = \det \begin{vmatrix} F_W^1 & F_Z^1 \\ F_W^2 & F_Z^2 \end{vmatrix}.$$

Note that if Π is high enough then from Lemma 1 we get that

$$D = F_W^1 F_Z^2 - F_W^2 F_Z^1 = F_W^1 F_Z^2 - (F_Z^1)^2 < 0.$$

We now report another set of computations. These will be required for our results later.

$$F_r^1 = \frac{\partial F^1}{\partial r} = \Pi_r Y_W + (Y - \underline{Y}) \Pi_{Wr} \qquad (11.8a)$$

$$F_r^2 = \frac{\partial F^2}{\partial r} = \Pi_r Y_Z \qquad (11.8b)$$

$$F_P^1 = \frac{\partial F^1}{\partial P} = \Pi_P Y_W + (Y - \underline{Y}) \Pi_{WP} \qquad (11.8c)$$

$$F_P^2 = \frac{\partial F^2}{\partial P} = Y_Z \Pi_P \qquad (11.8d)$$

$$F_{\underline{Y}}^1 = -\Pi_W \qquad (11.8e)$$

$$F_{\underline{Y}}^2 = -\Pi_Z = 1 \qquad (11.8f)$$

THE MAIN RESULTS

We now analyse the effects of changes in r, P and $\underline{Y}$ on the equilibrium levels of wage (W^*), employment (L^*) and (Z^*). It may be noted that our results will depend on the magnitude of ($Y - \underline{Y}$). There are situations where this magnitude can be low enough and situations where this can even be high enough. We will illustrate them briefly.

Although in this model, there is only one union leader doing all the wage bargaining with the firm, in reality, there are quite a few number of people in the race for the prime post in the labour union so that they can appropriate the cut money from wage bargaining. Competition among union leaders ultimately keeps Y as close to $\underline{Y}$ (pay-off to the union leader from directly joining politics). The higher the competition, the smaller would be the difference between Y and $\underline{Y}$. On the other hand, the pay-off from taking direct part in politics may be quite high, which is presently the case in India, where scams after scams are unfolding frequently, so that the difference ($Y - \underline{Y}$) may be sufficiently low. It is also possible for ($Y - \underline{Y}$) to be quite high if there is a single union with a party-dictated leader at the top (implying no competition among union leaders for the top post). In some industrial sectors in India, where the trade union of a certain political party is dominant, this may indeed be the case.

Effects on W^*

Using the implicit function theorem we get the following.

$$W_r^* = \frac{\partial W^*}{\partial r} = -\frac{\det \begin{vmatrix} F_r^1 & F_Z^1 \\ F_r^2 & F_Z^2 \end{vmatrix}}{D} = -\frac{F_r^1 F_Z^2 - F_r^2 F_Z^1}{D}$$

Since $D < 0$ (provided Π is high enough), the sign of $\frac{\partial W^*}{\partial r}$ is the same as the sign of $\left(F_r^1 F_Z^2 - F_r^2 F_Z^1\right)$. Similarly, the signs of $W_P^* = \frac{\partial W^*}{\partial P}$ and $W_{\underline{Y}}^* = \frac{\partial W^*}{\partial \underline{Y}}$ are the same as the signs of $\left(F_P^1 F_Z^2 - F_P^2 F_Z^1\right)$ and $(F_{\underline{Y}}^1 F_Z^2 - F_{\underline{Y}}^2 F_Z^1)$ respectively.

To analyse the effect of an increase in r, P and $\underline{Y}$ on equilibrium wage (W^*), we observe the following. Since $\Pi_r < 0$ (11.3d), $Y_W > 0$ (11.5a) and the sign of Π_{W_r} is ambiguous (11.4b), we get from (11.8a) that if Y is close enough to $\underline{Y}$, then $F_r^1 < 0$. We also have $F_Z^2 \leq 0$ (use 11.7d, 11.5b and 11.3b) and $F_r^2 \leq 0$ (from 11.8b, 11.3d, 11.5b). Since $Y_{WZ} > 0$ (from 11.5d), using (11.7b), we get that if Π is high enough $F_Z^1 > 0$. This implies that $F_r^1 F_Z^2 - F_r^2 F_Z^1 \geq 0$ if Π is high enough and if Y is close enough to $\underline{Y}$. Using similar logic, we can show that if Π is high enough, then $F_P^1 F_Z^2 - F_P^2 F_Z^1 < 0$ and $F_{\underline{Y}}^1 F_Z^2 - F_{\underline{Y}}^2 F_Z^1 < 0$. We summarise these results in terms of the following proposition.

Proposition 1. *(i) If Π is high enough and if Y is close enough to $\underline{Y}$, then $W_r^* \geq 0$, that is, an increase in r leads to an increase in the equilibrium wage W^*. (ii) If Π is high enough, then $W_P^* < 0$ and $W_{\underline{Y}}^* < 0$, that is, the equilibrium wage W^* decreases with increases in P and $\underline{Y}$.*

Effects on L^*

We now proceed to analyse the effects of increases in r, P and $\underline{Y}$ on the equilibrium level of employment L^*. Using 11.1a–11.1c, we get the following.

$$\frac{dL^*}{dr} = L_W^* W_r^* + L_r^* \tag{11.9a}$$

$$\frac{dL^*}{dP} = L_W^* W_P^* + L_P^* \tag{11.9b}$$

$$\frac{dL^*}{d\underline{Y}} = L_W^* W_{\underline{Y}}^* \tag{11.9c}$$

From 11.2a–11.2c, we know that $L_W^* < 0$, $L_r^* < 0$ and $L_P^* > 0$. From Proposition 1, we know that if Π is high enough and if Y is close enough to $\underline{Y}$, then $W_r^* \geq 0$. Also, if Π is high enough, then $W_P^* < 0$ and $W_{\underline{Y}}^* < 0$. Using this, we come to our next proposition.

Proposition 2. *(i) If Π is high enough and if Y is close enough to $\underline{Y}$, then $\frac{dL^*}{dr} < 0$. The equilibrium level of employment decreases with an increase in r. (ii) If Π is high enough then $\frac{dL^*}{dP} > 0$ and $\frac{dL^*}{d\underline{Y}} > 0$, that is, equilibrium level of employment **rises** decreases with increases in P and $\underline{Y}$.*

Effects on Z^*

We now analyse the effects of increases in r, P and $\underline{Y}$ on the equilibrium level of bribe Z^*. We show that the effects on Z^* will crucially depend on Π, W and $(Y - \underline{Y})$.

Using the implicit function theorem and some routine computations, we can show that the sign of $\frac{\partial Z^*}{\partial r}$, $\frac{\partial Z^*}{\partial P}$ and $\frac{\partial Z^*}{\partial \underline{Y}}$ are the same as the signs of $(F_W^1 F_r^2 - F_W^2 F_r^1)$, $(F_W^1 F_P^2 - F_W^2 F_P^1)$ and $(F_W^1 F_{\underline{Y}}^2 - F_W^2 F_{\underline{Y}}^1)$ respectively. If Π is high enough, then F_W^1, $F_W^2 > 0$. Also, $F_r^2 \leq 0$. Note that the sign of $F_r^1 = \Pi_r Y_W + (Y - \underline{Y})\Pi_{Wr}$ is ambiguous (as the sign of Π_{Wr} is ambiguous). But from (11.4b), we get that since $L_W^* < 0$, $\Pi_{Wr} > 0$ if W is high enough. This implies that if W is high enough and if $(Y - \underline{Y})$ is high enough (that is, the union leader's pay-off is much higher than his reservation pay-off), then $F_r^1 > 0$. This would imply that if Π, W and $(Y - \underline{Y})$ are high enough, then $\frac{\partial Z^*}{\partial r} < 0$. Using a similar logic, we can show that if Π and $(Y - \underline{Y})$ are high enough, then $\frac{\partial Z^*}{\partial P} > 0$ and $\frac{\partial Z^*}{\partial \underline{Y}} > 0$. We summarise these results in terms of another proposition.

Proposition 3. *(i) If Π, W and $(Y - \underline{Y})$ are high enough, then $\frac{\partial Z^*}{\partial r} < 0$, that is, an increase in r would lead to a decrease in equilibrium level of bribe (Z^*). (ii) If Π and $(Y - \underline{Y})$ are high enough, then $\frac{\partial Z^*}{\partial P} > 0$ and $\frac{\partial Z^*}{\partial \underline{Y}} > 0$, that is, the equilibrium bribe Z^* increases with increases in P and $\underline{Y}$.*

We now provide some intuition behind our main results.

1. A decrease in the interest rate on loans, r, lowers the real effective cost of hiring labour, which in turn induces the firm in employing more labour, L^*, than before. Besides as r falls, Π rises and, hence, the maximised joint income of the two players. The firm and the union leader grab this opportunity by lowering W^* and raising Z^*.

2. If P rises, the total revenue and the level of profit of the firm increase and, hence, the maximised joint income of the two players. This enables the two players to hike both W^* and Z^*. An increase in P raises the value of marginal product of labour, which induces the firm to employ more labour, L^*.

3. If $\underline{Y}$ rises, ceteris paribus, the opportunity income of the union leader from an alternative source, that is, income from directly joining politics rises. As the maxim and of the bargaining game falls, both the players would be trying to increase their maximised joint income, which is possible by raising Z^* and lowering W^*.

As W^* decreases, the cost of hiring labour, by the firm decreases, which, in turn, raises the employment of labour, L^*.

CONCLUSION

This theoretical essay builds up a model of a two-stage Nash bargaining game between a corrupt trade union leader and the firm. Being the representative of all the workers, the leader is entrusted with the task of bargaining for the workers' wage with the management of the firm. Since he is corrupt, he receives a bribe from the management for keeping wages as close as possible to the workers' reservation wage. But in case he is caught, he would be removed from his post. The analysis leads to some interesting results. For example, an increase in the interest rate on loans (product price) leads to an increase (a decrease) in the equilibrium unionised wage. On the other hand, the equilibrium employment level decreases with an increase in the interest rate on loans/product price. These results are important for designing appropriate policies to fight against corruption in trade union leadership.

REFERENCES

Banfield, E. 1975. 'Corruption as a Feature of Government Organization', *Journal of Law and Economics*, 18(3): 587–605.

Basu, K., S. Bhattacharya and A. Mishra. 1992. 'Notes on Bribery and the Control of Corruption', *Journal of Public Economics*, 48(3): 349–59.

Becker, G. S. and G. J. Stigler. 1974. 'Law Enforcement, Malfeasance, and the Compensation of Enforcers', *Journal of Legal Studies*, 3(1): 1–19.

Cadot, O. 1987. 'Corruption as a Gamble', *Journal of Public Economics*, 33(2): 223–44.

Klitgaard, R. 1988. *Controlling Corruption*. Berkeley, CA: University of California Press.

———. 1991. 'Gifts and Bribes', in R. Zeckhauser (ed.), *Strategy and Choice*. Cambridge, MA: MIT Press, pp. 211–40.

Rose-Ackerman, S. 1975. 'The Economics of Corruption', *Journal of Public Economics*, 4(2): 187–203.

———. 1978. *Corruption: A Study*. New York: Academic Press.

Shleifer, A. and R. W. Vishny. 1992. 'Pervasive Shortage under Socialism', *The Rand Journal of Economics*, 23(2): 237–46.

———. 1993. 'Corruption', *Quarterly Journal of Economics*, 108(3): 599–617.

PART V
DEVELOPMENT AND POLICY

12

Alternative Models for Structural Change and Unbalanced Growth*

Amitava Bose

INTRODUCTION

The resurgence of interest in the theory of economic growth was sparked off by the work of Romer (1986, 1990) and Lucas (1988). The flood of papers that followed concentrated on modelling knowledge creation and skill formation. The objective was to explain what prevents diminishing returns to material capital from eating into the growth of income per head. As it turns out, the outcome of this line of research can be summed up within the framework of the original Solow model itself. [1] A hallmark of the Solow family of models is balanced growth behaviour in the long run. Such behaviour conforms asymptotically to the following 'Kaldor facts': constancy of (*a*) the growth rate of per capita income, (*b*) the real return on capital, (*c*) the capital output ratio and (*d*) the factor shares (Kaldor 1961).

Kaldor's 'stylised facts' have significantly influenced thinking about economic growth. An equally influential work about the observed nature of growth is that of Simon Kuznets, the broad findings of whose Nobel Prize winning research constitute the 'Kuznets facts' (Kuznets 1957, 1966). The Kuznets facts discuss the typical sequence of changes in the sectoral composition of economic aggregates that characterises economic development. The emphasis is not on balanced sectoral growth but on *unbalanced* sectoral growth. If new growth theory was initially cast in the mould of balanced growth models, exploring 'structural change' has become a prominent preoccupation of growth economics in more recent years.

---

* An earlier version of this essay was presented at the Sixth Jawarharlal Nehru University and National Institute of Public Finance and Policy (JNU–NIPFP) Conference on Economic Theory and Policy, March 2013. The essay is dedicated to Professor Satish Jain with regards and affection.
[1] See Jones (2002) and Jones and Vollrath (2013).

The Kuznets hypothesis is that economic development is typically associated with a time sequence as follows: (a) Agriculture is the dominant sector in an underdeveloped economy; the first stage of development starts with a decline in the share of agriculture and an increase in the share of manufacturing. (b) This is followed by a leveling-off in the share of manufacturing as the economy moves from the low-income to the middle-income category; there is a continued fall in the share of agriculture and a rise in the share of the services sector. (c) Finally, there is a sustained increase in the share of the services sector which becomes the dominant sector as the country moves into the category of developed economies.

The theoretical literature on structural change is considerably large. The literature comprises two different methodological traditions. Several papers belong to the neoclassical tradition of dynamic optimising models of competitive equilibrium that can be tweaked to yield unbalanced growth. The objective in most of these neoclassical models is to obtain results that conform to the Kuznets facts, as revealed mainly in the US data. Some of the more recent papers include those by Kongsamut et al. (2001), Ngai and Pissarides (2007) and Acemoglu and Guerrieri (2008). The source of unbalanced growth lies, first, in differences in the income elasticities of demand for agricultural goods, manufactured goods and services respectively. On the production side, the three goods differ in terms of factor proportions and Hicks-neutral technical progress or total factor productivity (TFP). Mention should also be made of the earlier work of Rebelo (1991) that displays unbalanced output growth resulting from sectoral differences in the degree of diminishing returns to capital.

These papers attempt to reconcile the Kuznets facts at the sectoral level with the Kaldor facts at the aggregative level. In these models, structural change is driven by changes in relative prices. However, income effects are absent in these papers. Hence, they do not incorporate evidence from cross-section data (for instance, the US data) that show systematic differences in the expenditure structure across income groups. Such differences reflect the presence of income effects. In a recent paper, Boppart (2012) has introduced non-homothetic demand to capture the impact of income effects in addition to reconciling Kuznets facts with Kaldor facts. His paper also gives importance to persistent change in relative prices, something that the US data bring out.

The motivation of the present essay is to understand what explains the broad contours of India's economic development. Neoclassical models are not appropriate for this objective. The reasons for this are the following. First, in contrast to the Kaldor facts, the Indian economy is clearly in the phase of *transitional* rather than balanced growth dynamics. Second, a major contemporary concern is that high growth in India has proved not to be 'inclusive'. *Prima facie* the reason for this is the emerging *disconnect* between the growing parts of the economy (the services sector), on the one hand, and the rural agricultural sector, on the other. The surplus unskilled labour of the agricultural sector (growing through population growth) is not being sucked out through increased employment in the expanding parts of the economy, viz., the services sector. Full-employment models of the neoclassical variety—essentially generalised Solow models—do not fit the bill because these do not provide room for surplus labour. The literature on India's transition is also a bulging one. A recent contribution is Verma (2012); for the earlier period, one may also refer to Ghosh (1988). The emphasis in the present essay is on modelling and analytics that can be of use in explaining Indian growth. Since neoclassical models do not fit the bill, the present analysis is based on an alternative framework that allows for surplus labour and unemployment.

The benchmark surplus labour model is the classical dual economy model of Arthur Lewis (1954). However, the Lewis model—or others of the Lewis family such as the work of Ranis and Fei (1961)—also fails to fit the bill. The nub of the problem is that the non-agricultural sector has become less and less dependent for its growth on resources of the agricultural sector, especially unskilled labour.[2]

An alternative to the neoclassical and the Lewis traditions is the 'Cambridge School'. Here the research on structural change has been particularly influenced by the later papers of Kaldor, especially his Presidential Address to the Royal Economic Society (Kaldor 1976) and his paper in the Scitovsky festschrift (Kaldor 1979). Some of the papers that follow up on Kaldor are Dutt (1992), Bhaduri and Skarstein (2003) and Roberts and McCombie (2008). The setting is that of a two-sector dual economy, but the distinguishing characteristic of this tradition—in contrast to the Ricardian roots of the Lewis model—is emphasis on the role of *demand* factors.

None of the models discussed deal with *land* as an allocable resource and as a property. This is a serious drawback. As recent events in India have shown this drawback, one can scarcely discuss the role

---

[2] It is possible that the problem has been aggravated by increasing globalisation, but this is a hypothesis that needs to be verified systematically.

of agriculture in development without considering the role of land as a resource and without considering the political importance of property rights. However, the present essay has not been able to deal with this question and belongs to the tradition of classical dual economy models. These models may be termed as the 'landless dual economy models'.

The limited purpose of the present essay is to discuss some of the more 'classical' issues of modelling that need to be addressed in analysing the structural transformation that the contemporary Indian economy is experiencing. This essay is complementary to Bose (2012); hence, we begin by summarising that earlier piece.

INTERSECTORAL DISPARITIES AND GROWTH IN A DUAL ECONOMY

This section summarizes the argument in Bose (2012). There are two sectors: 'agriculture' and 'industry' (including the services sector). The output of the agricultural sector net of internal demand (the agricultural surplus) is determined exogenously at a level $X(t) = X(0)e^{xt}$. The output of industry is $Y(t) = AK(t)^\alpha$, where $K(t)$ is the capital stock at date t. The two 'state variables' are X and K.

The rates of growth of these variables are x, a given constant, and $g = g(p)$ respectively. Here p is the relative price of the agricultural good and g is inversely related to p. This inverse relationship could be explained in different ways. One explanation is that an increase in p redistributes industrial income in favour of wages (these are linked to food prices) and that reduces the saving ratio. At any given date t, $p(t)$ is determined by the demand for the agricultural surplus. In a closed economy, this demand comes from the industrial sector. Denoting the demand by D, it is assumed that D depends on Y and p. With separability, a particular form for D is: $D(p, Y) = Y^\sigma h(p)$, with $0 < \sigma \le 1$ and $h'(p) < 0$. The market clearing condition (suppressing t) is $X = Y^\sigma h(p)$. Using the production function $Y = AK^\alpha$, this reduces to $X/K^\theta = m(p)$, where $0 < \theta = \alpha\sigma \le 1$ and $m(p) = A^\sigma h(p)$, $m'(p) < 0$. Since $X(t)$ and $K(t)$ are historically given at any date t, it follows that market clearing for the agricultural good determines $p(t)$.

A decisive feature of this model is that *long-run equilibrium* (the limit of the instantaneous market clearing equilibrium programme) *is characterised by the existence of a constant p*, say $\hat{p}$. From usual continuity properties, it follows that there is a long-run equilibrium level to which (X/K^θ) converges over time. Let that number be $\hat{\eta}$. Constancy of $\hat{\eta}$ implies that $x = \theta g(\hat{p}) < g(\hat{p})$ which demonstrates that the X and K grow at unequal rates in the long run. Moreover, as asymptotic constancy of p

implies asymptotic constancy of (X/Y^σ) hence in the limit $x = \sigma g_Y$ where g_Y is the rate of growth of Y. The 'growth gap' $[g_Y - x] = [\{(1/\sigma) - 1\}x]$ is positive. It is decreasing in σ, vanishing in the limit as $\sigma \to 1$ or blowing up indefinitely for $\sigma \to 0$. In the long run, the ratio of outputs (Y/X) and the relative sectoral GDP share (Y/pX) depend on demand characteristics and not on supply-side features such as α, the exponent of K.

As an example, consider the following special functional forms: $h(p) = p^{-\varepsilon}, g(p) = 1/p$ and $x = 1 - (1/p)$ (allowing for x to be positively influenced by p as in, say, Dutt [1992]). Then $\dot{p}(t) = a - bp(t)$, where $a \equiv (1 + \theta)/\varepsilon$, $b = 1/\varepsilon$. This has the solution

$$p(t) = \hat{p} + [p(0) - \hat{p}]e^{-bt} \text{ where } \hat{p} = \frac{a}{b} = (1 + \theta).$$

Therefore,

$$\lim_{t\to\infty} p(t) = \hat{p}; \ \lim_{t\to\infty} g(t) = 1/(1 + \theta); \ \lim_{t\to\infty} x(t) = \theta/(1 + \theta),$$

and

$$\lim_{t\to\infty} [g(t) - x(t)] = (1 - \theta)/(1 + \theta).$$

COMPARISON WITH A NEOCLASSICAL MODEL OF INTERSECTORAL GROWTH

The aforementioned discussion can be contrasted with that in Rebelo (1991). It is instructive to do so both because the Rebelo model belongs to the neoclassical tradition and the long-run character of inter-sectoral growth is driven by supply-side factors rather than demand-side factors. In Rebelo's model, the sectors are not agriculture and industry, but consumption goods (C) and investment goods (I). The I-sector has constant returns to K but the C-sector suffers from diminishing returns to $K : I = AK_I, C = B(KC)^\alpha$. Capital is homogeneous $[K_C + K_I] = K$, and $\dot{K} = I$. The main difference from Bose (2012) lies not in the fact that demand conditions are derived by an exercise of dynamic optimisation by a representative agent, but in (a) the determination of growth rates and in (b) the modelling of the supply side. Unlike the Kaldorian analysis that takes the growth curves $g(p)$ and x (or $x(p)$) as *primary* decisions, in the Rebelo model, growth is a *consequence* of instantaneous capital (re)allocation at successive moments (to equate the rentals on capital services across sectors—the result of free entry or perfect capital mobility). When capital is fully mobile between the sectors—in contrast to irreversibility of I or sector-specificity of K—then there is no reason for the investor to plan ahead how much capital would be optimal for each sector in future. Second, since the rental rate of capital in units of the I-good is a constant $= A$, it follows that the value of the marginal product of capital in the C-sector must be constant in units of the I-good: $p.MPK_C = $ constant, where $p = P_C/P_I$. This condition yields an equilibrium locus that relates the relative price p not to the output *ratio* (C/I)—as in standard two-sector models—but to the *absolute level* of one of the outputs, viz., C: the supply curve is of the form $C = C(p)$.[3]

The demand side in the Rebelo model can be reduced to a general relation of the form $C = Iz(p)$ based on optimising a constant elasticity utility function. The model yields a constant growth rate of $K : I = gK$ from which it follows that K_I/K and K_C/K are constant and equal to (g/A) and $[1 - (g/A)]$ respectively. Therefore, both K_C and K_I grow at a constant positive rate. Hence, the output of C grows at the rate $\alpha g > 0$. From this, it follows that the equilibrium $p(t)$ is an increasing function. This conclusion contrasts sharply with the asymptotic results of Bose (2012) described earlier.

In the Rebelo model, there is no transitional dynamics. Both capital stocks grow at a common rate right from the beginning. Now $p = A(K_C)^{1-\alpha}/\alpha B$ from capital mobility; hence, $pC = AK_C/\alpha = AK_I(K_C/K_I)/\alpha$ which simplifies to $pC = \mu I$, where μ is a constant since (K_C/K_I) is constant. Thus, the sector shares remain constant in value terms: the values of the two outputs grow at the same rate. In this specific sense, there is 'balanced growth' in the aggregate.

However, the terms of trade $p(t)$ keep increasing over time. As a consequence, the ratio of real outputs (C/I) keeps falling over time. This latter conclusion is similar to the result derived in Bose (2012) that (X/Y) keeps falling over time when the income elasticity of demand for primary consumption goods is less than unity. This brief discussion illustrates two sides to the explanation of unbalanced growth—the supply-side reasons and the demand side.

---

[3] Consider the standard production possibilities curve for given K and L in a two-factor, two-good neoclassical constant returns to scale (CRS) model. Given the property of 'factor price equalisation', if p is held fixed, then so would be the factor price ratio w/r. In the (C, I) plane, the 'Rybczynski line' would normally be a ray through the origin, the slope of which would be determined by relative factor intensities. In the Rebelo model with $L_i/K_i = 0$, the Rybczynski line is vertical.

EFFECTIVE DEMAND AND TERMS OF TRADE

Kaldor (1979) points to the neglect of demand factors in neoclassical and Lewis–Ricardo models. In these models, market clearing is achieved through variations in the inter-sectoral terms of trade. Kaldor points out that the terms of trade may fail to be flexible because (a) wages in the industrial sector are indexed to the price of food and (b) industrial prices are fixed in terms of a mark-up on unit wage costs. Together this results in p being *given*.[4]

Consider a two-sector model of 'agriculture' and 'industry' (the latter sector is an amalgam of manufacturing and services). Let X stand for the net supply (net of internal demand) from agriculture—also called the 'marketable surplus'. Let D_x be the demand for agricultural goods from the industrial sector measured in units of the industrial good. Then market clearing for the agricultural good in a closed economy is $pX = D_x$, where p is the relative price of the agricultural good in terms of industrial good. In one class of dual economy models—summed up in Bose (2012)—market clearing is achieved through appropriate adjustments in p.

Suppose, however, that p is given and does not respond to current excess demands. This is the possibility raised by Kaldor (1979) and emphasised by others including Bhaduri and Skarstein (2003). For this alternative class of models, it is the level of industrial production Y that is the sole equilibrating variable. The supply curve of the Y sector is taken to be flat (mark-up pricing) and, therefore, the level of Y is demand-determined. The external demand for Y comes from sellers of the agricultural surplus X. *The role of the agricultural sector is to produce demand for the non-agricultural sector.* Kaldor, and others following him, underline this as capturing the essence of the effective demand problem for a dual economy. However, there remain some modelling issues to be sorted out.

Within this class of fixed price models,[5] there are two distinct categories with quite different economic implications. In one category, the assumption is that expenditure is *always* equal to income. The equality is regarded not as the outcome of *market* adjustments, but as an internal budget constraint. An example of the budget constraint at work

---

[4] We, however, question this later. See the section on A Difficulty with the Kaldor Argument.

[5] Note that it is not fixity of nominal prices as in Kalecki (1976), but fixity of the relative price (that is, the inter-sectoral terms of trade) that Kaldor is highlighting.

is the requirement that investment be financed by the investor's own savings.[6] This is, of course, at sharp variance with the Keynesian models that constitute the second category. Keynesian models regard saving and investment (hence also income and expenditure) as outcomes of *independent* decisions;[7] equality between the two is brought about by a market clearing adjustment and not imposed by a budget constraint. In what follows the first category of models is said to use *Ricardian* expenditure functions and the second category *Keynesian* expenditure functions. Each category is now taken up one by one.

To proceed with the analysis, the notation has to be fixed.

<u>Notation</u>: The index used for agriculture is x and that for industry is y. (*a*) Supply side: The marketable surplus of agricultural goods is denoted as X and industrial output is denoted as Y. (*b*) Demand side: Aggregate demand for y goods measured in units of y goods is denoted as AD. AD consists partly of demand from the y sector for y (D_y) and partly of the demand from the x sector for y (F). The y sector's demand for the two goods is D_y for y goods and D_x for x goods. The rates of growth of Y and X are g_y and g_x respectively. The relative price of the x good in terms of the y good is denoted by p.[8]

The contrast in conclusions as between using Ricardian and Keynesian expenditure functions is now worked out.

Ricardian Expenditure Functions

The two *budget constraints* that D_y, D_x and F must respect are:

$$D_y + D_x = Y \tag{12.1}$$

l.h.s. is the industrial sector's demand for the two goods.

$$F = pX \tag{12.2}$$

l.h.s. is the agricultural sector's demand for the industrial good.

Definition of aggregate demand for the y good is:

$$AD = D_y + F. \tag{12.3}$$

---

[6] This reflects a borrowing constraint on investors.

[7] To see this sharply, assume there are no borrowing constraints and the capital market is perfect.

[8] There is no harm setting $p = 1$ for the fix-price case, but for ease of comparison with the flex-price model, this has not been done.

Using (12.2), the Ricardian form for (12.3) is

$$AD = D_y + pX. \qquad (12.4)$$

(12.1) and (12.4) together imply—this is Walras' law:

$$AD - Y = pX - D_x. \qquad (12.5)$$

Thus, if the market for x goods is cleared, then the market for y goods is cleared as well. Here the focus is on the market for x goods. In that context, (12.5) is useful in clarifying how adjustments in Y—the 'other market' so to say—help to clear the market for x goods. The following condition clears both markets simultaneously:

$$D_x = pX \qquad (12.6)$$

To see how the market for x goods works the factors influencing demand and supply have to be put in. It is assumed that the level of X over time is given—p might have affected X, but p is given. On the demand side, given that p is fixed, assume that D_x depends only on Y : $D_x = D(Y)$. Then (12.6) implies that $Y = D^{-1}(pX) = G(X)$, say. This clarifies Kaldor's identification of X as the determinant of the effective demand for Y.

$$D_x = D(Y) \qquad (12.7)$$

Let $G(X) = D^{-1}(pX)$. Then (12.6) and (12.7) imply

$$Y = G(X) \qquad (12.8)$$

Causation and the Foreign Trade Multiplier: How Y Adjusts to Clear the x Market

The character of the model depends on which variables are flexible, that is, adjust to bring about the equality in (12.6), and which variables are fixed, that is, are autonomous. Here, it is assumed that pX is given and that Y is the equilibrating variable. Then it follows from (12.6) and (12.7) that Y is determined by pX. It appears that the Kaldor-type models have been 'inspired' by the Harrodian 'foreign trade multiplier'. The interpretation of (12.8) as a 'foreign trade multiplier' for the y sector is straightforward.[9]

---

[9] See, for instance, Bhaduri and Skarstein (2003). Note that the 'foreign trade balance' between exports and imports to the neglect of the capital account is a Ricardian legacy.

246 I Amitava Bose

Starting from an equilibrium position, suppose that pX goes up. This creates an excess supply of x goods at the initial level of Y. However, the budget constraint (12.2) implies that the increased pX stimulates F, the external demand for y goods.[10] That boosts AD as per (12.3). Now, in these models, the basic short-run adjustment is that Y adjusts to AD. The increase in AD stimulates Y and this, in turn, creates additional demand for x, thereby reducing the excess supply.

Using Δ to denote change, what ensures that $\Delta D_x = \Delta(pX)$ exactly? It is important to stress that the Ricardian form of the demand functions are responsible for this. In the section on 'Keynesian Demand Functions', it is shown that this kind of adjustment mechanism does not hold if demand functions are Keynesian. Before going into that, consider briefly the problem of growth, sticking to the Ricardian case.

Balanced and Unbalanced Growth
To be specific, first consider the example:

$$D_x = mY, 0 < m < 1. \tag{12.9}$$

Then, $G(X) = (pX/m)$ and for the x market to clear, it is required that

$$Y = pX/m. \tag{12.10}$$

As long as p is fixed, (12.10) implies that if X has a rate of growth g_x, then Y must also grow at the same rate: $g_x = g_y$. Market clearing adjustments in Y at fixed p implies 'balanced growth'.

This balanced growth result, however, is rather special. Apart from the fact that p is fixed, the demand function in (12.9) implies that the income elasticity of demand for agricultural goods ('food') is unity. That could be an unrealistic supposition. If the growth process is such that additional incomes accrue mostly to better paid workers, then this income elasticity is very likely less than unity.[11] Replace (12.7) by the following strictly concave function:

$$D_x = mY^\sigma, 0 < \sigma < 1 \tag{12.11}$$

---

[10] Supply creates demand. Note that there is no 'realisation problem': producers do not wait for pX to be realised into profits. For the 'realisation problem', see the section on 'The Realisation Problem'.

[11] A more explicit account would divide wages into 'skilled' and 'unskilled' components and accordingly demand for food would have to be specified differently for the two components.

Then x equilibrium entails

$$mY^\sigma = pX. \tag{12.12}$$

Log-differentiating both sides w.r.t. time,

$$\sigma g_y = g_x. \tag{12.13}$$

Since $\sigma < 1$, this implies that $g_y > g_x$.

Thus, when growth is biased in favour of upper- and middle-income groups, the non-agricultural sector (the 'modern sector') persistently maintains a higher rate of growth than the agricultural sector ('traditional sector').[12]

In general, the condition $D(Y) = pX$ implies that $\sigma(Y)g_y = g_x$, where $\sigma(Y) = YD'(Y)/D(Y)$. Thus, if $\sigma(Y) < 1$ (that is, the marginal propensity to consume < the average propensity to consume), then $g_y > g_x$.

Contemporary Relevance: Growth of the Services Sector

The conclusion is that growth has to be unbalanced to ensure market clearing. This observation is of considerable contemporary relevance for India. The two noteworthy characteristics of recent Indian growth are its impressively high rate, together with its unimpressively low inclusiveness. The growth process has also been accompanied by structural changes that do not conform to the sequence predicted by the Kuznets hypothesis. India appears to have entered the phase of services-led growth ahead of schedule. The share of the services sector in non-agricultural output has been increasing at the expense of the manufacturing sector. This has been causing significant changes in the composition of employment, resulting from the fact that the skilled-to-unskilled labour ratio is much higher in services (such as information technology [IT] and banking) than it is in manufacturing (and ancillaries). Growth has been accompanied, therefore, by a redistribution of income in favour of better-paid skilled workers in preference to poorly paid unskilled labour. As a consequence, the fraction of additional incomes that are re-spent on food has been coming down, given the fact that the marginal propensity to consume food is higher for lower-income groups.

---

[12] An alternative inelastic function is $D_x = M + mY$. Then equilibrium entails $mY = pX - M$ and, therefore, once again, $[g_y - g_x] = g_x(M/mY) > 0$.

This reasoning justifies adopting the assumption that food demand is less-than-unit-elastic when growth is services-oriented. Growth redistributes income and induces changes in the composition of demand. If relative prices are constant, then to maintain supply—demand equality, such continuing shifts in demand—away from food and other primary products—must be matched by equivalent changes in the composition of outputs.[13] Such changes in output composition over time require appropriate *disequalisation* of sectoral growth rates. Uneven output growth is a corollary of changes in the composition of demand.

Role of Agriculture and 'Is the Services Sector the Leading Sector?'

It has been assumed that Y is flexible and X is given. It follows from (12.8) and/or (12.10) that Y is determined by X, and g_y is determined by g_x. The non-agricultural/modern sector may be the faster growing sector, but that does not mean it is the *leading sector*. On the contrary, the modern sector (that is, services-'led') is logically subservient to the traditional agricultural sector. The role of Y is to adjust so as to create sufficient demand for the given X. It follows that in this model, the agricultural growth rate has a decisive influence on overall growth.

To sum up, though the growth rate of the modern sector persistently outstrips that of the backward sector, it is the latter that determines the former. In the simple framework adopted here, the only way in which the modern sector can increase its growth rate, *given* the agricultural growth rate, is by making its growth income-wise more top-heavy. This will reduce the income elasticity of demand for food (s), thereby raising g_y for unchanged g_x.

The Realisation Problem

The budget constraint (12.2) implies that suppliers of agricultural goods ('farmers') decide on their expenditure on non-agricultural goods (y) depending on the *potential* income pX, regardless of whether this will in fact be *realised* in terms of sales revenue.[14] This budget constraint is crucial for operation of the 'foreign trade multiplier'—in contrast to the 'Keynesian multiplier' that depends on income-independent

---

[13] All this is summed up in the dictum 'output is demand-determined'.

[14] pX could correspond to some trend value.

'autonomous spending' (autonomous consumption or investment or export demand).

Consider the scenario where farmers' demand for y depends instead on *realised* revenue from sales of X rather than on potential income. Then when pX goes up, there is no direct impact on the demand for y and, hence, on the levels of Y and D_x. The realised income of farmers will still be the previous value of D_x, say, $mY(0)^\sigma$. In this case, there is no multiplier on pX. The general lesson is that one cannot assume that increases in X stimulate Y—that depends on the extent to which the increase in X is accompanied by an essentially autonomous increase (independent of realised incomes) in sector X's demand for y.[15]

To see this explicitly, replace (12.2), that is, $F = pX$, by

$$F = D_x. \tag{12.2'}$$

Then (12.3), that is, $AD = Dy + F$, gets replaced by

$$AD = D_y + D_x. \tag{12.3'}$$

Neither D_y nor D_x depends on pX. Consequently, there is no effect of a change in pX on AD. In fact, given the budget constraint (12.1), it follows that $AD = Y$ always. The level of Y is indeterminate from the demand side and has to be determined from supply constraints.

It is not so much that the budget constraint (or a borrowing constraint) is in conflict with the foreign trade multiplier, but the fact that the budget constraint is defined on *realised* income and not potential income is what disrupts the foreign trade multiplier. The foreign trade multiplier argument conflicts with Keynesian effective demand considerations.

KEYNESIAN DEMAND FUNCTIONS

The point of departure for Keynesian macroeconomics is a rejection of Say's Law and Walras' Law. To follow Keynes, one assumes that some components of demand in the Y sector (such as investment demand) are autonomous (that is, not income-constrained). The reason for this could be the existence of a well-developed financial sector. That will obviate the need for investment to be financed by the investor's own savings.

---

[15] Relevant in this context is the Kalecki—Robinson dictum: 'capitalists get what they spend', implying that spending is independent of income. Here pX is essentially non-wage income in agriculture. See Kalecki (1976).

The demand for the y good (AD) can be written as the sum of the following: (a) investment demand (I), (b) consumption demand (bY) and (c) external demand (F).[16]

$$AD = I + bY + F \qquad (12.14)$$

For simplicity, retain (12.2), that is, farmers' demand for y is assumed to depend on potential income: $F = pX$.[17]

The level of y is demand-determined, that is, Y adjusts to AD. Therefore,

$$Y = (I + pX)/(1 - b). \qquad (12.15)$$

This shows that improvements in agricultural production stimulate non-agricultural production in much the same way that increases in autonomous investment do.

Next, define saving S (out of y income) residually as follows:

$$Y = S + bY + D_x \qquad (12.16)$$

The following property is important: While (12.15) and (12.16) imply that $[S + D_x = I + pX]$, it does *not* follow that $D_x = pX$ (food market is cleared)—unless it is *additionally* the case that $S = I$, that is,

$$I = S(Y), \text{ where } S(Y) = (1 - b)Y - D(Y) \text{ and } D(Y) = D_x. \quad (12.17)$$

This is unlike the Ricardian case in which (12.17) would be an identity. There is now an inconsistency between (12.15) and (12.17)—there is only one variable (viz., Y) to play around with (see Figure12.1).[18] While (12.15) asserts that pX has a multiplier impact on Y, (12.17) implies that Y is independent of pX. *We cannot insist on both markets being cleared.*

If Y is determined by AD (that is, there is Y equilibrium), then $I > S$ implies $pX < D(Y)$, an excess demand for food. If $I < S$ in Y equilibrium, then $pX > D(Y)$ (as in Figure 12.1), implying there is an excess

---

[16] 'External demand' is demand for y from the x sector. 'Internal demand' is the demand for y from the y sector itself. It is assumed that there is no investment demand for y from farmers.

[17] A more substantive reason for this is to be found in the section on Resolving the Inconsistency: The Credit Market.

[18] Typically in such two-sector dual economy models, one requires a pair of equilibrating variables—for instance, Bose (1989) and Rakshit (1989)—since the market clearing conditions for the two goods are independent equations. See also Jha (2010) for a recent account of a class of similar models.

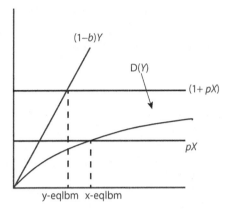

Figure 12.1 Alternative equilibria in the Keynesian case

supply of food. In the former case, farmers would end up with some extra financial saving if they run down food stocks to meet the increased demand, but stick to an expenditure of pX on the non-agricultural good (instead of increasing that to $D(Y)$). In the latter case, they would have to either borrow to maintain demand at pX or cut down their demand from pX to $D(Y)$. Farmers now face a 'realisation problem'. Whether F is sensitive to pX depends on the extent to which farmers' expenditure is linked to current sales of food and this has an important bearing on determination of Y.[19]

Growth Consequences

There are two possible solutions for Y as is clear from Figure 12.1. These two solutions will be denoted as Y_d and Y_x. Let Y_d solve (12.15), that is, when Y is determined by AD. Let Y_x solve (12.6): $D(Y_x) = pX$, then Y_x is determined by pX.

Case I: $Y = Y_d$

From (12.15), $(1 - b)Y = I + pX$, it follows that

$$g_y = \lambda g_I + (1 - \lambda)g_x, 0 \leq \lambda \leq 1 \text{ where } \lambda = I/(I + pX). \quad (12.18)$$

---

[19] This, in turn, would seem to depend on whether the excess of pX over $D(Y)$ is regarded as temporary or not.

Assume that g_I and g_x are given constants. Then differentiation with respect to time yields[20]

$$\dot{g}_y = \lambda(1 - \lambda)(g_I - g_x)^2 > 0 \text{ for } 0 < \lambda < 1. \tag{12.19}$$

Therefore,

$$g_y \to \max(g_I, g_x) \text{ as } t \to \infty. \tag{12.20}$$

(a) Thus, for $g_I > g_x$, it follows that $g_y > g_x$ for all t, and not only is there persistently uneven growth, but also, since $\lambda \to 1$ as $t \to \infty$, there is *divergently uneven* growth over time.

(b) However, for $g_I \leq g_x$, it follows that $g_y \to g_x$ from below and there is balanced growth in the long run (the disparity is temporary).

Case II: $Y = Y_x$
In this case, with $D(Y) = mY^\sigma$,

$$mY^\sigma = pX, 0 < \sigma = 1. \tag{12.21}$$

Therefore, $\sigma g_y = g_x$ and it follows that $[g_y - g_x] = [(1 - \sigma)g_x/\sigma]$ is constant and non-negative.

Comparing Y_d and Y_x:
From the definitions, it follows that

$$Y_d = [I + m(Y_x)^\sigma]/(1 - b) = A + a(Y_x)^\sigma. \tag{12.22}$$

Therefore,

$$Y_x - Y_d = [(1 - b)Y_x - I - m(Y_x)^\sigma]/(1 - b) \tag{12.23}$$

is increasing in Y_x; it is negative for small values and positive for large values of Y_x. Let Y_z solve

$$Y_z = [I + m(Y_z)^\sigma]/(1 - b). \tag{12.24}$$

Then $Y_x < Y_z \Rightarrow Y_x < Y_d; Y_x > Y_z \Rightarrow Y_x > Y_d$ and $Y_x = Y_z \Rightarrow Y_x = Y_d$.

Consider the respective influences of I and X on Y_z and Y_x. From (12.21), Y_x is independent of I, and from (12.24), Y_z is increasing in I. If I is small and X is large, as would be the case in the initial stages of development, then $Y_x > Y_z$ is likely to result in $Y_x > Y_d$. In such a case, there would be too little demand for X from the non-agricultural

---

[20] Noting that $\dot{\lambda} = \lambda(1 - \lambda)(g_I - g_x)$.

sector: the agricultural surplus would fail to find a market. On the other hand, if I is large and X is small, there would be an excess demand for agricultural goods; growth is likely to lead to 'food inflation'.

A Difficulty with the Kaldor Argument

The Kaldor argument justifying fixity of p depends on a severely aggregative framework. In general, changes in the composition of output would lead to a change in the inter-sectoral terms of trade 'p' despite mark-up pricing and indexing of wages to the price of food. That argument would fix the price ratio for a particular industry, but when the composition of outputs change, the 'average' degree of monopoly would change as well.

However, the fixity of p may here be regarded as approximately empirically established.

Resolving the Inconsistency: The Credit Market

In the Keynesian case, one encounters the problem that both markets cannot clear at the same time. It follows from (12.13) that $S - I = pX - D_x$. There are two possible repercussions of $pX \neq D_x$. The first is a change in—this has been ruled out. But there is another possibility. An excess supply of food would mean an excess supply of saving over investment. That indicates that the loanable funds market (financial flows) has not cleared—there is an excess flow of funds. To get over this, one can introduce an interest rate mechanism and invoke an investment function such as $I = I(r)$. Then the model becomes

$$I(r) + pX = (1 - b)Y. \tag{12.25}$$

$$D(Y) = pX \tag{12.26}$$

Now, there is no necessary inconsistency between the two market clearing conditions. The latter equation is a sub-system that determines $Y : Y = Y_x$. Inserting this value in (12.25) yields the equilibrium value of r.

The Open Economy and the Agenda for Future Research

There is possibly a better alternative. Excess demand and excess supply in the domestic market reflect potential demand for imports from the rest of the world and potential supply of exports to the rest of the world.

Moreover, if we invoke the small country assumption for the domestic economy then that gives a natural reason for p and r to be given.[21]

Consider excess supply of x goods (the $Y_d < Y_x$ case when I/X is 'relatively small'). Suppose that the home country is a small country following a fixed exchange rate regime. Then the domestic prices P_x and P_y are given and the home country can export and import any amount of either good in the world market. An excess supply of the x good in the domestic market means an equivalent amount of export of that good to the rest of the world.

It may be the case that there are restrictions on exportability of the agricultural good—to guard against food inflation. Consider the extreme case where export of primary products is not permitted at all. Excess supply reflects a downward rigidity of p perhaps as a result of policy measures—'support price' for farmers. If such is the case, then the excess supply is likely to end up in state warehouses as addition to 'buffer stocks'.

With the small country assumption, it is hard to maintain the 'demand determined output' scenario. However, the small country assumption may not be accurate in specific markets. The hue and cry in the US over outsourcing suggests that India cannot really be that small when it comes to IT-intensive services.

The relevance for India of considering the open economy case is that the services-led growth here has been fuelled by an increase in exports. However, there are numerous details that need to be put in place to obtain an open economy model that would be satisfactory in explaining growth and changes in the composition of gross domestic product in contemporary India. This is what we propose to do in a future project.

REFERENCES

Acemoglu, D. and V. Guerrieri. 2008. 'Capital Deepening and Non-balanced Economic Growth', *Journal of Political Economy*, 116(3): 467–97.

Bhaduri, A. and R. Skarstein. 2003. 'Effective Demand and the Terms of Trade in a Dual Economy: A Kaldorian Perspective', *Cambridge Journal of Economics*, 27: 583–95.

---

[21] Thus, for the interest mechanism to be active, we need to assume a large country or a lack of full convertibility on the capital account.

Boppart, T. 2012. 'Structural Change and the Kaldor Facts in a Growth Model with Relative Price Effects and Non-Gorman Preferences', University of Zurich, Department of Economics, December.

Bose, A. 1989. 'Short-Period Equilibrium in a Less Developed Economy', in M. K. Rakshit (ed.), *Studies in the Macroeconomics of Developing Countries*. New Delhi: Oxford University Press, pp. 26–41.

———. 2012. 'Intersectoral Disparities and Growth', paper presented at the Fifth Conference on Economic Theory and Policy, JNU–NIPFP, March.

Dutt, A. K. 1992. 'A Kaldorian Model of Growth and Development Revisited: A Comment on Thirlwall', *Oxford Economic Papers*, No. 44, pp. 156–68.

Ghosh, Jayati. 1988. 'Intersectoral Terms of Trade, Agricultural Growth and the Pattern of Demand', *Social Scientist*, 16(4): 9–27.

Jha, Rajiv. 2010. 'The Analytics of the Agriculture–Industry Relationship in a Closed Economy: A Case Study of India', *Economic and Political Weekly*, 45(17): 94–98.

Jones, C. I. 2002. *Introduction to Economic Growth*, second edition. New York: W. W. Norton.

Jones, C. I. and D. Vollrath. 2013. *Introduction to Economic Growth*, third edition. New York: W. W. Norton E-Book.

———. 1976. 'Inflation and Recession in the World Economy', *Economic Journal*, 86(44): 703–14.

Kaldor, N. 1961. 'Capital Accumulation and Economic Growth', in F. A. Lutz and D. C. Hague (eds.) *The Theory of Capital*, London: Macmillan, 177–222.

———. 1979. 'Equilibrium Theory and Growth Theory', in N. J. Baskin (ed.), *Economics and Human Welfare: Essays in Honor of Tibor Scitovsky*. New York: Academic Press.

Kalecki, M. 1976. 'The Problem of Financing Development', in his *Essays on Developing Economies*, Brighton, UK: Harvester Press. Reprinted in vol. V of J. Osiatynski (ed.), *The Collected Works of M. Kalecki*. Oxford: Oxford University Press, 1993.

Kongsamut, P., S. Rebelo and D. Xie. 2001. 'Beyond Balanced Growth', *Review of Economic Studies*, 68(237): 869–82.

Kuznets, S. 1966. *Modern Economic Growth: Rate, Structure and Spread*. New Haven: Yale University Press.

———. 1957. 'Quantitative Aspects of the Economic Growth of Nations II: Industrial Distribution of National Product and Labour Force', *Economic Development and Cultural Change*, 5(4): 81–139.

Lewis, W. A. 1954. 'Economic Development with Unlimited Supplies of Labour', *The Manchester School*, 22(2): 139–91.

Lucas, R. E. Jr. 1988. 'On the Mechanics of Economic Development', *Journal of Monetary Economics*, 22(1): 3–42.

Ngai, R. and C. Pissarides. 2007. 'Structural Change in a Multi-sector Model of Growth', *American Economic Review*, 97(1): 429–43.

Rakshit, M. K. 1989. 'Effective Demand in a Developing Country: Approaches and Issues', in M. K. Rakshit (ed.), *Studies in the Macroeconomics of Developing Countries*. New Delhi: Oxford University Press, pp. 1–25.

Ranis, G. and J. C. Fei. 1961. 'A Theory of Economic Development', *American Economic Review*, 51(4): 533–58.

Rebelo, S. 1991. 'Long-Run Policy Analysis and Long-Run Growth', *Journal of Political Economy*, 99(3): 500–21.

Roberts, M. and John S. L. McCombie. 2008. 'Effective Demand Constrained Growth in a Two-Sector Kaldorian Model', *Journal of Post Keynesian Economics*, 31(1): 57–78.

Romer, P. 1986. 'Increasing Returns and Long-Run Growth', *Journal of Political Economy* 94(5): 1002–37.

———. 1990. 'Endogenous Technological Change', *Journal of Political Economy* 98(5): 71–102.

Verma, Rubin. 2012. 'Structural Transformation and Jobless Growth in the Indian Economy', in C. Ghate (ed.), *The Oxford Handbook of the Indian Economy*. New York: Oxford University Press.

13

Public Expansion of Higher Education and a Dynamic Todaro Paradox

Subrata Guha

An old tradition in the literature on economic development represented most notably by Lewis (1954) views a developing economy as 'a dual economy' in which a relatively small part of the labour force is employed in a high productivity 'advanced', 'modern' or 'formal' sector, and a large majority are forced to seek their livelihood in a low productivity 'backward', 'traditional' or 'informal' sector. Viewed from this perspective, the process of economic development consists of generating a sufficiently high rate of growth of employment in the high productivity sector, allowing for a sustained rise in its share of employment.

Traditionally the rate of investment in physical capital has been perceived to be the major constraint on the growth of employment in the high productivity sector of the economy. It has, however, been progressively realised that the level of education and training of the labour force plays a crucial role in determining the rate of investment in physical capital.[1] In particular, if a threshold level of skills and learning is required for most employment in the high productivity sector or if there is a fixed requirement of workers with such skills per unit of productive capacity in the high productivity sector, the size of the labour force with the required level of skills can itself become a constraint on the amount

---

[1] See, for example, Lucas (1990), Ranis and Stewart (2000) and World Bank (2005).

of employment.[2,3] Not only does investment in education then become a major driver for economic development, but also education matters from this perspective only if it is provided up to a sufficiently high level.

This perspective suggests that the pace of economic development might be crucially affected by the rate of growth in the number of students graduating from the education system with the level of education required for work in the high productivity sector. There is no doubt that it is this view which informs the recent emphasis on post-primary education as a tool of development policy (World Bank 2007). In China the rate of enrollment in institutions of higher education increased almost fourfold between 1998 and 2004 (Bai 2006). In India, the National Knowledge Commission (2009) recommended in its final report that 1,500 universities be created by 2015, the number of universities in the country in 2006 being 355. This argument is, however, a general one, which could be used to justify a policy emphasis on education at any *sufficiently high level*. It does not necessarily entail an emphasis on education at the tertiary level, which is what is usually understood by 'higher education'.

Despite significant variations between countries, much of post-primary education in developing economies is still publicly provided (World Bank 2007). A policy designed to increase the rate of growth of workers qualified to work in the high productivity sector naturally takes the form of an expansion in the size of the public education system relative to the size of the economy as a whole. It is, for example, not uncommon to find a demand for greater public involvement in education at a given level being expressed simply in terms of a demand that public expenditure on education at that level be some given percentage of GDP.[4]

---

[2] Cole and Sanders (1985) make the related but distinct argument that employment (as opposed to the actual work done) in the modern sector requires a threshold level of educational attainment, whereas this is not true of the traditional sector.

[3] The strength of this argument has probably been reinforced in recent times by evidence of a shift in output composition of the high productivity sector in many developing economies in favour of human-capital-intensive services and away from physical-capital-intensive industries.

[4] A typical example is the following quote from the final report of the National Knowledge Commission of India: 'Public expenditure (Centre and States) on education is only around 3.6 per cent of GDP. Government funding of higher education is still below 1 per cent of GDP.... Various committees have unanimously

A significant section of the dual economy literature beginning with the important contributions of Todaro (1969) and Harris and Todaro (1970) also gives explicit recognition to the possibility that a process of continuous labour transfers from the low productivity to the high productivity sector might coexist with unemployment of workers who have failed to find jobs in the high productivity sector. In the context of developing economies, a large proportion of such failed job seekers are not openly unemployed, but in a state of underemployment in the informal sector, a part of the low productivity sector of the economy.[5]

The coexistence of employment growth with unemployment or underemployment of job seekers raises the possibility that policies designed to increase employment in the high productivity sector of a dual economy may also increase the number of job seekers who fail to get employment in the sector. This possibility has been called the Todaro Paradox[6] in the literature on rural–urban migration and has been analysed in various contributions to that literature (recent contributions include Satchi and Temple [2009] and Zenou [2008, 2011]).

A policy of expansion of the public education system which is designed to increase employment growth in the high productivity sector of a dual economy might also have an effect on the rate of employment of job seekers (workers with the required level of education) in the high productivity sector. There are two major reasons why this may be true even if their are no constraints on employment in terms of scarcity of physical capital. One, any expansion in the size of the public education system relative to the economy as a whole would imply a possibly greater claim by the government on private incomes in the high productivity sector. This could adversely affect incentives for employment in the sector. Two, any expansion in the relative size of the public education system would require an expansion in the relative

---

recommended that state funding be increased to 6 per cent. While the Central Advisory Board for Education (CABE) recommends spending 1 per cent to higher education and 0.5 per cent to technical education, the proportions in 2004–05 were 0.34 per cent for higher education and 0.03 per cent for technical education' (National Knowledge Commission 2009: 186).

[5] See, for example, Günther and Launov (2012) and Martin (2000).

[6] Todaro (1976: 212) noted that one of the important implications of the Harris–Todaro model of rural–urban migration was that 'efforts to create more urban jobs to cope with rising unemployment may in fact, through induced migration, lead to even more urban unemployment and perhaps even to higher unemployment rates as well.'

size of the population of teachers. This could lead to an adverse impact on the average quality and, therefore, employability of students as less motivated or less capable teachers are recruited.

That high rates of expansion of the public education system can have potentially massive adverse impacts on the employment prospects of graduating students, at least in the short term, is dramatically illustrated by the experience of China at the beginning of this century. As noted by Bai (2006), tertiary enrollment in China increased from 0.86 million students to 1.08 million students between 1978 and 1998. Subsequently, enrollment jumped to 5.4 million students in 2006. Li and Zhang (2010: 39) cite reports of the Ministry of Education published in 2003 and 2004 and of the Ministry of Labour and Social Security published in 2006 to conclude that: 'Massive graduate unemployment followed reform and college expansion. At the national level, the statistics [on the graduate unemployment rate] reported by different government ministries have relatively large variations, though they seem to be at least as high as 30%.'

The objective of this essay is to study the possibility that a *relative or dynamic* version of the Todaro Paradox might hold true in the long run when the size of the public education system is expanded in a dual economy in which growth of the high productivity sector is constrained by the availability of adequately qualified workers. The 'relative or dynamic version' of the paradox refers to the possibility that a policy which increases the rate of growth of employment in the high productivity sector might also decrease the proportion of adequately qualified workers employed in the high productivity sector. This is in contrast to normal interpretations of the Todaro Paradox which consider absolute changes in numbers of urban workers employed and not employed in the sector. The 'long run' refers to a situation of steady state growth in the high productivity sector of the economy.

Note also that the presence of a public education sector in the economy, in effect, converts the dual economy with two sectors of private economic activity into an economy with three sectors. However, the necessary conditions for employment in the public education sector are not too dissimilar from those in the case of the high productivity commodity producing sector of the economy. Most job seekers in the high productivity sector might consider employment in the public education sector a more than adequate substitute for employment in the former. Therefore, in analysing the possibility of a dynamic Todaro Paradox, it is probably more appropriate to consider the rate of growth of employment and the rate of employment of job seekers not only for the high productivity private sector, but also for a larger sector comprising both the high productivity private sector and the public education sector. In subsequent discussion we refer to this larger sector as the *knowledge-intensive sector* of the economy because, unlike the low productivity sector, work in these sectors requires a higher threshold level of formal learning.

The analysis in the essay is based on some crucial assumptions which considerably simplify the problem studied. In particular, the essay assumes a small open economy facing a perfectly elastic supply curve for physical capital, neglects the existence of private avenues for higher education, implies that individuals are always willing to seek the education necessary for employment in the high productivity sector and assumes that both private and public employers know the threshold wage rates at which workers could be induced not to shirk at their jobs. The essay also assumes that public expenditure on education is financed wholly by tax revenues whereas developing countries often have access to various forms of concessionary financing. This 'balanced budget' assumption is, however, not essential. The analysis can, for example, easily be extended to consider cases where taxes finance only a constant positive fraction of expenditures and the rest is financed through grants from external sources.

There is a substantial difference in approach between the analysis of the Todaro Paradox in models of rural–urban migration and that of this essay. Discussions of the paradox in most of these models do not involve consideration of any specific policy, but simply analyse the effects of exogenous increases in formal sector employment on unemployment or informal sector employment. Moreover, whether a worker can enter the high productivity sector is determined by her geographical location and not by her level of education. Therefore, even when the effects of specific policies (and their budgetary implications) are considered[7] there is no analysis in these models of policies which directly control the number of people having the opportunity of entry into the high productivity sector.

The remainder of the essay is structured as follows. The next section describes the model considered in the essay. The third section of the essay characterises the nature of the equilibrium in a single period and derives a necessary and sufficient condition for the existence of a trade-off between increases in the the rate of expansion of the public education sector and increases in the rate of employment of qualified

---

[7] See, for example, Zenou (2008, 2011).

job seekers in the knowledge-intensive sector. The fourth section considers the long-run implications of alternative policies which fix the size of the public education sector relative to the high productivity sector in the economy. A necessary and sufficient condition is derived for the existence of a dynamic Todaro Paradox in the model. The final section interprets this condition to highlight the role played by teacher quality, in particular, and the quality of public education, in general, in the existence of a dynamic Todaro Paradox in the economy.

THE MODEL

Types of Workers and Sectors of Employment

Consider an economy with one producible good and two types of workers. Workers may be of type-l (workers with a 'low' level of education) or type-h (workers with a 'high' level of education). In a single time period, employed workers can put in an effort level 0 (when a worker 'shirks' and the amount of effective labour performed is 0 units) or 1 (when a worker 'works' and a unit of effective labour is performed). There are three sectors in the economy: sector H ('high productivity' commodity producing sector), sector L ('low productivity' commodity producing sector) and sector G (the 'high education' sector or, equivalently, the 'government' sector).

Both type-l and type-h workers can work in sector L. Workers are self-employed and produce and earn a fixed amount $a > 0$ in a time period.[8] A worker does not incur any disutility from effort while working in sector L.

In sector H, output is produced using capital (stocks of the single good) and type-h workers in fixed proportions. Production is subject to constant returns to scale and a unit of capital together with a unit of effective labour is required to produce A units of output.

In any time period, there is in sector H a continuum of homogeneous firms of finite size (Lebesgue measure). Each firm in the economy is assigned a number and the numbers occupy a bounded interval on the real line. Firms, in any time period, aim to maximise profits in that period

---

[8] One can assume that no physical capital is required for production in the sector, an assumption commonly made in dual economy models to represent the relatively low capital intensity of production in the sector. Alternatively, since we consider a small open economy facing a fixed rental price of capital, one can assume that one unit of labour works with a fixed amount of physical capital to produce a level of output, which net of rental payments is equal to a.

and hire capital and type-h workers in the necessary proportion to carry on production. Each worker incurs, a particular disutility from putting in a positive level of effort while working in sector H. If a worker shirks, no output is produced by her. In such a case, the firm can dismiss the worker without any wage payment with a probability $p \in (0, 1)$. Since in the formal sector workers enjoy some degree of social protection[9] of employment, we assume that there is a positive probability $1 - p$ with which a worker will be able to prevent or successfully contest dismissal and be entitled to receive the full wage. If a worker does not shirk, she is paid her full wage.

Firms simultaneously post a wage offer for each type-h worker in the economy in any given time period. For any given worker, we assume that the set of wage offers from firms always has a maximum. If a worker who decides to work in sector H is indifferent between accepting employment in a set of firms, she chooses her employer at random. In case the set is countable, there is a positive probability associated with the choice of any single firm. In case the set is uncountable, the number of the firm chosen by the worker is a random variable which is distributed with positive probability density throughout. The random variables defined by the choices of workers are assumed to be independent.

We assume that the economy under consideration is a small open economy and the world interest rate is fixed at r. Firms in the economy, therefore, face a perfectly elastic supply curve of capital at a fixed rental price r. We assume that $A - r > a$.

In sector G, the government employs type-h workers as teachers to provide high education to selected individuals from the next generation. We assume that the pupil–teacher ratio is fixed and constant at some value θ. This means that if a type-h worker employed in period t in sector G chooses not to shirk, she generates θ type-h workers for the economy in period $t + 1$ through her teaching. Every type-h worker incurs the same disutility from effort in sector G as in sector H. If a type-h worker employed in sector G chooses to shirk, no type-h worker is generated by her teaching in period $t + 1$. We will assume that if an employed worker shirks, the probability that the government can dismiss the worker without payment of any wage is the same as for firms in sector-h and equal to p.

The government finances its wage payments to teachers by taxing the wage incomes of type-h workers in sectors G and H at a proportional

---

[9] This need not necessarily imply protection by a formal legal system, but could, for example, be protection afforded by people or organisations directly enjoying social or political power.

rate τ. At the beginning of each period, the government notifies the tax rate which is known to firms when they post their wage schedules. The government then, simultaneously with firms, posts a wage offer for each type-h worker in the economy.

This discussion implies that work in sectors G and H require the application of knowledge gained from a high level of education, while this knowledge is not necessary for work in sector L. We, therefore, refer to sectors G and H taken together as the *knowledge-intensive sector* of the economy. We refer to work performed in the knowledge-intensive sector as type-h or knowledge-intensive work.

Government and Individuals in the Economy

The economy is populated in any period by three overlapping generations of individuals. Every individual lives for three periods. Individuals work in the second period and consume in the last two periods of their lives. In the first period, an individual acquires a low level of education or a high level of education. A low level of education can be acquired by everybody privately and free of cost, whereas the government offers a high level of education for free to a certain number of individuals in every generation. We leave the mechanism by which the government selects these individuals unspecified under the assumption that whatever be the selection mechanism, the distribution of learning outcomes is the same in any selected group of a given size.

In the next period of their lives, individuals with a low level of education become type-l workers, work in sector L and earn a real income a. Individuals with a high level of education become type-h workers and consider the wage offers from the government and the firms in sector H. An individual worker then compares the expected lifetime utility from working in the three sectors, G, H and L, and seeks employment in these sectors in descending order of expected lifetime utility. If a worker is initially employed in either sector H or sector G and is dismissed due to shirking, the worker can subsequently work in sector L in the same period and earn an income a. This ensures that every individual in the economy who is offered the opportunity of acquiring a high education would be interested in doing so.

We further assume that if a type-h worker is indifferent between accepting a job offer in sector H and a job offer in sector G, the worker chooses to accept the job in sector G. As will be seen later, this ensures that there is a determinate wage offer on the basis of which the government can achieve for certain any desired and feasible level of employment in sector G.

Individuals who acquire a low level of education in any given period $t - 1 \geq 0$, become type-l workers in period t and go to work in sector L are identical and their lifetime utility is a function $U(c_1(t), c_2(t + 1))$ of their consumption in period t, denoted by $c_1(t)$, and their consumption in period $t + 1$, denoted by $c_2(t + 1)$. We assume that $U_1(c_1, c_2) > 0$, $U_2(c_1, c_2) > 0$, $U_{11}(c_1, c_2) < 0$ and $U_{22}(c_1, c_2) < 0$ for all $c_1 > 0$ and for all $c_2 > 0$. Further, we assume that U is homogeneous of degree one and satisfies the Inada conditions. These individuals choose $c_1(t)$ and $c_2(t + 1)$ by solving the following decision-making problem:

$$\max_{c_1(t), c_2(t+1)} U(c_1(t), c_2(t + 1))$$

$$s.t. \quad c_1(t) + \frac{c_2(t + 1)}{1 + r} = a$$

$$c_1(t) \geq 0, \quad c_2(t + 1) \geq 0$$

It can be shown that the lifetime utility of any type-l worker in the economy is equal to $B(r)a$, where $B(r) > 0$ and $B'(r) > 0$.

Individuals who acquire a high education in any given period $t - 1 \geq 0$ enter the labour force in period t as type-h workers. A type-h worker incurs disutility if she is employed in the knowledge-intensive sector and does not shirk. We will assume that type-h workers entering the labour force in period t are identical in all respects except in the disutility of effort incurred by them from working in the knowledge-intensive sector.

We assume that in period t, $[0, N(t)]$ is the set of numbers which is used to denote type-h workers and the population of type-h workers forms a continuum of size $N(t)$. Let $v(i, t)$ denote the disutility of effort in knowledge-intensive work incurred by type-h worker i of period t when she is employed in the knowledge-intensive sector and does not shirk. We assume that for all $t \geq 0$ and for all $i \in [0, N(t)]$,

$$v(i, t) = \frac{i}{N(t)} b(t), \tag{13.1}$$

where $b(t)$ is the maximum possible disutility which can be incurred by a type-h worker in period t. It follows that in any period t disutility of effort in type-h work is distributed uniformly in the population of type-h workers in the interval $[0, b(t)]$.

In this model, an individual type-h worker's disutility of effort in type-h work is assumed to reflect the degree of her interest in work which requires the application of knowledge acquired from high education. Less the interest an individual type-h worker finds in type-h work, the greater her disutility of effort. The degree of interest that type-h workers, find in type-h work is, in turn, assumed to be a reflection of the degree of interest that their teachers in the high education sector had taken in their work. In particular, we assume that the average disutility of effort in type-h work of type-h workers in period t is a linear function of the average disutility of effort of type-h workers employed in sector G in period $t - 1$ (denoted by $z(t - 1)$):

$$\frac{b(t)}{2} = \frac{\beta_0}{2} + \beta_1 z(t - 1), \qquad (13.2)$$

where β_0 and β_1 are positive constants.

The lifetime utility function for an individual joining the labour force in period t as type-h worker $i \in [0, N(t)]$ is assumed to be of the form

$$U(c_1(i, t), c_2(i, t + 1)) - v(i, t)e(i, t),$$

where $c_1(i, t)$ and $c_2(i, t + 1)$ are worker i's consumption levels in periods t and $t + 1$ respectively, and $e(i, t)$ is the level of effort in type-h work put in by worker i. Thus, $e(i, t) = 0$ if worker i is employed in the knowledge-intensive sector and shirks or if worker i is not employed in the knowledge-intensive sector. $e(i, t) = 1$ if worker i is employed in the knowledge-intensive sector and does not shirk.

For any given value of $e(i, t)$ and any given value of $y(i, t)$, the income earned by worker i in period t, the utility-maximising values of $c_1(i, t)$ and $c_2(i, t + 1)$ are given by the solution to the decision-making problem:

$$\max_{c_1(i,t),c_2(i,t+1)} U(c_1(i, t), c_2(i, t + 1))$$

$$s.t. \ c_1(i, t) + \frac{c_2(i, t + 1)}{1 + r} = y(i, t)$$

$$c_1(i, t) \geq 0, \ c_2(i, t + 1) \geq 0$$

This implies that, for any given level of income $y(i, t)$ and for any given level of effort in type-h work $e(i, t)$, the lifetime utility of worker i of period t is equal to $B(r)y(i, t) - v(i, t)e(i, t)$.

Given a tax rate τ on wage incomes in the knowledge-intensive sector, the type-h worker i of period t ($i \in [0, N(t)]$; $t \geq 0$) employed in sector j ($j \in \{G, H\}$) at a wage w_j will decide whether to shirk or not depending on whether expected lifetime utility from shirking given by $(1 - p)B(r)(1 - \tau)w_j + pB(r)a$ is greater or less than the lifetime utility from not shirking, which is given by $B(r)(1 - \tau)w_j - v(i, t)$. It follows that worker i of period t will prefer to shirk, be indifferent between shirking and not shirking or prefer not to shirk according to whether

$$w_j \lessgtr \frac{1}{pB(r)(1-\tau)}[pB(r)a + v(i,t)] = w(i,t,\tau). \quad (13.3)$$

We refer to $w(i, t, \tau)$ as the effort reservation wage for worker i of period t when the tax rate is τ. We will assume that type-h workers do not shirk when they are employed in the knowledge-intensive sector at their effort reservation wage.

We make the strong assumption that in any given time period, the government as well as all firms know the effort reservation wage of every type-h worker. We will assume, in addition, that the government is *cost-efficient*. We take this to mean two things. One, the government is not going to hire any type-h worker at a wage less than her effort reservation wage or greater than the maximum wage she is offered in sector H. Two, no type-h worker will be in employment in sector G if there exists another type-h worker not in employment in sector G who has a lower effort reservation wage and is willing to work in sector G at a wage not higher than that paid to the former.

THE ECONOMY IN A SINGLE TIME PERIOD

In a given time period t, the size of the population of type-h workers $N(t)$ and the distribution of the disutility of effort in type-h work in the population of type-h workers (uniformly distributed with support $[0, b(t)]$) is historically determined.

The Equilibrium Distribution of Wages and Employment

In this section, we derive, for any given period t and for any given value of τ chosen by the government, the equilibrium wage rates paid to type-h workers in sectors G and H and the equilibrium distribution of type-h workers by sector of employment.

An equilibrium in a given time period and for a given tax rate is a state of the economy specified by a government wage schedule, a collection of firm wage schedules, one for each firm in sector H, and a distribution of type-h workers by initial employer (government, firms or self) such that, given that the other elements of the state remain unchanged, no firm has an incentive to change its wage schedule, no worker has an incentive to change her employer, the assumption of a cost-efficient government is satisfied and the wage payments in sector G are exactly equal to government tax revenue. We consider only equilibria in which there is a positive amount of employment in sector G.

Since both profit-maximising firms and the cost-efficient government know the effort reservation wages of type-h workers, neither the government nor any firm will employ a type-h worker at a wage less than that worker's effort reservation wage. This implies that no type-h worker employed in the knowledge-intensive sector will shirk. Thus, the addition to firm output resulting from the employment of any type-h worker will be equal to A and firms will be willing to hire type-h workers so long as the wage paid does not exceed $A - r$. If any type-h worker is employed in the knowledge-intensive sector at a wage less than $A - r$, it would be profitable for firms not employing the worker to rent one more unit of capital and offer the worker employment at a slightly higher wage. Given that the disutility of effort for any worker is the same in all knowledge-intensive jobs, the worker will also be willing to accept such job offers. On the other hand, profit-maximising firms will not hire any worker at a wage greater than $A - r$. It follows that the wage paid to any given type-h worker employed in sector H must in equilibrium be equal to

$$A - r = w. \tag{13.4}$$

In equilibrium, therefore, the wage paid to all type-h workers employed in sector H is uniform and firms' profits are equal to zero. Also, in equilibrium, the wage paid to any worker employed in sector G cannot be less than w.

From (13.3) and (13.4), for all $i \in [0, N(t)]$, $w(i, t, \tau) \leq w$ if and only if $v(i, t) \leq pB(r)[(1 - \tau)w - a]$. Let for all $\tau \in [0, 1]$,

$$\lambda(\tau) = pB(r)[(1 - \tau)w - a]. \tag{13.5}$$

It follows that any type-h worker i will be offered employment in sector H only if $v(i, t) \leq \lambda(\tau)$.

Note, however, that if the tax rate τ is such that $(1 - \tau)w < a$, every type-h worker in the economy will prefer to work in sector L. Further, if $(1 - \tau)w = a$, then from (13.5), the size of the population of type-h workers employed in sector H will be zero. Since a positive fraction of wage payments to type-h workers employed in sector G are financed by taxation of type-h workers employed in sector H, it follows that for an equilibrium to exist with a positive amount of employment in sector G the tax rate τ must satisfy

$$\tau < 1 - \frac{a}{w} = \tau_{\max} \tag{13.6}$$

Note also that because any type-h worker employed in sector H will receive wage w and prefer not to shirk, the lifetime utility of type-h worker i, if employed in sector H, will be equal to $B(r)(1 - \tau)w - v(i, t)$. On the other hand, the lifetime utility of any type-h worker working in sector L will be equal to $B(r)a$. It follows that type-h worker $i \in [0, b(t)]$ will prefer to work in sector H rather than sector L if and only if

$$v(i, t) < B(r)[(1 - \tau)w - a].$$

Since $\lambda(\tau) < B(r)[(1 - \tau)w - a]$, it follows that the only type-h workers who will prefer self-employment in sector L over employment in sector H are those who will never find employment in sector H. Therefore, every type-h worker with effort reservation wage less than or equal to w will be employed either in sector H at a wage w or in sector G with a wage not less than w.

We next argue that all workers employed in sector G will also receive the wage w in equilibrium and then proceed to derive the equilibrium distribution of type-h workers by sector of employment.

We first prove that the only type-h workers who will be employed in sector G are those with effort reservation wage less than or equal to w. Suppose that is not the case. Then, there must exist some worker $i \in [0, N(t)]$ such that $v(i, t) > \lambda(\tau)$ and i is employed in sector G. When $\lambda(\tau) > b(t)$, this is clearly not possible. Next suppose that $\lambda(\tau) < b(t)$. Since the government is assumed to be cost-efficient, it follows that the wage paid to worker i cannot be less than $w(i, t, \tau)$, which is greater than w, the wage received by employed workers in sector H. The assumption of a cost-efficient government then also implies that any type-h worker $j \in [0, \lambda(\tau)]$ must either not be willing to work in sector G at a wage lower than $w(i, t, \tau)$ or must also be employed in sector G. Since $w(i, t, \tau) > w$, this implies that for all $j \in [0, \lambda(\tau)]$, j must be employed in sector G. This, in turn, implies that there is zero employment in sector H, which violates the condition that wage payments in sector G are met by taxation of wage incomes of all type-h workers employed in the knowledge-intensive sector.

It follows that if $i \in [0, N(t)]$ is employed in sector G, then $v(i, t) \leq \lambda(\tau)$. Given that the government is cost-efficient and that type-h workers take up employment in sector G whenever they are indifferent between job offers from sector G and sector H, two conclusions follow: One, the wage paid to every worker employed in sector G is w and, two, if we denote the size of the workforce in sector G in period t by $x(t)$, then type-h worker $i \in [0, N(t)]$ is employed in sector G if and only if $i \in [0, x(t)]$. Let,

$$\lambda_H(t) = \min\{\lambda(\tau), b(t)\}. \tag{13.7}$$

Since for any worker i employed in sector G, $v(i, t) \leq \lambda(\tau)$, it must be true that $\frac{x(t)b(t)}{N(t)} \leq \lambda_H(t)$.

Let $\lambda_G(t) = \frac{x(t)b(t)}{N(t)}$. It follows that, for all $i \in [0, N(t)]$, i is employed in sector G if and only if $v(i, t) \in [0, \lambda_G(t)]$ and i is employed in sector H if and only if $v(i, t) \in (\lambda_G(t), \lambda_H(t)]$. Since the disutility of effort in type-h work is uniformly distributed in the population of type-h workers, it follows that the rate of employment of type-h workers in the knowledge-intensive sector of the economy is equal to $\frac{\lambda_H(t)}{b(t)}$, the fraction of type-h workers employed in sector G is equal to $\frac{\lambda_G(t)}{b(t)}$ and the share of sector G in the total employment of type-h workers in the knowledge-intensive sector is $\frac{\lambda_G(t)}{\lambda_H(t)}$.

Note that (13.2) can now be rewritten as

$$b(t) = \beta_0 + \beta_1 \lambda_G(t - 1). \tag{13.8}$$

Since wage incomes of workers in sectors G and H are taxed at a proportional rate τ and the tax revenue is equal to public expenditure on wages in sector G it follows that

$$w \frac{\lambda_G(t)}{b(t)} N(t) = \tau w \frac{\lambda_H(t)}{b(t)} N(t).$$

This implies that sector G's share in the total employment of the knowledge-intensive sector is equal to the tax rate:

$$\frac{\lambda_G(t)}{\lambda_H(t)} = \tau \tag{13.9}$$

Our analysis in this section indicates that the wage rates received by employed workers in the knowledge-intensive sector and the distribution of type-h workers by sector of employment is the same in any equilibrium in a given period t (with given values of $b(t)$ and $N(t)$) and for a given tax rate τ. However, so long as (13.6) is satisfied, it is clear that an infinite number of equilibria will exist. All of the equilibria will be characterised by the fact that for all $i \in [0, \lambda_G(t)]$, the maximum wage offer received by worker i is w and the wage offer received from the government is w; for all $i \in [\lambda_G(t), \lambda_H(t)]$ the maximum wage offer received by worker i is w, there is at least one firm in sector H which makes this wage offer and the government makes a lower wage offer; where $\lambda_H(t) \leq b(t)$, for all $i \in [\lambda_H(t), b(t)]$, the maximum wage offer received by worker i is less than the wage rate which would leave her indifferent between employment in the knowledge-intensive sector and employment in sector L.

Note that, while this is strictly not necessary for our purpose, the equilibrium distribution of type-h workers employed in sector H across firms in the sector is, in fact, left unspecified in this analysis. Given that firms are homogeneous, one can choose to concentrate on equilibria in which the posted wage schedules of firms are the same. If one then assumes that the random variable defined by the number of the firm selected by any type-h worker $i \in [\lambda_G(t), \lambda_H(t)]$ is uniformly distributed on the bounded interval occupied by firm numbers, employed workers in sector H will be uniformly distributed in equilibrium across firms in the sector.

The Rate of Expansion of High Education and the Rate of Employment in the Knowledge-Intensive Sector

Let the size of sector G in a period be measured by the size of the population of students receiving a high level of education in that period. In this section we consider how, within any given period, the government's choice of the tax rate, τ, affects the growth in the size of sector G and the rate of employment of type-h workers in the knowledge-intensive sector, $\frac{\lambda_H(t)}{b(t)}$.

The rate of growth in the size of sector G in period t is given by

$$\frac{N(t+1)}{N(t)} = \frac{\theta \frac{\lambda_G(t)}{b(t)} N(t)}{N(t)} = \theta \tau \frac{\lambda_H(t)}{b(t)}. \tag{13.10}$$

Note that $\frac{\lambda_G(t)}{b(t)} N(t)$ is the size of the teaching population in period t.

From (13.5)–(13.7), it follows that the employment rate of type-h workers in the knowledge-intensive sector is given by

$$\frac{\lambda_H(t)}{b(t)} = 1, \text{ if } \tau_{\max} > \frac{b(t)}{pB(r)w} \text{ and } \tau \in \left[0, \tau_{\max} - \frac{b(t)}{pB(r)w}\right]$$

$$= \frac{\lambda(\tau)}{b(t)}, \text{ if } \tau_{\max} > \frac{b(t)}{pB(r)w} \text{ and } \tau \in \left[\tau_{\max} - \frac{b(t)}{pB(r)w}, \tau_{\max}\right]$$

$$= \frac{\lambda(\tau)}{b(t)}, \text{ if } \tau_{\max} \leq \frac{b(t)}{pB(r)w} \tag{13.11}$$

Figure 13.1 shows that the relationship between the rate of employment in the knowledge-intensive sector and the tax rate will depend on whether $b(t) < \tau_{\max} pB(r)w$ (Figure 13.1a) or whether $b(t) \geq \tau_{\max} pB(r)w$ (Figure 13.1b). In the former case, there would be full employment of type-h workers in the knowledge-intensive sector so long as the tax rate

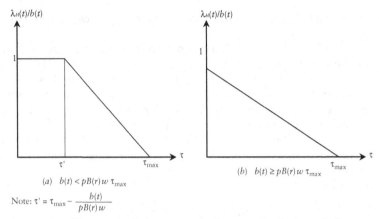

(a) $b(t) < pB(r)w\,\tau_{\max}$

(b) $b(t) \geq pB(r)w\,\tau_{\max}$

Note: $\tau' = \tau_{\max} - \dfrac{b(t)}{pB(r)w}$

Figure 13.1 Tax rate and short-run employment in the knowledge-intensive sector

is below a critical positive value. Subsequently, the rate of employment decreases linearly with the tax rate approaching a value of zero as τ approaches $\tau_{\max}$. In the latter case, there is no tax rate at which all type-h workers are employed in the knowledge-intensive sector and the negative relation between the tax rate and the employment rate extends over the entire range of values of the tax rate. The negative relation reflects the fact that higher tax rates on type-h workers employed in the knowledge-intensive sector make a greater proportion of such workers prefer to shirk at the equilibrium wage w and, therefore, make a greater proportion of them unemployable in this sector.

From (13.10) and (13.11), we get

$$\frac{N(t+1)}{N(t)} = \theta\tau, \ \text{if } \tau_{\max} > \frac{b(t)}{pB(r)w} \ \text{and } \tau \in \left[0, \tau_{\max} - \frac{b(t)}{pB(r)w}\right]$$

$$= \theta\tau\frac{\lambda(\tau)}{b(t)}, \ \text{if } \tau_{\max} > \frac{b(t)}{pB(r)w} \ \text{and } \tau \in \left[\tau_{\max} - \frac{b(t)}{pB(r)w}, \tau_{\max}\right]$$

$$= \theta\tau\frac{\lambda(\tau)}{b(t)}, \ \text{if } \tau_{\max} \leq \frac{b(t)}{pB(r)w}. \tag{13.12}$$

(13.12) implies that if $\tau_{\max} > \frac{b(t)}{pB(r)w}$, the rate of expansion of the high education sector increases proportionately with the tax rate (the share of sector G in the total employment of the knowledge-intensive sector) till a threshold value given by $\tau_{\max} - \frac{b(t)}{pB(r)w}$. From (13.5), (13.6) and (13.12), it follows that for values of τ greater than this value in case

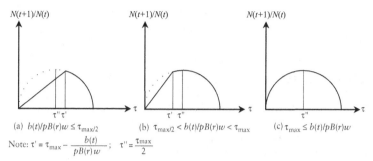

(a) $b(t)/pB(r)w \leq \tau_{max/2}$ (b) $\tau_{max/2} < b(t)/pB(r)w < \tau_{max}$ (c) $\tau_{max} \leq b(t)/pB(r)w$

Note: $\tau' = \tau_{max} - \dfrac{b(t)}{pB(r)w}$; $\tau'' = \dfrac{\tau_{max}}{2}$

Figure 13.2 Tax rate and rate of expansion of higher education in the short run

$\tau_{max} > \dfrac{b(t)}{pB(r)w}$ and for all values of τ otherwise, the relationship between the rate of growth in the size of sector G and the tax rate is given by

$$\frac{N(t+1)}{N(t)} = \frac{\theta p B(r)}{b(t)}[(w - a)\tau - w\tau^2]. \tag{13.13}$$

The function on the right-hand side of equation (13.13) is a strictly concave function of τ with a global maximum at $\tau_{max}/2$. Therefore, if $\frac{b(t)}{pB(r)w} \leq \frac{\tau_{max}}{2}$, it follows that for all values of τ greater than $\tau_{max} - \frac{b(t)}{pB(r)w}$, the rate of growth in the size of sector G is a decreasing function of τ. In contrast, if $\frac{b(t)}{pB(r)w} \geq \tau_{max}$ then for values of τ in $[0, \tau_{max})$ and if $\tau_{max} > \frac{b(t)}{pB(r)w} > \frac{\tau_{max}}{2}$ then for values of τ in $(\tau_{max} - \frac{b(t)}{pB(r)w}, \tau_{max})$, the rate of growth in the size of sector G initially increases with τ and then decreases. The alternative cases are represented in Figure 13.2.

From the preceding discussion, it is clear that it is only in the case $\frac{b(t)}{pB(r)w} \leq \frac{\tau_{max}}{2}$ that increases in the rate of expansion of the high education sector can always be secured without any decrease in the rate of employment of type-h workers in the knowledge-intensive sector. Otherwise, there always exists some value for the rate of growth in the size of sector G such that any increase in the rate beyond this value requires a decrease in the employment rate of type-h workers. Similarly, there exists some value of the employment rate such that increases in the employment rate beyond this value entails a sacrifice in terms of the rate of growth of the high education sector. The conclusion of the argument in this section can, therefore, be stated in the form of the following proposition.

Proposition 1. The necessary and sufficient condition for the existence of a trade-off in a period t between increasing the rate of growth in the size of the high education sector and increasing the rate of employment of type-h workers in the knowledge-intensive sector is that

$$b(t) > \frac{pB(r)(w - a)}{2}.$$

Suppose we interpret $b(t)$ as an indicator of the average quality of type-h workers in the economy in period t (a higher value of $b(t)$ signalling lower quality). The preceding result then implies that the poorer the average quality of type-h workers in the economy, the greater is the possibility of a trade-off between the objective of increasing the rate of expansion of the high education sector and that of increasing the rate of employment of workers with high education.

THE LONG-RUN IMPLICATIONS OF ALTERNATIVE TAX RATES

The tax rate on wage incomes in the knowledge-intensive sector also represents in our model the employment share of the high education sector in the total employment of the knowledge-intensive sector in the economy. The tax rate fixes the proportion between the size of the workforce in the high education sector and the size of the workforce in the high productivity commodity producing sector of the economy.

In the previous section, we considered the implications of choosing alternative tax rates in a single time period for the rate of expansion of the high education sector and for the rate of employment of workers with high education in the knowledge-intensive sector in that period. The choice of a tax rate in a given period t, however, also has intertemporal effects on employment in the knowledge-intensive sector through its effect on $N(t + 1)$, the size of the type-h labour force in the next period and on $b(t + 1)/2$, the average disutility of effort in knowledge-intensive work characterising type-h workers in the next period.

In this section, we consider the long-run implications of maintaining alternative tax rates in the economy, that is, following alternative policies each of which fixes the ratio between the number of teachers in the high education sector and the number of employees in the high productivity commodity producing sector at a given level over time. In particular, we focus on what happens in the long run to the rate of growth of employment as well as the rate of employment of type-h workers in the knowledge-intensive sector when the tax rate in the economy is held fixed.

Long-Run Growth and Employment Rate for a Given Tax Rate

We begin by deriving, for any given $\tau \in (0, \tau_{\max})$, the relation between $b(t + 1)$ and $b(t)$. Note that if $\tau = 0$ in period t, no type-h workers exist in the economy period $t + 1$ onwards.

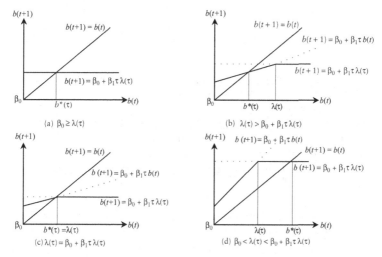

Figure 13.3 Relation between $b(t+1)$ and $b(t)$: Alternative cases

From (13.7) and (13.9), we know that

$$\lambda_G(t) = \tau b(t), \quad \text{if } b(t) \leq \lambda(\tau)$$
$$= \tau \lambda(\tau), \quad \text{if } b(t) \geq \lambda(\tau). \tag{13.14}$$

From (13.8) and (13.14), it, therefore, follows that

$$b(t+1) = \beta_0 + \beta_1 \tau b(t), \quad \text{if } b(t) \leq \lambda(\tau)$$
$$= \beta_0 + \beta_1 \tau \lambda(\tau), \quad \text{if } b(t) \geq \lambda(\tau). \tag{13.15}$$

$b(t) \geq 0$ by definition and, from (13.5) and (13.6), $\lambda(\tau) > 0$ because $\tau < \tau_{\max}$. Note, therefore, that β_0 is the minimum possible value of $b(t+1)$ in any period $t+1$. Moreover, (13.15) implies that for $b(t) = \beta_0$, $b(t+1) > b(t)$.

The graph of (13.15) in the $b(t) - b(t+1)$ plane is presented in Figure 13.3 distinguishing between the two cases: $\beta_0 \geq \lambda(\tau)$ and $\beta_0 < \lambda(\tau)$. It is clear that in both cases there must exist a unique equilibrium for the dynamic system in (13.15) since there is one and only one point of intersection of the graph with the line of equality. Let $b^*(\tau)$ denote the equilibrium state for all $\tau \in (0, \tau_{\max})$. The equilibrium of the dynamic system is globally stable because for all $b(t) \in [\beta_0, b^*(\tau)]$, $b(t+1) > b(t)$ and for all $b(t) \in (b^*(\tau), \infty)$, $b(t+1) < b(t)$.

Further, since $b(t + 1) > b(t)$ for $b(t) = \beta_0$, it follows that

$$b^*(\tau) > \beta_0, \quad \text{for all } \tau \in (0, \tau_{\max}). \qquad (13.16)$$

If for any given t, $b(t) = b^*(\tau)$, it follows that for all $v \geq t$, $b(v) = b^*(\tau)$. From (13.11) and (13.12), given a constant tax rate, we can, therefore, conclude that the rate of employment of type-h workers in the knowledge-intensive sector and the rate of growth of the type-h labour force must remain constant time period $t + 1$ onwards. The rate of growth of employment in the knowledge-intensive sector and the rate of growth of output and employment in sector H in any given period v are both equal to $N(v)\frac{\lambda_H(v)}{b(v)}/N(v-1)\frac{\lambda_H(v-1)}{b(v-1)}$ when the tax rate is the same in periods v and $v - 1$. Since the values of $N(v)/N(v-1)$ and $\lambda_H(v)/b(v)$ are the same for all $v \geq t + 1$, it follows that the values of $N(v)\frac{\lambda_H(v)}{b(v)}/N(v-1)\frac{\lambda_H(v-1)}{b(v-1)}$ must be the same for all $v \geq t + 1$ and must be equal to the rate of growth of the type-h labour force $N(v)/N(v-1)$.

Thus, global stability of the equilibrium for the dynamic system (13.15) implies that the economy in the long run approaches a situation in which the size of the type-h labour force, output and employment in sector H, and employment in sector G all grow at the same steady rate and the rate of employment of type-h workers in the knowledge-intensive sector remains constant. For any given tax rate τ, let us denote the limiting value of the rate of growth of the type-h labour force by $n(\tau)$ and the limiting value of the rate of employment of type-h workers in the knowledge-intensive sector by $\varepsilon(\tau)$.

We next derive a set of conditions governing the values of $b^*(\tau)$, $\varepsilon(\tau)$ and $n(\tau)$ for any given $\tau \in (0, \tau_{\max})$. We can distinguish usefully between two cases: the case where $pB(r)(w - a) \leq \beta_0$ and the case where $\beta_0 < pB(r)(w - a)$.

Case I. Suppose $\beta_0 \geq pB(r)(w - a)$.

In this case, from (13.5), it follows that $\beta_0 \geq \lambda(\tau)$ for all $\tau \in (0, \tau_{\max})$. From (13.16) it then follows that:

$$\text{if } \beta_0 \geq pB(r)(w - a) \text{ then, for all } \tau \in (0, \tau_{\max}), b^*(\tau) > \lambda(\tau). \quad (13.17)$$

Case II. Next, suppose that $\beta_0 < pB(r)(w - a)$ i.e. $\tau_{\max} > \frac{\beta_0}{pB(r)w}$.

From (13.5), it follows that $\beta_0 \geq \lambda(\tau)$ if and only if $pB(r)w\tau \geq pB(r)(w - a) - \beta_0$. Therefore, given (13.6) and (13.16), it follows that:

if $\beta_0 < pB(r)(w - a)$ then, for all $\tau \in \left[\tau_{\max} - \dfrac{\beta_0}{pB(r)w}, \tau_{\max} \right]$,

$$b^*(\tau) > \lambda(\tau). \tag{13.18}$$

Now suppose that $pB(r)w\tau < pB(r)(w - a) - \beta_0$ so that $\beta_0 < \lambda(\tau)$. Note from (13.15) that $\frac{b(t+1)}{b(t)}$ is a continuous strictly decreasing function of $b(t)$ on the interval $[\beta_0, \lambda(\tau)]$. $\frac{b(t+1)}{b(t)}$ has the value $1 + \beta_1\tau$ at the lower endpoint of the interval and the value $\frac{\beta_0}{\lambda(\tau)} + \beta_1\tau$ at the upper endpoint of the interval. Since $b^*(\tau)$ is that value of $b(t)$ at which $\frac{b(t+1)}{b(t)} = 1$, it follows that $b^*(\tau) < \lambda(\tau)$ if and only if it is true that $\frac{b(t+1)}{b(t)} < 1$ at $b(t) = \lambda(\tau)$, that is, $\lambda(\tau) > \beta_0 + \beta_1\tau\lambda(\tau)$. Similarly, $b^*(\tau) = \lambda(\tau)$ if and only if $\lambda(\tau) = \beta_0 + \beta_1\tau\lambda(\tau)$. We can, therefore, conclude that

$$b^*(\tau) \lessgtr \lambda(\tau) \text{ according to whether } \lambda(\tau)(1 - \beta_1\tau) \gtrless \beta_0. \tag{13.19}$$

From (13.5) and (13.6),

$$\lambda(\tau) = pB(r)w(\tau_{\max} - \tau). \tag{13.20}$$

From (13.19) and (13.20), it then follows that

$$b^*(\tau) \lessgtr \lambda(\tau) \text{ according to whether } (\tau_{\max} - \tau)(1 - \beta_1\tau) \gtrless \frac{\beta_0}{pB(r)w}. \tag{13.21}$$

(13.6) and (13.21) imply that

$$b^*(\tau) \lessgtr \lambda(\tau) \text{ according as } \beta_1\tau^2 - (1 + \beta_1\tau_{\max})\tau \gtrless \frac{\beta_0 - pB(r)(w - a)}{pB(r)w}. \tag{13.22}$$

Let $\phi : \mathbf{R} \to \mathbf{R}$ be a function such that for all $\tau \in \mathbf{R}$,

$$\phi(\tau) = \beta_1\tau^2 - (1 + \beta_1\tau_{\max})\tau. \tag{13.23}$$

Since we are considering the case where $\beta_0 < pB(r)(w - a)$, it follows that

$$\phi(0) = 0 > \frac{\beta_0 - pB(r)(w - a)}{pB(r)w}. \tag{13.24}$$

Note also that for $\tau = \tau_{max} - \frac{\beta_0}{pB(r)w}$, $(\tau_{max} - \tau)(1 - \beta_1\tau) = \frac{\beta_0}{pB(r)w}(1 - \beta_1\tau) < \frac{\beta_0}{pB(r)w}$. This, given (13.6), implies that

$$\phi\left(\tau_{max} - \frac{\beta_0}{pB(r)w}\right) < \frac{\beta_0 - pB(r)(w - a)}{pB(r)w}. \tag{13.25}$$

Further,

$$\phi'(\tau) \lesseqgtr 0 \text{ according to whether } \tau \lesseqgtr \frac{1 + \beta_1\tau_{max}}{2\beta_1} \tag{13.26}$$

$\phi(\tau)$ has a global minimum at $\tau = \frac{1 + \beta_1\tau_{max}}{2\beta_1}$.

From (13.24)–(13.26), it then follows that there exists a unique value of τ in the interval $(0, \tau_{max} - \frac{\beta_0}{pB(r)w})$ for which $\phi(\tau) = \frac{\beta_0 - pB(r)(w - a)}{pB(r)w}$. Let

$$\hat{\tau} \in \left(0, \tau_{max} - \frac{\beta_0}{pB(r)w}\right) \text{ such that } \phi(\hat{\tau}) = \frac{\beta_0 - pB(r)(w - a)}{pB(r)w}. \tag{13.27}$$

Then, from (13.22)–(13.27), we get:

if $\beta_0 < pB(r)(w - a)$ then
$b^*(\tau) \lesseqgtr \lambda(\tau)$ according to whether $\tau \lesseqgtr \hat{\tau}$.

Given (13.18), this implies that:

if $\beta_0 < pB(r)(w - a)$ then for all $\tau \in (0, \tau_{max})$,
$b^*(\tau) \lesseqgtr \lambda(\tau)$ according to whether $\tau \lesseqgtr \hat{\tau}$. \qquad (13.28)

If $b^*(\tau) \leq \lambda(\tau)$ then, in the long run, all type-h workers will be employed in the knowledge-intensive sector. Given (13.7) and (13.10), it follows that:

if $b^*(\tau) \leq \lambda(\tau)$ then $\varepsilon(\tau) = 1$ and $n(\tau) = \theta\tau$. \qquad (13.29)

Similarly, we get:

$$\text{if } b^*(\tau) \geq \lambda(\tau) \text{ then } \varepsilon(\tau) = \frac{\lambda(\tau)}{b^*(\tau)} = \frac{\lambda(\tau)}{\beta_0 + \beta_1 \tau \lambda(\tau)} \text{ and}$$

$$n(\tau) = \frac{\theta \tau \lambda(\tau)}{\beta_0 + \beta_1 \tau \lambda(\tau)}. \tag{13.30}$$

Long-Run Trade-Offs between the Employment Rate and the Growth Rate of Employment

In this section, we consider how the long-run values of the rate of employment in the knowledge-intensive sector $\varepsilon(\tau)$ and the growth rate of employment in the knowledge-intensive sector $n(\tau)$ vary with the tax rate τ. From (13.29) and (13.30), we know that for any given τ, the relation between $\varepsilon(\tau)$, $n(\tau)$ and τ depends on whether $b^*(\tau) \leq \lambda(\tau)$ or whether $b^*(\tau) \geq \lambda(\tau)$.

We consider two cases separately: the case where $\beta_0 - pB(r)(w - a) \geq 0$ and the case where $\beta_0 - pB(r)(w - a) < 0$.

Suppose $\beta_0 - pB(r)(w - a) \geq 0$. From (13.17) and (13.30) it follows that

$$\varepsilon(\tau) = \frac{\lambda(\tau)}{\beta_0 + \beta_1 \tau \lambda(\tau)} \text{ and } n(\tau) = \frac{\theta \tau \lambda(\tau)}{\beta_0 + \beta_1 \tau \lambda(\tau)}, \text{ for all } \tau \in (0, \tau_{max}). \tag{13.31}$$

From inspection it is obvious that $n(\tau)$ is increasing in $\tau \lambda(\tau)$ and it can be shown that

$$\varepsilon'(\tau) = \frac{-pB(r)w\beta_0 - [pB(r)w]^2(\tau_{max} - \tau)^2 \beta_1}{[\beta_0 + \beta_1 \tau \lambda(\tau)]^2} < 0, \text{ for all } \tau \in (0, \tau_{max}) \tag{13.32}$$

We know that the function $\tau \lambda(\tau) = pB(r)w(\tau_{max}\tau - \tau^2)$ has a global maximum at $\tau = \frac{\tau_{max}}{2}$. It follows that $n(\tau)$ is increasing on $(0, \frac{\tau_{max}}{2})$ and decreasing on $(\frac{\tau_{max}}{2}, \tau)$. This together with the fact that the rate of employment in the knowledge-intensive sector $\varepsilon(\tau)$ is strictly decreasing on $(0, \tau_{max})$ implies that in the case where $\beta_0 - pB(r)(w - a) \geq 0$, any increase in the long-run rate of growth of employment $n(\tau)$ can only be secured by a reduction in $\varepsilon(\tau)$.

Next consider the case where $\beta_0 - pB(r)(w - a) < 0$.

From (13.28)–(13.30), it follows that

$$\varepsilon(\tau) = 1 \text{ and } n(\tau) = \theta\tau, \text{ for all } \tau \in (0, \hat{\tau})$$

$$\varepsilon(\tau) = \frac{\lambda(\tau)}{\beta_0 + \beta_1 \tau \lambda(\tau)} \text{ and } n(\tau) = \theta\tau\varepsilon(\tau), \text{ for all } \tau \in (\hat{\tau}, \tau_{max}).$$

$$(13.33)$$

$\varepsilon(\tau)$ is a constant function of τ on $(0, \hat{\tau})$ and $n(\tau)$ is strictly increasing in τ on $(0, \hat{\tau})$. (13.31) and (13.33) imply that the conditions governing the relation between τ, $\varepsilon(\tau)$ and $n(\tau)$ on the interval $(\hat{\tau}, \tau_{max})$ are the same as on the interval $(0, \tau_{max})$ in the case $\beta_0 - pB(r)(w - a) \geq 0$. From our discussion of that case, we can, therefore, infer that $\varepsilon(\tau)$ must be strictly decreasing in τ on $(\hat{\tau}, \tau_{max})$. We also know that if $\hat{\tau} \geq \frac{\tau_{max}}{2}$, then $n(\tau)$ is strictly decreasing in τ on $(\hat{\tau}, \tau_{max})$. If $\hat{\tau} < \frac{\tau_{max}}{2}$, however, $n(\tau)$ is strictly increasing in τ on $(\hat{\tau}, \frac{\tau_{max}}{2})$ and strictly decreasing in τ on $(\frac{\tau_{max}}{2}, \tau_{max})$.

Therefore, it follows that if $\beta_0 - pB(r)(w - a) < 0$, then just in the case that $\hat{\tau} \geq \frac{\tau_{max}}{2}$ it is true that any increase in the long-run rate of growth of employment in the knowledge-intensive sector can be secured without any sacrifice in terms of the long-run rate of employment of type-h workers in the knowledge-intensive sector. Otherwise, there would always exist a value of the rate of growth of employment such that any increase beyond this value would necessarily require a reduction in the rate of employment.

From (13.26), we know that for all $\tau \in (0, \tau_{max})$, $\phi'(\tau) \lesseqgtr 0$ according to whether $\tau \lesseqgtr \frac{1}{2\beta_1} + \frac{\tau_{max}}{2}$. Therefore, $\phi'(\frac{\tau_{max}}{2}) < 0$. Further, from (13.6), (13.24)–(13.25) and (13.27), we know that $\hat{\tau} \in (0, \tau_{max} - \frac{\beta_0}{pB(r)w})$ and $\phi(0) > \phi(\hat{\tau}) = \frac{\beta_0}{pB(r)w} - \tau_{max} > \phi(\tau_{max} - \frac{\beta_0}{pB(r)w})$. Given (13.26), it, therefore, follows that $\phi'(\hat{\tau}) < 0$ and

$$\hat{\tau} \lesseqgtr \frac{\tau_{max}}{2} \text{ according to whether } \phi\left(\frac{\tau_{max}}{2}\right) \lesseqgtr \frac{\beta_0}{pB(r)w} - \tau_{max}.$$

Simplifying, it follows that

$$\hat{\tau} \lesseqgtr \frac{\tau_{max}}{2} \text{ according to whether } \frac{\beta_0}{pB(r)(w - a)} \gtreqless \frac{1}{2}\left(1 - \beta_1\frac{\tau_{max}}{2}\right).$$

Note that $\frac{1}{2}(1 - \beta_1\frac{\tau_{max}}{2}) < 1$. The conclusion of the argument in this section can, therefore, be stated in the form of the following proposition.

Proposition 2. *The necessary and sufficient condition for the existence of a trade-off between increasing the long-run rate of growth of employment in the knowledge-intensive sector and increasing the long-run rate* *of employment of type-h workers in the knowledge-intensive sector is that*

$$\frac{\beta_0}{pB(r)(w-a)} > \frac{1}{2}\left(1 - \beta_1\frac{w-a}{2w}\right).$$

From an inspection of the inequality in Proposition 2, it is clear that higher values of β_0 and β_1 make the existence of a long-run trade-off more likely in this model. Note also that if the ratio of individual worker incomes in the knowledge-intensive sector and the low productivity sector is kept constant, a rise in the size of the income differential between the sectors reduces the prospect of a trade-off in the model.

CONCLUSION

The essay derives a necessary and sufficient condition for the existence of a dynamic Todaro Paradox in the long run (Proposition 2) in a dual economy where the possibility of employment in the high productivity sector is governed by the opportunity to acquire a threshold level of education in a public education system.

Proposition 2 can be used to infer that in the case of two economies with the same ratio of individual labour earnings between the high productivity and the low productivity sectors, the possibility of the dynamic Todaro Paradox is greater in the economy with lower absolute levels of labour earnings and labour productivity in both sectors. One could, therefore, argue that poorer developing economies are more vulnerable to the policy trade-offs implied by the paradox.

Finally, Proposition 2 implies that the possibility of a dynamic Todaro Paradox is greater the larger the values of the parameters β_0 and β_1. From equation (13.8), the parameter β_1 can be interpreted as a measure of how the levels of motivation of teachers in the public education system and the extent of interest taken by them in their work affect the motivation and, therefore, employability of prospective workers in the knowledge-intensive sector. The parameter β_0 can then be interpreted as a measure of the effect of other important features of the public education system (for example, appropriate design of curricula and availability of adequate infrastructure) on the interest that formally qualified workers in the knowledge-intensive sector take in their work. One finds, not surprisingly, that these are also the factors often emphasised as crucial for improving the employment prospects of students in relatively high-income sectors of developing economies.[10]

ACKNOWLEDGEMENT

Helpful comments from Mausumi Das, Krishnendu Ghosh Dastidar, Ranja Sengupta and Tridip Ray are gratefully acknowledged.

REFERENCES

Bai, Limin. 2006. 'Graduate Unemployment: Dilemmas and Challenges in China's Move to Mass Higher Education', *China Quarterly*, 185: 128–44.

Cole, W. E. and R. D. Sanders. 1985. 'Internal Migration and Urban Employment in the Third World', *American Economic Review*, 75(3): 481–94.

Günther, I. and A. Launov. 2012. 'Informal Employment in Developing Countries: Opportunity or last resort?' *Journal of Development Economics*, 97(1): 88–98.

Harris, J. R. and M. P. Todaro. 1970. 'Migration, Unemployment and Development: A Two-Sector Analysis', *American Economic Review*, 60(1): 126–42.

Lewis, W. Arthur. 1954. 'Economic Development with Unlimited Supplies of Labour', *Manchester School*, 22(2): 139–91.

Li, T. and J. Zhang. 2010. 'What Determines Employment Opportunity for College Graduates in China after Higher Education Reform?' *China Economic Review*, 21(1): 38–50.

Lucas, Jr., Robert E. 1990. 'Why Doesn't Capital Flow from Rich to Poor Countries?' *American Economic Review*, 80(2): 92–6.

Martin, Gary. 2000. 'Employment and Unemployment in Mexico in the 1990s,' *Monthly Labor Review*, November, pp. 3–18.

National Knowledge Commission. 2009. *Report to the Nation 2006–2009*, New Delhi: Government of India.

Ranis, G. and F. Stewart. 2000. 'Economic Growth and Human Development', *World Development*, 28(2): 197–219.

Satchi, M. and J. Temple. 2009. 'Labor Markets and Productivity in Developing Countries', *Review of Economic Dynamics*, 12(1): 183–204.

Todaro, Michael P. 1969. 'A Model of Labor Migration and Urban Unemployment in Less Developed Countries', *American Economic Review*, 59(1): 138–48.

———. 1976. 'Urban Job Expansion, Induced Migration and Rising Unemployment: A Formulation and Simplified Empirical Test for LDCs', *Journal of Development Economics*, 3(3): 211–25.

---

[10] See, for example, World Bank (2007).

World Bank. 2005. *World Development Report 2005: A Better Investment Climate for Everyone*, Washington D.C.: World Bank.

———. 2007. *World Development Report 2007: Development and the Next Generation*, Washington D.C.: World Bank.

Zenou, Yves. 2008. 'Job Search and Mobility in Developing Countries. Theory and Policy Implications', *Journal of Development Economics*, 86(2): 336–55.

———. 2011. 'Rural–Urban Migration and Unemployment: Theory and Policy Implications', *Journal of Regional Science*, 51(1): 65–82.

PART VI
SOCIAL AND ECONOMIC MEASUREMENT

14

On a Family of Indices for Envy in Situations of Income Inequality

Ravindra Ranade and Yukie Shimono

The coefficient of inequality in Gini (1912) was initially defined for a finite population—a discrete income distribution. Its calculation was a statistician's exercise. The income distribution in larger societies, on the other hand, was always thought to be of the lognormal variety. In the literature, including Sen (1973), these two different situations are pooled together by assuming the latter case as an approximation for the former. The lognormal distribution is not very amenable to explicit analysis and manipulability. Making complete sense of the Lorenz curve (Lorenz 1905) and the Gini coefficient for a continuous distribution is not the easiest of things to achieve for a student exposed to these matters for the first time (see item A1 in the Appendix for some interesting personal history). In this essay, as an approximation, we assume the simplest unimodal income distribution—the triangular one. After all, societies do not have zero and infinity as the extreme incomes as required in the lognormal case. This assumption here allows us to use the minimum level, modal level and the maximum level as parameters for further analysis. The essay is an attempt to propose a family of envy indices based on the Lorenz curve which can be seen to be a quantification of the magnitude of society-wide relative deprivation (or envy) arising from the presence of inequality in an income distribution. In the context of the particular distribution we employ, the index can be related to a number of other elementary statistical measures of central tendency and dispersion.

ASSUMPTIONS AND FORMAL ANALYSIS

We assume a triangular income distribution with the minimum, modal and maximum income as a\$, d\$ and b\$ respectively—all positive and distinct. Also, the distribution is assumed to be skewed to the left. The density is given by:

For

$$a \leq x \leq d, f(x) = \frac{2(x-a)}{(b-a)(d-a)}$$

For

$$d \leq x \leq b, f(x) = \frac{2(b-x)}{(b-a)(b-d)}.$$

As the textbooks on statistics point out, the range, the mean income, the second moment and the variance are respectively given by the terms,

$$r = (b-a)$$

$$\mu = E(x) = \frac{a+b+d}{3}$$

$$E(x^2) = \frac{1}{6}(a^2 + b^2 + d^2 + ab + bd + da)$$

$$\sigma^2 = V(x) = \frac{a^2 + b^2 + d^2 - ab - bd - da}{18}$$

The four expressions for percentages of population with income less than x, where x is smaller than the mode, is exactly equal to mode d, bigger than the mode and is exactly equal to the maximum income b are given by the following respectively.

$$\int_a^x f(x)dx = \frac{(x-a)^2}{(b-a)(d-a)}$$

$$\int_a^d f(x)dx = \frac{(d-a)}{(b-a)}$$

$$\int_a^d f(x)dx + \int_d^x f(x)dx = \frac{(d-a)}{(b-a)} + \frac{(x-d)(2b-x-d)}{(b-a)(b-d)}$$

$$= 1 - \frac{(b-x)^2}{(b-a)(b-d)}$$

$$\int_a^d f(x)dx + \int_d^b f(x)dx = 1$$

The respective total incomes for these four populations are, in turn, given by the following four expressions.

$$\int_a^x xf(x)dx = \frac{(x-a)^2(2x+a)}{3(b-a)(d-a)}$$

$$\int_a^d x f(x) dx = \frac{(d-a)(2d+a)}{3(b-a)}$$

$$\int_a^d x f(x) dx + \int_x^x x f(x) dx = \frac{a+b+d}{3} - \frac{(b-x)^2 (b+2x)}{3 (b-a)(b-d)}$$

$$\int_a^d x f(x) dx + \int_d^b x f(x) dx = \frac{a+b+d}{3}$$

In order to transfer this into the Lorenz curve, these expressions need to be carefully transformed into cumulative variables (see item A2 in the Appendix). As a threshold point, at x equal to the modal level d, the bottom y per cent of the population is given by:

$$y = \frac{d-a}{b-a}$$

and has the percentage of total income given by the expression

$$\frac{(d-a)(2d+a)}{(b-a)(a+b+d)}.$$

Then the bottom y per cent of the population has $g(y)$ per cent of the total income. That is to say, the lower part of the Lorenz curve lies between the limits

$$0 < y < \frac{d-a}{b-a}$$

$$0 < g(y) < \frac{(d-a)(2d+a)}{(b-a)(a+b+d)}.$$

The actual values of the cumulative variable and its function are given by

$$y = \frac{(x-a)^2}{(b-a)(d-a)}$$

$$g(y) = \frac{(x-a)^2 (2x+a)}{(b-a)(d-a)(a+b+d)}.$$

We manipulate to get rid of the original variable x and obtain the functional form of the lower part of the Lorenz curve as:

$$g(y) = \frac{3ay + 2y\sqrt{y(b-a)(d-a)}}{(a+b+d)}.$$

For x between the modal level d and the maximum income b, the percentage of the population that is richer is given by

$$\int_x^b f(x)dx = \frac{(b-x)^2}{(b-a)(b-d)}.$$

And they have the total income and the percentage of income respectively as

$$\int_x^b xf(x)dx = \frac{(b-x)^2(b+2x)}{3(b-a)(b-d)}$$

$$\frac{(b-x)^2(b+2x)}{(a+b+d)(b-a)(b-d)}.$$

In other words the bottom y per cent of the population with x bigger than the mode is

$$y = 1 - \frac{(b-x)^2}{(b-a)(b-d)}.$$

And they have the percentage of income given by

$$1 - \frac{(b-x)^2(b+2x)}{(a+b+d)(b-a)(b-d)}.$$

Again manipulating the expression to get rid of x, we get the higher part of the Lorenz curve as

$$g(y) = 1 - \frac{3b(1-y)}{(a+b+d)} + \frac{2(1-y)\sqrt{(1-y)(b-a)(b-d)}}{(a+b+d)}.$$

It is worth noting here (in the light of item A3 in the Appendix) that the curve is continuous and contrary to a possible intuition has no kink at the point that corresponds to the mode. It can be checked that the curve has the same slope in the left neighbourhood than on the right side. Thus, neither the differentiability of the curve nor its integrability are a problem. If we think from the point of view of the bottom y per cent of the population, the higher the $g(y)$, the happier they are. Or in other words, the envy in the society is inversely related to $g(y)$. Using some simple experimental economics tools, it is easily possible to ask the people in the society about the envy they feel for different levels of $g(y)$. Using some simple experimental economics tools, it should be possible to ascertain from the people in the society the extent of relative deprivation they feel at different levels of $g(y)$. Then armed with this relative deprivation metric—related inversely to $g(y)$—and integrating over the range from 0 to1, we can obtain an estimate of the aggregate relative deprivation (which can also be seen to be linked to a measure of aggregate envy or discontent in that society). For alternative functional relations linking relative deprivation to $g(y)$, we can derive a family of alternative indices of aggregate inequality which, in turn, are linked, along the lines described earlier, to individual levels of comparative deprivation or envy. In this essay, we present the simplest possible index.

A Simple Index

Here we look at the straightforward and simple possibility. For a given y, the happiest situation for the bottom y per cent of the population is that $g(y)$ be equal to y. The simple distance measure of envy would be $y - g(y)$ (see item A1 of the Appendix for a wisecrack). The integral of this measure over the range will then yield a concrete measure of social envy. Towards that,

$$\int_0^{\frac{(d-a)}{(b-a)}} g(y)dy$$

and

$$\int_{\frac{d-a}{b-a}}^1 g(y)dy$$

are respectively given by

$$\frac{(d-a)^2 (7a + 8d)}{10 (b-a)^2 (a+b+d)}$$

$$\frac{(b-d)}{(b-a)} - \frac{3b (b-d)^2}{2 (a+b+d) (b-a)^2} + \frac{4}{5} \frac{(b-d)^3}{(a+b+d) (b-a)^2}.$$

And our measure of social envy is then

$$\frac{1}{2} - \frac{(d-a)^2 \, (7a+8d)}{10 \, (a+b+d) \, (b-a)^2} - \frac{(b-d)}{(b-a)} + \frac{3b \, (b-d)^2}{2 \, (a+b+d) \, (b-a)^2}$$
$$- \frac{4}{5} \frac{(b-d)^3}{(a+b+d) \, (b-a)^2}.$$

After some manipulation, this comes to

$$\frac{1}{10(a+b+d)(b-a)^2}$$
$$\times \left[5(a+b+d)(b-a)^2 - (d-a)^2 \, (7a+8d) \right.$$
$$\left. -10 \, (a+b+d) \, (b-a) \, (b-d) + 15b \, (b-d)^2 - 8(b-d)^3 \right]$$
$$= \frac{(b-a)(2b^2 + 2a^2 + d^2 - 3ab - bd - ad)}{10(a+b+d)(b-a)^2}$$
$$= \frac{1}{10 \, (a+b+d) \, (b-a)} \left[a^2 + b^2 + d^2 - ab - bd - ad + (b-a)^2 \right]$$
$$= \frac{18\sigma^2 + r^2}{30\mu r}.$$

Despite the complicated looking calculations, this is essentially the area between the diagonal and the Lorenz curve—in other words, half of the Gini coefficient. We conclude by some comments on this index. First, the index allows us to compare different societies by just knowing the range, variance and mean of the distribution or, equivalently, looking at the minimum, modal and maximum levels of income. It also allows us to look at effects of parametric changes on the social envy and discontent. Second, theoretically, the Gini coefficient ranges between 0 and 1 or the area between curves ranges between 0 and half. But most societies have neither the perfect equality nor the perfect inequality of income. It has been always felt that the range was rather wide to realise the significance of the actual coefficient. Our assumption of the left skewed triangular distribution, which seems a reasonable approximation of the lognormal density, allows us to reduce the range of the coefficient for meaningful comparisons of societies. It is easily checked that our index lies between the values $\frac{(b-a)}{5(b+2a)}$ and $\frac{2(b-a)^2 - ab}{15(a+b)(b-a)}$, giving us some additional goalposts for comparisons. It goes without saying that there is a major assumption about subjectivity in the analysis of envy in this essay. The notion itself, however, is decidedly based on emotions and, hence, it is inevitable that we end up incorporating the subjectivity in the construction of the index. Finally, this index or its parent family can be used for actual empirical work provided some evidence—depending on the results of experimental economics data—is available to substantiate the assumptions of subjectivity. This task, however, is not part of this essay and seems best left to the future (see item A4 of the Appendix). Finally, it seems important to point out the relevance of this index making in real societies. We now live in a fast information society. Social activities including demonstrations and agitations are aided ably by the internet. Social discontent these days get channelled into very concrete forms very fast. This makes issues like income inequality and envy in the society rather important. One only has to look at agitations and demonstrations in the USA, France, Thailand, Egypt, India and so on for proof. From the standpoint of controlling discontent in the society for the ruling class and inciting agitations by its counterparts as well, the measurement of discontent or envy in the society is important. Long ago, when Lorenz and Gini talked about inequality, it was more of an academic exercise in the index making. In this essay, we have tried to look at it from a different perspective. There is a certain amount of subjective element in the notion of envy. There are poor economies with little envy, for example, Bhutan, as also rich economies, for example, Japan. It seemed worthwhile to think about quantifying envy so that societies about to get into turmoil can be predicted.

APPENDIX

A1. I first met Professor Jain when I was an impressionable 19-year-old graduate student at the Indian Statistical Institute (Delhi), and he was a 27-year-old returnee from Rochester. He was a young faculty member and stayed in the same wing of my hostel room. It was quite natural to interact with him outside the classroom. There were long walks in the evenings, and he used to have opinions on most issues under the sun (a predilection that has not changed with time). We—being ISI students and P. C. Mahalanobis followers—used to measure the *gyan* (knowledge/wisdom) we got from him by the distance walked with him. In a lighter vein, it could be said that some of us were rather possessive about Professor Jain, and our envy vis-à-vis each other was clearly measurable by the difference in distance walked with him! He has always had a knack of attracting devoted friends and followers and—I insist—completely without deliberate intent.

The main theme of this essay has a history—and it also highlights Professor Jain's nous. It has been nearly 40 years and my memory by now may have become very selective. The situation at ISI in those days was quite different from what it is today. The faculty seminars in 1976 were converted into a course for the graduate students; the faculty members were not always very kind to each other; a bad grade for the student meant getting thrown out of the institute quite unceremoniously. Everyone was on tenterhooks. One day there was a presentation on the issues of Gini–Lorenz economic Inequality, and the speaker was taken to task by some of our other mentors for not being sufficiently careful or nuanced about such phenomena as step functions, kinked polygonal Lorenz curves, the transformation of the income variable into the cumulative form, differentiability and integrability. It was bewildering and unnerving. And we were going to be graded on the basis of what we had understood in the seminar. In the evening, I asked Professor Jain what to make of it. He tugged at his beard, puffed at his Borkum Riff-filled pipe a couple of times, and then said 'All these issues of real analysis and topology are complicated and one has to be extra careful. But the beauty of welfare economics is more in the discreteness and the logic used—look at the Arrow impossibility theorem...' And I guess that day I was converted, and became his prospective graduate student. This fact should explain the eccentricities of the present essay.

A2. The income variable and the cumulative population variable are positive monotonic transformations of each other. The conversion could be complicated, but it should be possible to do it —as Professor Jain assured me on the occasion dealt with in A1. Even in the simple case of a triangular distribution, as in this essay, the conversion is tricky. With other complicated densities, the relevant calculations may simply not be easy to perform.

A3. The kink in the Lorenz curve can actually be almost smoothed out by a simple trick, involving the peak of the triangular distribution being replaced by a circular distribution, as long as both sides of the triangle get smoothly into the circle at the top. I would, however, expect Professor Jain to remind me that the unnecessary complication would merely come in the way of simple analysis. (As it is, the analysis is probably not up to his expected levels of elegance and neatness.)

A4. I conclude by wishing Professor Jain a long and fruitful life after his retirement. Despite the fact that I agree that he and Dr Ram Manohar Lohia—and not Raj Narain—are the most original thinkers that Uttar Pradesh/India/the World has produced, I venture to offer some advice. Just go to 3/4/5...doctors if necessary—so that we can again walk with, and receive some more *gyan* from, you. This comes from someone who hates going to doctors.

A5. I would like to express my heartfelt thanks to the editors for suggesting improvements in the presentation despite my obstinacy.

REFERENCES

Gini, C. 1912. 'Variabilita e Mutabilita', Journal of Economic Studies, 3(2).

Lorenz, M. O. 1905. 'Methods of Measuring the Concentration of Wealth', *Publications of the American Statistical Association*, 9(70): 209–19.

Sen, A. K. 1973. *On Economic Inequality*. Oxford: Clarendon Press.

15

On a Distance Function-Based Inequality Measure in the Spirit of the Bonferroni and Gini Indices

S. Subramanian[*]

In this essay, I advance a measure of inequality which is very similar to the Bonferroni (1930) index, and also shares commonalities with the well-known Gini (1912) coefficient of inequality, and an attempt is made in the essay to flag the relevant links. The measure is derived, very simply, as a distance function, and since the specific distance function employed in the cause is the so-called Canberra function,[1] the resulting index is called the 'Canberra inequality measure'. Some features of the measure are discussed with specific reference to the properties of decomposability and transfer-sensitivity. Also discussed is a graphical representation of inequality, analogous to the Lorenz and Bonferroni curves, which is here called the Canberra curve, from which the Canberra measure can be derived, just as the Gini coefficient can be derived from the Lorenz curve and the Bonferroni index from the Bonferroni curve.[2]

At least four important contributions to reviving interest in, interpreting, characterising and analysing the properties of the Bonferroni inequality measure are the papers by Barcena and Imedio (2000), Chakravarty (2007), Giorgi and Crescenzi (2001) and Imedio-Olmedo et al. (2011). Also of relevance is a brief note by the present author (Subramanian 1989) which advanced what was called a 'simple

---

[*] I am indebted to R. Dharumaperumal and A. Arivazhagan for help with the figures, and to the United Nations University's World Institute for Development Economics Research (UNU-WIDER), Helsinki, for permission to publish this article here, an earlier version of which was written in the course of a sabbatical fellowship at UNU-WIDER, and appeared as Working Paper No. 2012/62 in its working papers series.
[1] See Lance and Williams (1967).
[2] On this, see Barcena and Imedio (2000).

transfer-sensitive index of inequality', in complete ignorance of the fact that the index in question was Bonferroni's!

NOTATION

An ordered income n-vector is a list $\mathbf{x}$ of n non-negative incomes $(x_1, ..., x_i, ..., x_n)$ arranged in non-decreasing sequence (so that $0 \leq x_i \leq x_{i+1}, i = 1, ..., n-1$), where x_i is the income of the ith poorest person in a community of n individuals, n being a member of the set of positive integers $\mathcal{N}$. The set of all n-vectors is $\mathbf{X}_n$ and the set of all income distributions is represented by $\mathbf{X} \equiv \bigcup_{n \in \mathcal{N}} \mathbf{X}_n$. For every $\mathbf{x} \in \mathbf{X}$, the set of individuals whose incomes are represented in $\mathbf{x}$ is designated by $N(\mathbf{x})$, the dimensionality of $\mathbf{x}$ by $n(\mathbf{x})$ and the mean of $\mathbf{x}$ by $\mu(\mathbf{x}) \equiv (1/n(\mathbf{x})) \sum_{i \in N(x)} x_i$. If $\mathcal{R}$ is the set of reals, then an inequality measure is a mapping $I : \mathbf{X} \to \mathcal{R}$ such that, for every $\mathbf{x} \in \mathbf{X}$, $I(\mathbf{x})$ is a unique real number that indicates the amount of inequality associated with the vector $\mathbf{x}$. Given any $\mathbf{x} \in \mathbf{X}$, we shall let $\mu_i(\mathbf{x}) \equiv (1/i) \sum_{j=1}^{i} x_j$ stand for the average income of those with incomes not exceeding the ith poorest person's income; in the interests of convenience, if not correctness in the use of language, we shall also refer to $\mu_i(\mathbf{x})$ as 'person i's mean income', as in Subramanian (1989). (Notice that $\mu_1(\mathbf{x}) \equiv x_1$ and $\mu_n(\mathbf{x}) \equiv \mu(\mathbf{x})$.) For any $\mathbf{x} \in \mathbf{X}$, we shall define two corresponding distinguished vectors (of the same dimensionality as $\mathbf{x}$), given, respectively by, $\boldsymbol{\mu}_\mathbf{x} \equiv (\mu(\mathbf{x}), ..., \mu(\mathbf{x}))$ and $\hat{\boldsymbol{\mu}}_\mathbf{x} \equiv (\mu_1(\mathbf{x}), ..., \mu_n(\mathbf{x}))$. Where there is no risk of ambiguity, we shall also write μ for $\mu(\mathbf{x})$, μ_i for $\mu_i(\mathbf{x})$, n for $n(\mathbf{x})$, and so on.

POVERTY AND INEQUALITY MEASURES AS DISTANCE FUNCTIONS

Given any three vectors $\mathbf{a}$, $\mathbf{b}$ and $\mathbf{c}$ in n-dimensional real space, the *distance* between the vectors $\mathbf{a}$ and $\mathbf{b}$, represented as $\delta(\mathbf{a}, \mathbf{b})$, is a metric which satisfies the properties of non-negativity (namely, $\delta(\mathbf{a}, \mathbf{b}) \geq 0$), identity (namely, $\delta(\mathbf{a}, \mathbf{a}) = 0$) symmetry (namely, $\delta(\mathbf{a}, \mathbf{b}) = \delta(\mathbf{b}, \mathbf{a})$) and triangle inequality (namely $\delta(\mathbf{a}, \mathbf{b}) + \delta(\mathbf{b}, \mathbf{c}) \geq \delta(\mathbf{a}, \mathbf{c})$). Measures of poverty and inequality are essentially measures of distance—between empirical vectors of income and certain idealised vectors, such as vectors of 'no poverty', in the case of poverty measurement, and vectors of equal incomes, in the case of inequality measurement. Given any ordered n-vector of incomes $\mathbf{x} = (x_1, ..., x_i, ..., x_n)$ and the corresponding equally distributed vector of incomes $\boldsymbol{\mu}_\mathbf{x} \equiv (\mu(\mathbf{x}), ..., \mu(\mathbf{x}))$, one can see that the distance between $\mathbf{x}$ and $\boldsymbol{\mu}_x$, averaged over the number of individuals in the society $n(\mathbf{x})$, could legitimately be interpreted as a measure of inequality. For any two vectors $\mathbf{x}$ and $\mathbf{y}$ in n-dimensional real space, the *Euclidean distance* between the vectors is given by:

$$\delta_E(\mathbf{x}, \mathbf{y}) = \left[\sum_{i=1}^{n(\mathbf{x})} (x_i - y_i)^2 \right]^{1/2}.$$

Note now that the well-known inequality measure yielded by the standard deviation (S) of incomes

$$\left(= (1/n(\mathbf{x}))^{1/2} \left[\sum_{i=1}^{n(\mathbf{x})} (x_i - \mu(\mathbf{x}))^2 \right]^{1/2} \right)$$

is simply proportional to the Euclidean distance between the income vector $\mathbf{x}$ one is confronted by and its corresponding $\boldsymbol{\mu}_x$ vector, viz.,

$$S(\mathbf{x}) = (1/\sqrt{n(\mathbf{x})})\delta_E(\mathbf{x}, \boldsymbol{\mu}_x).$$

Real analysis offers a number of distance functions to choose from—Wilson and Martinez (1997) provide a particularly useful review—and some of these have been employed in the economics measurement literature. Subramanian (2009), for instance, suggests a certain close correspondence between the well-known Foster–Greer–Thorbecke (Foster et al. 1984) family of poverty measures and the class of Minkowski distance functions. Of relevance for the purposes of the present essay is the so-called 'Canberra distance function', due to Lance and Williams (1967) (which has also been employed to derive a parametrised family of poverty indices in Subramanian [2009]). Given any two vectors $\mathbf{a}$ and $\mathbf{b}$ in n-Euclidean space, the Canberra distance between the two vectors is defined as:

$$\delta_C(\mathbf{a}, \mathbf{b}) = \sum_{i=1}^{N} \left| \frac{a_i - b_i}{a_i + b_i} \right|. \tag{15.1}$$

It is the distance function featured in Equation (15.1) which will be employed, in what follows, to derive a variant—the Canberra index—of the Bonferroni inequality measure.

THE CANBERRA INEQUALITY MEASURE

For any (ordered) income vector $\mathbf{x} \in \mathbf{X}$, and the corresponding vectors $\boldsymbol{\mu}_x$ and $\hat{\boldsymbol{\mu}}_x$ defined in an earlier section, we now define the Canberra inequality measure C as the Canberra distance between the vectors $\boldsymbol{\mu}_x$ and

$\hat{\boldsymbol{\mu}}_{\mathbf{x}}$, averaged across the n individuals constituting the society under review. For all $\mathbf{x} \in \mathbf{X}$:

$$C(\mathbf{x}) = (1/n(\mathbf{x}))\delta_C(\boldsymbol{\mu}_{\mathbf{x}}, \hat{\boldsymbol{\mu}}_{\mathbf{x}}) = (1/n(\mathbf{x})) \sum_{i=1}^{n(\mathbf{x})} \left[\frac{\mu(\mathbf{x}) - \mu_i(\mathbf{x})}{\mu(\mathbf{x}) + \mu_i(\mathbf{x})} \right]. \quad (15.2)$$

The (relative) Bonferroni index[3] is given by: for all $\mathbf{x} \in \mathbf{X}$,

$$B(\mathbf{x}) = (1/n(\mathbf{x})) \sum_{i=1}^{n(\mathbf{x})} \left[\frac{\mu(\mathbf{x}) - \mu_i(\mathbf{x})}{\mu(\mathbf{x})} \right]. \quad (15.3)$$

As one can see from expressions (15.2) and (15.3), the Canberra index is a close relative of the Bonferroni Index, with the difference reflected in the additional term μ_i in the denominator in the square bracket on the right-hand side of equation (15.2). One way of writing the Gini coefficient of inequality[4] is the following: for all $\mathbf{x} \in \mathbf{X}$,

$$G(\mathbf{x}) = \frac{n(\mathbf{x}) + 1}{n(\mathbf{x})} - \left(\frac{2}{n^2(\mathbf{x})\mu(\mathbf{x})} \right) \sum_{i=1}^{n(\mathbf{x})} (n(\mathbf{x}) + 1 - i)x_i. \quad (15.4)$$

To see the link between the Canberra and Gini measures, it can be verified from equation (15.2) that, for all $\mathbf{x} \in \mathbf{X}$,

$$C(\mathbf{x}) = (1/n(\mathbf{x})) \left[\begin{array}{l} \dfrac{\mu(\mathbf{x}) - x_1}{\mu(\mathbf{x}) + x_1} + \cdots + \dfrac{i\mu(\mathbf{x}) - (x_1 + \cdots + x_i)}{i\mu(\mathbf{x}) + (x_1 + \cdots + x_i)} \\[2ex] + \cdots + \dfrac{n(\mathbf{x})\mu(\mathbf{x}) - (x_1 + \cdots + x_n)}{n(\mathbf{x})\mu(\mathbf{x}) + (x_1 + \cdots + x_n)} \end{array} \right]. \quad (15.5)$$

It may be noted from expression (15.5) that the income level x_i is repeated $(n + 1 - i)$ times over, for every $i = 1, ..., n$: this corresponds exactly with the Borda rank-order weighting scheme that is a distinctive feature of the Gini coefficient; and the 'equity-consciousness' of these indices is captured precisely in a system of diminishing weights, given by the income levels' respective rank-orders, as one climbs up the income ladder.

---

[3] See, for example, Chakravarty (2007).
[4] See, for example, Sen (1973).

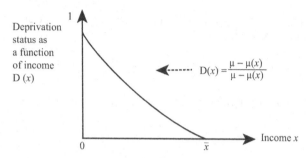

Figure 15.1 The Canberra deprivation function

There is another way of interpreting the Canberra index, which involves invoking the notion of income-related relative deprivation.[5] Specifically, consider an income-recipient with income x, in a situation where the highest income in the distribution is $\bar{x}$. Let $D(x)$ be an indicator of the distribution-relative deprivation status of the person with income x. It seems reasonable to require that $D(x)$ should decline with x and—if we are interested in equity sensitivity—that $D(x)$ should decline with x at an increasing rate. Further, in terms of a simple normalisation requirement which ensures that the deprivation status of an individual is encompassed in the interval $[0, 1]$, we can demand that $D(0) = 1$ and $D(\bar{x}) = 0$. Briefly, a reasonable perspective on how deprivation status might be expected to change with income would require the $D(x)$graph to be a declining and strictly convex curve over the range $[0, \bar{x}]$, with $D(0) = 1$ and $D(\bar{x}) = 0$, as featured in Figure 15.1. A specific deprivation function that satisfies these properties is what one may call the Canberra deprivation function, given by: $D^C(x) = [\mu - \mu(x)] / [\mu + \mu(x)]$ for all $x \in [0, \bar{x}]$, where μ is the mean of the distribution under study, and $\mu(x)$ is the mean income of all recipients with incomes not exceeding x. Thus, given any ordered income n-vector $\mathbf{x} = (x_1, ..., x_i, ..., x_n)$, an inequality measure associated with the vector can be written as a simple average of all the individuals' Canberra deprivation functions: $I(\mathbf{x}) = (1/n(\mathbf{x})) \sum_{i=1}^{n(\mathbf{x})} D^C(x_i)$. I is, precisely, the Canberra inequality measure C.

The use of individual deprivation functions is reminiscent of one widely employed method of constructing poverty measures. It is customary, in the construction of poverty indices, to specify a poverty line z as a level of income below which a person is considered impoverished; and

---

[5] See Chakravarty (2007) and Chakravarty et al. (1995).

given any $\mathbf{x} \in \mathbf{X}$, if $Q(\mathbf{x}) \equiv \{i \in N(\mathbf{x}) \,|\, x_i < z\}$ and $q(\mathbf{x}) \equiv \#Q(\mathbf{x})$, then the deprivation status of an individual i, if i is poor, is taken to be some increasing function of the shortfall of that person's income from the poverty line ($i = 1, ..., q(\mathbf{x})$), and zero if the person is non-poor ($i = q(\mathbf{x}) + 1, ..., n(\mathbf{x})$). A measure of poverty can then be taken to be a simple average of all individuals' deprivation functions. Unsurprisingly, under certain well-defined limits, poverty measures are transformed into inequality measures: thus, and as is well known, when the poverty line z is replaced by the mean income μ of a distribution, and when q is replaced by n, the Sen index of poverty becomes the Gini coefficient of inequality, the Watts index of poverty becomes one of Theil's inequality measures, and one member of the Foster–Greer–Thorbecke family of poverty measures becomes the squared coefficient of variation. The Bonferroni deprivation function has also been employed in the derivation of a poverty index, as has been demonstrated in Giorgi and Crescenzi (2001).

Indeed, in a distance function approach to the construction of a poverty index, Subramanian (2009) suggests the following procedure. Given any ordered income $\mathbf{x}$-vector $\mathbf{x} = (x_1, ..., x_q, x_{q+1}, ..., x_n) \in \mathbf{X}$, one can define the associated n-vectors $\mathbf{c_x} = (x_1, ..., x_q, z, ..., z)$ (which is what Takayama [1979] calls a 'censored' vector), $\mathbf{z_x} = (z, ..., z)$ (which is just a vector, of the same dimensionality as $\mathbf{x}$, with the smallest mean that is compatible with a complete absence of poverty), and $\mathbf{0_x} = (0, ..., 0)$ (which is the vector representing maximal poverty, with every person receiving zero income). A normalised index of poverty $P(\mathbf{x}; z)$ can now be derived as the ratio of two vector distances: the distance between the vectors $\mathbf{c_x}$ and $\mathbf{z_x}$ (which is the gap between the 'actual poverty situation' and the 'no poverty situation') and the distance between the vectors $\mathbf{0_x}$ and $\mathbf{z_x}$ (which is the gap between the 'complete poverty situation' and the 'no poverty situation'): $P(\mathbf{x}; z) = \delta(\mathbf{z_x}, \mathbf{c_x})/\delta(\mathbf{z_x}, \mathbf{0_x})$. Equally, one may write a poverty index as: $P(\mathbf{x}; z) = \delta(\mathbf{z_x}, \hat{\boldsymbol{\mu}}_{\mathbf{x}}^c)/\delta(\mathbf{z_x}, \mathbf{0_x})$, where $\hat{\boldsymbol{\mu}}_{\mathbf{x}}^c$ is derived from $\mathbf{c_x}$ as the n-vector $(\mu_1, ..., \mu_q, z, ..., z)$. If the distance function employed is the Canberra distance function δ_C, then we obtain the poverty index

$$P^C(\mathbf{x}; z) = (1/n(\mathbf{x})) \sum_{i=1}^{q(\mathbf{x})} \left[\frac{z - \mu_i(\mathbf{x})}{z + \mu_i(\mathbf{x})} \right].$$

The superscript C on P stands for 'Canberra', and the 'Canberra' poverty measure is analogous to the 'Bonferroni' poverty measure derived by Giorgi and Crescenzi (2001). When z is replaced by $\mu(\mathbf{x})$ and $q(\mathbf{x})$ by $n(\mathbf{x})$ in the expression for P^C, we just recover—as we might expect—the Canberra inequality measure C.

When all incomes are equal, the value of the Canberra inequality measure is zero, and when a single person appropriates the entire income, the measure assumes a value of $(n - 1)/n$. It is easy to verify that the index satisfies the commonly advanced properties of transfer, symmetry, continuity, and scale invariance. Of specific interest are the properties of subgroup decomposability and transfer-sensitivity, the first of which is violated by C, and the second is satisfied. This is elaborated on in the following two sections.

SUBGROUP DECOMPOSABILITY

The measure C cannot be expressed as an exact sum of a 'within-group' component and a 'between-group' component of inequality. The amenability of a poverty measure to such an additive split is what is commonly referred to as the property of subgroup decomposability. Indeed, the Canberra measure does not even satisfy the weaker property of subgroup consistency,[6] which requires that, other things being equal, an increase in any one subgroup's inequality should raise overall inequality. The following simple numerical example demonstrates this. Consider the two ordered 4-vectors of income $\mathbf{x} = (2, 4, 5, 5)$ and $\mathbf{y} = (2, 5, 5, 5)$. Assume that there are two groups 1 and 2, and that the subgroup vectors of income can be written as: $\mathbf{x}^1 = (2, 4)$, $\mathbf{y}^1 = (2, 5)$, and $\mathbf{x}^2 = \mathbf{y}^2 = (5, 5)$. Employing the expression for C provided in equation (15.2), it can be verified that $C(\mathbf{x}^1) = 0.1$, $C(\mathbf{y}^1) = 0.136$ and $C(\mathbf{x}^2) = C(\mathbf{y}^2) = 0$: since subgroup 1's inequality has gone up in $\mathbf{y}$ vis-à-vis $\mathbf{x}$, with subgroup 2's inequality level remaining unchanged, one should expect—by subgroup consistency—that $C(\mathbf{y}) > C(\mathbf{x})$. However, and as can be easily checked, it turns out that $C(\mathbf{y})(= 0.122) < C(\mathbf{x})(= 0.130)$: subgroup consistency is violated by C.

C violates subgroup consistency for the same reason that the Gini and Bonferroni indices violate the axiom, namely, via a violation of the property of 'independence of irrelevant alternatives', and—through that route—the property of 'contraction consistency'.[7] Specifically, and as the numerical example we have employed demonstrates, when we focus on any particular subgroup, the incomes outside of that subgroup ought—if one sets store by subgroup consistency—to become 'irrelevant' for an assessment of the subgroup's inequality level. However, these incomes do become material in the case of the Canberra

---

[6] See Shorrocks (1988).
[7] See Sen (1973).

measure because as a result of the contraction from the whole group to a subgroup, both the group-specific means (the $\mu's$) and the 'truncated means' (the $\mu_i's$) (could) change from what they were before the contraction. These changes amount to a violation of 'the independence of irrelevant alternatives', with a consequential violation of contraction consistency. The normative question, however, remains as to whether the incomes outside of the subgroup under consideration ought really to be treated as irrelevant alternatives such that the subgroup level of inequality must be seen to be independent of them.[8] An implication of this is the following. Suppose the population is partitioned into K mutually exclusive and completely exhaustive subgroups, and that μ^j is the mean income of subgroup j and μ_i^j the mean income of the ith poorest person in subgroup j, whose members constitute the set N^j of individuals ($j = 1, ..., K$). For every $j \in \{1, ..., K\}$, let $\lambda^j : N^j \to N$ be a one-to-one mapping such that the ith poorest person in N^j is the same as the $\lambda^j(i)$th poorest person in N, for every $i \in N^j$. 'Properly' speaking, the Canberra inequality measure for the jth group ought to be written as:

$$C^j = (1/n^j) \sum_{i \in N^j} \left[\frac{\mu^j - \mu_i^j}{\mu^j + \mu_i^j} \right]. \tag{15.6}$$

If, however, one believes that the relation of elements within each subgroup to the entire community *is* relevant to an assessment of subgroup inequality, then it would be legitimate to write the Canberra measure for subgroup j as in equation (15.7):

$$\hat{C}^j = (1/n^j) \sum_{i \in N^j} \left[\frac{\mu - \mu_{\lambda^j(i)}}{\mu + \mu_{\lambda^j(i)}} \right]. \tag{15.7}$$

Using equation (15.7), one can write the Canberra measure as an index that is decomposable after one fashion:

$$C = \sum_{j=1}^{K} (n^j/n)\hat{C}^j. \tag{15.8}$$

Equation (15.8) reflects the sort of subgroup decomposition which Podder (1993) performs for the Gini coefficient of inequality, wherein subgroup income ranks of individuals are replaced by the income ranks

---

[8] See Foster and Sen (1997).

of these same individuals in the overall vector of incomes. 'Decomposability', as in equation (15.8), is now interpreted in the same way in which the decomposability of a poverty measure is conventionally understood, namely, as the ability to write the measure as a population share-weighted sum of subgroup poverty levels. This enables one to identify the contribution of any particular subgroup to overall inequality: equation (15.8) suggests that the proportionate contribution of subgroup j to aggregate inequality is $((n^j/n)\hat{C}^j/C)$. This is not, of course, decomposability in the Theil (1967) sense of an exact additive sum of a 'within-group' and a 'between-group' component of inequality—but then, as Podder (1993: 263) sensibly observes, 'without questioning its usefulness, it can be contended that the Theil type of decomposition is not the only type of decomposition one can think of. If the general purpose is to get an idea of the contribution of each of the groups to total inequality . . . it is possible to think of other types of decomposition.'

TRANSFER-SENSITIVITY

Transfer-sensitivity is the requirement that an inequality measure should be more sensitive to income transfers at the lower than at the upper end of an income distribution. There are alternative ways of giving expression to this property which Kolm (1976) called the 'principle of diminishing transfers'. Under one version, a given income transfer between two individuals a fixed *number of persons* apart should have a greater effect on inequality, the poorer the pair of persons involved in the transfer is; under another version, a given income transfer between two individuals a fixed *income* apart should have a greater effect on inequality, the poorer the pair of persons involved in the transfer is.[9] For our purposes, we shall define transfer-sensitivity under the constraint that the pair of individuals involved in the transfer are both a fixed population *and* a fixed income apart. The following definitions are in order.

Given an ordered income n-vector $\mathbf{x} = (x_1, ..., x_j, ..., x_k, ..., x_n)$, a *progressive rank-preserving transfer* of income between two persons k and j is one in which $x_k > x_j$ and a transfer of $\Delta \leq (x_k - x_j)/2$ takes place from k to j.

The *transfer axiom* requires that for any two ordered income n-vectors $\mathbf{x}, \mathbf{y} \in \mathbf{X}$, if $\mathbf{y}$ has been derived from $\mathbf{x}$ through a progressive rank-preserving transfer of income from some person k to some

---

[9] See Foster (1985).

person j, that is, $y_i = x_i \forall i \notin \{j, k\}$ for some $j, k \in N(x)$ satisfying $y_j = x_j + \Delta, y_k = x_k - \Delta, x_k > x_j$ and $\Delta \leq (x_k - x_j)/2$, then $I(y) < I(x)$.

Transfer-sensitivity, as we define it, requires the following: For all ordered income n-vectors $x, y, w \in X$, if y is derived from x through a progressive rank-preserving transfer of income from some k to some j, and w is derived from x through a progressive rank-preserving transfer of income from some q to some p, with $k - j = q - p \equiv t > 0$, and $x_k - x_j = x_q - x_p \equiv \Delta > 0$, then $I(x) - I(y) > I(x) - I(w) > 0$.

It is well known that the Gini coefficient violates transfer-sensitivity: so long as the area enclosed by the Lorenz curve and the diagonal of the unit square in which the curve is drawn is the same for any intersecting pair of Lorenz curves, the value of the Gini coefficient will be the same for both distributions, irrespective of whether the Lorenz curve bulges at the top or at the bottom of the distribution. The Bonferroni index, however, *is* transfer-sensitive.[10] So is the Canberra measure.

To see this, imagine that the antecedents in the statement of the transfer-sensitivity axiom have been satisfied for some triple of n-vectors of income $x, y, w \in X$. Then, it can be verified that, if μ is the common mean shared by the three distributions,

$$C(x) - C(y) = (2\mu\Delta/n)$$

$$\times \left[\frac{1}{(\mu + \mu_j)\{j(\mu + \mu_j) + \Delta\}} + \cdots + \frac{1}{(\mu + \mu_{j+t-1})\{(j + t - 1)(\mu + \mu_{j+t-1}) + \Delta\}} \right]$$

$$(15.9)$$

and

$$C(x) - C(w)$$

$$= (2\mu\Delta/n) \left[\frac{1}{(\mu + \mu_p)\{p(\mu + \mu_p) + \Delta\}} + \cdots + \frac{1}{(\mu + \mu_{p+t-1})\{(p + t - 1)(\mu + \mu_{p+t-1}) + \Delta\}} \right]$$

$$(15.10)$$

Since the right-hand sides of equations (15.9) and (15.10) are positive, the transfer axiom is verified. Further, and since $j < p$ and the

---

[10] See Chakravarty (2007).

truncated means are arranged in non-descending order, it follows that $1/(\mu + \mu_{j+i})\{(j + i)(\mu + \mu_{j+i}) + \Delta\} > 1/(\mu + \mu_{p+i})\{(p + i)(\mu + \mu_{p+i}) + \Delta\}\forall i \in \{0, 1, ..., t - 1\}$, which is sufficient to verify that C satisfies transfer-sensitivity.

If transfer-sensitivity is regarded as an appealing property, then the Bonferroni and Canberra measures score over the Gini coefficient in this respect.

THE CANBERRA CURVE

Given any ordered n-vector of incomes $\mathbf{x} \in X$, we know that the Lorenz curve is defined by the relationship

$$L(\mathbf{x}; i/n) = (1/n\mu) \sum_{j=1}^{i} x_j. \tag{15.11}$$

Similarly, we can define the Canberra curve in terms of the following relationship:

$$R(\mathbf{x}; i/n) = \frac{(i/n) - (\sum_{j=1}^{i} x_j/n\mu)}{(i/n) + (\sum_{j=1}^{i} x_j/n\mu)} \left(= \frac{\mu - \mu_i}{\mu + \mu_i} \right). \tag{15.12}$$

If we designate i/n by P_i and $(1/n\mu) \sum_{j=1}^{i} x_j$ by L_i, then L_i is the cumulative income share of the poorest P_ith fraction of the population, and the plot of L_i against P_i is just the Lorenz curve. In like fashion, if we designate

$$\frac{(i/n) - (\sum_{j=1}^{i} x_j/n\mu)}{(i/n) + (\sum_{j=1}^{i} x_j/n\mu)}$$

by R_i, then we can see from (15.12) that the Canberra curve is obtained by plotting the points $R_i \equiv (P_i - L_i)/(P_i + L_i)$ against the points P_i ($i = 1, ..., n$). The curve can be drawn within the unit square as a non-increasing graph from $(0, 1)$ to $(1, 0)$ of the square. For an illustrative numerical example, consider the ordered 5-vector $\mathbf{x} = (10, 15, 20, 24, 41)$ whose mean μ is 22. The coordinates of the Canberra curve for the distribution $\mathbf{x}$ can be derived as in the last two columns of the following table.

A plot of the R_i against the P_i presented in the last two columns of Table 15.1 yields the Canberra curve as a step function—see Figure 15.2. It is easy to see that the area beneath the Canberra curve is just the value of the Canberra measure of inequality. One can also see that as

Table 15.1 Coordinates of the Canberra curve for the vector $x = (10, 15, 20, 24, 41)$

i	x_i	μ_i	$\mu - \mu_i$	$\mu + \mu_i$	$P_i \equiv i/n$	$R_i \equiv \frac{\mu - \mu_i}{\mu + \mu_i}$
1	10	10	12	32	0.2	0.38
2	15	12.5	9.5	34.5	0.4	0.28
3	20	15	7	37	0.6	0.19
4	24	17.25	4.75	39.25	0.8	0.12
5	41	22	0	44	1.0	0

n becomes large, the Canberra curve can be approximated by a continuous curve obtained by connecting the plotted points of the curve with 'piece-wise' linear segments. Two examples of possible Canberra curves are presented in Figure 15.3. One curve lies everywhere below what Kakwani (1980) calls the 'alternative diagonal' drawn from (0, 1) to (1, 0) of the unit square; the other curve lies everywhere above this diagonal.[11] A relationship analogous to that of Lorenz dominance can be defined for the Canberra curve: for any two distributions $x, y \in X$, x will be said to Canberra-dominate y, written $x \succ_C y$, if and only if the Canberra curve for x lies somewhere below and nowhere above the Canberra curve for x. For all $x, y \in X$, if $x \succ_C y$, then one can say that x displays unambiguously less inequality than y. In Figure 15.3, the strictly convex Canberra curve obviously dominates the strictly concave curve.

Finally, visual confirmation of the transfer-sensitivity of the Canberra measure is available from the following elementary numerical example. Suppose $a = (20, 30, 40, 50)$ and that x and y are derived from a through a transfer of 5 units of income from person 2 to person 1 and a transfer of 5 units from person 4 to person 3 respectively, so that $x = (25, 25, 40, 50)$, $y = (20, 30, 45, 45)$, and x and y share the same mean $\mu = 35$. The coordinates of both the Lorenz and the Canberra curves are derived in the tables following:

---

[11] It is straightforward that if the Canberra curve is uniformly convex, then it will lie everywhere below the alternative diagonal, while if it is uniformly concave, it will lie everywhere above the alternative diagonal. The area below the alternative diagonal is 0.5, which serves as a sort of benchmark: if the Canberra curve is uniformly convex, then the value of the Canberra measure is less than 0.5, and the other way around if the curve is uniformly concave.

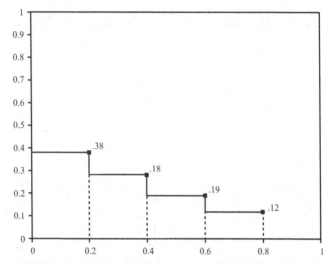

Figure 15.2 A step-function Canberra curve drawn for the vector (10, 15, 20, 24, 41)

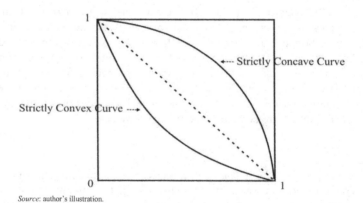

Source: author's illustration.

Figure 15.3 Two examples of possible Canberra curves

Table 15.2 Coordinates of the Lorenz and the Canberra curves for the vector $\mathbf{x} = (20, 25, 40, 50)$

i	x_i	μ_i	$\mu - \mu_i$	$\mu + \mu_i$	$P_i \equiv i/n$	$R_i \equiv \frac{\mu - \mu_i}{\mu + \mu_i}$	$L_i \equiv (1/n\mu) \sum_{j=1}^{i} x_j$
1	25	25	10	60	0.25	0.17	0.18
2	25	25	10	60	0.50	0.17	0.36
3	40	30	5	65	0.75	0.08	0.64
4	50	35	0	70	1.00	0	1.00

Table 15.3 Coordinates of the Lorenz and the Canberra curves for the vector $\mathbf{y} = (20, 30, 45, 45)$

i	x_i	μ_i	$\mu - \mu_i$	$\mu + \mu_i$	$P_i \equiv i/n$	$R_i \equiv \frac{\mu - \mu_i}{\mu + \mu_i}$	$L_i \equiv (1/n\mu) \sum_{j=1}^{i} x_j$
1	20	20	15	55	0.25	0.27	0.14
2	30	25	10	60	0.50	0.17	0.36
3	45	31.67	3.33	66.67	0.75	0.05	0.68
4	45	35	0.75	70	1.00	0	1.00

From the step functions representing the Lorenz and the Canberra curves for the two distributions, one can see that the Gini coefficients are the same for both $\mathbf{x}$ and $\mathbf{y}$ (the area a in Figure 15.4a is the same as the area b), while the Canberra measure is larger for $\mathbf{y}$ than for $\mathbf{x}$ (the area a in Figure 15.4b is larger than the area b).

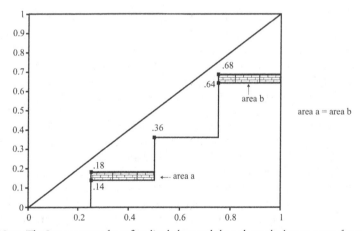

Note: The Lorenz curve for y *first lies below and then above the lorenz curve for* x.

Figure 15.4a Step-function Lorenz curves for the vectors $\mathbf{x} = (25, 25, 40, 50)$ and $\mathbf{y} = (20, 30, 45, 45)$

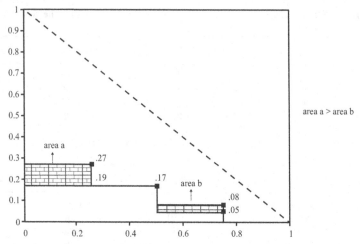

Note: The Canberra curve for y first lies above and then below the Canberra Curve for x.

Figure 15.4b Step-function Canberra curves for the vectors **x** = (25, 25, 40, 50) and **y** = (20, 30, 45, 45)

CONCLUSION

This essay has been a variation on the theme of the Bonferroni inequality index, which has been subjected to rigorous analysis by, among others, Barcena and Imedio (2000), Chakravarty (2007), Giorgi and Crescenzi (2001) and Imedio-Olmedo et al. (2011). The possible novelty of the essay resides in the use of a distance function—the Canberra distance function, as it happens—as a natural approach to take in the measurement of both inequality and poverty. An application of the Canberra distance function to an assessment of inequality leads to a measure of disparity—here called the 'Canberra measure'—which turns out to be closely related to the Bonferroni index, and also to the Gini coefficient of inequality. A curve analogous to the Lorenz curve, and referred to as the Canberra curve in the essay, is derived and discussed.

Also discussed are some properties of the Canberra inequality measure, with specific reference to the features of decomposability and transfer-sensitivity. The principal merit of the Canberra measure vis-à-vis the Gini coefficient is that, unlike the latter, it satisfies the property of transfer-sensitivity. The emphasis of the essay has been mainly on a simple and systematic derivation and presentation of an inequality measure with a known ancestry in two other distinguished measures. The essay is, thus, best viewed as an effort in consolidation and, it is hoped, useful exposition.

REFERENCES

Barcena, E. and L. J. Imedio. 2000. 'The Bonferroni, Gini, and De Vergottini Indices: Inequality, Welfare, and Deprivation in the European Union in 2000', in J. Bishop and B. Zheng (eds), *Inequality and Opportunity: Papers for the Second ECINEQ Society Meeting (Research on Economic Inequality)*, Vol. 16. Bingley: Emerald Group Publishing Limited, pp. 231–57.

Bonferroni, C. E. 1930. *Elementi di Statistica Generale*. Liberia Seeber: Firenze.

Chakravarty, S. R. 2007. 'A Deprivation-Based Axiomatic Characterization of the Absolute Bonferroni Index of Inequality', *Journal of Economic Inequality*, 5(3): 339–51.

Chakravarty, S. R., N. Chattopadhyay and A. Majumder. 1995. 'Income Inequality and Relative Deprivation', *Keio Economic Studies*, 32(1): 1–15.

Foster, J. E. 1985. 'Inequality Measurement', in H. Peyton Young (ed.), *Fair Allocation*. Providence: American Mathematical Society, pp. 31–68.

Foster, J. E., J. Greer and E. Thorbecke. 1984. 'A Class of Decomposable Poverty Measures', *Econometrica*, 52(3): 761–66.

Foster, J. E. and A. Sen. 1997. *On Economic Inequality after a Quarter Century*, Oxford: Clarendon Press.

Gini, C. 1912. 'Variabilita e Mutabilita', *Studi Economico-Giuridici dell'Universita di Cagliari*, 3(2): 1–158.

Giorgi, G. M. and M. Crescenzi. 2001. 'A Proposal of Poverty Measures Based on the Bonferroni Inequality Index', *Metron Journal of Statistics*, LIX(3–4): 3–16.

Imedio-Olmedo, L. J., E. Barcena-Martin and E. M. Parrado-Gallardo. 2011. 'A Class of Bonferroni Inequality Indices', *Journal of Public Economic Theory*, 13(1): 97–124.

Kakwani, N. C. 1980. *Income Inequality and Poverty: Methods of Estimation and Policy Applications*. New York: Oxford University Press.

Kolm, S. C. 1976. 'Unequal Inequalities II', *Journal of Economic Theory*, 13(1): 82–111.

Lance, G. N. and W. T. Williams. 1967. 'Mixed-Data Classificatory Programs I: Agglomerative Systems', *Australian Computer Journal*, 1(1): 15–20.

Podder, N. 1993. 'A New Decomposition of the Gini Coefficient among Groups and Its Interpretation with Applications to Australian Data', *Sankhya: The Indian Journal of Statistics*, 55(Series B, 2): 262–71.

Sen, A. 1973. *On Economic Inequality*. Oxford: Clarendon Press.

Shorrocks, A. F. 1988. 'Aggregation Issues in Inequality Measurement', in W. Eichorn (ed.), *Measurement in Economics*. New York: Physica-Verlag, pp. 429–52.

Subramanian, S. 1989. 'On a Simple, Transfer-Sensitive Index of Inequality', *Economics Letters*, 23(4): 389–92.

———. 2009. 'Poverty Measures as Normalized Distance Functions', *Indian Economic Review*, 44(2): 171–83.

Takayama, N. 1979. 'Poverty, Income Inequality, and Their Measures: Professor Sen's Axiomatic Approach Reconsidered', *Econometrica*, 47(3): 747–59.

Theil, H. 1967. *Economics and Information Theory*. Amsterdam: North-Holland.

Wilson, D. R. and T. R. Martinez. 1997. 'Improved Heterogeneous Distance Functions', *Journal of Artificial Intelligence Research*, 6(1): 1–34.

16

Measuring Vulnerability to Poverty
An Expected Poverty Index

Satya R. Chakravarty and Nachiketa Chattopadhyay*

Vulnerability refers to the inability to avoid risks. For instance, families with low incomes may not be poor currently, but are vulnerable to poverty in the sense that they live under a risky environment of becoming poor in the future. Likewise, some people may be vulnerable to unemployment, that is, there is a possibility that they may become unemployed in the future. This, therefore, indicates that vulnerability to poverty evaluations are forward-looking and, hence, are different from usual poverty evaluations because the latter is based on current observable information.

'The challenge of development includes not only the elimination of persistent and endemic deprivation, but also the removal of vulnerability to sudden and severe destitution' (Sen 1999a). Likewise, the World Bank (1997) stated that, 'Protecting vulnerable groups during episodes of macroeconomic contraction is vital to poverty reductions in developing countries.'

The existing voluminous literature on poverty measurement relies on the assumption of full certainty.[1] Until recently, the calculus of risk was not systematically incorporated into the normative economic analysis of poverty. Attempts to regard vulnerability indices as expected poverty indices were made, among others, by Calvo and Dercon (2013), Kamanou and Morduch (2002), and Ligon and Schechter (2003).[2] Dutta et al.

* The authors thank the participants of the National Seminar on 'Rural Consumers in Globalizing Market: Vulnerability and Choices', Kalyani University, December 2010, and 'Panchanan Chakraborty and Prabhat Sarbadhikari Memorial Lecture', Jadavpur University, December 2010.

[1] See Chakravarty (2009) for a recent survey.
[2] For related attempts, see Chaudhuri (2003), Chaudhuri et al. (2002), Christiaensen and Boisvert (2000) and Pritchett et al. (2000). See also Basu

(2011) suggested an index of vulnerability that incorporates the current standard of living and observed that (p. 745): 'Ligon and Schechter's measure is the expected poverty gap, whereas Calvo and Dercon's measure is the expected Chakravarty index and Kamanou and Morduch's (2002) employs the expected Foster–Greer–Thorbecke (FGT) index'.

In this essay, we develop an alternative axiomatic characterisation of the expected Chakravarty (1983) vulnerability index using a von Neumann–Morgenstern utility function. This characterisation is different from the Calvo–Dercon characterisation and enables us to view vulnerability as the burden of the threat of poverty, and interpret the index as an expected utility loss. We first measure vulnerability at the individual level and then aggregate these individual levels of vulnerability to get an overall measure of vulnerability for the society as a whole.

The next section of the essay presents the characterisation theorem and investigates properties of the index in details. The last section makes some concluding remarks.

FORMAL FRAMEWORK

At the individual level, vulnerability can be treated in terms of uncertainty in the outcomes of different indicators of well-being, such as income and consumption, that the individual faces in the future. For simplicity of exposition, we assume a framework in which income is the only attribute of well-being. Our index of vulnerability is an ex ante measure in the sense it should incorporate future uncertainty with respect to occurrence of income. The index has to take into account the downside risk, that is, the shortfalls from a given a reference point. More precisely, we look at an individual's vulnerability of income in terms of shortfall of income from the poverty line as a result of economic and other shocks. Since for a given shortfall, different individuals may have different levels of vulnerability, the index should be individual-specific.

Thus, we consider income as an uncertain prospect and there are different levels of returns on the prospect. We refer to the returns on the prospect as state contingent returns. A state contingent return means a return that depends on the outcome of the state. Assume that the society under consideration consists of m individuals and n states. For

---

and Nolen (2005), Calvo (2008), Christiaensen and Subbarao (2005), Dercon and Krishnan (2000), Morduch (1994) and Suryahadi and Sumarto (2003) for alternative notions.

individual j, $x^j = (x_1^j, x_2^j, ..., x_n^j)$ is the vector of state contingent returns on the prospect, $1 \leq j \leq m$. The level of income in each of these states represents the final amount that person j receives when a state occurs. So, if the individual becomes unemployed in one of the future states, then the income in the state will take into account any unemployment benefit that he may receive. Individual j assumes that state i, that is, x_i^j occurs with probability p_i^j, $1 \leq i \leq n$, $1 \leq j \leq m$. We denote the vector of probabilities by

$$(p_1^j, p_2^j, ..., p_n^j) = p^j.$$

Evidently,

$$0 \leq p_i^j \leq 1 \text{ for all } 1 \leq i \leq n, 1 \leq j \leq m \text{ and } \sum_{i=1}^{n} p_i^j = 1, 1 \leq j \leq m.$$

We say that the individual j is poor in state i, if $x_i^j < z$, where $z > 0$, is the exogenously given poverty line, a reference income level. The person is non-poor in the state if $x_i^j \geq z$.

Since we focus on the downside risk, when measuring vulnerability, we consider the shortfalls that the individual faces in different states of the world. These shortfalls are formulated using a von Neumann–Morgenstern utility function U, which is assumed to be continuous, increasing and strictly concave. It is assumed that the utility function U satisfies the 'cardinally measurable, fully comparable' measurability and comparability assumption (Sen 1977).

For any person j and state i with income x_i^j, the shortfall depends on the exogenously given poverty line z. For state i, the shortfall, more precisely utility shortfall, is given by the difference $d_j(z, x_i^j) = U(z) - U(x_i^j)$. Since each x_i^j has a chance of being less than z, the likelihood of future poverty episodes is considered in the formulation. Furthermore, the vulnerability deprivation indicator d_j incorporates the severity of poverty in such cases. These two issues are vulnerable counterparts to the identification and depth of poverty shortfall of a poor person considered in the context of income poverty (Chakravarty 1990, 2009; Foster et al. 1984; Sen 1976).

Thus, strictly speaking, when it comes to vulnerability, the individual faces the state-contingent deprivation vector or utility shortfalls $(d_j(z, x_1^j), d_j(z, x_2^j), ..., d_j(z, x_n^j))$ with probabilities $(p_1^j, p_2^j, ..., p_n^j)$.

Definition 1. *For any state-contingent incomes* $x^j = (x_1^j, x_2^j, ..., x_n^j)$ *and probabilities* $(p_1^j, p_2^j, ..., p_n^j)$, *the individual vulnerability index* $V_j(x^j, p^j, z)$ *is defined as the maximum of the normalised value of the expected utility shortfall and zero. Formally,*

$$V_j\left(x^j, p^j, z\right) = \max\left\{A\left(z, n\right) \sum_{i=1}^{n} p_i^j \left(U\left(z\right) - U\left(x_i^j\right)\right), 0\right\}, \quad (16.1)$$

where $A(z, n) > 0$ *is the coefficient of normalisation, assumed to depend on the number of states n and the threshold income z.*

Since in some of the states, the person may be non-poor, the corresponding utility gaps will be negative. If he is non-poor in all the states, the expected utility shortfall is clearly negative. In order to rule out such states from our formulation, we look at the maximum value of the normalised expected utility gap or zero. This definition is similar to the definition of vulnerability considered by Ligon and Schechter (2003).

While in the von Neumann–Morgernstern framework, the decision maker looks at the expected utility value from different states, in the present context, we consider expected utility shortfall. Thus, our index can be regarded as the vulnerable counterpart to the expected utilitarian rule that ranks two situations on the basis of their expected utility values (Blackorby et al. 1984).

For deriving the explicit form of $V_j(x^j, p^j, z)$, we consider the following axioms.

Normalisation (NOM): For a given p^j and z, if $x_i^j = 0$ for all i, $1 \leq i \leq n$, then $V_j\left(x^j, p^j, z\right) = 1$.

Homogeneity (HOM): For a given p^j, and for all z and x^j, $V_j\left(x^j, p^j, z\right) = V_j\left(cx^j, p^j, cz\right)$, where $c > 0$ is arbitrary.

According to NOM, the vulnerability index achieves its maximal value unity when the state contingent outcomes are zero, the minimum. This is the situation of maximum vulnerability because it is not possible to reduce the state contingent returns further. Given the state contingent probabilities and the threshold income, increasingness of the utility function indicates that as we reduce the return in one or more states, the utility gap or deprivation increases. Consequently, if income in each state becomes minimal, the utility gaps and, hence, their expected value will be the maximum. HOM demands that given the state contingent

probabilities, the vulnerable index remains invariant under scale transformations of all the state contingent returns and the threshold income.
Thus, given the vector p^j, if the currency unit in which income is measured changes, the vulnerability index remains unaltered.

We now state and prove our characterisation theorem for individual
vulnerability.

Theorem 1. *The only individual vulnerability index of the form (16.1)*
that satisfies axioms NOM and HOM is given by

$$V_j\left(x^j, p^j, z\right) = \max\left\{\sum_{i=1}^{n} p_i^j\left[1 - \left(\frac{x_i^j}{z}\right)^e\right], 0\right\}, \qquad (16.2)$$

where $0 < e < 1$ is a constant.

Proof: The index $V_j\left(x^j, p^j, z\right)$ in (16.1) satisfying NOM becomes

$$V_j(x^j, p^j, z) = \max\{A(z, n)(U(z) - U(0)), 0\}. \qquad (16.3)$$

Since $z > 0$ and U is increasing, V_j in (16.3) is in fact given by
$A(z, n)(U(z) - U(0))$. But by NOM, V_j in this particular case takes on
the value 1. Hence, we have

$$A(z, n) = \frac{1}{[U(z) - U(0)]}, \qquad (16.4)$$

which, on substitution into (16.1) yields

$$V_j(x^j, p^j, z) = \max\left\{\frac{\sum_{i=1}^{n} p_i^j\left[U(z) - U(x_i^j)\right]}{[U(z) - U(0)]}, 0\right\}.$$

$$= \max\left\{\sum_{i=1}^{n} p_i^j\left[1 - \frac{f(x_i^j)}{f(z)}\right], 0\right\}, \qquad (16.5)$$

where $f(v) = U(v) - U(0)$.

Since the axioms hold for any number of states and any arbitrarily given state contingent probability vector p^j, they hold as well if
$n = 1$ and $p_1^j = 1$. For $n = 1$ and $0 < x_1^j < z$, the index in (16.5) is
$1 - f(x_1^j)/f(z)$. But HOM demands that $V_j\left(x^j, p^j, z\right)$ should depend only
on x_1^j/z in such a case. Therefore, $f(v)/f(t)$ is of the form $g(v/t)$ for some
continuous function g. This shows that $f(t) = \beta t^e$, where β and e are

constants.[3] Increasingness and strict concavity of f require that $\beta > 0$, and $0 < e < 1$. Substituting $U(t) = a + \beta t^e$, where $a = U(0)$, in (16.5), we get the desired form of $V_j(x^j, p^j, z)$. This establishes the necessity part of the theorem. The sufficiency can be verified by checking that $V_j(x^j, p^j, z)$ in (16.2) satisfies NOM and HOM.

The individual vulnerable index V_j has some additional properties. Some of these properties have been discussed by Calvo and Dercon (2013):

1. The index is bounded between 0 and 1, where the lower bound is achieved when the incomes are risk-free in all states, that is, for any p^j, $x_i^j \geq z$ for all i, $1 \leq i \leq n$. The upper bound is specified in NOM.

2. Since U is cardinal, it is necessary that V_j remains invariant under affine transformations of U. This is because U and its transformation $\hat{U} = a + bU$, where $b > 0$ and a are constants, essentially convey the same information in terms of ranking. From (16.5), it follows that V_j based on U and $\hat{U}$ coincide. We apply the same transformation for all individuals because of full comparability assumption.

3. For a given p^j and x^j, an increase in z does not decrease V_j. Since given p^j and x^j, utility shortfall in each state increases as z increases, expected utility shortfall cannot decrease.

4. For a given p^j and x^j, where $p_i^j > 0$, a reduction in $x_i^j < z$ increases V_j. This is the vulnerable counterpart to Sen's (1976) monotonocity axiom.

5. The index V_j satisfies a restricted anonymity condition, which says that if we consider a reordering of x_js and the same reordering of p_js, then V_j remains unchanged. That is, given z, any information other than state-contingent probabilities and returns are irrelevant to the measurement of individual vulnerability.

6. If $z > x_i^j > x_l^j$, then a reduction in p_i^j by $0 < \varepsilon < p_i^j$ and an increase in p_l^j by ε will increase V_j, that is, if the chance of being vulnerable in a state with low returns increases and the chance of being vulnerable in a state with high returns decreases, then vulnerability increases.

7. If $z > x_i^j > x_l^j$, then a reduction in x_l^j by $0 < \varepsilon < x_l^j$ and an increase in x_i^j by ε, where $0 < p_i^j < p_l^j$, will increase vulnerability. This

---

[3] See Aczel (1966: 144).

property says that vulnerability increases if there is a transfer of income from a state with low income and high probability to one with a higher income and lower probability. This is sensible because the higher utility gap has a higher probability in state l and the transfer increases the gap in the state and decreases that further in state i, which has a lower probability. Hence, expected utility gap increases. This is the vulnerable counterpart to the transfer axiom of Sen (1976).

8. For a given p^j and x^j, V_j increases as the parameter e increases. For $e = 0$, $V_j = 0$. On the other hand, if $e = 1$, $V_j = \max \left\{ \sum_{i=1}^{n} p_i^j \left(1 - \left(x_i^j / z \right) \right), 0 \right\}$, the maximum of the expected value of relative income shortfalls and zero. The constant $(1 - e)$ is the absolute Arrow (1971) and Pratt (1964) measure of risk aversion. For a given p^j and x^j, as e decreases, the individual becomes more and more risk averse.

9. For simplicity of exposition, we have assumed that the reference income level is constant across states. However, our framework allows variability of the reference income over states.

We define the global vulnerability index G as the arithmetic average of individual vulnerability indices. We assume that the type and number of states, and the reference income are fixed. Then if there are m individuals in a society, the global vulnerability index G is defined as

$$G = \frac{1}{m} \sum_{i=1}^{m} V_j \left(x^j, p^j, z \right). \tag{16.6}$$

This index can be characterised using axioms similar to those employed for characterising the generalised human development index suggested by Chakravarty (2003). It possesses the following interesting properties.

1. It is bounded between 0 and 1, where the lower bound is attained if nobody is vulnerable in the society. The upper bound is achieved if all the individuals are subject to maximum vulnerability.

2. It is increasing in its arguments, that is, if one person becomes more vulnerable and the vulnerability levels of the remaining individuals are unchanged, then G increases.

3. G remains invariant under any reordering of its arguments. Thus, in measuring global vulnerability we are concerned with only individual vulnerability levels.

4. It satisfies a global homogeneity condition in the sense that given the vector $(p^1, p^2, ..., p^m)$, any rescaling of x^j and z, $1 \leq j \leq m$, does not change G.
5. The index G is population replication invariant. It remains invariant under any replication of the population. Thus, it becomes helpful for cross-population comparison of vulnerability. However, the comparison should be made under the assumption that the type and the number of states are the same.
6. It is subgroup decomposable, that is, for any partitioning of the population into $k \geq 2$ subgroups with respect to some characteristics like region, religion and gender, national vulnerability becomes the weighted average of subgroup vulnerability levels, where the weights are the population shares of different subgroups. Formally, let m_i be the population size of subgroup i, $1 \leq i \leq k$. Thus, $\sum_{i=1}^{k} m_i = m$. Then subgroup decomposability of G means that

$$G = \sum_{i=1}^{k} \frac{m_i}{m} G^i, \tag{16.7}$$

where G^i is the vulnerability level of subgroup i, that is, formula (16.6) applied to the individuals in the ith subgroup. This property is quite useful for practical purposes. The contribution of subgroup i to total vulnerability is given by the quantity $(m_i/m) G^i$. This is precisely the amount by which overall vulnerability will fall if vulnerability in the ith subgroup is eliminated. The percentage contribution of subgroup i to total vulnerability is $100(\frac{m_i G^i}{mG})$. This property becomes helpful in identifying the subgroups that are more afflicted by vulnerability and, hence, in formulating anti-vulnerability policies. Therefore, each of these statistics is important for policy purpose. Evidently, according to this non-welfarist notion of policy, an assessment of vulnerability becomes contingent on the valuation of the index. However, following Sen (1985), this approach to policy applications is quite popular by now. Therefore, it will be worthwhile to examine what kind of policy would be implied by the use of a particular vulnerability index.

CONCLUSION

Sen (1992) argued that the proper space for social evaluation is that of 'functionings', the different things—such as adequate nourishment, having self-respect, environmental factors and communing with friends—a person may value having or doing (or being). While the sets of functionings of different persons constitute an important ingredient of social evaluation, it is more necessary to get a complete picture of well-being. The 'capability set' of an individual provides information on the set of functionings that the individual could achieve. The set of alternative functioning vectors from which a person can choose, when the resource allocation is given, gives his capability set. The determination of living standards of a person then depends on the opportunity set of the available basic capabilities of the person to function. In the capability-functioning approach, vulnerability is a problem of expected capability failure. According to Sen (1999b), capability failure captures the notion of deprivation that people experience in day-to-day living conditions. This notion of expected capability failure is a multidimensional phenomenon. We leave axiomatic characterisation of vulnerability as an expected capability failure as a future research programme.[4] In the framework considered in the essay, income is the only functioning and poverty arises simply from the lowness of income. Consequently, the vulnerability index in (16.1) can be interpreted as the expected income utility failure.

REFERENCES

Aczel, J. 1966. *Lectures on Functional Equations and Their Applications*. London: Academic Press.

Alkire, S. and J. E. Foster. 2011. 'Counting and Multidimensional Poverty Measurement', *Journal of Public Economics*, 95: 476–87.

Arrow, K. 1971. *Essays on the Theory of Risk Bearing*. Chicago: Markham.

Basu, K. and P. Nolen. 2005. 'Vulnerability, Unemployment and Poverty: A New Class of Measures, Its Axiomatic Properties and Applications', BREAD Working Paper 38.

Blackorby, C., D. Donaldson and J. A. Weymark. 1984. 'Social Choice Theory with Interpersonal Utility Comparisons: A Diagrammatic Introduction', *International Economic Review*, 25: 327–56.

Bourguignon, F. and S. R. Chakravarty. 2003. 'The Measurement of Multidimensional Poverty', *Journal of Economic Inequality*, 1: 25–49.

Calvo, C. 2008. 'Vulnerability to Multidimensional Poverty: Peru, 1998–2002', *World Development*, 36: 1011–20.

---

[4] For treatment of multidimensional poverty as capability failure, see Alkire and Foster (2011), Bourguignon and Chakravarty (2003) and Tsui (2002).

Calvo, C. and S. Dercon. 2013. 'Vulnerability, Risk, and Poverty', *Social Choice and Welfare*, 40: 721–40.

Chakravarty, S. R. 1983. 'A New Index of Poverty', *Mathematical Social Sciences*, 6: 307–13.

———. 1990. *Ethical Social Index Numbers*. New York: Springer.

———. 2003. 'A Generalized Human Development Index', *Review of Development Economics*, 7: 99–114.

———. 2009. *Inequality, Polarization and Poverty: Advances in Distributional Analysis*. New York: Springer.

Chaudhuri, S. 2003. 'Assessing Vulnerability to Poverty: Concepts, Empirical Methods and Illustrative Examples', mimeo, Columbia University.

Chaudhuri, S., J. Jalan and A. Suryahadi. 2002. 'Assessing Household Vulnerability to Poverty from Cross-Sectional Data: A Methodology and Estimates from Indonesia', Discussion Paper No. 0102-52, Columbia University.

Christiaensen, L. and R. N. Boisvert. 2000. 'On Measuring Household Food Vulnerability: Case Evidence from Northern Mali', Working Paper, World Bank.

Christiaensen, L. and K. Subbarao. 2005. 'Towards an Understanding of Household Vulnerability in Rural Kenya', *Journal of African Economies*, 14: 520–58.

Dercon, S. and P. Krishnan. 2000. 'In Sickness and in Health: Risk Sharing within Households in Rural Ethiopia', *Journal of Political Economy*, 108: 688–727.

Dutta, I., J. E. Foster and A. Mishra. 2011. 'On Measuring Vulnerability to Poverty', *Social Choice and Welfare*, 37: 743–61.

Foster, J., J. Greer and E. Thorbecke. 1984. 'A Class of Decomposable Poverty Measures', *Econometrica*, 52: 761–66.

Kamanou, G. and J. Morduch. 2002. 'Measuring Vulnerability to Poverty', WIDER Discussion Paper, No. 2002/58.

Ligon, E. and L. Schechter. 2003. 'Measuring Vulnerability', *Economic Journal*, 113: C95–C102.

Morduch, J. 1994. 'Poverty and Vulnerability', *American Economic Review, Papers and Proceedings*, 84: 221–25.

Pratt, J. W. 1964. 'Risk Aversion in the Small and in the Large', *Econometrica*, 32: 122–36.

Pritchett, L., A. Suryahadi and S. Sumarto. 2000. 'Quantifying Vulnerability to Poverty', World Bank, Research Working Paper, No. 2437.

Sen, A. K. 1976. 'Poverty: An Ordinal Approach to Measurement', *Econometrica*, 44: 219–31.

———. 1977. 'On Weights and Measures: Information Constraints in Social Welfare Analysis', *Econometrica* 45, 1539–72.

———. 1985. 'Commodities and Capabilities', North Holland, Amsterdam.

———. 1992. 'Inequality Re-examined', Harvard University Press, Cambridge.

———. 1999a. 'A Plan for Asia's Growth', *Asia Week*, 8 October, p. 25. Available at:http://www.asiaweek.com/asiaweek/magazine/99/1008/viewpoint.html.

———. 1999b. *Development as Freedom*. Oxford: Oxford University Press.

Suryahadi, A. and S. Sumarto. 2003. 'Poverty and Vulnerability in Indonesia before and after the Economic Crisis', *Asian Economic Journal*, 17(1): 45–64.

Tsui, K-Y. 2002. 'Multidimensional Poverty Indices', *Social Choice and Welfare*, 19: 69–93.

World Bank. 1997. 'Poverty Lines', Policy Research and Poverty and Social Policy Department, World Bank, No. 6. Available at http://www.worldbank.org/html/prdph/ls

17

On Literacy Rankings*

Tapan Mitra

The importance of literacy in the process of economic development of a society is well recognised. The standard measure of literacy of a society is the percentage of literates in the adult population, called the *literacy rate*. This measure has been the subject of careful scrutiny in recent years. Basu and Foster (1998) have argued that literates in a household provide a positive externality to the illiterates in that household. Thus, an illiterate person in a household which has some literate person, is *effectively more literate* than an illiterate person in a household which has no literate person. Consequently, some account needs to be taken of this externality in capturing the *effective* literacy of the household.

Empirical work shows that such an intra-household externality of literacy is present, and can be quite large. In an early essay in this area, Green et al. (1985) studied the role of 'shared literacy' in the adoption of modern farm practices in Guatemala. More recent work include Gibson (2001), who studied the effects of adult literacy on children's nutritional status in Papua New Guinea, and Basu et al. (2002), who studied the effects of education on individual earnings in the non-farm sector in Bangladesh.

This essay is primarily concerned with the observation of Basu and Foster (1998) that, taking into account the fact that literate household members generate a positive externality for illiterate members, 'a more even distribution of literacy across households leads to greater effective literacy'. The observation would be of greater interest if its validity (*a*) does not depend on the choice of a specific externality function, but applies to an entire class of externality functions, consistent with literacy indices satisfying a set of reasonable axioms, and (*b*) the distributions

---

* This essay is dedicated, with affection and admiration, to Satish Jain. For comments on an earlier version of this essay, I am grateful to Paola Valenti. For encouragement in preparing the current revised version, I am greatly indebted to S. Subramanian.

of literacy that are being compared encompass a broad class and are not confined merely to extreme polar cases.

With this objective in mind, we present an axiomatic study of the class of decomposable literacy indices in the second section of the essay. Four axioms are imposed on the literacy indices, reflecting monotonicity with respect to literates, scale invariance (to capture the idea that the index is a relative measure, not an absolute one), a standard normalisation rule and, crucially, a positive externality axiom (reflecting the fact that literates generate an externality within a household for its illiterate members). Theorem 1 in the second section presents our main representation result for decomposable literacy indices. It shows that any decomposable literacy index of a society (satisfying the set of four axioms) can be written as the weighted sum of a *concave* and *increasing* function of the *literacy rates* of the individual households of that society, and that this form of representation in fact characterises decomposable literacy indices, satisfying the four axioms. We view this result as an extension of the standard mathematical theory relating *gauge functions* to *convex functions*.

Equipped with this result, one can develop a theory of super majorisation along the lines of the well-known Tomic–Weyl theorem. The standard theory cannot be directly applied, because the number of literates or illiterates in a household are integers, and so variables like literacy rates take on rational values only. Thus, the natural domain of measures of literacy of societies is not a convex set. The relevant material, covering this technical part of the essay, is presented in the Appendix. It leads to Theorem 2 in the second section, which can be considered to be the principal theoretical application of Theorem 1. It asserts that, given two societies A and B, if the distribution of the literacy rates of the households in society A is more equitable than the distribution of the literacy rates of the households in society B, in the sense of the standard Lorenz quasi-order, then society A has a higher effective literacy index compared to society B.[1]

Theorem 2 meets the primary objective of the essay, described earlier. The distributions of literacy that can be compared are as numerous

---

[1] Expressions like 'higher' and 'more equitable' are used in the weak sense. So, a more precise formulation of the result would be that if society B has a strictly less equitable distribution of literacy rates than society A in the sense of the standard Lorenz quasi-order, then society B cannot have a strictly higher literacy index compared to society A.

as those that are Lorenz comparable. And, the result does not depend on a choice of a specific externality function, but on the positive externality axiom which asserts merely the presence of an intra-household externality of literacy. However, Theorems 1 and 2 naturally lead to the explicit characterisation of externality functions implicit in our set of four axioms on decomposable literacy indices; this is presented in Theorem 3 in the third section 3. It would appear from our results in the second and third sections that the crucial variable of interest in literacy rankings, even after taking the externality aspect of literacy into account, is the literacy rate, although now at the micro-level of the household.

In the fourth section, we compare our characterisation result in Theorem 3, with those proposed by Dutta (2004) and Valenti (2002).[2] The framework used in these essays is comparable to but somewhat different from ours, and we describe it explicitly in the section 'The Alternative Framework'. The axiom system used by Valenti (2002) implies that all four of our axioms hold, and is slightly stronger. Thus, our main conclusion with respect to the distribution of literacy (Theorem 2) holds under her axiom system. Further, using our characterisation of externality functions (Theorem 3), we can present (in Theorem 4) the main contribution in her essay: a characterisation of externality functions implicit in her axiom system.

The axiom system used by Dutta (2004) is weaker than the one in Valenti (2002) and, in particular, the 'weak externality' axiom used by him asserts the presence of an intra-household externality of literacy only in more restricted circumstances. As a result, the characterisation of externality functions implicit in his axiom system (presented in Theorem 5) imposes less structure on the externality functions. In particular, our principal result on the distribution of literates (Theorem 2) does not hold under his axiom system, and we demonstrate this with a simple example. In the example, a society with an unequal distribution of literates among households is seen to have a *strictly higher* effective

---

[2] An earlier version (Mitra 2002) of the current essay was circulated as a CAE Working paper in 2002. In the decade that has followed, there has been considerable research in this area. In terms of axiomatic analysis, the contributions by Valenti (2002) and Dutta (2004) are noteworthy. The purpose of the fourth section is to provide the reader with a better perspective of alternative axiomatic approaches that have been pursued in studying literacy indices with intra-household externality to literacy.

literacy index than a society with a completely equal distribution of literates, and this literacy index is consistent with the axiom set used by Dutta (2004).

LITERACY INDICES

Notation

Let $\mathbb{N}$ denote the set of natural numbers $\{1, 2, 3, ...\}$, and let $\mathbb{M}$ denote the set $\{0, 1, 2, 3, ...\}$. We define the set $\mathbb{X} = \{(x, y) : x \in \mathbb{M}, y \in \mathbb{N}$, and $x \leq y\}$. Let $\mathbb{Q}$ denote the set of rational numbers, and $\mathbb{R}$ the set of real numbers. We denote by $\mathbb{Q}_+$ the set of non-negative rational numbers $\{z = p/q$, where $p \in \mathbb{M}$, and $q \in \mathbb{N}\}$, and by $\mathbb{Y}$ the set $\mathbb{Q} \cap [0, 1]$; the set $\mathbb{Q} \cap (0, 1)$ is denoted by $\underline{Y}$.

Decomposable Literacy Indices

A *household* is a pair $(r, n) \in \mathbb{X}$. Here n is to be interpreted as the total number of individuals in the household, and r is to be interpreted as the number of *literate* individuals in the household. Thus, $s = r - n$ is the number of *illiterate* individuals in the household.

A *society* is a (non-empty) collection of households; a society consisting of $m \in \mathbb{N}$ households is denoted by the set $\{(r_1, n_1), ..., (r_m, n_m)\}$.

A literacy index is a function from the set of all possible societies to the reals. To formalise this, we define the set of all possible societies to be:

$$\mathbb{U} = \bigcup_{k=1}^{\infty} \mathbb{X}^k \qquad (17.1)$$

and we define a *literacy index* as a function, $L : \mathbb{U} \to \mathbb{R}$. We will confine our attention exclusively to *decomposable literacy indices*, that is, those which satisfy:

$$L(\{(r_1, n_1), ..., (r_m, n_m)\}) = \sum_{i=1}^{m} (n_i/n)L(\{(r_i, n_i)\}), \qquad (17.2)$$

where $n = (n_1 + \cdots + n_m)$.

Given our restriction to decomposable literacy indices, it is clear that any axiom system on literacy indices of a society can be expressed as an axiom system on the literacy indices of the single-household society. This allows us to focus on the micro-level, and see what reasonable restrictions one might wish to impose on the literacy index of a household.

We shall impose four such axioms, and provide some justification for each one.

Remark 1.

1. *The restriction of the exercise to decomposable literacy indices is a serious one. There is little in the way of a theoretical justification for this restriction. This is especially true in a context in which externalities of literates on illiterates within a household is being emphasised, for the restriction rules out any inter-household externality of literates on illiterates. One would think that such externalities are prevalent, even when they are not formalised in the institution of a school. Of course, formally, one can think of a 'household' more broadly as the unit in which the externalities are prevalent. But, this creates problems in defining precisely the boundaries of 'households' and, therefore, in using the theory on standard household data. From the practical point of view, one might argue that decomposable indices are the only indices which stand a chance of being used by policy makers.*

2. *The depiction of a household as a pair (r, n) hides a lot of relevant information about the household. For example, there is no special significance attached to whether the father (or the mother) in the household is literate. A whole range of policy issues which are tied to such aspects of the household cannot, therefore, be addressed in our framework. However, the representation of a household as $(1, 3)$ in my notation for example, conveys all the relevant information that is conveyed by its alternative representation, used in Basu and Foster (1998), as $(0, 0, 1)$ (or equivalently as $(0, 1, 0)$ or $(1, 0, 0)$, using their anonymity axiom) in which each 0 represents an illiterate and each 1 represents a literate person in the household.*

Axioms on Decomposable Literacy Indices

Consider a single household, with a single literate member (and no illiterate member). If we compare this with a single household, with a single illiterate member (and no literate member), it should be obvious that any reasonable literacy index would pronounce the first one more literate than the second. If we are to assign higher numbers for higher literacy, then any reasonable literacy index would assign a higher number to the first household than to the second. Our first axiom treats these two households as 'benchmarks' relative to which other households are evaluated, by assigning the number 1 to the first household, and 0 to the second household.

Axiom N (Normalisation Axiom):

$$L(\{(1, 1)\}) = 1; L(\{(0, 1)\}) = 0.$$

Consider, next, a comparison of one household, (r, n), with another household, (r', n), where the number of literates in the second household (r') exceeds the number of literates in the first household (r), while the total number of individuals in both households is the same. It should be obvious that any reasonable literacy index should assign a higher number to the second household relative to the first. This is the content of the monotonicity axiom.

Axiom RM (Monotonicity Axiom):

If $(r, n) \in \mathbb{X}$, and $(r', n) \in \mathbb{X}$, and $r' > r$, then $L(\{(r', n)\}) > L(\{(r, n)\})$.

We now come to an axiom, which might be viewed as an extension of the idea that there is a positive externality of literates on the illiterates in a household. Consider a society $A = \{(1, 1), (0, 1)\}$, with two households: a household consisting of a literate person, and no illiterate person, and another household consisting of an illiterate person and no literate person. Contrast this with a society $B = \{(1, 2)\}$, consisting of a single household, obtained by merging the two households of society A into one. The presence of positive externality of literates on illiterates in the same household means precisely that a literacy index should assign at least as high a number (possibly higher) to society B relative to society A.

Notice that the literate in the first household cannot have a positive externality on the illiterate in the second household in society A. The decomposability of the literacy index rules out an inter-household externality. But, when the two individuals are part of the same household, as in society B, then the illiterate can gain from the literate.

Thus, we might view the presence of a positive intra-household externality as saying that $L(\{1 + 0, 1 + 1\}) \geq L(\{(1, 1), (0, 1)\})$. Extending this idea, we could say that if society C consists of two households, and is described by $\{(r_1, n_1), (r_2, n_2)\}$, and society $D = \{(r_1 + r_2), (n_1 + n_2)\}$ is obtained by merging the two households of society C into one, then we should have $L(D) \geq L(C)$; that is, $L(\{(r_1 + r_2), (n_1 + n_2)\}) \geq L(\{(r_1, n_1), (r_2, n_2)\})$. After all, the single household society of D can always function like two households living under one roof, that is, without any interaction between the literates of the first household (r_1) and the illiterates of the second household $(n_2 - r_2)$, and without any interaction between the literates of the second household (r_2) and the illiterates of the first household $(n_1 - r_1)$. But, in general, there is the *possibility* of these positive interactions in society D, which are absent in society C; that is, society D is capable of doing everything that society C is capable of doing, in terms of positive effects of its literates on its illiterates, and possibly more. We formalise these ideas in the positive externality axiom.

Axiom PE (Positive Externality Axiom):

If $(r_1, n_1) \in \mathbb{X}$, and $(r_2, n_2) \in \mathbb{X}$, then $L(\{(r_1 + r_2), (n_1 + n_2)\})$
$\geq L(\{(r_1, n_1), (r_2, n_2)\})$.

Our final axiom pertains to scale invariance. Consider society A, consisting of a single household, with one literate and no illiterate person. Contrast this with society B, consisting again of a single household, with two literates and no illiterate person. We agreed to assign a literacy index of 1 to society A (by **Axiom N**). It would seem reasonable to assign the same literacy index to society B. Similarly, society C, consisting of a single household, with one illiterate, and no literate person, gets a literacy index of 0 by **Axiom N**. And, it again seems reasonable to assign the same index of 0 to society D, consisting of a single household, with two illiterates and no literate person. These are rather clear-cut cases of invariance of the literacy index to the scale of the household in question (in a single-household society). The next axiom postulates that such scale invariance holds for all single household societies.

Axiom SI (Scale Invariance Axiom):

If $(r, n) \in \mathbb{X}$, and $k \in \mathbb{N}$, then $L(\{(kr, kn)\}) = L(\{(r, n)\})$.

Remark 2.

1. *The usual statement of the normalisation axiom (in Basu and Foster [1998], Dutta [2004], and Valenti [2002]) is stronger than our **Axiom N**, asserting that if $n \in \mathbb{N}$, then $L(\{(n, n)\}) = 1$, and $L(\{(0, n)\}) = 0$, that is, it combines our **Axiom N** with a scale invariance property for some particular single household societies.*

2. *The monotonicity axiom (**Axiom RM**) is basically the same as the one used in Basu and Foster (1998) and Valenti (2002).*

3. *Valenti (2002) uses an 'equality axiom' instead of **Axiom PE** and **Axiom SI**. Her equality axiom implies PE and SI, but is stronger than axioms **PE** and **SI** combined. I have found it more useful to separate the two axioms. This makes **Axiom PE** acceptable, if one believes in the positive externality of literates on illiterates in the same household. And, it makes **Axiom SI** acceptable, if one believes that a literacy index should be a relative (not an absolute) index. The interpretation given in Valenti (2002) for the equality axiom is somewhat different from that provided in the discussion above. A detailed description of Valenti's axiom system can be found in the fourth section.*

4. *The externality axiom in Basu and Foster (1998) implies **Axiom PE**, but is stronger. The first part of their externality axiom also implies **Axiom SI**.*

Representation of Decomposable Literacy Indices

In this subsection, we discuss the main representation result of the class of decomposable literacy indices, satisfying the set of four axioms introduced in the previous subsection.

To formulate the result precisely, let us define the following properties that a function $\phi : \mathbb{Q}_+ \to \mathbb{R}$ might satisfy.[3]

Concavity(C): If $z, z' \in \mathbb{Q}_+$, and $t \in Y$, then $\phi(tz + (1 - t)z') \geq t\phi(z) + (1 - t)\phi(z')$.

Monotonicity(M): If $z, z' \in \mathbb{Q}_+$, and $z' > z$, then $\phi(z') > \phi(z)$.

End Point Condition(E): $\phi(0) = 0$ and $\phi(1) = 1$.

Recall that we defined the set of all possible societies to be:

$$\mathbb{U} = \bigcup_{k=1}^{\infty} \mathbb{X}^k$$

and a literacy index as a function from $\mathbb{U}$ to the reals. We will establish the following representation result.

Theorem 1. *Given a decomposable literacy index, $L : \mathbb{U} \to \mathbb{R}$ which satisfies Axioms **N**, **RM**, **PE** and **SI**, there is a function $f : Y \to \mathbb{R}$ satisfying properties **C**, **M** and **E**, such that for any society*

---

[3] Here, the names 'concavity' and 'monotonicity' are deliberately used, even though the domain of ϕ is not an interval of the real line, unlike the usual setting for concave and monotone functions of a real variable.

$\{(r_1, n_1), ..., (r_m, n_m)\} \in \mathbb{U}$, *we have:*

$$L(\{(r_1, n_1), ..., (r_m, n_m)\}) = \sum_{i=1}^{m} (n_i/n)f(r_i/n_i) \qquad (17.3)$$

Conversely, any literacy index $L : \mathbb{U} \to \mathbb{R}$, *defined by (17.3), where* $f :$ $\mathbb{Y} \to \mathbb{R}$ *satisfies properties* **C, M** *and* **E**, *must satisfy Axioms* **N, RM, PE** *and* **SI**.

Proof: The second statement in Theorem 1 is, of course, trivial to verify. So, we proceed to demonstrate the first statement. To this end, given a decomposable literacy index, $L : \mathbb{U} \to \mathbb{R}$, let us associate with it a *literacy measure*, M, defined on $\mathbb{U}$ by:

$$M(\{(r_1, n_1), ..., (r_m, n_m)\}) = L(\{(r_1, n_1), ..., (r_m, n_m)\})(n_1 + \cdots + n_m). \qquad (17.4)$$

Thus, M is also a real-valued function on $\mathbb{U}$. Since L is decomposable (that is, it satisfies (17.2)), M must be *additively separable*; that is, it must satisfy:

$$M(\{(r_1, n_1), ..., (r_m, n_m)\}) = \sum_{i=1}^{m} M(\{(r_i, n_i)\}). \qquad (17.5)$$

We now proceed to infer properties on the literacy measure, M, associated with a decomposable literacy index, L, which satisfies Axioms **N, RM, PE** and **SI**. Using Axiom **N**, it follows that:

$$M(\{(1, 1)\}) = 1, \quad M(\{(0, 1)\}) = 0. \qquad (17.6)$$

Using Axiom **RM**, it follows that:

if $(r, n) \in \mathbb{X}$, and $(r', n) \in \mathbb{X}$, then $M(\{(r', n)\}) > M(\{(r, n)\})$. (17.7)

Using Axiom **PE**, and the additive separability of M, we can infer that:

if $(r_1, n_1), (r_2, n_2) \in \mathbb{X}$, then
$$M(\{(r_1 + r_2, n_1 + n_2)\}) \geq M(\{(r_1, n_1)\}) + M(\{(r_2, n_2)\}). \quad (17.8)$$

Finally, using Axiom **SI**, we can deduce that:

if $(r, n) \in \mathbb{X}$, and $k \in \mathbb{N}$, then $M(\{(kr, kn)\}) = kM(\{(r, n)\})$. (17.9)

Let us now define a function, $F : \mathbb{X} \to \mathbb{R}$ by:

$$F(r, n) = M(\{(r, n)\}). \qquad (17.10)$$

Notice that the domain of F is $\mathbb{X}$, while the domain of M is the set of all societies, $\mathbb{U}$; F is defined by restricting the domain of M to single-household societies.

Given F, one can define a function $f : \mathbb{Y} \to \mathbb{R}$ by:

$$f(z) = F(p, q)/q \text{ where } z = p/q, \text{ and } (p, q) \in \mathbb{X}, \qquad (17.11)$$

as formally demonstrated in the Appendix. Further, it follows from (17.6),(17.7), (17.8) and (17.9) that f satisfies properties **C**, **M** and **E**, by Proposition 1 in the Appendix.

Clearly, (17.10) and (17.11) imply that $[M(\{(r, n)\})/n]$ is a function, f, of the single variable (r/n), and that this function, f, satisfies properties **C**, **M** and **E**. But, by (17.4), $[M(\{(r, n)\})/n]$ is $L(\{(r, n)\})$, and so any decomposable literacy index, L, satisfying the axioms **N**, **RM**, **PE** and **SI** can be written as:

$$L(\{(r_1, n_1), ..., (r_m, n_m)\}) = \sum_{i=1}^{m} (n_i/n) f(r_i/n_i),$$

where $n = (n_1 + \cdots + n_m)$, and $f : \mathbb{Y} \to \mathbb{R}$ satisfies properties **C**, **M** and **E**.

Distribution of Literacy

Our representation theorem shows that any decomposable literacy index of a society (satisfying a set of reasonable axioms) can be written as the weighted sum of a *concave* and *increasing* function of the *literacy rates* of the individual households of that society. This representation has the advantage that it can provide a formal demonstration of one of the principal themes of the recent literature on literacy that 'effective literacy is enhanced by a more, rather than less, equitable distribution of literates across households.' (Subramanian 2008: 839). A particularly appealing aspect of this result (stated formally in Theorem 2) is that its validity does not depend on the choice of a specific literacy index of a society, but applies to the *entire class* of literacy indices of society, satisfying the set of four axioms described in subsection on 'Axioms on Decomposable Literacy Indices'. Specifically, the result states that, given two societies A and B, if the distribution of the literacy rates of the households in society A is more equitable than the distribution of the literacy rates of the households in society B, in the sense of the standard Lorenz quasi-order, then society A has a higher literacy index compared to society B.

Theorem 2. *Let $L : \mathbb{U} \to \mathbb{R}$ be any decomposable literacy index satisfying **Axioms N, RM, PE** and **SI**. Consider two societies, $A = \{(r_1, n_1), ..., (r_m, n_m)\}$ and $B = \{(r_1', n_1'), ..., (r_k', n_k')\}$. Let $n = (n_1 + \cdots + n_m)$, and $n' = (n_1' + \cdots + n_k')$. Define two vectors, x and y, in $\mathbb{Y}^{nn'}$ as follows:*

$$x=(\underbrace{(r_1/n_1), \ldots, (r_1/n_1)}_{n'n_1 \text{ times}}, \underbrace{(r_2/n_2), \ldots, (r_2/n_2)}_{n'n_2 \text{ times}}, \ldots, \underbrace{(r_m/n_m), \ldots, (r_m/n_m)}_{n'n_m \text{ times}})$$

$$y=(\underbrace{(r_1'/n_1'), \ldots, (r_1'/n_1')}_{nn_1' \text{ times}}, \underbrace{(r_2'/n_2'), \ldots, (r_2'/n_2')}_{nn_2' \text{ times}}, \ldots, \underbrace{(r_k'/n_k'), \ldots, (r_k'/n_k')}_{nn_k' \text{ times}}).$$

$$\text{(17.12)}$$

Denote by $\hat{x}$ the increasing rearrangement of x, and by $\hat{y}$ the increasing rearrangement of y. Assume that for each $K \in \{1, \ldots, nn'\}$, the following inequalities hold:

$$\sum_{i=1}^{K} \hat{x}_i \geq \sum_{i=1}^{K} \hat{y}_i \qquad (17.13)$$

Then, we have:

$$L(\{(r_1, n_1), ..., (r_m, n_m)\}) \geq L(\{(r_1', n_1'), ..., (r_k', n_k')\}), \qquad (17.14)$$

that is, society A is at least as literate as society B, according to the literacy index, L.

Proof: Given (17.13), we can apply Proposition 2 of the Appendix to obtain:

$$\sum_{i=1}^{nn'} f(\hat{x}_i) \geq \sum_{i=1}^{nn'} f(\hat{y}_i) \qquad (17.15)$$

whenever $f : \mathbb{Y} \to \mathbb{R}$ satisfies properties **C** and **M**. This can be rewritten as:

$$\sum_{j=1}^{m} (n'n_j)f(r_j/n_j) \geq \sum_{j=1}^{k} (nn_j')f(r_j'/n_j'). \qquad (17.16)$$

Dividing (17.16) by nn', we obtain:

$$\sum_{j=1}^{m} (n_j/n)f(r_j/n_j) \geq \sum_{j=1}^{k} (n_j'/n')f(r_j'/n_j'). \qquad (17.17)$$

Given the literacy index, $L : U \to \mathbb{R}$, we know that there is $f : Y \to \mathbb{R}$ satisfying conditions **C**, **M** and **E**, such that (17.3) holds. Thus, using (17.3) and (17.17), we have:

$$L(\{(r_1, n_1), ..., (r_m, n_m)\}) \geq L(\{(r'_1, n'_1), ..., (r'_k, n'_k)\}).$$

This means, of course, that society A is at least as literate as society B, according to the literacy index, L.

Remark 3. *To illustrate Theorem 2, consider two societies A and B, defined as follows:*

$$A = \{(r_1, n_1), (r_2, n_2), (r_3, n_3)\} = \{(3, 10), (4, 10), (6, 10)\}$$

$$B = \{(r'_1, n'_1), (r'_2, n'_2), (r'_3, n'_3)\} = \{(1, 10), (5, 10), (7, 10)\}$$

The vectors x and y (and $\hat{x}$ and $\hat{y}$) associated with societies A and B respectively are as follows:

$$\hat{x} = x = (\underbrace{(0.3, \dots, 0.3)}_{300 \; times}, \underbrace{(0.4, \dots, 0.4)}_{300 \; times}, \underbrace{(0.6, \dots, 0.6)}_{300 \; times})$$

$$\hat{y} = y = (\underbrace{(0.1, \dots, 0.1)}_{300 \; times}, \underbrace{(0.5, \dots, 0.5)}_{300 \; times}, \underbrace{(0.7, \dots, 0.7)}_{300 \; times})$$

Then, $\hat{x}, \hat{y}$ satisfy (17.13) if and only if the vector $(0.3, 0.4, 0.6)$ Lorenz-dominates the vector $(0.1, 0.5, 0.7)$, which it does, since $0.3 > 0.1$, $0.3 + 0.4 > 0.1 + 0.5$ and $0.3 + 0.4 + 0.6 = 0.1 + 0.5 + 0.7$. Thus, $L(A) \geq L(B)$ for *every* decomposable literacy index L satisfying **Axioms N, RM, PE** and **SI**.

EXTERNALITY FUNCTIONS

We have defined the class of decomposable literacy indices $L : U \to \mathbb{R}$ by:

$$L(\{(r_1, n_1), ..., (r_m, n_m)\}) = \sum_{i=1}^{m} (n_i/n) L(\{(r_i, n_i)\}). \qquad (17.18)$$

Note that for any household $i \in \{1, ..., m\}$, we can write:

$$(n_i/n)L(\{(r_i, n_i)\}) = (n_i/n)[(r_i/n_i) + L(\{(r_i, n_i)\}) - (r_i/n_i)]$$
$$= \frac{n_i[(r_i/n_i) + L(\{(r_i, n_i)\}) - (r_i/n_i)]}{n}$$
$$= \frac{[r_i + n_i L(\{(r_i, n_i)\}) - r_i]}{n}$$
$$\equiv \frac{[r_i + E(r_i, n_i)]}{n}, \qquad (17.19)$$

where we have defined the function $E : \mathbb{X} \to \mathbb{R}$ by:

$$E(r, n) \equiv nL(\{(r, n)\}) - r \text{ for all } (r, n) \in \mathbb{X}. \qquad (17.20)$$

Thus, any decomposable literacy index $L : \mathbb{U} \to \mathbb{R}$ can be written as:

$$L(\{(r_1, n_1), ..., (r_m, n_m)\}) = \frac{\sum_{i=1}^{m}[r_i + E(r_i, n_i)]}{n}, \qquad (17.21)$$

where $n = (n_1 + \cdots + n_m)$, and $E : \mathbb{X} \to \mathbb{R}$ is defined by (17.20).

Conversely, if E is a map from $\mathbb{X}$ to $\mathbb{R}$, and $L : \mathbb{U} \to \mathbb{R}$ is defined by (17.21), then clearly E satisfies (17.20), and:

$$L(\{(r_1, n_1), ..., (r_m, n_m)\}) = \frac{\sum_{i=1}^{m}[r_i + E(r_i, n_i)]}{n}$$
$$= \frac{\sum_{i=1}^{m}[r_i + n_i L(\{(r_i, n_i)\}) - r_i]}{n}$$
$$= \sum_{i=1}^{m}(n_i/n)L(\{(r_i, n_i)\}), \qquad (17.22)$$

so that L is a decomposable literacy index.

Note that the expression (17.21) is valid for any decomposable literacy index $L : \mathbb{U} \to \mathbb{R}$, independent of the four axioms imposed on L discussed earlier. The form (17.21) of decomposable literacy indices is useful for the discussion of externality in measuring literacy, which follows.[4]

Crucial to the representation result stated in Theorem 1, and its principal application (stated in Theorem 2), is the recognition of the fact that the literates in a household bestow on the illiterates of that household

---

[4] If E (defined by [17.20]) happens to be a map from $\mathbb{X}$ to $\mathbb{R}_+$ (that is, it is non-negative on its domain), then it can be interpreted as an intra-household *externality measure*.

an *externality*, so that the effective literacy rate of a household is typically different from the literacy rate measured in the standard way as the percentage of literates in a household. This key observation of Basu and Foster (1998) has been formalised in different ways in the literature on literacy. In our formulation, it appears in the form of the positive externality axiom. Because of the extremely convenient form of the representation of decomposable literacy indices (satisfying **Axioms N, RM, PE and SI**) obtained in Theorem 1, the externality implicit in **Axiom PE** can be given an explicit form. This section is devoted to studying the form of the *class of externality functions*, associated with the class of decomposable literacy indices satisfying **Axioms N, RM, PE and SI**.

Given a decomposable literacy index, $L : \mathbb{U} \to \mathbb{R}$, satisfying the axioms **N, RM, PE and SI**, we can associate an *externality function* with it in the following way. Note that the literacy measure, $M : \mathbb{U} \to \mathbb{R}$, associated with L, satisfies (17.6)–(17.9). Consider any $(r, n) \in \mathbb{X}$. If $r = n$, then clearly $L(\{(r, n)\}) = 1 = (r/n)$. And, if $r = 0$, then $L(\{(r, n)\}) = 0 = (r/n)$. Finally, if $0 < r < n$, then $(n - r) \in \mathbb{N}$, and $r \in \mathbb{N}$, so we have $M(\{(r, n)\}) \geq M(\{(r, r)\}) + M(\{(0, n - r)\})$ (by [17.8]) $= rM(\{(1, 1)\}) + (n - r)M(\{(0, 1)\})$ (by [17.6]) $= r$ (by [17.9]), and $L(\{(r, n)\}) \geq (r/n)$. Thus, we have:

$$L(\{(r, n)\}) \geq (r/n) \text{ for all } (r, n) \in \mathbb{X} \qquad (17.23)$$

and so by (17.20),

$$E(r, n) \geq 0 \text{ for all } (r, n) \in \mathbb{X}.$$

As noted earlier, associated with L is a function, $f : \mathbb{Y} \to \mathbb{R}$, such that $L(\{(r, n)\}) = f(r/n)$ for all $(r, n) \in \mathbb{X}$. We can, therefore, define an *externality function* $e : \mathbb{Y} \to \mathbb{R}$ associated with L as:

$$e(r/n) \equiv f(r/n) - (r/n) = L(\{(r, n)\}) - (r/n) \text{ for all } (r, n) \in \mathbb{X} \quad (17.24)$$

and so by (17.20),

$$E(r, n) = ne(r/n) \text{ for all } (r, n) \in \mathbb{X} \qquad (17.25)$$

Clearly, using (17.23) and (17.24), e is a function from $\mathbb{Y}$ to $\mathbb{R}_+$, and using (17.25), E is a function from $\mathbb{X}$ to $\mathbb{R}_+$. We refer to E as an *externality measure*.

Since f satisfies property **C**, so does e. And, since $f(0) = 0$, while $f(1) = 1$, we have $e(0) = e(1) = 0$. Note that e is *not* a monotone increasing function on $\mathbb{Y}$, but since f is a monotone increasing function on $\mathbb{Y}$, so is the function $e(z) + z$. To summarise, e is a function from $\mathbb{Y}$

to $\mathbb{R}_+$, which satisfies the following:

1. $e(0) = e(1) = 0$
2. $e(z) + z$ satisfies property **M** on $\mathbb{Y}$
3. e satisfies property **C** on $\mathbb{Y}$

$$(17.26)$$

These three properties, in fact, *characterise* externality functions consistent with decomposable literacy indices, satisfying axioms **N, RM, PE** and **SI**. That is, if e is a function from $\mathbb{Y}$ to $\mathbb{R}_+$, which satisfies (17.26), and $E : \mathbb{X} \to \mathbb{R}$ is of the form given in (17.25), then $L : \mathbb{U} \to \mathbb{R}$ defined by (17.21), where $n = (n_1 + \cdots + n_m)$, is a decomposable literacy index which satisfies axioms **N, RM, PE** and **SI**.

To verify this claim, note that since L is defined by (17.21), $E : \mathbb{X} \to \mathbb{R}$ must satisfy (17.20), so that

$$L(\{(r, n)\}) = [E(r, n)/n] + (r/n) = e(r/n) + (r/n) \text{ for all } (r, n) \in \mathbb{X},$$
$$(17.27)$$

the second equality in (17.27) following from (17.25). Further, since L is defined by (17.21), we have:

$$L(\{(r_1, n_1), \ldots, (r_m, n_m)\}) = \sum_{i=1}^{m} (n_i/n)L(\{(r_i, n_i)\}) \qquad (17.28)$$

for all $\{(r_1, n_1), \ldots, (r_m, n_m)\} \in \mathbb{U}$, with $n = (n_1 + \cdots + n_m)$, as verified in (17.22), so that L is a decomposable literacy index. Now, using (17.27), axiom **N** follows from (17.26) (1), axiom **RM** follows from (17.26)(2). Axiom **SI** follows directly from (17.27). To verify axiom **PE**, let (r_1, n_1) and (r_2, n_2) belong to $\mathbb{X}$, and denote $(n_1 + n_2)$ by n. Then,

$$\begin{aligned} L(\{(r_1 + r_2), (n_1 + n_2)\}) &= e((r_1 + r_2)/(n_1 + n_2)) + ((r_1 + r_2)/(n_1 + n_2)) \\ &= e((n_1/n)(r_1/n_1) + (n_2/n)(r_2/n_2)) \\ &\quad + ((n_1/n)(r_1/n_1) + (n_2/n)(r_2/n_2)) \\ &\geq (n_1/n)e(r_1/n_1) + (n_2/n)e(r_2/n_2) \\ &\quad + ((n_1/n)(r_1/n_1) + (n_2/n)(r_2/n_2)) \\ &= (n_1/n)L(\{(r_1, n_1)\}) + (n_2/n)L(\{(r_2, n_2)\}) \\ &= L(\{(r_1, n_1), (r_2, n_2)\}), \end{aligned}$$

where the first equality uses (17.27), the single inequality follows from (17.26)(3), and the last two equalities use (17.27) and (17.28) respectively.

We can summarise the findings in the following characterisation of decomposable literacy indices in terms of externality functions.

Theorem 3. *1. If $L : \mathbb{U} \to \mathbb{R}$ is any decomposable literacy index, then it can be written as:*

$$L(\{(r_1, n_1), ..., (r_m, n_m)\}) = \frac{\sum_{i=1}^{m} [r_i + E(r_i, n_i)]}{n}, \qquad (17.29)$$

where $(n_1 + \cdots + n_m) = n$ and $E : \mathbb{X} \to \mathbb{R}$ is defined by:

$$E(r, n) \equiv nL(\{(r, n)\}) - r \text{ for all } (r, n) \in \mathbb{X}. \qquad (17.30)$$

Conversely, if E is a map from $\mathbb{X}$ to $\mathbb{R}$, and $L : \mathbb{U} \to \mathbb{R}$ is defined by (17.29), then E satisfies (17.30) and L is a decomposable literacy index.

2. If $L : \mathbb{U} \to \mathbb{R}$ is a decomposable literacy index, which satisfies Axioms N, RM, PE and SI, then L can be written as (17.29), where $(n_1 + \cdots + n_m) = n$ and $E : \mathbb{X} \to \mathbb{R}$ is defined by (17.30), and there is a function $e : \mathbb{Y} \to \mathbb{R}_+$ satisfying (17.26), such that $E : \mathbb{X} \to \mathbb{R}$ takes the form:

$$E(r, n) = ne(r/n) \text{ for all } (r, n) \in \mathbb{X} \qquad (17.31)$$

Conversely, if e is a function from $\mathbb{Y}$ to $\mathbb{R}_+$, which satisfies (17.26), and $E : \mathbb{X} \to \mathbb{R}$ is of the form given in (17.31), then $L : \mathbb{U} \to \mathbb{R}$ defined by (17.29), where $n = (n_1 + \cdots + n_m)$, is a decomposable literacy index which satisfies axioms N, RM, PE and SI.

Remark 4.

1. *The traditional index of literacy, the literacy rate, arises by defining the externality function to be: $e(z) = 0$ for all $z \in \mathbb{Y}$. Clearly, this e satisfies (17.26).*
2. *The literacy index used by Basu and Foster (1998) arises by defining the externality function to be: $e(z) = \alpha(1 - z)$ for $z \neq 0$, and $e(0) = 0$, where α is a number in $(0, 1)$. It is easy to verify that this e satisfies (17.26).*
3. *The literacy index proposed by Subramanian (2004: 456) arises by defining the externality function to be: $e(z) = z(1 - z)$. It can be checked that this e satisfies (17.26).*

ALTERNATIVE CHARACTERISATIONS

Alternative axiomatic characterisations of literacy indices have been proposed in the literature, with the aim of generalising the Basu–Foster analysis to appropriate *classes* of externality functions. In this section, we compare our characterisation results, provided in Theorems 1 and 3, with those proposed by Valenti (2002) and Dutta (2004). The basic framework is somewhat different from ours, and the axiom systems used also differ from ours in some respects. It turns out that the characterisation result of Valenti (2002) is essentially similar to the result stated in Theorem 3. In contrast, the result of Dutta (2004) is different from ours in a crucial respect, so that the result on the distribution of literates (contained in our Theorem 2) does not follow from his characterisation. The connection between our analysis (of the second and third sections) and these alternative approaches might provide the reader with a better perspective of axiomatic characterisations of literacy indices.

The Alternative Framework

The framework used by both Valenti (2002) and Dutta (2004) may be presented as follows. A household is described by the number of literates (r) and the number of illiterates (s).[5] This description might appear to be equivalent to the one presented in the second section. However, a difference arises when considering a *change* in literates only in a household. Thus, an increase of literates in a household depicted as (r, n), with n remaining constant, reflects a situation in which some illiterates in the household become literates. On the other hand, an increase of literates in a household depicted as (r, s), with s remaining constant, reflects a situation in which new members are added to the household (so that the total number of persons in the household $(r + s)$ goes up) and all of the newly added members are literates.

Let us define a set:

$$\mathbb{Z} = \{(r, s) \in \mathbb{M} \times \mathbb{M} : (r + s) \in \mathbb{N}\}$$

In this alternative framework, a *household* is a pair $(r, s) \in \mathbb{Z}$. Here r is to be interpreted as the number of *literate* individuals in the household, and s is to be interpreted as the number of *illiterate* individuals in the household. Thus, $n \equiv r + s$ is the total number of individuals in the household.

A *society* is a (non-empty) collection of households; a society consisting of $m \in \mathbb{N}$ households is denoted by the set $\{(r_1, s_1), ..., (r_m, s_m)\}$.

---

[5] Actually, Valenti (2002) employs the more extensive form representation of the household used by Basu and Foster (1998), but her analysis can be adequately presented as described here.

A literacy index is a function from the set of all possible societies to the reals. To formalise this, we define the set of all possible societies to be:

$$\mathbb{V} = \bigcup_{k=1}^{\infty} \mathbb{Z}^k \qquad (17.32)$$

and we define a *literacy index* as a function, $\Lambda : \mathbb{V} \to \mathbb{R}$. We can confine our attention exclusively to *decomposable literacy indices*, that is, those which satisfy:

$$\Lambda(\{(r_1, s_1), ..., (r_m, s_m)\}) = \sum_{i=1}^{m} (n_i/n)\Lambda(\{(r_i, s_i)\}), \qquad (17.33)$$

where $n_i = r_i + s_i$ for all $i \in \{1, ..., m\}$ and $n = (n_1 + \cdots + n_m)$. Both Valenti (2002) and Dutta (2004) impose the restriction (17.33) in their analysis, by including a 'decomposability axiom' in their set of axioms; I prefer not to state it as an axiom, but as a restriction on the scope of the analysis.

To relate this framework to the one we have used in the second section, we can define $L : \mathbb{U} \to \mathbb{R}$ in terms of Λ by:

$$L(\{(r_1, n_1), ..., (r_m, n_m)\}) = \sum_{i=1}^{m} (n_i/n)\Lambda(\{(r_i, n_i - r_i)\}), \qquad (17.34)$$

where $n = (n_1 + \cdots + n_m)$. Then, clearly, we have:

$$L(\{(r, n)\}) = \Lambda(\{(r, n - r)\}) \text{ for all } (r, n) \in \mathbb{X} \qquad (17.35)$$

and so (using (17.34) and (17.35)) $L : \mathbb{U} \to \mathbb{R}$ is decomposable:

$$L(\{(r_1, n_1), ..., (r_m, n_m)\}) = \sum_{i=1}^{m} (n_i/n)L(\{(r_i, n_i)\}) \qquad (17.36)$$

in exactly the sense described in (17.2).

Both Valenti (2002) and Dutta (2004) include a 'normalisation axiom' in their axiom systems;[6] this can be written as:

$$\Lambda(\{(1, 0)\}) = 1; \ \Lambda(\{(0, 1)\}) = 0. \tag{17.37}$$

This translates, using (17.35), to:

$$L(\{(1, 1)\}) = 1; \ L(\{(0, 1)\}) = 0, \tag{17.38}$$

which is precisely our **Axiom N**, described in section 2.3.

Beyond this point, the approaches of Valenti (2002) and Dutta (2004) differ from each other, and we highlight the differences in the next two subsections.

Monotonicity and Equality

Valenti (2002) uses a 'monotonicity axiom' which can be stated as follows:

$$\Lambda(\{(r + 1, s - 1)\}) > \Lambda(\{(r, s)\}) \ \text{for all } (r, s) \in \mathbb{Z} \text{ with } s \in \mathbb{N}, \tag{17.39}$$

that is, the household on the left side of (17.39) is obtained from the household on the right side of (17.39) by a 'simple increment', involving an illiterate becoming literate. Notice that the total number of persons in the household remains unchanged in such a comparison, and we see that (17.39) translates, using (17.35), to:

$$L(\{(r + 1, n)\}) > L(\{(r, n)\}) \ \text{for all } (r, n) \in \mathbb{X}, \text{ with } r < n \tag{17.40}$$

This yields our **Axiom RM**, described earlier, by induction.

---

[6] Actually, Valenti (2002) and Dutta (2004) state a stronger normalisation axiom, which assigns a literacy index of 1 to all households which have only literates, and a literacy index of 0 to all households which have only illiterates. This is superfluous in Valenti's axiom system, because of (17.33) and (17.41) (1). It is superfluous in Dutta's axiom system because of (17.33) and (17.63).

Crucial to Valenti's axiom system is the 'equality axiom', which can be stated as follows.[7] If $(r_1, s_1) \in \mathbb{Z}$, and $(r_2, s_2) \in \mathbb{Z}$, then:

1. $\Lambda(\{\{(r_1+r_2), (s_1+s_2)\}\}) = \Lambda(\{(r_1, s_1), (r_2, s_2)\})$ when $(r_1, s_1) = (r_2, s_2)$

2. $\Lambda(\{\{(r_1+r_2), (s_1+s_2)\}\}) > \Lambda(\{(r_1, s_1), (r_2, s_2)\})$ when $(r_1, s_1) \neq (r_2, s_2)$

(17.41)

Note that (17.41)(1) translates, using (17.33) and (17.34), to the following condition. If $(r_1, n_1) \in \mathbb{X}$ and $(r_2, n_2) \in \mathbb{X}$, then:

$$L(\{\{(r_1 + r_2), (n_1 + n_2)\}\}) = L(\{\{(r_1, n_1), (r_2, n_2)\}\}) \text{ when } (r_1, n_1) = (r_2, n_2).$$

(17.42)

Using (17.36) and (17.42), and using induction, it follows that if $(r, n) \in \mathbb{X}$ and $k \in \mathbb{N}$, then:

$$L(\{\{(kr, kn)\}\}) = L(\{\{(r, n)\}\}),$$ (17.43)

which is our **Axiom SI**, described earlier.

Also, (17.41) implies, using (17.33) and (17.34), that the following condition holds. If $(r_1, n_1) \in \mathbb{X}$ and $(r_2, n_2) \in \mathbb{X}$, then:

$$L(\{\{(r_1 + r_2), (n_1 + n_2)\}\}) \geq L(\{\{(r_1, n_1), (r_2, n_2)\}\}),$$ (17.44)

which is our **Axiom PE**, described earlier. Thus, Valenti's axiom system on $\Lambda : \mathbb{V} \to \mathbb{R}$ implies that $L : \mathbb{U} \to \mathbb{R}$, defined by (17.34), is a decomposable literacy index, which satisfies our axioms **N**, **RM**, **PE** and **SI**.

It follows that, under Valenti's axiom system, the literacy index L (associated with Λ) satisfies (17.3) of Theorem 1 and, therefore, its principal application on the distribution of literacy rates (Theorem 2) holds.

Valenti's principal contribution (contained in her Theorem, p. 14) is a characterisation of literacy indices $\Lambda : \mathbb{V} \to \mathbb{R}$ satisfying the decomposability, normalisation, monotonicity and equality axioms (written as (17.33), (17.37), (17.39) and (17.41)) in terms of *externality functions* $\alpha : \mathbb{Q}_+ \to [0, 1)$ satisfying concavity, monotonicity and an endpoint condition. [See remark (2) following Theorem 4 for a more precise statement].

---

[7] The wording is somewhat different in Valenti (2002). However, note that a single household always satisfies 'perfect literacy equality', according to her terminology. And, the society appearing on the right side of (17.41) satisfies 'perfect literacy equality', when $(r_1, s_1) = (r_2, s_2)$, while it violates 'perfect literacy equality', when $(r_1, s_1) \neq (r_2, s_2)$.

We show how a characterisation result similar to Valenti's can be obtained, by using our characterisation result in Theorem 3. This will clarify the connection between the externality function $e : \mathbb{Y} \to \mathbb{R}_+$ appearing in Theorem 3 and the externality function $\alpha : \mathbb{Q}_+ \to [0, 1)$ which appears in her characterisation result. In accordance with our own axiom system used in the second section, we work with a slightly weaker axiom set than Valenti's. Specifically, we replace her equality axiom (17.41), with the following weaker version.[8] If $(r_1, s_1) \in \mathbb{Z}$, and $(r_2, s_2) \in \mathbb{Z}$, then:

1. $\Lambda(\{(r_1+r_2), (s_1+s_2)\})=\Lambda(\{(r_1, s_1), (r_2, s_2)\})$ when $(r_1, s_1)=(r_2, s_2)$
2. $\Lambda(\{(r_1+r_2), (s_1+s_2)\}) \geq \Lambda(\{(r_1, s_1), (r_2, s_2)\})$ when $(r_1, s_1) \neq (r_2, s_2)$

$$(17.45)$$

Our preference for this weaker version arises from the fact that the characterisation result on the class of literacy indices can thereby accommodate the standard literacy rate and the Basu–Foster literacy index as special cases. (For further elaboration on this point see remark (3) following Theorem 4).

Theorem 4. [Valenti]

1. *Suppose* $\Lambda : \mathbb{V} \to \mathbb{R}$ *is a literacy index satisfying the axioms* *(17.33), (17.34), (17.39) and (17.45). Then,* $\Lambda : \mathbb{V} \to \mathbb{R}$ *can be written as*

$$\Lambda(\{(r_1, s_1), ..., (r_m, s_m)\}) = \frac{\sum_{i=1}^{m}[r_i + \eta(r_i, s_i)]}{n}, \qquad (17.46)$$

where $n_i = r_i + s_i$ *for all* $i \in \{1, ..., m\}$ *and* $(n_1 + \cdots + n_m) = n$ *and* $\eta : \mathbb{Z} \to \mathbb{R}$ *satisfies:*

$$\eta(r, s) = (r + s)\Lambda(\{(r, s)\}) - r \text{ for all } (r, s) \in \mathbb{Z}. \qquad (17.47)$$

Further, there is a function $\alpha : \mathbb{Q}_+ \to [0, 1)$, *satisfying (a)* $\alpha(0) = 0$, *(b) If* $z, z' \in \mathbb{Q}_+$, *and* $z' > z$, *then* $\alpha(z') \geq \alpha(z)$, *(c)* α *satisfies*

---

[8] Note that the weaker axiom set on $\Lambda : \mathbb{V} \to \mathbb{R}$, given by (17.33), (17.37), (17.39) and (17.45), is enough to ensure that $L : \mathbb{U} \to \mathbb{R}$, defined by (17.34), is a decomposable literacy index, which satisfies our axioms N, RM, PE and SI. Thus, under this weaker axiom system, the literacy index L (associated with Λ) satisfies (17.3) of Theorem 1 and, therefore, the result on the distribution of literacy rates (Theorem 2) holds.

property C on $\mathbb{Q}_+$, *such that* $\eta : \mathbb{Z} \to \mathbb{R}$ *takes the form:*

$$\eta(r, s) = \begin{cases} s\alpha(r/s) & \text{for all } (r, s) \in \mathbb{Z}, \text{ with } s \in \mathbb{N} \\ 0 & \text{for all } (r, s) \in \mathbb{Z}, \text{ with } s = 0 \end{cases} \qquad (17.48)$$

2. *Conversely, if there is a function* $\alpha : \mathbb{Q}_+ \to (0, 1)$, *satisfying (a)* $\alpha(0) = 0$; *(b) if* $z, z' \in \mathbb{Q}_+$, *and* $z' > z$, *then* $\alpha(z') \geq \alpha(z)$; *(c)* α *satisfies property C on* $\mathbb{Q}_+$, *and* $\eta : \mathbb{Z} \to \mathbb{R}$ *is of the form given in (17.48), then* $\Lambda : \mathbb{V} \to \mathbb{R}$ *defined by (17.46), where* $n_i = r_i + s_i$ *for all* $i \in \{1, ..., m\}$ *and* $n = (n_1 + \cdots + n_m)$, *is a literacy index which satisfies axioms (17.33), (17.37), (17.39) and (17.45).*

Proof: 1. Given $\Lambda : \mathbb{V} \to \mathbb{R}$ satisfying the axioms (17.33), (17.37), (17.39) and (17.45), we define $L : \mathbb{U} \to \mathbb{R}$ by (17.34) where $n = (n_1 + \cdots + n_m)$. Then, as verified earlier, $L : \mathbb{U} \to \mathbb{R}$ is a decomposable literacy index satisfying axioms **N**, **RM**, **PE** and **SI**. Applying Theorem 3, L can be written as:

$$L(\{(r_1, n_1), ..., (r_m, n_m)\}) = \frac{\sum_{i=1}^{m} [r_i + E(r_i, n_i)]}{n}, \qquad (17.49)$$

where $(n_1 + \cdots + n_m) = n$ and $E : \mathbb{X} \to \mathbb{R}$ is defined by:

$$E(r, n) \equiv nL(\{(r, n)\}) - r \text{ for all } (r, n) \in \mathbb{X}. \qquad (17.50)$$

Further, there is a function $e : \mathbb{Y} \to \mathbb{R}_+$ satisfying (17.27), such that $E : \mathbb{X} \to \mathbb{R}$ takes the form:

$$E(r, n) = ne(r/n) \text{ for all } (r, n) \in \mathbb{X}. \qquad (17.51)$$

Using (17.33), (17.34) and (17.49), $\Lambda : \mathbb{V} \to \mathbb{R}$ can be written as:

$$\Lambda(\{(r_1, s_1), ..., (r_m, s_m)\}) = \frac{\sum_{i=1}^{m} [r_i + \eta(r_i, s_i)]}{n},$$

where $n_i = r_i + s_i$ for all $i \in \{1, ..., m\}$ and $(n_1 + \cdots + n_m) = n$ and $\eta : \mathbb{Z} \to \mathbb{R}$ is defined by:

$$\eta(r, s) = E(r, r + s) \text{ for all } (r, s) \in \mathbb{Z}, \qquad (17.52)$$

Then, by (17.34), (17.40) and (17.52),

$$\eta(r, s) = (r + s)L(\{(r, r + s)\}) - r = (r + s)\Lambda(\{(r, s)\}) - r \text{ for all } (r, s) \in \mathbb{Z},$$

which is (17.47).

Now, define $\alpha : \mathbb{Q}_+ \to \mathbb{R}_+$ by:

$$\alpha(w) = (1 + w)e(w/(1 + w)) \text{ for all } w \in \mathbb{Q}_+$$

Then, since $e : \mathbb{Y} \to \mathbb{R}_+$ satisfies (17.30), Proposition 3 of the Appendix can be used to show that $\alpha : \mathbb{Q}_+ \to \mathbb{R}_+$ maps from $\mathbb{Q}_+$ to $[0, 1)$, and that (a) $\alpha(0) = 0$; (b) If $w, w' \in \mathbb{Q}_+$, and $w' > w$, then $\alpha(w') \geq \alpha(w)$; (c) α satisfies property **C** on $\mathbb{Q}_+$.

Further, using (17.51) and (17.52),

$$\eta(r, s) = E(r, r + s) = (r + s)e(r/(r + s)) \text{ for all } (r, s) \in \mathbb{Z}. \quad (17.53)$$

Thus, for all $(r, s) \in \mathbb{Z}$ with $s = 0$, we have $\eta(r, s) = 0$. And, for all $(r, s) \in \mathbb{Z}$ with $s \in \mathbb{N}$, we have:

$$\eta(r, s)/s = [(r + s)/s]e(r/(r + s)) = \alpha(r/s) \text{ for all } (r, s) \in \mathbb{Z}$$

which establishes (17.48).

2. Since $\alpha : \mathbb{Q}_+ \to (0, 1)$, satisfies (a) $\alpha(0) = 0$; (b) If $z, z' \in \mathbb{Q}_+$, and $z' > z$, then $\alpha(z') \geq \alpha(z)$; (c) α satisfies property **C** on $\mathbb{Q}_+$, Proposition 4 in the Appendix can be applied to show that the function $e : \mathbb{Y} \to \mathbb{R}_+$ defined by:

$$e(z) = \begin{cases} \alpha(z/(1 - z))(1 - z) & \text{for } z \neq 1 \\ 0 & \text{for } z = 1 \end{cases} \quad (17.54)$$

has the following properties: (a) $e(0) = e(1) = 0$, (b) $e(z) + z$ satisfies property **M** on $\mathbb{Y}$, (c) e satisfies property **C** on $\mathbb{Y}$. Thus, by (2) of Theorem 3, if $E : \mathbb{X} \to \mathbb{R}$ is defined by:

$$E(r, n) = ne(r/n) \text{ for all } (r, n) \in \mathbb{X} \quad (17.55)$$

and $L : \mathbb{U} \to \mathbb{R}$ is defined as:

$$L(\{(r_1, n_1), ..., (r_m, n_m)\}) = \frac{\sum_{i=1}^{m}[r_i + E(r_i, n_i)]}{n}, \quad (17.56)$$

where $(n_1 + \cdots + n_m) = n$, then $L : \mathbb{U} \to \mathbb{R}$ is a decomposable literacy index which satisfies axioms **N, RM, PE** and **SI**.

Since $\eta : \mathbb{Z} \to \mathbb{R}$ is of the form (17.48), we must have for all $(r, s) \in \mathbb{Z}$ with $s \in \mathbb{N}$,

$$\frac{\eta(r, s)}{(r + s)} = \frac{s}{(r + s)}\alpha(r/s) = \frac{(n - r)}{n}\alpha(r/(n - r))$$

$$= (1 - \frac{r}{n})\alpha\left(\frac{(r/n)}{1 - (r/n)}\right) = e(r/n) = \frac{E(r, n)}{n}, \quad (17.57)$$

where $n = r + s$, and we have used (17.54) and (17.55) in the second line of (17.57). Also, for all $(r, s) \in \mathbb{Z}$ with $s = 0$, we have:

$$\frac{\eta(r, s)}{(r + s)} = \frac{\eta(r, 0)}{r} = 0 = \frac{E(n, n)}{n} = \frac{E(r, n)}{n}, \qquad (17.58)$$

where $n = r + s = r$.

Since $\Lambda : \mathbb{V} \to \mathbb{R}$ is defined by (17.46), where $n_i = r_i + s_i$ for all $i \in \{1, ..., m\}$ and $n = (n_1 + \cdots + n_m)$, we must have:

$$\eta(r, s) = (r + s)\Lambda(\{(r, s)\}) - r \text{ for all } (r, s) \in \mathbb{Z}, \qquad (17.59)$$

so using this in (17.46), we see that (17.33) must hold. Further, we obtain by using (17.57) and (17.58),

$$\Lambda(\{(r_1, s_1), ..., (r_m, s_m)\}) = \frac{\sum_{i=1}^{m}[r_i + \eta(r_i, s_i)]}{n} = \frac{\sum_{i=1}^{m}[r_i + E(r_i, n_i)]}{n}$$
$$= L(\{(r_1, n_1), ..., (r_m, n_m)\}). \qquad (17.60)$$

It remains to verify that Λ satisfies (17.37), (17.39) and (17.45). Since L satisfies axiom **N**, we obtain from (17.60) that $\Lambda(\{(1, 0)\}) = L(\{(1, 1)\}) = 1$ and $\Lambda(\{(0, 1)\}) = L(\{(0, 1)\}) = 0$, so that (17.37) must hold. Since L satisfies axiom **RM**, we obtain from (17.60) that for all $(r, s) \in \mathbb{Z}$ with $s \in \mathbb{N}$,

$$\Lambda(\{(r + 1, s - 1)\}) = L(\{(r + 1, r + s)\}) > L(\{(r, r + s)\}) = \Lambda(\{(r, s)\})$$

so that (17.39) must hold. Since L satisfies axiom **SI**, when $(r_1, s_1) \in \mathbb{Z}$, and $(r_2, s_2) \in \mathbb{Z}$, with $(r_1, s_1) = (r_2, s_2)$, we obtain from (17.60):

$$\Lambda(\{(r_1 + r_2), (s_1 + s_2)\})$$
$$= \Lambda(\{(2r_1, 2s_1)\}) = L(\{(2r_1, 2r_1 + 2s_1)\})$$
$$= L(\{(r_1, r_1 + s_1)\}) = (\tfrac{1}{2})L(\{(r_1, r_1 + s_1)\}) + (\tfrac{1}{2})L(\{(r_2, r_2 + s_2)\})$$
$$= (\tfrac{1}{2})\Lambda(\{(r_1, s_1)\}) + (\tfrac{1}{2})\Lambda(\{(r_2, s_2)\}) = \Lambda(\{(r_1, s_1)\}, \{(r_2, s_2)\}),$$
$$(17.61)$$

where we have used the fact that Λ satisfies (17.33) in the third line of (17.61). Thus, (17.45)(1) must hold. Finally, since L satisfies axiom **PE**, when $(r_1, s_1) \in \mathbb{Z}$, and $(r_2, s_2) \in \mathbb{Z}$, with $(r_1, s_1) \neq (r_2, s_2)$, we obtain from (17.60):

$$\Lambda(\{(r_1 + r_2), (s_1 + s_2)\}) = L(\{(r_1 + r_2), (n_1 + n_2)\})$$
$$\geq L(\{(r_1, n_1), (r_2, n_2)\}) = \Lambda(\{(r_1, s_1), (r_2, s_2)\}),$$

where we have denoted $(r_1 + s_1)$ by n_1 and $(r_2 + s_2)$ by n_2. Thus, (17.45)(2) must hold.

Remark 5.

1. *The externality functions $e : \mathbb{Y} \to \mathbb{R}_+$ and $\alpha : \mathbb{Q}_+ \to [0, 1)$ appearing in Theorems 3 and 4 respectively can be interpreted as follows. If (r, n) is a household, then the total externality generated (by the literates on the illiterates) is measured by $e(r/n)$. If there are some illiterates in the household, so that $s \equiv n - r \neq 0$, then $\alpha(r/s) \equiv \alpha(r/(n - r))$ measures the externality generated as a proportion of the fraction who are illiterate in the household. Thus, if the household is $(r, n) = (2, 3)$, then the fraction of the illiterates in the household is $(1/3)$, and $\alpha(r/s) = \alpha(2)$ measures $[e(2/3)/(1/3)]$. Note that $\alpha(r/s)$ does not measure the externality per illiterate. For the household $(r, n) = (2, 3)$, the externality per illiterate is $e(2/3)$ itself, since there is only one illiterate, while $\alpha(r/s) = \alpha(2) = e(2/3)/(1/3)$.*

    The relationship between the functions $e : \mathbb{Y} \to \mathbb{R}_+$ and $\alpha : \mathbb{Q}_+ \to [0, 1)$ is used in the proof of Theorem 4, which relates them technically. This can be conveniently illustrated with the specific externality function $\alpha : \mathbb{Q}_+ \to [0, 1)$ proposed by Subramanian (2004: 456), where $\alpha(y) = y/(1 + y)$; that is,

$$\alpha(r/s) = \frac{r}{r + s} = \frac{(r/s)}{(r/s) + 1}.$$

    The corresponding externality function $e : \mathbb{Y} \to \mathbb{R}_+$ is then given by:

$$e(z) = (1 - z)\alpha\left(\frac{z}{1 - z}\right) = (1 - z)z \ \text{ so that } e(r/n) = \frac{r}{n}\left(1 - \frac{r}{n}\right)$$

    and

$$ne(r/n) = \frac{r(n - r)}{n} = \frac{rs}{r + s} = s\alpha(r/s).$$

2. *The statement of the actual characterisation theorem presented in Valenti (2002: 14) differs from the statement of Theorem 4 in the following respects. The equality axiom (17.45) is replaced by the stronger equality axiom (17.41) in Valenti's Theorem. Further, for the class of externality functions $\alpha : \mathbb{Q}_+ \to [0, 1)$, property (b) is replaced by the stronger property:*

    (b+) If $z, z' \in \mathbb{Q}_+$, and $z' > z$, then $\alpha(z') > \alpha(z)$

and property (c) is replaced by the stronger property:

(c+) *If* $z, z' \in \mathbb{Q}_+$, *with* $z \neq z'$, *and* $t \in Y$, *then* $\alpha(tz + (1 - t)z')$
$> t\alpha(z) + (1 - t)\alpha(z')$

in Valenti's theorem.

3. *The traditional index of literacy, the literacy rate, arises by defining the externality function (in Theorem 4) to be:* $\alpha(z) = 0$ *for all* $z \in \mathbb{Q}_+$. *This* α *does not satisfy property* (b+), *and it also does not satisfy property* (c+). *Similarly, the literacy index used by Basu and Foster (1998) arises by defining the externality function (in Theorem 4) to be:* $\alpha(z) = \alpha$ *for all* $z \in \mathbb{Q}_{++}$ *and* $\alpha(z) = 0$ *for* $z = 0$. *Thus, this* α *also violates property* (b+) *and property* (c+).

4. *Valenti's characterisation is in terms of externality functions,* α, *defined on the ratio* (r/s), *the ratio of literates to* illiterates *in a household, rather than on* (r/n), *the literacy rate of the household. This makes it difficult to see the literacy ranking result of Theorem 2 directly* from *her characterisation theorem, or from Theorem 4.*

Weak Externality

Dutta (2004) examines literacy indices which satisfy decomposability (that is, [17.33]) and the normalisation axiom (that is, [17.37]), and imposes in addition a *weak externality* axiom. We will find it convenient to present this axiom in two parts.

The first part of the weak externality axiom can be stated as follows.

$$\left.\begin{array}{l} 1.\ \Lambda(\{(r_1 + r_2, 0)\}) = \Lambda(\{(r_1, 0), (r_2, 0)\}) \text{ when } (r_1, 0), (r_2, 0) \in Z \\ 2.\ \Lambda(\{(0, s_1 + s_2)\}) = \Lambda(\{(0, s_1), (0, s_2)\}) \text{ when } (0, s_1), (0, s_2) \in Z \end{array}\right\} \tag{17.62}$$

So, when a household consisting only of literates is split up into two households, this is an 'externality neutral' split and, therefore there is no loss of literacy from such a split. A similar explanation holds if a household consisting only of illiterates is split in two.

Given the decomposability of Λ, and the normalisation axiom, it is easy to verify by induction that (17.62) is equivalent to:

$$\Lambda(\{(r, 0)\}) = 1 \text{ for all } r \in \mathbb{N}; \ \Lambda(\{(0, s)\}) = 0 \text{ for all } s \in \mathbb{N} \tag{17.63}$$

that is, it combines the normalisation axiom (17.37) with a scale invariance property for some particular single household societies.

The second part of the weak externality axiom considers a split of a household which has both literates and illiterates. If the household is split up into two households in such a way that one of these two households has all the illiterates (that is, only the literates are split up), then this is an 'externality reducing' split and, consequently, there is a loss of literacy when such a split occurs.

$$\Lambda(\{(r_1 + r_2, s)\}) > \Lambda(\{(r_1, s), (r_2, 0)\}) \text{ when } (r_1, s), (r_2, 0) \in \mathbb{Z}, s \in \mathbb{N}$$
(17.64)

Note that this is a strictly weaker restriction than that imposed in (17.41)(2) (the second part of the equality axiom) by Valenti (2002). It is not directly comparable to (17.45)(2) because of the weak inequality in that version of the equality axiom.

Literacy indices satisfying (17.33), (17.37), (17.62) and (17.64) (that is, the decomposability, normalisation and weak externality axioms) have been characterised by Dutta (2004: 75; Theorem 1) in terms of a class of externality functions. We can state and prove his result as follows.

Theorem 5. [Dutta] 1. *Suppose* $\Lambda : V \to \mathbb{R}$ *is a literacy index satisfying the axioms (17.33), (17.37), (17.62) and (17.64). Then,* $\Lambda : V \to \mathbb{R}$ *can be written as*

$$\Lambda(\{(r_1, s_1), ..., (r_m, s_m)\}) = \frac{\sum_{i=1}^{m} [r_i + a(r_i, s_i)]}{n}, \qquad (17.65)$$

where $n_i = r_i + s_i$ *for all* $i \in \{1, ..., m\}$ *and* $(n_1 + \cdots + n_m) = n$ *and* $a : \mathbb{Z} \to \mathbb{R}$ *is defined by:*

$$a(r, s) = (r + s)\Lambda(\{(r, s)\}) - r \text{ for all } (r, s) \in \mathbb{Z}. \qquad (17.66)$$

Further, $a : \mathbb{Z} \to \mathbb{R}$, *satisfies (a)* $a(r, 0) = 0 = a(0, s)$ *for all* $r, s \in \mathbb{N}$; *(b)* $a(r, s) \geq 0$ *for all* $(r, s) \in \mathbb{Z}$; *(c)* $a(r + r', s) > a(r, s)$ *for all* $(r, s) \in \mathbb{Z}$, *and* $(r', s) \in \mathbb{N}^2$.

2. *Conversely, if there is a function* $a : \mathbb{Z} \to \mathbb{R}$, *satisfying (a)* $a(r, 0) = 0 = a(0, s)$ *for all* $r, s \in \mathbb{N}$; *(b)* $a(r, s) \geq 0$ *for all* $(r, s) \in \mathbb{Z}$; *(c)* $a(r + r', s) > a(r, s)$ *for all* $(r, s) \in \mathbb{Z}$, *and* $(r', s) \in \mathbb{N}^2$, *then* $\Lambda : V \to \mathbb{R}$ *defined by (17.65), where* $n_i = r_i + s_i$ *for all* $i \in \{1, ..., m\}$ *and* $n = (n_1 + \cdots + n_m)$, *is a literacy index which satisfies axioms (17.33), (17.37), (17.62) and (17.64).*

Proof: 1. Since $\Lambda : V \to \mathbb{R}$ is a literacy index satisfying (17.33), we can write (using the notation $n_i = r_i + s_i$ for all $i \in \{1, ..., m\}$ and

$$n = (n_1 + \cdots + n_m)),$$

$$\Lambda(\{(r_1, s_1), ..., (r_m, s_m)\}) = \sum_{i=1}^{m} (n_i/n)\Lambda(\{(r_i, s_i)\})$$

$$= \frac{\sum_{i=1}^{m}[r_i + n_i\Lambda(\{(r_i, s_i)\}) - r_i]}{n}$$

$$= \frac{\sum_{i=1}^{m}[r_i + a(r_i, s_i)]}{n}, \tag{17.67}$$

where $a : \mathbb{Z} \to \mathbb{R}$ is defined by (17.66). Thus, it only remains to verify the properties $(a),(b)$ and (c) of the function a.

Using (17.33), (17.37) and (17.62), we know that (17.63) must hold. Using (17.63), (a) follows from (17.66). To verify (b), note that this is clearly true when $(r, s) \in \mathbb{Z}$ and either $r = 0$ or $s = 0$, by using (a). Thus, consider $(r, s) \in \mathbb{Z}$ with $(r, s) \in \mathbb{N}^2$. Then, by (17.33) and (17.64),

$$\Lambda(\{(r, s)\}) > \Lambda(\{(r, 0), (0, s)\})$$

$$= \frac{r}{r+s}\Lambda(\{(r, 0)\}) + \frac{s}{r+s}\Lambda(\{(0, s)\})$$

$$= \frac{r}{r+s}, \tag{17.68}$$

the last line of (17.68) following from (17.63). Now, it follows from (17.66) that $a(r, s) > 0$. This establishes (b).

To establish (c), note that for $(r, s) \in \mathbb{Z}$, and $(r', s) \in \mathbb{N}^2$, we have by (17.33) and (17.64),

$$\Lambda(\{(r + r', s)\}) > \Lambda(\{(r, s), (r', 0)\})$$

$$= \frac{r+s}{r+r'+s}\Lambda(\{(r, s)\}) + \frac{r'}{r+r'+s}\Lambda(\{(r', 0)\})$$

$$= \frac{r+s}{r+r'+s}\Lambda(\{(r, s)\}) + \frac{r'}{r+r'+s}. \tag{17.69}$$

Thus, we get, from (17.66) and (17.69),

$$a(r + r', s) = (r + r' + s)\Lambda(\{(r + r', s)\}) - (r + r')$$

$$> (r + s)\Lambda(\{(r, s)\}) + r' - (r + r')$$

$$= (r + s)\Lambda(\{(r, s)\}) - r = a(r, s)$$

which proves property (c).

2. Since $\Lambda : \mathbb{V} \to \mathbb{R}$ is defined by (17.65), where $n_i = r_i + s_i$ for all $i \in \{1, ..., m\}$ and $n = (n_1 + \cdots + n_m)$, we know that $a : \mathbb{Z} \to \mathbb{R}$ must

satisfy (17.66). Using (17.66) in (17.65), we obtain:

$$\Lambda(\{(r_1, s_1), ..., (r_m, s_m)\}) = \sum_{i=1}^{m} (n_i/n)\Lambda(\{(r_i, s_i)\})$$

so that Λ satisfies (17.33). Given property (a) of a, we get (17.63) directly by using (17.66). This establishes (17.37) as well as (17.62) since, as we have already noted under (17.33), the conditions (17.62) and (17.63) are equivalent.

It remains to establish (17.64). When $(r_1, s), (r_2, 0) \in \mathbb{Z}, s \in \mathbb{N}$, we have by property (c) of a,

$$\begin{aligned}
(r_1 + r_2 + s)\Lambda(\{(r_1 + r_2, s)\}) - (r_1 + r_2) &= a(r_1 + r_2, s) \\
&> a(r_1, s) \\
&= (r_1 + s)\Lambda(\{(r_1, s)\}) - r_1
\end{aligned}$$

$$(17.70)$$

so that, by using (17.33), (17.63) and (17.70),

$$\begin{aligned}
\Lambda(\{(r_1 + r_2, s)\}) &> \frac{(r_1 + s)}{(r_1 + r_2 + s)}\Lambda(\{(r_1, s)\}) + \frac{r_2}{(r_1 + r_2 + s)} \\
&= \frac{(r_1 + s)}{(r_1 + r_2 + s)}\Lambda(\{(r_1, s)\}) + \frac{r_2}{(r_1 + r_2 + s)}\Lambda(\{(r_2, 0)\}) \\
&= \Lambda(\{(r_1, s), (r_2, 0)\}),
\end{aligned}$$

which proves (17.64).

Comparing Theorems 4 and 5, and, therefore, the functions $\eta : \mathbb{Z} \to \mathbb{R}$ and $a : \mathbb{Z} \to \mathbb{R}$, we see that the crucial difference is that in Theorem 4, one gets η in the form described in (17.48), where α is a concave, non-decreasing function on $\mathbb{Q}_+$, and there is no such corresponding restriction on the function a in Theorem 5. It is this feature of Theorem 4 which ensures that the literacy index $\Lambda : \mathbb{V} \to \mathbb{R}$ satisfies the monotonicity and equality axioms, and, consequently, the corresponding literacy index $L : \mathbb{U} \to \mathbb{R}$ satisfies axioms N, SI, RM and PE. This, in turn, implies that the literacy index L satisfies Theorem 1, and its principal application on the distribution of literacy rates (Theorem 2) holds. This important application, that a more equal distribution of literacy rates across households produces a higher overall literacy index for society, *cannot* be derived from Theorem 5.

We can make this point more precise by specifying a particular choice of the function $a : \mathbb{Z} \to \mathbb{R}$ as follows:

$$a(r, s) = \frac{sr^2}{r^2 + s^2} \quad \text{for all } (r, s) \in \mathbb{Z} \tag{17.71}$$

It is easy to check then that $a : \mathbb{Z} \to \mathbb{R}$ satisfies properties $(a),(b)$ and (c) listed in Theorem 5. Thus, if we now define $\Lambda : V \to \mathbb{R}$ by (17.35), where $n_i = r_i + s_i$ for all $i \in \{1, ..., m\}$ and $n = (n_1 + \cdots + n_m)$, then Λ is a literacy index which satisfies all of Dutta's axioms, namely, (17.33), (17.37), (17.62) and (17.64), by directly applying Theorem 5.

For a two-household society $\{(r_1, s_1), (r_2, s_2)\}$, we would then have (by (17.65)):

$$n\Lambda(\{(r_1, s_1), (r_2, s_2)\}) = \left[r_1 + \frac{s_1 r_1^2}{r_1^2 + s_1^2} \right] + \left[r_2 + \frac{s_2 r_2^2}{r_2^2 + s_2^2} \right]. \quad (17.72)$$

Consider now two societies specified as follows:

$$\left. \begin{array}{l} 1.\ \{(r_1, s_1), (r_2, s_2)\} = \{(1, 19), (3, 17)\} \\ 2.\ \{(r_1', s_1'), (r_2', s_2')\} = \{(2, 18), (2, 18)\} \end{array} \right\} \quad (17.73)$$

Note that in the second society, there is complete equality in the literacy rates in the two households. In the first society, the literacy rates clearly differ among the households, with the second household having a higher literacy rate. Now, using the formula (17.72), one can easily verify that:

$$\Lambda(\{(r_1, s_1), (r_2, s_2)\}) = 4.56 \text{ and } \Lambda(\{(r_1', s_1'), (r_2', s_2')\}) = 4.43$$

so that the society with the more *unequal* distribution of literacy rates has a higher overall literacy index.

APPENDIX: MATHEMATICAL CONCEPTS AND RESULTS

Here, we provide an exposition of the mathematical concepts and results used in the second, third and fourth sections of the essay. We have tried to keep the exposition entirely elementary and self-contained. The reader who is familiar with the standard results on concave functions on the real line will be able to shorten the exposition considerably.

Super-Additive and Concave Functions

In the standard mathematical theory of convex functions, it is known that *gauge functions* defined on convex cones are also convex functions.[9] Thus, for example, if F is a gauge function on $\mathbb{R}_+^2$ (that is, F is sub-additive and homogeneous of degree one), then F is convex on $\mathbb{R}_+^2$. This

---

[9] See, for example, Green (1954), Roberts and Varberg (1973) and Rosenbaum (1950).

means that the function $f(z) = F(z, 1)$ is a convex function of z, for $z \in \mathbb{R}_+$. A similar theory can be developed for functions, defined on a subset of $\mathbb{M}^2$, where $\mathbb{M}$ is the set of non-negative integers.[10]

Let $\mathbb{N}$ denote the set of natural numbers $\{1, 2, 3, \ldots\}$, and let $\mathbb{M}$ denote the set $\{0, 1, 2, 3, \ldots\}$. We define the set $\mathbb{X} = \{(x, y) : x \in \mathbb{M}, y \in \mathbb{N}$, and $x \le y\}$. Let $\mathbb{Q}$ denote the set of rational numbers, and $\mathbb{R}$ the set of real numbers. We denote by $\mathbb{Q}_+$ the set of non-negative rational numbers $\{z = p/q$, where $p \in \mathbb{M}$, and $q \in \mathbb{N}\}$, and by $\mathbb{Y}$ the set $\mathbb{Q} \cap [0, 1]$; the set $\mathbb{Q} \cap (0, 1)$ is denoted by Y.

Let F be a function from $\mathbb{X}$ to $\mathbb{R}$. Consider the following properties, which may be satisfied by such a function:

Homogeneity of Degree One(H): If $(x, y) \in \mathbb{X}$, and $t \in \mathbb{N}$, then $F(tx, ty) = tF(x, y)$.

Super Additivity (SA): If $(x, y) \in \mathbb{X}$, and $(x', y') \in \mathbb{X}$, then $F(x + x', y + y') \ge F(x, y) + F(x', y')$.

X-Monotonicity (XM): If $(x, y) \in \mathbb{X}$, and $(x', y) \in \mathbb{X}$, with $x' > x$, then $F(x', y) > F(x, y)$.

Origin and Scale (OS): $F(1, 1) = 1$, $F(0, 1) = 0$.

Given any $F : \mathbb{X} \to \mathbb{R}$, satisfying **H**, we can define $f : \mathbb{Y} \to \mathbb{R}$ as follows:

$$f(z) = F(p, q)/q \quad \text{where} \quad z = (p/q), \text{ with } (p, q) \in \mathbb{X} \quad (17.74)$$

Note that the function, f, is well defined by (17.73). For, if $z = (p/q)$, with $(p, q) \in \mathbb{X}$, and if z is also equal to (p'/q'), with $(p', q') \in \mathbb{X}$, then we have $F(p', q')/q' = qF(p', q')/qq' = F(qp', qq')/qq'$ (by **H**) $= F(pq', qq')/qq' = q'F(p, q)/qq'$ (by **H**) $= F(p, q)/q$.

Suppose $F : \mathbb{X} \to \mathbb{R}$ satisfies properties **H, SA, XM** and **OS**. We can show that the function, $f : \mathbb{Y} \to \mathbb{R}$ must satisfy the following properties:[11]

Concavity (C): If $z, z' \in \mathbb{Y}$, and $t \in Y$, then $f(tz + (1 - t)z') \ge tf(z) + (1 - t)f(z')$.

---

[10] Properties of such functions, discussed later, are called by familiar names such as 'homogeneity of degree one', 'super-additivity', even though the domains are restricted. This is deliberately done to show the similarity of the theory presented here to the one usually developed for domains not so restricted.

[11] Here, as indicated in an earlier footnote, the terms 'concavity' and 'monotonicity' are deliberately used, even though the domain of f is not an interval of the real line, unlike the usual setting for concave and monotone functions of a real variable.

Monotonicity (M): If $z, z' \in \mathbb{Y}$, and $z' > z$, then $f(z') > f(z)$.
End Point Condition (E): $f(0) = 0$ and $f(1) = 1$.

Conversely, given any $f : \mathbb{Y} \to \mathbb{R}$, we can associate with it a function, $F : \mathbb{X} \to \mathbb{R}$, defined as follows:

$$F(p, q) = qf(p/q) \quad \text{where} \quad (p, q) \in \mathbb{X} \qquad (17.75)$$

If $f : \mathbb{Y} \to \mathbb{R}$ satisfies the properties **C**, **M** and **E**, then we can show that the associated function, $F : \mathbb{X} \to \mathbb{R}$, defined by (17.75), satisfies properties **H**, **SA**, **XM** and **OS**.

We summarise this discussion in the following proposition.

Proposition 1. *(a) Suppose $F : \mathbb{X} \to \mathbb{R}$ satisfies properties H, SA, XM and OS. Then, the function, $f : \mathbb{Y} \to \mathbb{R}$, defined by (17.74), satisfies properties C, M and E. (b) Suppose $f : \mathbb{Y} \to \mathbb{R}$ satisfies properties C, M and E. Then, the function, $F : \mathbb{X} \to \mathbb{R}$, defined by (17.75), satisfies properties H, SA, XM and OS.*

Majorisation Theory

In the standard theory of convex functions, defined on convex subsets of the real line, the class of functions which are convex and monotone is of special significance because a very useful *majorisation* theory can be developed for it. The main result of this theory is known as the Tomic–Weyl theorem.[12] Something similar can be achieved for functions, $f : \mathbb{Y} \to \mathbb{R}$, which satisfy properties **C** and **M**. We summarise this theory in the following proposition.

Proposition 2. *Let z and z' be vectors in $\mathbb{Y}^n$, such that $z_1 \leq z_2 \leq \ldots \leq z_n$, and $z'_1 \leq z'_2 \leq \ldots \leq z'_n$. Let $f : \mathbb{Y} \to \mathbb{R}$ be a function satisfying properties C and M. Suppose, for each integer $k \in \{1, 2, ..., n\}$, we have:*

$$\sum_{i=1}^{k} z'_i \leq \sum_{i=1}^{k} z_i. \qquad (17.76)$$

Then, we must have:

$$\sum_{i=1}^{n} f(z'_i) \leq \sum_{i=1}^{n} f(z_i). \qquad (17.77)$$

---

[12] See, for example, Mitrinovic-Vasic (1970: 165) for this result, as well as some of the important variations of it.

Remark: In Proposition 2, if there is a strict inequality in (17.76) when $k = n$, then we can infer that (17.77) must also hold with a strict inequality, by using property **M** of the function f.

Concave and Monotone Functions
In this subsection, we note two results relating to two classes of concave and monotone functions. These results are used to establish Theorem 4.

Proposition 3. *Suppose $e : \mathbb{Y} \to \mathbb{R}_+$ is a function such that (a) $e(0) = e(1) = 0$, (b) $e(z) + z$ satisfies property **M** on $\mathbb{Y}$ and (c) e satisfies property **C** on $\mathbb{Y}$. Then, $\alpha : \mathbb{Q}_+ \to \mathbb{R}_+$, defined by:*

$$\alpha(w) = (1 + w)e(w/(1 + w))$$

*satisfies: (a) $\alpha(0) = 0$, (b) If $w, w' \in \mathbb{Q}_+$, and $w' > w$, then $\alpha(w') \geq \alpha(w)$ and (c) α satisfies property **C** on $\mathbb{Q}_+$. Further, α maps from $\mathbb{Q}_+$ to $[0, 1)$.*

Proposition 4. *Suppose α is a function from $\mathbb{Q}_+$ to $[0, 1)$, such that: (a) $\alpha(0) = 0$, (b) if $w, w' \in \mathbb{Q}_+$, and $w' > w$, then $\alpha(w') \geq \alpha(w)$ and (c) α satisfies property **C** on $\mathbb{Q}_+$. If $e : \mathbb{Y} \to \mathbb{R}_+$ is a function defined as follows:*

$$e(z) = \begin{cases} \alpha(z/(1 - z))(1 - z) & \text{for } z \neq 1 \\ 0 & \text{for } z = 1 \end{cases}$$

*then (a) $e(0) = e(1) = 0$, (b) $e(z) + z$ satisfies property **M** on $\mathbb{Y}$ and (c) e satisfies property **C** on $\mathbb{Y}$.*

Proofs
In this section, the proofs of the mathematical results of the previous three subsections are presented.

Proof of Proposition 1. 1. Suppose $F : \mathbb{X} \to \mathbb{R}$ satisfies properties **H**, **SA**, **XM** and **OS**. Define the function, $f : \mathbb{Y} \to \mathbb{R}$ by (17.74). Then, we have $f(0) = F(0, 1) = 0$ and $f(1) = F(1, 1) = 1$ by **OS**, so property **E** is verified.

To verify property **M**, let $z, z' \in \mathbb{Y}$, with $z' > z$. Then there exist $(p, q) \in \mathbb{X}$ and $(p', q') \in \mathbb{X}$, with $z' = (p'/q')$ and $z = (p/q)$. Then, we have $qq' \in \mathbb{N}$, $pq' \in \mathbb{M}$, $p'q \in \mathbb{M}$ and $pq' < p'q \leq q'q$. Thus, we can write $f(z') = f(p'/q') = f(p'q/q'q) = F(p'q, q'q)/q'q > F(pq', qq')/qq' = f(pq'/qq') = f(p/q) = f(z)$, the inequality following from property **XM** of F.

To verify property **C**, let $z, z' \in \mathbb{Y}$, and $t \in Y$. Then there exist $(p, q) \in \mathbb{X}$, $(p', q') \in \mathbb{X}$ and $(s, r) \in \mathbb{X}$, with $z = (p/q)$, $z' = (p'/q')$ and $t = (s/r)$.

Then, we have:

$$f(tz + (1-t)z') = f\left(\frac{spq'}{rqq'} + \frac{(r-s)p'q}{rq'q}\right)$$

$$= f\left(\frac{spq' + (r-s)p'q}{rqq'}\right)$$

$$= F(spq' + (r-s)p'q, rqq')/rqq'$$

$$= F(spq' + (r-s)p'q, sqq' + (r-s)qq')/rqq'$$

$$\geq \frac{F(spq', sqq') + F((r-s)p'q, (r-s)qq')}{rqq'}$$

$$= \frac{sq'F(p,q)}{rqq'} + \frac{(r-s)qF(p',q')}{rqq'}$$

$$= (s/r)\frac{F(p,q)}{q} + (1 - (s/r))\frac{F(p',q')}{q'}$$

$$= (s/r)f(p/q) + (1 - (s/r))f(p'/q')$$

$$= tf(z) + (1-t)f(z'),$$

where property **SA** of F is used to obtain the inequality, and property **H** of F is used in the very next line in the previous computations.

2. To establish the converse, given any $f : \mathbb{Y} \to \mathbb{R}$, satisfying properties **C**, **M** and **E**, we associate with it a function, $F : \mathbb{X} \to \mathbb{R}$, defined by (17.75). Then, $F(1,1) = f(1) = 1$, and $F(0,1) = f(0) = 0$, verifying property **OS** of F.

To verify property **H** of F, let $(x,y) \in \mathbb{X}$ and $t \in \mathbb{N}$. Then, $(tx, ty) \in \mathbb{X}$ and $F(tx, ty) = tyf(tx/ty) = tyf(x/y) = tF(x,y)$.

To verify property **XM** of F, let $(x,y) \in \mathbb{X}$ and $(x',y) \in \mathbb{X}$, with $x' > x$. Then, by property **M** of f, we have $F(x',y) = yf(x'/y) > yf(x/y) = F(x,y)$.

Finally, to verify property **SA** of F, let $(x,y) \in \mathbb{X}$ and $(x',y') \in \mathbb{X}$. Then,

$$F(x+x', y+y') = (y+y')f\left(\frac{x+x'}{y+y'}\right)$$

$$= (y+y')f\left((x/y)\frac{y}{y+y'} + (x'/y')\frac{y'}{y+y'}\right)$$

$$\geq yf(x/y) + y'f(x'/y')$$

$$= F(x,y) + F(x',y'),$$

where property **C** of f was used to obtain the inequality in the above computations.

Proposition 2 is established by using three lemmas, which we state and prove subsequently. The three lemmas are analogous to the basic results for concave functions defined on an interval of the real line.[13] The first lemma relates to the comparison of slopes of chords.

Lemma 1. *Let $f : \mathbb{Y} \to \mathbb{R}$ be a function satisfying property* **C**. *Then:*

1. *If $a, b, c \in \mathbb{Y}$, and $a < b \leq c$, then $[f(b) - f(a)]/[b - a] \geq$ $[f(c) - f(a)]/[c - a]$.*
2. *If $a, b, c \in \mathbb{Y}$, and $a \leq b < c$, then $[f(c) - f(a)]/[c - a] \geq$ $[f(c) - f(b)]/[c - b]$.*
3. *If $a, b, c \in \mathbb{Y}$, and $a < b < c$, then $[f(b) - f(a)]/[b - a] \geq$ $[f(c) - f(a)]/[c - a] \geq [f(c) - f(b)]/[c - b]$.*

Proof: We will only prove (1). The proof of (2) is similar; (3) follows directly from (1) and (2). We are given that $a, b, c \in \mathbb{Y}$ and $a < b \leq c$. Then, there is a real number $\lambda \in (0, 1]$, such that $b = (1 - \lambda)a + \lambda c$. Then, $\lambda(c - a) = (b - a)$, so that:

$$\lambda = \frac{b - a}{c - a}. \tag{17.78}$$

Thus, λ must be a rational number in $(0, 1]$. Using property **C** of the function f, we then have: $f(b) \geq (1 - \lambda)f(a) + \lambda f(c)$, which can be rewritten as:

$$\lambda[f(c) - f(a)] \leq [f(b) - f(a)]. \tag{17.79}$$

Using (17.78) in (17.79), and dividing through by $(b - a) > 0$, we get:

$$\frac{[f(c) - f(a)]}{(c - a)} \leq \frac{[f(b) - f(a)]}{(b - a)}. \tag{17.80}$$

This establishes (1).

The second lemma is analogous to the result for concave functions (defined on an interval of the real line) that the right-hand derivative is well defined in the interior of the interval and is non-increasing.

Lemma 2. *Let $f : \mathbb{Y} \to \mathbb{R}$ be a function satisfying property* **C**. *Then, the function, $g : Y \to \mathbb{R}$ is well defined by:*

$$g(y) \equiv \lim_{\substack{\varepsilon \downarrow 0 \\ y + \varepsilon \in Y}} \{[f(y + \varepsilon) - f(y)]/\varepsilon\}. \tag{17.81}$$

Further, g is monotone non-increasing on Y.

---

[13] See, for example, Nikaido (1968: 47, Theorem 3.15) for comparison.

Proof: For $y \in Y$, we can pick $\delta \in Y$, such that $y - \delta > 0$, and $y + \delta < 1$. For all $\varepsilon \in Y$, with $\varepsilon < \delta$, we have by Lemma 1,

$$\frac{f(y) - f(y - \delta)}{\delta} \geq \frac{f(y + \varepsilon) - f(y)}{\varepsilon}. \tag{17.82}$$

Also, by Lemma 1, the right-hand side expression in (17.81) is non-decreasing as ε decreases to zero. Since it is bounded above by the left-hand side expression in (17.82), it must converge to a limit. Thus, $g : Y \rightarrow \mathbb{R}$, is well defined by:

$$g(y) \equiv \lim_{\substack{\varepsilon \downarrow 0 \\ y + \varepsilon \in Y}} \{[f(y + \varepsilon) - f(y)]/\varepsilon\}. \tag{17.83}$$

Let $y, z \in Y$ with $y < z$. We can pick $\delta \in Y$, such that $0 < y + \delta < z < z + \delta < 1$. Then, for all $n \in \mathbb{N}$, we have $0 < y + (\delta/n) < z < z + (\delta/n) < 1$, and so by Lemma 1,

$$\frac{f(y + (\delta/n)) - f(y)}{(\delta/n)} \geq \frac{f(z + (\delta/n)) - f(z)}{(\delta/n)}. \tag{17.84}$$

Letting $n \rightarrow \infty$ in (17.84), and using (17.83), we have $g(y) \geq g(z)$.

The third lemma is analogous to the result for concave functions (defined on an interval of the real line) comparing the slope of a chord with the (right-hand) derivative at an end point of the chord.

Lemma 3. *Let $f : \mathbb{Y} \rightarrow \mathbb{R}$ be a function satisfying property C. Then for $x \in \mathbb{Y}$, $y \in Y$, we have:*

$$f(x) - f(y) \leq g(y)(x - y). \tag{17.85}$$

Proof: The result is trivial for $x = y$. So, we consider two cases (a) $x > y$ and (b) $x < y$. In case (a), we can choose $\delta \in Y$, such that $x > y + \delta$. Then, for all $n \in \mathbb{N}$, $x > y + (\delta/n)$. Consequently, for all $n \in \mathbb{N}$, we have:

$$\frac{f(x) - f(y)}{(x - y)} \leq \frac{f(y + (\delta/n)) - f(y)}{(\delta/n)} \tag{17.86}$$

by Lemma 1. Letting $n \rightarrow \infty$ in (17.86), and using Lemma 2, we have:

$$\frac{f(x) - f(y)}{(x - y)} \leq g(y) \tag{17.87}$$

Multiplying through in (17.87) by $(x - y) > 0$, we get the desired result.

In case (b), we can choose $\delta \in Y$, such that $x < y - \delta$. Then, for all $n \in \mathbb{N}$, $x < y - (\delta/n)$. Therefore, for all $n \in \mathbb{N}$, we obtain:

$$\frac{f(y) - f(x)}{(y - x)} \geq \frac{f(y) - f(y - (\delta/n))}{(\delta/n)} \geq \frac{f(y + (\delta/n)) - f(y)}{(\delta/n)} \qquad (17.88)$$

by Lemma 1. Letting $n \to \infty$ in (17.90), and using Lemma 2, we get:

$$\frac{f(y) - f(x)}{(y - x)} \geq g(y). \qquad (17.89)$$

Multiplying through in (17.89) by $(y - x) > 0$, we obtain:

$$f(y) - f(x) \geq g(y)(y - x). \qquad (17.90)$$

Transposing terms in (17.90) yields the desired result.

The aforementioned lemmas, together with Abel's inequality, can be used to establish Proposition 2, which we now proceed to prove.

Proof of Proposition 2. We first show the result under the assumption that $z_i \in Y$ for all $i \in \{1, \ldots, n\}$. Then, we show that the general case (without this assumption) follows easily.

Since $z_i \in Y$ and $z_i' \in \mathbb{Y}$, we can use Lemma 3 to write, for each $i \in \{1, \ldots, n\}$,

$$f(z_i') - f(z_i) \leq g(z_i)(z_i' - z_i). \qquad (17.91)$$

Summing over $i \in \{1, \ldots, n\}$, we get:

$$\sum_{i=1}^{n} [f(z_i') - f(z_i)] \leq \sum_{i=1}^{n} g(z_i)(z_i' - z_i). \qquad (17.92)$$

Using Lemma 2, we have:

$$g(z_1) \geq g(z_2) \geq \cdots \geq g(z_n). \qquad (17.93)$$

Using the fact that f satisfies property **M** in Lemma 2, we also have:

$$g(z_i) \geq 0 \text{ for } i \in \{1, \ldots, n\}. \qquad (17.94)$$

Thus, we can use Abel's inequality (Mitrinovic and Vasic (1970: 32)) to write:

$$\sum_{i=1}^{n} g(z_i)(z_i' - z_i) \leq g(z_1)[\max_{1 \leq k \leq n} \sum_{i=1}^{k} (z_i' - z_i)]. \qquad (17.95)$$

By (17.76), we have:

$$[\max_{1 \le k \le n} \sum_{i=1}^{k} (z_i' - z_i)] \le 0. \tag{17.96}$$

Thus, using (17.94) and (17.96) in (17.95), we have:

$$\sum_{i=1}^{n} g(z_i)(z_i' - z_i) \le 0. \tag{17.97}$$

Using (17.97) in (17.92), we obtain (17.77), the desired result.

Turning now to the more general situation, we see that the following cases can arise: (a) $z_i \in Y$ for $i \in \{1, \ldots, n\}$; (b) $z_i = 0$ for $i \in \{1, \ldots, n\}$; (c) $z_i = 1$ for $i \in \{1, \ldots, n\}$; (d) there is $1 \le p < n$ such that $z_i = 0$ for $i \in \{1, \ldots, p\}$ and $z_i = 1$ for $i \in \{p+1, \ldots, n\}$; (e) there is $1 \le p < n$ such that $z_i = 0$ for $i \in \{1, \ldots, p\}$ and $z_i \in Y$ for $i \in \{p+1, \ldots, n\}$; (f) there is $1 \le q < n$ such that $z_i \in Y$ for $i \in \{1, \ldots, q\}$ and $z_i = 1$ for $i \in \{p+1, \ldots, n\}$; (g) there exist $1 \le p < q < n$ such that $z_i = 0$ for $i \in \{1, \ldots, p\}$, $z_i \in Y$ for $i \in \{p+1, \ldots, q\}$ and $z_i = 1$ for $i \in \{q+1, \ldots, n\}$.

We have already established the result in case (a). In case (b), (17.76) implies that $z_i' = 0$ for $i \in \{1, \ldots, n\}$, so (17.77) follows trivially. In case (c), $z_i' \le z_i$ for $i \in \{1, \ldots, n\}$, so (17.76) follows from property **M** of f. In case (d), we have $z_i' = 0$ for $i \in \{1, \ldots, p\}$ by (17.76), while $z_i' \le z_i$ for $i \in \{p+1, \ldots, n\}$, so (17.77) follows again from property **M** of f.

In case (e), we have $z_i' = 0$ for $i \in \{1, \ldots, p\}$ by (17.76), so we can define $j = i - p$ for $i = p+1, \ldots, n$, and $m = n - p$. Then, by (17.78), we have for $k = 1, \ldots, m$,

$$\sum_{j=1}^{k} z_j' \le \sum_{j=1}^{k} z_j$$

so that by the analysis of case (a), we obtain:

$$\sum_{j=1}^{m} f(z_j') \le \sum_{j=1}^{m} f(z_j)$$

and this yields (17.77), since $z_i' = z_i = 0$ for $i = 1, \ldots, p$.

In case (f), using the analysis of case (a), we have:

$$\sum_{i=1}^{q} f(z_i') \le \sum_{i=1}^{q} f(z_i)$$

and this yields (17.77), by using property **M** of f, since $z_i' \leq z_i = 1$ for $i = q+1, \ldots, n$.

In case (g), we have $z_i' = 0$ for $i \in \{1, \ldots, p\}$ by (17.76), so we can define $j = i - p$ for $i = p+1, \ldots, q$, and $m = q - p$. Then, by (17.76), we have for $k = 1, \ldots, m$,

$$\sum_{j=1}^{k} z_j' \leq \sum_{j=1}^{k} z_j$$

so that by the analysis of case (a), we have:

$$\sum_{j=1}^{m} f(z_j') \leq \sum_{j=1}^{m} f(z_j).$$

This yields (17.77), by (A) using property **M** of f, and $z_i' \leq z_i = 1$ for $i = q+1, \ldots, n$, while noting that (A) $z_i' = z_i = 0$ for $i = 1, \ldots, p$.

We now present the proof of Proposition 3, which is used to establish part (1) of Theorem 4 in the text.

Proof of Proposition 3. Property (a) of the function α is clear from its definition and property (1) of the function e. We proceed to verify property (c) of α. Let $w, w' \in \mathbb{Q}_+$, and let $t \in Y$. Define $w'' = tw + (1 - t)w'$, and note that $w'' \in \mathbb{Q}_+$, and:

$$(1 + w'') = t(1 + w) + (1 - t)(1 + w') \tag{17.98}$$

Clearly, we have $[w/(1+w)]$, $[w'/(1+w')]$, $[w''/(1+w'')]$ in $\mathbb{Y}$. Using the definition of α, we can write:

$$
\begin{aligned}
\alpha(w'') &= e(w''/(1+w''))(1+w'') \\
&= e\left(\frac{tw(1+w)}{(1+w'')(1+w)} + \frac{(1-t)w'(1+w')}{(1+w'')(1+w')} \right)(1+w'') \\
&= e\left(\frac{t(1+w)}{(1+w'')} \frac{w}{(1+w)} + \frac{(1-t)(1+w')}{(1+w'')} \frac{w'}{(1+w')} \right)(1+w'') \\
&\geq \left[\frac{t(1+w)}{(1+w'')} e\left(\frac{w}{(1+w)} \right) + \frac{(1-t)(1+w')}{(1+w'')} e\left(\frac{w'}{(1+w')} \right) \right](1+w'') \\
&= t\alpha(w) + (1-t)\alpha(w')
\end{aligned}
$$

the inequality following from property (3) of e, after using (17.98).

We now turn to property (b) of the function, α. Let $w, w' \in \mathbb{Q}_+$, with $w' > w$. We claim that $\alpha(w') \geq \alpha(w)$. Suppose, on the contrary, that $\alpha(w') < \alpha(w)$. Define $\delta = [\alpha(w) - \alpha(w')]/(w' - w)$; then $\delta > 0$.

Using property (c) of α (which has already been established), and using the proof of Lemma 1, we have for all $n \in \mathbb{N}$,

$$-\delta = \frac{\alpha(w') - \alpha(w)}{(w' - w)} \geq \frac{\alpha(w' + n) - \alpha(w)}{(w' + n - w)}.$$

This yields the inequality:

$$-\alpha(w) \leq \alpha(w' + n) - \alpha(w) \leq (w' + n - w)(-\delta) < -n\delta \qquad (17.99)$$

using the facts that $\alpha(w' + n) \geq 0$ and $(w' - w) > 0$. But (17.99) clearly leads to a contradiction for large n. This establishes our claim, and hence property (b) of α.

To verify that α maps from $\mathbb{Q}_+$ to $[0, 1)$, suppose on the contrary there is some $w \in \mathbb{Q}_+$, with $\alpha(w) \geq 1$. Define $z = w/(1 + w)$; then, we have $z \in (0, 1)$, and $(1 - z) = 1/(1 + w)$. Using the definition of α, we then have $e(z) = (1 - z)\alpha(w) \geq (1 - z)$, so that $e(z) + z \geq 1$. But, by property $\mathbf{M}$ of e, we must have $e(z) + z < e(1) + 1 = 1$, since $e(1) = 0$ by property (1) of e. This contradiction establishes the result.

We now present the proof of Proposition 4, which is used to establish part (2) of Theorem 4 in the text.

Proof of Proposition 4. Property (1) of e being clear from its definition, we proceed to prove property (2). Let $z, z' \in \mathbb{Y}$, with $z' > z$. There are two cases to consider: (I) $z' = 1$, (II) $z' < 1$. In case (I), $e(z') + z' = 1$, while $e(z) + z = \alpha(z/(1 - z))(1 - z) + z < (1 - z) + z$ (since $z < 1$, and $\alpha(z/(1 - z)) \in [0, 1)) = 1$.

In case (II), we have:

$$\begin{aligned}
e(z') + z' &= \alpha(z'/(1 - z'))(1 - z') + z' \\
&\geq \alpha(z/(1 - z))(1 - z') + z' \\
&= \alpha(z/(1 - z))(1 - z) + z + \alpha(z/(1 - z))(z - z') + (z' - z) \\
&= e(z) + z + (z' - z)[1 - \alpha(z/(1 - z))] \\
&> e(z) + z,
\end{aligned}$$

the first inequality following from property (b) of α and the fact that $z'/(1 - z') > z/(1 - z)$ (using $1 > z' > z$), and the second inequality following from the fact that $\alpha(z/(1 - z)) \in [0, 1)$ and $z' > z$.

We turn now to property (3) of the function e. Let $z, z' \in \mathbb{Y}$, and let $t \in Y$. We will first prove the property, assuming that z and z' are both less than 1. Then, we will show that the property is also valid without this assumption. When $z, z' < 1$, let us denote $[1 - (tz + (1 - t)z')]$ by

Δ. Then, we have:

$$\Delta = t(1 - z) + (1 - t)(1 - z') \qquad (17.100)$$

Then, we can write:

$$
\begin{aligned}
e(tz + (1 - t)z') &= \alpha \left(\frac{(tz + (1 - t)z')}{\Delta} \right) \Delta \\
&= \alpha \left(\frac{tz(1 - z)}{\Delta(1 - z)} + \frac{(1 - t)z'(1 - z')}{\Delta(1 - z')} \right) \Delta \\
&= \alpha \left(\frac{t(1 - z)}{\Delta} \frac{z}{1 - z} + \frac{(1 - t)(1 - z')}{\Delta} \frac{z'}{1 - z'} \right) \Delta \\
&\geq \left[\frac{t(1-z)}{\Delta} \alpha \left(\frac{z}{1-z} \right) + \frac{(1-t)(1-z')}{\Delta} \alpha \left(\frac{z'}{1-z'} \right) \right] \Delta \\
&= te(z) + (1 - t)e(z'),
\end{aligned}
$$

the inequality following from property C of the function, α, after using (17.100).

In the general case, where z, z' are not necessarily less than 1, we proceed as follows. Define, for all $n \in \mathbb{N}$, $z(n) = z$ if $z < 1$, and $z(n) = [n/(1 + n)]z$, when $z = 1$; similarly, define for all $n \in \mathbb{N}$, $z'(n) = z'$ if $z' < 1$, and $z'(n) = [n/(1 + n)]z'$, when $z' = 1$. Then, $z(n)$ and $z'(n)$ are both less than 1 for all $n \in \mathbb{N}$, with $z(n) \leq z$ and $z'(n) \leq z'$ for all $n \in \mathbb{N}$. Thus, we can write:

$$
\begin{aligned}
e(tz + (1 - t)z') + [tz + (1 - t)z'] &\geq e(tz(n) + (1 - t)z'(n)) \\
&\quad + [tz(n) + (1 - t)z'(n)] \\
&\geq te(z(n)) + (1 - t)e(z'(n)) \\
&\quad + [tz(n) + (1 - t)z'(n)], \quad (17.101)
\end{aligned}
$$

the first inequality following from property (2) of e (already established earlier), and the second inequality from the earlier analysis of property (3) of e, since $z(n), z'(n)$ are both less than 1. The inequality (17.101) yields:

$$
\begin{aligned}
e(tz + (1 - t)z') &\geq te(z(n)) + (1 - t)e(z'(n)) \\
&\quad + t(z(n) - z) + (1 - t)(z'(n) - z') \\
&\geq te(z) + (1 - t)e(z') \\
&\quad + t(z(n) - z) + (1 - t)(z'(n) - z'), \quad (17.102)
\end{aligned}
$$

the second inequality following from the fact that $e(1) = 0$, while e maps to $\mathbb{R}_+$. Now, letting $n \to \infty$ in (17.102), we obtain the desired result.

REFERENCES

Basu, K. and J. E. Foster (1998), 'On Measuring Literacy', *Economic Journal*, 108(451): 1733–49.

Basu, K., A. Narayan and M. Ravallion (2002), 'Is Literacy Shared within Households? Theory and Evidence for Bangladesh', *Labour Economics* 8(6): 649–65.

Dutta, I. (2004), 'Generalized Measures of Literacy', *Mathematical Social Sciences*, 48, 69–80.

Gibson, J. (2001), 'Literacy and Intrahousehold Externalities', *World Development* 29, 155–66.

Green, J.W. (1954), 'Recent Applications of Convex Functions', *American Mathematical Monthly*, 61(7): 449–54.

Green, S. E., T.A. Rich and E.G. Nesman (1985), 'Beyond Individual Literacy: the Role of Shared Literacy for Innovation in Guatemala', *Human Organisation* 44(4): 313–21.

Mitra, T. (2002), 'On Literacy Rankings', CAE Working Paper 02-16, Cornell University.

Mitrinovic, D.S. and P.M. Vasic (1970), *Analytic Inequalities*, Heidelberg: Springer-Verlag.

Nikaido, H. (1968), *Convex Structures and Economic Theory*, Academic Press, New York.

Roberts, A.W. and D.E. Varberg (1973), *Convex Functions*, New York: Academic Press.

Rosenbaum, R.A. (1950), "Sub-Additive Functions", *Duke Mathematical Journal*, 17: 227–47.

Subramanian, S. (2004), 'Measuring Literacy: Some Extensions of the Basu–Foster Framework', *Journal of Development Economics*, 73(1): 453–63.

——— (2008), 'Externality and Literacy: A Note', *Journal of Development Studies*, 44(6): 839–48.

Valenti, P.M. (2002), "Should We Be Concerned about the Distribution of Literacy across Households? An Axiomatic Characterisation", CAE Working paper 02-15, Cornell University.

Epilogue:
The Stability of Binary Social
Decision Rules*

The problem of strategic manipulation of social decision rules has been extensively discussed in recent years. The major contributions on this problem are those of Gibbard (1973), Pattanaik (1973, 1974, 1975) and Satterthwaite (1975). Gibbard and Satterthwaite are concerned with the stability of voting schemes which yield one and only one social alternative as the outcome for any given set of individual orderings. Voting schemes can be viewed as social decision rules. Then a voting scheme is a social decision rule whose structure is such that for every situation it yields a social preference relation such that the choice set (the set of best elements) contains exactly one element. It can be easily seen that every voting scheme which satisfies the condition of independence of irrelevant alternatives is either dictatorial or violates the weak Pareto criterion. So, the Gibbard–Satterthwaite theorem essentially considers the stability of a class of non-binary social decision rules.

Pattanaik (1973, 1974, 1975) has considered the stability of various classes of neutral functions. However, there are two problems with Pattanaik's formulation of the problem. If by stability is meant the property of immunity from strategic manipulation then Pattanaik's definition of stability is not a correct formalisation of the notion of stability. Pattanaik defines a sincere situation $< \overline{R}_i >$ belonging to W_A (the set of $< R_i >$ such that the choice set $C(A, R)$ is non-empty) to be unstable only if it is vulnerable to some situation $< R_i >$ also belonging to W_A. Now, a sincere situation $< \overline{R}_i > \in W_A$ might not be vulnerable to any $< R_i > \in W_A$, but might be vulnerable to some situation $< R_i > \notin W_A$.

---

* This is an abridged version of Chapter 5 of Satish Jain's doctoral dissertation titled 'The Game-Theoretic Stability of Binary Social Decision Rules' (1975). Introduction, definitions, assumptions and such like are taken from other chapters (eds.).

Whether a sincere situation $< \overline{R}_i > \in W_A$ is vulnerable to a situation $< R_i > \in W_A$ or a situation $< R_i > \notin W_A$ is, in our opinion, immaterial. What is relevant is whether $< \overline{R}_i >$ is such that there exists a set of individuals such that it is beneficial for them to misrepresent their preferences. Clearly, the restriction to set W_A is quite arbitrary. Pattanaik defines a social decision rule to be stable iff for every environment A, every situation which belongs to W_A and is a sincere situation is stable. This definition leaves out the situations not belonging to W_A from consideration altogether. Clearly, stability should be defined in such a way that the statement that f is stable is equivalent to the statement that the structure of f is such that no strategic distortion of preferences can be beneficial. For this one has to consider all sincere situations whether they belong to W_A or not. We shall illustrate the point by an example.

Example 1. *Let $S = \{x, y, z\}$.*
Let f be characterised as follows:

(a) *xPy*

(b) *yPz*

(c) *$xR_1z \rightarrow xPz$*
    $zP_1x \rightarrow zPx$

(d) *If the choice set is empty, $x_o \notin \{x, y, z\}$ is the outcome. Assume that individual 1's preference ordering is xP_1yP_1z and that individual 1 prefers x_o to x, y, z. If individual 1 reveals his true preferences, the outcome will be x. However, if his revealed preferences are zP_1xP_1y, then the outcome will be x_o. As individual 1 prefers x_o to x, the aforementioned situation is subject to strategic manipulation. However, it can be checked that no sincere situation belonging to W_A is vulnerable to any situation belonging to W_A. Thus, according to Pattanaik's definition of stability, this function is stable.*

In fact, Pattanaik (1975) states the following theorem.

Theorem: If f is binary, monotonic and resolute[1] then f is stable.

It can be checked that the f in the above example satisfies all conditions of the theorem. However, it is obvious that this function is not stable if by stability we mean that the structure of f is such that there is never any incentive to misrepresent one's preferences.

Pattanaik assumes that under risky situations individuals follow the maximin rule. The maximin rule is very plausible under uncertain

---

[1] A function is resolute iff it never allows social indifference.

situations. However, under risky situations the maximin rule is inconsistent with rational behaviour. We shall illustrate the inconsistency by an example.

Example 2. *Let* $S = \{x_1, x_2, x_3, x_4, x_5\}$. *Let individual i's preference ordering of S be* $x_1 I_i x_2 I_i x_3 P_i x_4 P_i x_5$. *Consider the following two lotteries:* $C^* = (x_1, x_2, x_3, x_4, x_5, \frac{1}{5}, \frac{1}{5}, \frac{1}{5}, \frac{1}{5}, \frac{1}{5})$
$\hat{C}^* = (x_3, x_5, \frac{1}{2}, \frac{1}{2})$.

As $x_3 P_i x_4$, *by maximin criterion we infer that individual i would prefer* $\hat{C}^*$ *to* C^*. *However, for any given level of satisfaction, the probability that the individual will obtain an outcome which will give him at least the given level of satisfaction is in the case of C^* at least as great as it is in the case of $\hat{C}^*$, and in some cases is actually greater. Thus, C^* is unconditionally better than $\hat{C}^*$. Clearly, a rational individual will prefer C^* to $\hat{C}^*$.*

So, in some situations the preference relation inferred from the maximin rule would conflict with individual rationality. Thus, any stability analysis which is based on the maximin rule might declare certain situations to be unstable which might otherwise be perfectly stable, and on the other hand might declare some unstable situations to be stable.

In this work we shall prove that every binary social decision rule is either dictatorial or imposed or unstable. In other words, it will be shown that every non-trivial binary social decision rule is unstable.

DEFINITIONS AND ASSUMPTIONS

The set of social alternatives (S) will be assumed to be finite. The number of elements (n) in S will be assumed to be at least 3. Alternatives are defined in such a way that they are mutually exclusive. We denote the finite set of individuals by N and assume that $\#N = \nu \geq 2$. Each individual $i \in N$ will be assumed to have a binary weak preference relation R_i over S. The asymmetric parts of binary relations $R_i, R_i', R, R' \ldots$ will be denoted by $P_i, P_i', P, P' \ldots$ respectively; and the symmetric parts by $I_i, I_i', I, I' \ldots$ respectively.

An element x in S is a best element of S with respect to a binary relation R iff $\forall y: (y \in S \rightarrow xRy)$. The set of best elements in S is called its choice set and is denoted by $C(S, R)$.

We define a binary relation R over a set S to be (*a*) reflexive iff $(\forall x \in S)(xRx)$, (*b*) connected iff $(\forall x, y \in S)[x \neq y \rightarrow xRy \vee yRx]$,

(c) acyclic iff $(\forall x_1, x_2, \ldots, x_m \in S)[x_1 P x_2 \wedge \ldots \wedge x_{m-1} P x_m \rightarrow x_1 R x_m]$, where m is a positive integer ≥ 3, (d) quasi-transitive iff $(\forall x, y, z \in S)[x P y \wedge y P z \rightarrow x P z]$, (e) transitive iff $(\forall x, y, z \in S)[x R y \wedge y R z \rightarrow x R z]$, (f) an ordering iff R is reflexive, connected and transitive, and (g) a strong ordering iff R is an ordering and $(\forall x, y \in S)(x I y \leftrightarrow x = y)$.

The set of all logically possible orderings of the alternatives in the set S will be denoted by π. The set of all logically possible strong orderings of the alternatives in the set S will be denoted by π'. π^ν and π'^ν will denote the Cartesian products $\pi \times \ldots \times \pi$ (ν times) and $\pi' \times \ldots \times \pi'$ (ν times) respectively.

A social decision rule (SDR) is a functional relation f such that for any ν-tuple of individual orderings $(R_1, \ldots, R_\nu)$ in the domain one and only one reflexive and connected social preference relation R is determined; $R = f(R_1, \ldots, R_\nu)$. The social binary weak preference relations corresponding to $(R_1, \ldots, R_\nu), (R'_1, \ldots, R'_\nu) \ldots$ will be denoted by $R, R' \ldots$ respectively. At times, $(R_1, \ldots, R_\nu), (R'_1, \ldots, R'_\nu) \ldots$ will be written in abbreviated form as $< R_i >, < R'_i > \ldots$ respectively. f satisfies the condition of unrestricted domain (U) iff the domain includes all logically possible ν-tuples of individual orderings. An SDR f with unrestricted domain (a) satisfies the weak Pareto criterion (P) iff $(\forall (R_1, \ldots, R_\nu) \in \pi^\nu)(\forall x, y \in S)[(\forall i \in N)(x P_i y) \rightarrow x P y]$, (b) is dictatorial iff $(\exists j \in N)(\forall (R_1, \ldots, R_\nu) \in \pi^\nu)(\forall x, y \in S)(x P_j y \rightarrow x P y)$, (c) is imposed iff $(\exists x, y \in S)(\forall (R_1, \ldots, R_\nu) \in \pi^\nu)(\sim x P y)$, and (d) is trivial iff it is dictatorial or imposed.

f satisfies independence of irrelevant alternatives (I) iff $(\forall (R_1, \ldots, R_\nu), (R'_1, \ldots, R'_\nu) \in \pi^\nu) [(\forall i \in N) (\forall x, y \in A \subset S) (x R_i y \leftrightarrow x R'_i y) \rightarrow (\forall x, y \in A)(x R y \leftrightarrow x R' y)]$. An SDR which satisfies condition I will be called a binary SDR. A binary SDR with unrestricted domain satisfies (a) monotonicity (M) iff $(\forall (R_1, \ldots, R_\nu), (R'_1, \ldots, R'_\nu) \in \pi^\nu)(\forall x, y \in S)[(\forall i \in N)[(x P_i y \rightarrow x P'_i y) \wedge (x I_i y \rightarrow x R'_i y)] \rightarrow [(x P y \rightarrow x P' y) \wedge (x I y \rightarrow x R' y)]]$, and (b) weak monotonicity (WM) iff $(\forall (R_1, \ldots, R_\nu), (R'_1, \ldots, R'_\nu) \in \pi^\nu)(\forall x, y \in S)(\forall k \in N)[(\forall i \in N - \{k\})[(x R_i y \leftrightarrow x R'_i y) \wedge (y R_i x \leftrightarrow y R'_i x)] \wedge [(y P_k x \wedge x R'_k y) \vee (x I_k y \wedge x P'_k y)] \rightarrow [(x P y \rightarrow x P' y) \wedge (x I y \rightarrow x R' y)]]$.

Let $x, y \in S$ and $x \neq y$. We define a set of individuals V to be (a) decisive for $(x, y)[\overline{D}^V(x, y)]$ iff $(\forall (R_1, \ldots, R_\nu) \in \pi^\nu)[(\forall i \in V)(x P_i y) \rightarrow x P y]$, (b) minimally decisive for (x, y) iff it is decisive for (x, y) and no proper subset of it is decisive for (x, y), (c) a decisive set iff it is decisive for all $(x, y) \in S \times S, x \neq y$, and (d) a minimal decisive set iff it is a decisive set and no proper subset of it is a decisive set.

THE CHOICE MECHANISM

As has been noted earlier, the alternatives are defined in such a way that they are mutually exclusive. If the SDR is such that for every situation it yields a choice set containing exactly one element, then there is no problem as the unique element of the choice set becomes the final outcome. However, in general, such will not be the case. So, we have to specify how the final outcome is selected when the choice set is not univalent.[2] When the choice set contains more than one element, we would assume that a random mechanism is employed to select one element from the choice set such that the probability of any particular element of the choice set being selected is $\frac{1}{m}$, where m is the number of elements in the choice set. If the choice set is empty we assume that a distinguished alternative $x_0 \notin S$ is selected. The lottery corresponding to choice set C will be denoted by C^*. The set of all possible outcomes will be denoted by S^*.

The following is a formal restatement of the choice procedure: (a) For every configuration of individual orderings over S, SDR assigns a unique reflexive and connected R over S. (b) For every reflexive and connected R over S function C assigns a unique subset of S. C is the function which selects the best elements of S according to the binary preference relation R over S. (c) Finally, we have function r which for every subset of S assigns a unique element of S^*.

Let $r \circ C \circ f = g$. Thus, for every configuration of individual orderings, g assigns an outcome.

We will assume that every individual i has an ordering R_i^* defined over S^*. Throughout this work we assume that the domain of f is such that for every individual i any logically possible ordering of S is admissible. Now, we state the corresponding assumption with respect to set S^*. We will assume that for every individual i every logically possible ordering of $S^*(R_i^*)$ is admissible which satisfies the following two conditions:

1. The restriction of R_i^* over S must agree with R_i.
2. The R_i^* must be consistent with the expected utility maximisation principle.

Throughout this work, we shall denote individual i's true preference ordering over the set S by $\overline{R}_i$ and over the set S^* by $\overline{R}_i^*$.

---

[2] A set is called univalent if it contains a single element.

THE NOTION OF STABILITY

We define an SDR to be stable iff its structure is such that no individual ever has any incentive to misrepresent his preferences. This is equivalent to requiring that every $< \overline{R}_i >$ situation be a Nash equilibrium.

Suppose f is unstable, then for some k there must exist:

$(R_1, \ldots, R_{k-1}, R_k, R_{k+1}, \ldots, R_v)$ and $(R_1, \ldots, R_{k-1}, \overline{R}_k, R_{k+1}, \ldots, R_v)$ such that $g(R_1, \ldots, R_{k-1}, R_k, R_{k+1}, \ldots, R_v)\overline{P}_k^* g(R_1, \ldots, R_{k-1}, \overline{R}_k, R_{k+1}, \ldots, R_v)$.

Now assume for $\forall i \neq k : R_i = \overline{R}_i$. This means that $< \overline{R}_i >$ is not a Nash equilibrium. We have demonstrated that if f is unstable then there must exist an $< \overline{R}_i >$ situation which is not a Nash equilibrium. Now suppose that there exists an $< \overline{R}_i >$ situation which is not a Nash equilibrium. So, for some k and R_k, we must have

$g(\overline{R}_1, \ldots, \overline{R}_{k-1}, R_k, \overline{R}_{k+1}, \ldots, \overline{R}_v)\overline{P}_k^* g(\overline{R}_1, \ldots, \overline{R}_{k-1}, \overline{R}_k, \overline{R}_{k+1}, \ldots, \overline{R}_v)$.

Given that $\forall i \neq k$ are going to reveal their true preferences, k can obtain a better outcome by misrepresenting his preferences. Therefore, f is unstable. So, we have shown that if there exists an $< \overline{R}_i >$ situation which is not a Nash equilibrium then f is unstable. In view of this, the notion of stability can be defined as follows.

An SDR f is stable iff every $< \overline{R}_i >$ situation is a Nash equilibrium.

STABILITY OF BINARY SOCIAL DECISION RULES

Theorem 1. *Every non-trivial SDR satisfying conditions U and I is unstable.*

Proof of the Theorem. As every SDR which is imposed is by definition trivial, we need consider only the class of SDRs which satisfy conditions U and I and are non-imposed.

Lemma 1. *Let f be non-imposed. If f belongs to the class of SDRs which satisfy conditions U and I, then a necessary condition for the stability of f is that it satisfy condition P.*

Proof: Let $S = \{x, y, z_1, \ldots, z_{n-2}\}$. If f violates P, then there exists an ordered pair of alternatives, say, (x, y), such that $\forall i \in N: xP_iy \rightarrow yRx$. Now, construct $< R_i >$ as follows: (*a*) As f is non-imposed, for every ordered pair $(y, z_j), j = 1, \ldots, n-2$, there exists a configuration of individual preferences such that yPz_j. For all (y, z_j), assume these preferences (*b*) $\forall i \in N: xP_iy, z_1, \ldots, z_{n-2}$. So we obtain: $yRx, yPz_j, j = 1, \ldots, n-2$. Therefore, $< R_i >$ yields the outcome y or $(x, y)^*$.

Now, construct $< R_i' >$ as follows. As f is non-imposed, for every ordered pair (x, t), $t = y, z_1, \ldots, z_{n-2}$, there exists a configuration of individual preferences such that $xP't$. For all (x, t), assume these preferences. So, the outcome for the situation $< R_i' >$ is x.

Let N' be the set of individuals for whom $R_i \neq R_i'$. Let N' contain v' individuals. Order these individuals as follows $(i_1, \ldots, i_{v'})$. Rename $< R_i >$ as $< R_i^0 >$ and construct a sequence of situations $< R_i^t >$, $t = 1, \ldots, v'$, where $< R_i^t >$ is characterised as follows: $\forall i \in N - \{i_t\} : R_i^t = R_i^{t-1}$ and $R_i^t = R_i'$. Thus, $< R_i^{v'} > = < R_i' >$.

$< R_i >$ yields an outcome which is different from x. $< R_i' >$ yields the outcome x. Let $< R_i^p >$ be the first situation in the sequence which yields the outcome x. Let $< R_i^{p-1} > = < \overline{R}_i >$. Assume $x\overline{P}_{i_p}^* x_0$. By construction, $< \overline{R}_i >$ yields an outcome which is different from x, that is to say, if every individual i employs strategy $\overline{R}_i$, an outcome different from x is obtained. Now, given that every individual $i \neq i_p$ is going to employ strategy $\overline{R}_i$, if individual i_p uses the strategy $R_{i_p}' \neq \overline{R}_{i_p}$, the situation $< R_i^p >$ is obtained yielding the outcome x. Individual i_p prefers x to any other outcome. Therefore, $< \overline{R}_{i_p} >$ is not a Nash equilibrium. This proves the necessity of condition P.

Thus, the set of non-trivial binary SDRs which are stable is contained in the set of SDRs which satisfy conditions U, I and P.

Lemma 2. *If an SDR satisfies conditions U and I, then it is monotonic iff it is weakly monotonic.*

Proof: By the definitions of monotonicity and weak monotonicity, if f is monotonic then it is weakly monotonic. Now, let f satisfy weak monotonicity. Let $(R_1, \ldots, R_v)$ and $(R_1', \ldots, R_v')$ be two configurations of individual orderings such that: $(\forall i \in N)[(xP_i y \to xP_i' y) \wedge (xI_i y \to xR_i' y)]$. We shall show that this implies $[(xPy \to xP'y) \wedge (xIy \to xR'y)]$, which will prove monotonicity of f.

Partition N into N_1 and N_2 such that $N_1 = \{i \in N | (xR_i y \leftrightarrow xR_i' y) \wedge (yR_i x \leftrightarrow yR_i' x)\}$, $N_2 = N - N_1$. N_1 is the set of individuals whose preferences over the pair $\{x, y\}$ remain unchanged. N_2 is the set of individuals in whose esteem x has risen vis-à-vis y.

If N_2 is empty, the required conclusion follows from Condition I. So, we need consider only the case when N_2 is nonempty. Without any loss of generality, assume $N_2 = \{1, \ldots, m\}$. Rename $< R_i >$ and $< R_i' >$ as $< R_i^0 >$ and $< R_i^m >$ respectively. Now, construct $< R_i^1 >, \ldots, < R_i^{m-1} >$ as follows.
For $t = 1, \ldots, m - 1$,

$\forall i \neq t : R_i^t = R_i^{t-1}$ and for $i = t : R_i^t = R_i^m$.

For $t = 1, \ldots, m$, we have, by WM, $[(xP^{t-1}y \rightarrow xP^t y) \wedge (xI^{t-1}y \rightarrow xR^t y)]$. Thus, $[(xPy \rightarrow xP'y) \wedge (xIy \rightarrow xR'y)]$.

Lemma 3. *If f satisfies U, P and I, then a necessary condition for the stability of f is that it satisfy condition M.*

Proof: Let $S = \{x, y, z_1, \ldots, z_{n-2}\}$. Suppose f violates M, then by Lemma 2, there exists a pair of alternatives, say, x, y, and two situations $< R_i >$ and $< R_i' >$ such that for some k,

$\forall i \neq k : [(xR_i y \leftrightarrow xR_i'y) \wedge (yR_i x \leftrightarrow yR_i'x)]$

$k : [(yP_k x \wedge xI_k'y) \vee (yP_k x \wedge xP_k'y) \vee (xI_k y \wedge xP_k'y)]$,

however, we have

$(xPy \wedge yP'x) \vee (xPy \wedge xI'y) \vee (xIy \wedge yP'x)$.

Suppose $(xPy \wedge yP'x)$ and $(yP_k x \wedge xI_k'y)$. Let the restriction of $< R_i >$ over $\{x, y\}$ be characterised as follows: $\forall i \in N_1 : xP_i y; \forall i \in N_2 : xI_i y; \forall i \in N_3 : yP_i x$, where $\cup_{t=1}^3 N_t = N$ and $k \in N_3$.

Now let $< \overline{R}_i >$ be as follows:

$\forall i \in N_1 : x\overline{P}_i y\overline{P}_i z_1 \overline{P}_i \ldots \overline{P}_i z_{n-2}$

$\forall i \in N_2 : x\overline{I}_i y\overline{P}_i z_1 \overline{P}_i \ldots \overline{P}_i z_{n-2}$

$\forall i \in N_3 : y\overline{P}_i x\overline{P}_i z_1 \overline{P}_i \ldots \overline{P}_i z_{n-2}$.

By condition I and the fact that $< \overline{R}_i >$ is identical with $< R_i >$ over $\{x, y\}$, we conclude that $\overline{R}$ and R are identical over $\{x, y\}$. This together with condition P completely determines $\overline{R}$.

$\overline{R} = x\overline{P}y\overline{P}z_1\overline{P} \ldots \overline{P}z_{n-2}$.

Now construct $< R_i^0 >$ as follows:

$\forall i \in N_1 : xP_i^0 yP_i^0 z_1 P_i^0 \ldots P_i^0 z_{n-2}$

$\forall i \in N_2 \cup \{k\} : xI_i^0 yP_i^0 z_1 P_i^0 \ldots P_i^0 z_{n-2}$

$\forall i \in N_3 - \{k\} : yP_i^0 xP_i^0 z_1 P_i^0 \ldots P_i^0 z_{n-2}$.

$< R_i^0 >$ and $< R_i' >$ are identical over $\{x, y\}$. So, R^0 and R' must be identical over $\{x, y\}$ by condition I. This, in conjunction with condition P, determines R^0 completely. $R^0 = yP^0 xP^0 z_1 P^0 \ldots P^0 z_{n-2}$.

If every individual reveals his true preferences, we obtain the situation $< \overline{R}_i >$ which yields the outcome x. Now, given that every $i \neq k$ is going to reveal his true preferences, if individual k's revealed preferences are $R_k^0 \neq \overline{R}_k$, then the situation $< R_i^0 >$ is obtained which yields the outcome y. As individual k prefers y to x, it follows that the situation $< \overline{R}_i >$ is not a Nash equilibrium.

For the case $(xPy \wedge yP'x)$ and $(yP_kx \wedge xI'_ky)$, we have shown that there exists an $< \overline{R}_i >$ situation which is not a Nash equilibrium. Similarly, the existence of an $< \overline{R}_i >$ situation which is not a Nash equilibrium can be demonstrated in each of the remaining 8 cases. This completes the proof.

In view of Lemma 3, we conclude that the set of non-trivial binary SDRs which are stable is contained in the set of SDRs which satisfy conditions U, I, P and M.

Lemma 4. *If f belongs to the class of SDRs which satisfy U, P, I and M, then a necessary condition for the stability of f is that it always yield acyclic R.*

Proof: Let $S = \{x_1, \ldots, x_n\}$. Suppose acyclicity is violated. Then there exists a situation $< R_i >$ such that the choice set $C(A, R)$ is empty for some $A \subset S$, where $A \neq \emptyset$. Let A^0 be the smallest non-empty subset (or one of the smallest non-empty subsets) of S for which choice set $C(A, R)$ is empty. Let A^0 contain m elements. Without any loss of generality, assume $A^0 = \{x_1, \ldots, x_m\}$. As A^0 is the smallest non-empty subset of S for which choice set $C(A, R)$ is empty, we must have a P-cycle of the m-th order over A^0. Without any loss of generality, assume $x_1 P x_2 P \ldots P x_{m-1} P x_m P x_1$. Let the restriction of $< R_i >$ over $\{x_m, x_1\}$ be as follows: $\forall i \in N_1: x_1 P_i x_m; \forall i \in N_2: x_m R_i x_1$; where $\cup_{t=1}^2 N_t = N$. Now construct $< R_i^0 >$ as follows:

(a) $\forall i \in N: x_1, x_2, \ldots, x_{m-1}, x_m P_i^0 x_{m+1} P_i^0 x_{m+2} P_i^0 \ldots P_i^0 x_n$
(b) $\forall i \in N: x_k R_i^0 x_l \leftrightarrow x_k R_i x_l$, for all $x_k, x_l \in A^0$.

By condition P we obtain $x_1, x_2, \ldots, x_{m-1}, x_m P^0 x_{m+1} P^0 x_{m+2} P^0 \ldots P^0 x_n$. As $< R_i >$ and $< R_i^0 >$ are identical over A^0, we must have by condition I, $x_1 P^0 x_2 P^0 \ldots P^0 x_{m-1} P^0 x_m P^0 x_1$.

Let N_2 contain p members. Order these individuals as follows, $(i_1, \ldots, i_p)$. Now construct a sequence $< R_i^t >, t = 1, \ldots, p$, of p situations, where $< R_i^t >$ is characterised as follows:

(a) $\forall i \in N - \{i_t\}: R_i^t = R_i^{t-1}$
(b) $x_k R_{i_t}^t x_l \leftrightarrow x_k R_{i_t}^{t-1} x_l$, for all $x_k, x_l \in S - \{x_1\}$
(c) $x_1 P_{i_t}^t x_j, j = 2, \ldots, n$.

Let $s, 1 \leq s \leq p$, be the smallest integer such that $< R_i^t >$ yields $x_1 R^t x_m$. Such an s must exist in view of condition $P (< R_i^p >$ yields $x_1 P^p x_m$ as $\forall i \in N: x_1 P_i^p x_m)$.

Now, $< R_i^s >$ is identical to $< R_i^0 >$ over $S - \{x_1\}$, so R^s and R^0 must be identical over $S - \{x_1\}$. Thus, we have

$x_2 P^s \ldots P^s x_m P^s x_{m+1} P^s \ldots P^s x_n$. Therefore, no $x_j, 3 \leq j \leq n$, belongs to $C(S, R^s)$. We have for all $(x_1, x_j), j = 2 \ldots n, (\forall i \in N)[(x_1 P_i^0 x_j \to x_1 P_i^s x_j) \wedge (x_1 I_i^0 x_j \to x_1 R_i^s x_j)]$. As $x_1 P^0 x_2$, by condition M, $x_1 P^s x_2$ must hold, so x_2 does not belong to $C(S, R^s)$.

We have $x_1 P^0 x_j, j = m + 1, \ldots, n$. We must have $x_1 P^s x_j, j = m + 1, \ldots, n$, by condition M. Furthermore, $x_1 I x_j, j = 3, \ldots, m - 1$, must be true, otherwise the supposition that A^0 is the smallest subset of S for which $C(A, R)$ is empty would be contradicted. Also, for all x_j, $j = 3, \ldots, m - 1, (\forall i \in N)[(x_1 P_i x_j \to x_1 P_i^s x_j) \wedge (x_1 I_i x_j \to x_1 R_i^s x_j)]$. So by condition M, we obtain $x_1 R^s x_j, j = 3, \ldots, m - 1$. Thus, for all $x_j \in S$, we have $x_1 R^s x_j$. Therefore, $C(S, R^s) = \{x_1\}$.

Let $< R_i^{s-1} > = < \overline{R}_i >$ and suppose that individual i_s prefers x_1 to x_0. Now, $< \overline{R}_i >$ and $< R_i^0 >$ are identical over $S - \{x_1\}$. Therefore, in view of condition I, we must have $x_2 \overline{P} x_3 \overline{P} \ldots \overline{P} x_{m-1} \overline{P} x_m \overline{P} x_{m+1} \overline{P} \ldots \overline{P} x_n$. Therefore, no $x_j, 3 \leq j \leq n$, belongs to $C(S, \overline{R})$. Furthermore, we have, $(\forall i \in N)[(x_1 P_i^0 x_2 \to x_1 \overline{P}_i x_2) \wedge (x_1 I_i^0 x_2 \to x_1 \overline{R}_i x_2)]$. As $x_1 P^0 x_2$, we must have $x_1 \overline{P} x_2$. Thus, x_2 does not belong to the choice set $C(S, \overline{R})$. By construction $x_m \overline{P} x_1$. Therefore, x_1 does not belong to $C(S, \overline{R})$. Hence, $C(S, \overline{R})$ is empty and the situation $< \overline{R}_i >$ yields the outcome x_0.

As individual i_s prefers x_1 to x_0, it follows that the situation $< \overline{R}_i >$ is not a Nash equilibrium being vulnerable to the situation $< R_i^s >$. This proves the necessity of acyclicity for stability.

In view of Lemma 4, we conclude that the set of non-trivial binary stable SDRs is contained in the set of SDRs which satisfy conditions U, I, P and M and are such that they always yield acyclic R. Therefore, we can restrict our attention to the latter class of SDRs.

Lemma 5. *Let f satisfy conditions U, I, P and M, and always yield acyclic R. Then a necessary condition for the stability of f is that every situation $< R_i >$ belonging to $(\pi')^v$ yield quasi-transitive R.*

Proof: Let $S = \{x, y, z, w_1, \ldots, w_{n-3}\}$. Suppose there exists a situation $< R_i' >$ belonging to $(\pi')^v$ which violates quasi-transitivity. Without any loss of generality assume, $x P' y \wedge y P' z \wedge \sim (x P' z)$. $\sim (x P' z)$ is equivalent to $(x I' z \vee z P' x)$. However, $z P' x$ is impossible, otherwise acyclicity would be violated. So $x I' z$ must hold. The restriction of $< R_i' >$ over $\{x, y, z\}$ can be characterized as follows:

$\forall i \in N_1 : x P_i' y P_i' z$
$\forall i \in N_2 : x P_i' z P_i' y$
$\forall i \in N_3 : y P_i' x P_i' z$

$\forall i \in N_4 : yP_i'zP_i'x$
$\forall i \in N_5 : zP_i'xP_i'y$
$\forall i \in N_6 : zP_i'yP_i'x,$
where $\cup_{t=1}^{6} N_t = N.$

As $xP'y$, by condition P, $N_1 \cup N_2 \cup N_5$ is non-empty. In view of condition M, $N_1 \cup N_2 \cup N_5$ is a decisive set for x against y. Hence, as a consequence of condition P, there exists a non-empty set $V_{xy} \subset N_1 \cup N_2 \cup N_5$ which is minimally decisive for x against y. By an analogous argument, there exists a non-empty set $V_{yz} \subset N_1 \cup N_3 \cup N_4$ which is minimally decisive for y against z. Now let situation $< R_i >$ be as follows:

$\forall i \in V_{xy} \cap V_{yz} : xP_iyP_izP_iw_1P_i \ldots P_iw_{n-3}$
$\forall i \in V_{xy} - V_{yz} : zP_ixP_iyP_iw_1P_i \ldots P_iw_{n-3}$
$\forall i \in V_{yz} - V_{xy} : yP_izP_ixP_iw_1P_i \ldots P_iw_{n-3}$
$\forall i \in N - (V_{xy} \cup V_{yz}): zP_iyP_ixP_iw_1P_i \ldots P_iw_{n-3}.$

By condition P, we have $x, y, zPw_1P \ldots Pw_{n-3}$. We obtain xPy and yPz as $\forall i \in V_{xy}: xP_iy$ and $\forall i \in V_{yz}: yP_iz$. Now, $(\forall i \in N)[(zP_i'x \rightarrow zP_ix) \wedge (zI_i'x \rightarrow zR_ix)]$. Therefore, in view of condition M ($zPx \vee xIz$) must hold as we have $xI'z$. However, zPx is impossible because f always yields acyclic R. Therefore, xIz holds. Thus, R is as follows:
$x, y, zPw_1P \ldots Pw_{n-3}; xPy, yPz, xIz.$

As has already been argued, both V_{xy} and V_{yz} are non-empty thanks to condition P. Furthermore, $V_{xy} \cap V_{yz}$ must be non-empty, otherwise we will get a contradiction as follows. Assume $V_{xy} \cap V_{yz} = \emptyset$. Then the restriction of $< R_i >$ over $\{x, y, z\}$ becomes as follows: $\forall i \in V_{xy} :$ zP_ixP_iy; $\forall i \in V_{yz} : yP_izP_ix$; $\forall i \in N - (V_{xy} \cup V_{yz}): zP_iyP_ix$. But then we must have zPx as $\forall i : zP_ix$. This contradicts xIz. Hence, $V_{xy} \cap V_{yz}$ must be non-empty.

Let individual $j \in V_{xy} \cap V_{yz}$ and let $< \overline{R}_i >$ be as follows:

(a) $\forall i \neq j : \overline{R}_i = R_i$
(b) $x\overline{P}_jz\overline{P}_jy\overline{P}_jw_1\overline{P}_j \ldots \overline{P}_jw_{n-3}.$

Now $< \overline{R}_i >$ and $< R_i >$ are identical for all pairs of alternatives $\{s, t\} \neq \{y, z\}$. Suppose $y\overline{P}z$. Then $V_{yz} - \{j\}$ is a decisive set for y against z, in view of condition M. However, this contradicts the fact that V_{yz} is a minimal decisive set for y against z. Therefore, $y\overline{P}z$ is false, that is to say, $z\overline{R}y$ holds. Thus, $\overline{R}$ is as follows: $x, y, z\overline{P}w_1\overline{P} \ldots \overline{P}w_{n-3}; x\overline{P}y, z\overline{R}y, x\overline{I}z.$

If every individual i employs the strategy $\overline{R}_i$, the situation $< \overline{R}_i >$ results which yields the outcome $(x, z)^*$. Now given that every individual $i \neq j$ is going to use strategy $\overline{R}_i$, if individual j uses the strategy $R_j \neq \overline{R}_j$, the situation $< R_i >$ obtains with the outcome x. Individual j prefers the outcome x to $(x, z)^*$. Therefore, $< \overline{R}_i >$ is not a Nash equilibrium and hence f is unstable. This completes the proof of the lemma.

In view of Lemma 5, we conclude that the set of non-trivial binary stable SDRs is contained in the set of SDRs which satisfy conditions U, I, P and M and always yield acyclic R and are such that every situation belonging to $(\pi')^v$ yields quasi-transitive R.

Remark 1. *For the class of functions which satisfy conditions U, I, P and M and always yield acyclic R, quasi-transitivity is not a necessary condition for stability as can be seen by the following example.*

Example 3. *Let $S = \{x, y, z\}$. Let f be characterised as follows:*
(a) *Individual 1 is decisive for every ordered pair of alternatives, that is to say, for all ordered pairs of alternatives (s, t), $sP_1t \rightarrow sPt$.*
(b) $xI_1y \rightarrow xPy$
   $yI_1z \rightarrow yPz$
   $xI_1z \rightarrow xIz$.

It is easy to see that this function is stable. Also f satisfies conditions U, I, P and M and always yields acyclic R. If individual 1 is indifferent among all the alternatives then the social preference relation R is xPy, yPz, xIz, which is not quasi-transitive. It can be checked that for every situation belonging to $(\pi')^v$ f yields quasi-transitive R.

Lemma 6. *Let f satisfy conditions U, P, I and M. If f is such that for every situation belonging to $(\pi')^v$ it yields quasi-transitive R, then if a set of individuals V is decisive for some ordered pair of distinct alternatives, it is decisive for all ordered pairs of distinct alternatives.*

Proof: Let V be decisive for (x, y), $x \neq y, x, y \in S$. Let z be an alternative distinct from x and y, and consider the following configuration of individual preferences:
$\forall i \in V : xP_iyP_iz$
$\forall i \in N - V : yP_izP_ix$.
Now, $\overline{D}^V(x, y) \wedge \forall i \in V: xP_iy \rightarrow xPy$
$\forall i \in N : yP_iz \rightarrow yPz$.

Every situation $< R_i >$ belonging to $(\pi')^v$ yields quasi-transitive R. Then, by condition I, if a situation is such that every individual has a strong ordering over the set $A \subset S$, then the social preferences over A must be quasi-transitive. Now, the situation under consideration is such that every individual has a strong ordering over $\{x, y, z\}$. Therefore, social preferences over $\{x, y, z\}$ must be quasi-transitive. $xPy \wedge yPz \rightarrow xPz$, by quasi-transitivity. In view of monotonicity, it follows that V is decisive for (x, z). Therefore, $\overline{D}^V(x, y) \rightarrow \overline{D}^V(x, z)$. Similarly, by considering the configuration

$$\forall i \in V : zP_i x P_i y$$
$$\forall i \in N - V : yP_i z P_i x$$

we can show $[\overline{D}^V(x, y) \rightarrow \overline{D}^V(z, y)]$. By appropriate interchanges of alternatives, it follows that $\overline{D}^V(x, y) \rightarrow \overline{D}^V(a, b)$, for all $(a, b) \in \{x, y, z\} \times \{x, y, z\}$, where $a \neq b$. To prove the assertion for any $(a, b) \in S \times S, a \neq b$, first we note that if $[(a = x \vee a = y) \vee (b = x \vee b = y)]$, the desired conclusion $\overline{D}^V(a, b)$ can be obtained by considering a triple which includes all of x, y, a and b. If both a and b are different from x and y, then one first considers the triple $\{x, y, a\}$ and deduces $\overline{D}^V(x, a)$, and then considers the triple $\{x, a, b\}$ and obtains $\overline{D}^V(a, b)$.

Remark 2. *Lemma 6 is similar to the Arrow lemma which is used in proving the General Possibility Theorem.[3] The two lemmas are, however, independent of each other.*

Lemma 7. *Let f satisfy U, P, I and M. If f is such that for every situation belonging to $(\pi')^v$ it yields quasi-transitive R, then there is a unique minimal decisive set.*

Proof: The set of all individuals is decisive, by condition P. Therefore, a minimal decisive set exists. Suppose that the lemma is false, then there are at least two minimal decisive sets. Let V_1 and V_2 be two minimal decisive sets. Now $V_1 \cap V_2 \neq \emptyset$; otherwise we will get a contradiction as follows. Suppose $V_1 \cap V_2 = \emptyset$. Assume the following configuration of preferences: $\forall i \in V_1: xP_i y, \forall i \in V_2: yP_i x$. By the definition of a decisive set xPy and yPx, which is impossible. Therefore, $V_1 \cap V_2 \neq \emptyset$.

Now, assume the following configuration of preferences:
$$\forall i \in V_1 \cap V_2: xP_i y P_i z$$
$$\forall i \in V_1 - V_2 : zP_i x P_i y$$
$$\forall i \in V_2 - V_1 : yP_i z P_i x$$
$$\forall i \in N - (V_1 \cup V_2): zP_i y P_i x.$$

We obtain xPy and yPz as we have $\forall i \in V_1: xP_i y$ and $\forall i \in V_2 : yP_i z$. Now f is such that for every situation which belongs to $(\pi')^v$, it yields quasi-transitive R. Then by condition I, if every individual has a strong ordering over $A \subset S$, the social preferences over A must be quasi-transitive. In this situation, every individual has a

---

[3] See Arrow (1963 [1951]) and Sen (1970).

strong ordering over $\{x, y, z\}$; therefore R must be quasi-transitive over $\{x, y, z\}$. $xPy \wedge yPz \rightarrow xPz$, by quasi-transitivity. We have $\forall i \in V_1 \cap V_2$: $xP_iz; \forall i \in N - (V_1 \cap V_2): zP_ix$. Thus, in view of condition M, $V_1 \cap V_2$ is a decisive set for (x, z). Therefore, by Lemma 6, $V_1 \cap V_2$ is a decisive set for all ordered pairs of alternatives. However, $V_1 \cap V_2$ is a proper subset of both V_1 and V_2 which were assumed to be minimal decisive sets. This contradiction establishes the lemma.

Remark 3. *The above Lemma 7 is similar to the Gibbard result. The two results are, however, independent of each other.*

Lemma 8. *Let f satisfy conditions U, I, P and M, and always yield acyclic R. Also let f be such that for every situation $< R_i >$ belonging to $(\pi')^v$, it yields quasi-transitive R. Then, a necessary condition for the stability of f is that for every situation belonging to $(\pi')^v$ it yield transitive R.*

Proof: Let $S = \{x, y, z, w_1, \ldots, w_{n-3}\}$. Let $< R'_i >$ belonging to $(\pi')^v$ violate transitivity for some triple, say, $\{x, y, z\}$. Without any loss of generality, assume $yR'z \wedge zR'x \wedge \sim (yR'x)$. $\sim (yR'x)$ is equivalent to $xP'y$. Suppose $yP'z$, then by quasi-transitivity we obtain $xP'z$ ($xP'y \wedge yP'z \rightarrow xP'z$). However $xP'z$ is false, so $yP'z$ must be false. Therefore $yI'z$ is true. By an analogous argument $xI'z$ holds. So R' over $\{x, y, z\}$ is as follows: $xP'y, yI'z, xI'z$. The restriction of $< R'_i >$ over $\{x, y, z\}$ can be characterised as follows:

$\forall i \in N_1 : xP'_iyP'_iz$
$\forall i \in N_2 : xP'_izP'_iy$
$\forall i \in N_3 : yP'_ixP'_iz$
$\forall i \in N_4 : yP'_izP'_ix$
$\forall i \in N_5 : zP'_ixP'_iy$
$\forall i \in N_6 : zP'_iyP'_ix,$
where $\cup_{t=1}^{6} N_t = N$.

We have $\forall i \in N_1 \cup N_2 \cup N_5: xP'_iy$ and $\forall i \in N_3 \cup N_4 \cup N_6: yP'_ix$. This yields $xP'y$. Therefore, $N_1 \cup N_2 \cup N_5$ is decisive for (x, y) in view of condition M. By Lemma 6, this implies that $N_1 \cup N_2 \cup N_5$ is a decisive set. Now, by Lemma 7, there exists a unique minimal decisive set V. Therefore, $V \subset N_1 \cup N_2 \cup N_5$. Now $N_1 \cap V$ must be non-empty. Suppose not, then $V \subset N_2 \cup N_5$. As $\forall i \in N_2 \cup N_5: zP'_iy$, we must have $zP'y$ by the decisiveness of V. However $zP'y$ is false. This proves that $N_1 \cap V$ is non-empty. By an analogous argument, $N_5 \cap V$ can be shown to be non-empty.

Now let situation $< \overline{R}_i >$ be as follows:

$\forall i \in (N_1 \cap V) \cup (N_2 \cap V): x\overline{P}_i y\overline{P}_i z\overline{P}_i w_1\overline{P}_i \ldots \overline{P}_i w_{n-3}$

$\forall i \in N_5 \cap V: z\overline{P}_i x\overline{P}_i y\overline{P}_i w_1\overline{P}_i \ldots \overline{P}_i w_{n-3}$

$\forall i \in N - V: y\overline{P}_i z\overline{P}_i x\overline{P}_i w_1\overline{P}_i \ldots \overline{P}_i w_{n-3}.$

Let $N_1^0 = (N_1 \cap V) \cup (N_2 \cap V)$, $N_2^0 = N_5 \cap V$, $N_3^0 = N - V$. As $\forall i \in V : x\overline{P}_i y$, we must have $x\overline{P}y$. Suppose $y\overline{P}z$. This implies that $N_1^0 \cup N_3^0$ is a decisive set for (y, z). Then, by Lemma 6, $N_1^0 \cup N_3^0$ is a decisive set. Hence, there exists a minimal decisive set $V' \subset N_1^0 \cup N_3^0$. As $V' \cap N_2^0 = \emptyset$ and N_2^0 is non-empty, it follows that $V \neq V'$. However, this contradicts the result of Lemma 7, that there is a unique minimal decisive set. Therefore, $y\overline{P}z$ is false. Now, suppose $z\overline{P}y$. Then, N_2^0 is a decisive set for (z, y) and, hence, a decisive set in view of Lemma 6. Therefore, there exists a minimal decisive set $V' \subset N_2^0$. As $V' \cap N_1^0 = \emptyset$ and $N_1^0 \neq \emptyset$, it follows that $V \neq V'$. However, it contradicts the result of Lemma 7 that there is a unique minimal decisive set. Therefore, $z\overline{P}y$ is false. Hence, by the completeness of $\overline{R}$, $y\overline{I}z$ must hold. By an analogous argument, it can be shown that $x\overline{I}z$ must hold. Thus $\overline{R}$ is as follows: $x, y, z\overline{P}w_1\overline{P}\ldots\overline{P}w_{n-3}; x\overline{P}y, y\overline{I}z, x\overline{I}z.$

Let $j \in N_1^0$ and assume that individual j prefers $(x, y, z)^*$ to $(x, z)^*$. Construct the situation $< R_i >$ as follows:

(a) $\forall i \neq j : R_i = \overline{R}_i$
(b) $yP_j xP_j zP_j w_1P_j \ldots P_j w_{n-3}.$

$< \overline{R}_i >$ and $< R_i >$ are identical for all pairs $\{s, t\} \neq \{x, y\}$. Therefore, $\overline{R}$ and R must be identical for all pairs $\{s, t\} \neq \{x, y\}$. Suppose xPy. Then $V - \{j\}$ is a decisive set in view of Lemma 6. However, this contradicts the fact that V is a minimal decisive set. Therefore, xPy is false. Next, suppose yPx. This implies that $N_3^0 \cup \{j\}$ is a decisive set. Therefore there exists a minimal decisive set $V' \subset N_3^0 \cup \{j\}$. As $(N_3^0 \cup \{j\}) \cap N_2^0 = \emptyset$ and $N_2^0 \neq \emptyset$, it follows that $V \neq V'$. This contradicts the result of Lemma 7 that there is a unique minimal decisive set. Therefore, yPx is false. Hence, xIy must hold. Thus R is as follows: $x, y, zPw_1P\ldots Pw_{n-3}; xIy, yIz, xIz.$

$< \overline{R}_i >$ yields the outcome $(x, z)^*$ and $< R_i >$ the outcome $(x, y, z)^*$. As individual j prefers $(x, y, z)^*$ to $(x, z)^*$, it follows that $< \overline{R}_i >$ is not a Nash equilibrium being vulnerable to $< R_i >$. This completes the proof.

In view of this result, we conclude that the set of non-trivial binary stable SDRs is contained in the set of SDRs which satisfy conditions U, I, P, M and always yield acyclic R and are such that they yield transitive R for every situation which belongs to $(\pi')^v$.

Remark 4. *In Lemma 8 we have shown that for the class of SDRs which satisfy conditions U, I, P, M and always yield acyclic R and are such that they yield quasi-transitive R for every situation belonging to $(\pi')^v$, a necessary condition for the stability is that f yield transitive R for every situation belonging to $(\pi')^v$. The following example shows that for this class of SDRs transitivity is not a necessary condition for stability. In fact, transitivity is not a necessary condition for stability even for the class of SDRs which satisfy U, I, P, M and always yield quasi-transitive R.*

Example 4. *Let $S = \{x, y, z\}$. Let f be characterised as follows:*

(a) *Individual 1 is decisive for every ordered pair of alternatives, that is to say, for all ordered pairs of alternatives (s, t), $sP_1t \rightarrow sPt$.*

(b) $xI_1y \rightarrow xPy$
$yI_1z \rightarrow yIz$
$xI_1z \rightarrow xIz.$

This SDR satisfies U, I, P and M and always yields quasi-transitive R. It can be checked that this SDR is stable. However, this SDR does not always yield transitive R. If individual 1 is indifferent among all the alternatives then we obtain xPy, yIz, xIz, which violates transitivity. Of course, every situation belonging to $(\pi')^v$ yields transitive R.

Lemma 9. *Let f satisfy U, P, I and M. If f is such that every situation belonging to $(\pi')^v$ yields transitive R, then there is a unique minimal decisive set which consists of a single individual.*

Proof: By Lemma 7, there exists a unique minimal decisive set V. So, the only thing that we have to prove is that V consists of a single individual. Suppose that the lemma is false, then V contains at least two members. Let $j \in V$. We have $V - \{j\} \neq \emptyset$.

Assume the following configuration of preferences:
$\forall i \in \{j\} : xP_iyP_iz$
$\forall i \in V - \{j\} : zP_ixP_iy$
$\forall i \in N - V : yP_izP_ix.$

By the decisiveness of V, we obtain xPy. As $V - \{j\}$ is a proper subset of V and we have $\forall i \in V - \{j\}: zP_iy \wedge \forall i \in N - (V - \{j\}): yP_iz$, we must have yRz in view of Lemma 6. Now f yields transitive R for every situation which belongs to $(\pi')^v$. By condition I then, if every individual has a strong ordering over $A \subset S$, R must be transitive over A. In this situation, every individual has a strong ordering over the set $\{x, y, z\}$. Therefore, R must be transitive over $\{x, y, z\}$. $xPy \wedge yRz \rightarrow xPz$, by transitivity. However, only individual j prefers x to z, all others prefer z to x. So individual j is decisive for (x, z) in view of condition M. This, by Lemma 6, implies that j is decisive for all ordered pairs of alternatives. However, this contradicts the fact that V is a minimal decisive set. This contradiction establishes the lemma.

We have already demonstrated that the set of non-trivial binary SDRs which are stable is contained in the set of SDRs which satisfy conditions U, I, P, M and always yield acyclic R, and are such that they yield transitive R for every situation which belongs to $(\pi')^v$. However, by Lemma 9, every SDR belonging to the aforementioned class of SDRs is trivial. Therefore, the set of non-trivial binary stable SDRs is empty.

REFERENCES

Arrow, K. J. 1963 [1951]. *Social Choice and Individual Values*, second edition. New York: Wiley.

Gibbard, A. 1973. 'Manipulation of Voting Schemes: A General Result', *Econometrica*, 41(4): 587–601.

Pattanaik, P. K. 1973. 'On the Stability of Sincere Voting Situations', *Journal of Economic Theory*, 6 (6): 558–74.

———. 1974. 'Stability of Sincere Voting under Some Classes of Non-binary Group Decision Procedures', *Journal of Economic Theory*, 8(2): 206–24.

———. 1975. 'Strategic Voting without Collusion under Binary and Democratic Group Decision Rules', *Review of Economic Studies*, 42(1): 93–103.

Satterthwaite, M. A. 1975. 'Strategy-Proofness and Arrow's Conditions: Existence and Correspondence Theorems for Voting Procedures and Social Welfare Functions', *Journal of Economic Theory*, 10 (2): 187–217.

Sen, A. K. 1970. *Collective Choice and Social Welfare*. San Francisco: Holden-Day.

Printed in the United States
by Baker & Taylor Publisher Services